The Road to Daulis

The Road to DAULIS

Psychoanalysis, Psychology, and Classical Mythology

Robert Eisner

SYRACUSE UNIVERSITY PRESS

The paper used in this publication meets the minimum requirements of American National Standard for Information Sciences—Permanence of Paper for Printed Library Materials, ANSI Z39.48-1984. ∞™

Library of Congress Cataloging-in-Publication Data

Eisner, Robert, 1945–
    The road to Daulis.

    Bibliography: p.
    Includes index.
    1. Mythology, Classical—Psychological aspects.
I. Title.
BL727.E37   1987   292'.13'019   86-32304
ISBN 0-8156-0210-3 (alk. paper)

Contents

To Elaine

And to the Memory of
Eileen
and
Susannah

Preface

T HIS BOOK will examine the use by psychoanalysis of some classical figures, the validity of the correspondences alleged between the myths and the elements of psychology, the presuppositions and methods used to arrive at those correspondences. What, the question I shall attempt to answer runs, is the therapeutic value and philosophical significance of the myths for post-Freudian man? I have not tried to explain every aspect of every myth treated in the analytical writings nor even every aspect of each myth here given space. An attempt to account for all facets of a problem leads to dogmatism, and this book will show that myth resists all dogmatic advances while appearing to consort with each passing catechist.

As the chapters progress, merits and demerits for interpretation and use of the myths will be handed out to the analysts. This may distress some readers who will see in such evaluations a careless eclecticism, a lack of system building. But consistent theorizing at the expense of the inconsistent myths has often done violence to the truth. The point is not to pension off the veterans and raise a younger, fresher, army to follow a revolutionary banner, but to refurbish the old outfit and prepare it for new maneuvers—with a revised set of orders. The book proceeds on the assumption that attention to the details of the myths in their rich original contexts will suggest more psychological insights than will any attempt to create our own myths by misappropriating those of another age and deleting their cultural and social codes.

"An animus against the systematizers has been a recurrent feature of intellectual good taste for more than a century," Susan Sontag observes approvingly in her introduction to *A Barthes Reader*. Such a bias has encouraged the proper answer to those who wonder what god I have chosen to serve when caught between obligations to classical scholarship and to psychoanalysis. Neither; instead, I have been true to the nature of the work in progress. Nevertheless, the reader will notice two voices—the narrative and the critical ones—speaking alternately in the text that follows. This discontinuity, while beneficial to grasping the subject matter, is in any case inevitable.

deconstruction

Since literary fashion (based in Paris, but some American houses are on the upswing) now decrees that a primary text should be read through a secondary one—literature through theory rather than a theory of literature—which is putting the cart before the horse, or the professor before the poet, I must emphasize my eccentric regard for the creative act over the analytical act. On the other hand, if one wants to use the scholars' data, as they themselves rarely do, to draw some conclusions in the realm of ideas instead of lingering forever over the facts, then one will regularly be tempted beyond the facts. But the mythical trail of crumbling footprints and cold droppings must be followed as far as it leads. Psychoanalysis should strike a bargain between fact and fancy, very much the way the modern realistic novel does—caught by the dilemma of making it new and fresh without abandoning tradition and the world as given. Let us attend not to Pound's poetic motto, no ideas but in things, but to the novelist's—no ideas but *from* things. Analysis can validate or check the imperative of tradition. Tradition can restrain or enfranchise the otherwise cavalier brio of analysis. So at my most critical I wish to destroy neither psychoanalysis nor the classics, but to poise a rhetoric of psychological theory against a rhetoric of archaeological fact.

Lévi-Strauss said that a myth consists of all its versions, and thus the Oedipus myth should include Freud's analysis of it. By this logic no one, not even the anthropologist, could ever observe a myth without participating in it. The mythological investigator, peering through the devilish lens of this or that theory, would always find only his own eyeball staring blandly up at him from the Petri dish. I shall presume, while admitting a certain truth in this observation, that some objectivity is possible—albeit rarely attained—even in this age of self-conscious novelists and self-conscious physicists. For the myth of Oedipus, this confusion of all the versions with Sophocles' version with Freud's version must be cleaned up, since Sophocles was an artist and his play should not be identified with someone else's intentions. But myth is a slippery matter, and we shall find (even in the process of making distinctions) that a story must still be told as though it happened once, at least in a particular author's mind, and that the details from many tellings tend to creep in and coalesce into a single, paradigmatic, authorless amalgam.

Late (Hellenistic and Roman) sources for the myths must be taken with a grain of salt, for they tend to be *recherché*. The deeper the learning exercised in an account, the shallower the meaning oftentimes attained. There is a kind of rough virtue in the primitive. But in some cases those late sources are all we have; in others, a sudden gloss from the scholarly lamp flames up and obliquely illuminates the truth.

I have tried to supply background material for those who need it, without boring those who have it. I have kept references to a minimum, citing ancient authors in the text, by book and chapter or line, and modern authors in the Notes. The Bibliography lists all works cited. All translations not immediately acknowledged in the text are mine. Italicized words and peculiarities of spelling in quotes are those of the person cited.

I am grateful to the National Endowment for the Humanities for a Fellowship during the tenure of which I completed a draft of this book.

Robert Eisner

The Road to Daulis

1

Oedipus and His Kind

ON AN ETRUSCAN SEAL RING, carved about 400 B.C., we see Oedipus confronting the Sphinx. The size of the gem stone left no room for the artist to inscribe an anchoring text, let alone a dramatic one. Yet he was determined that those who viewed his work be able to hear the dialogue between monster and hero: the famous question which she, at once lion, bird of prey, and woman, posed to all who would safely pass her roost by the road (no one had until now), "What walks on four legs in the morning, two at noon, and three at evening?"—and the equally famous answer, "Man crawling as a child, walking as an adult, and hobbling as an elder." Oedipus, ignorant at this point in his career that he is the murderer of his father and about to become the husband of his mother, looks almost innocently up at the monster. His head is a little too large. His eyes bulge—"sphinx" means "strangler." She returns his gaze, fearing (but it is only a pretense of fear) that he will make the correct response; and he does. The artist, lacking words, shows us this answer in a language that comes naturally to the Greeks. Oedipus raises his right hand and curls one finger back at himself to pronounce the gesture, "Me."

In the next scene of the myth, presented in the mind's eye as, still holding the gem before us, we shift our gaze inward, the Sphinx lies on the ground below her column, apparently dead of shock at Oedipus' wisdom in understanding the riddle; and the hero strides victoriously (strides? did he ever walk without a limp?) into Thebes to be given the throne and the old queen in marriage. Half a generation later (sphinxes sleep long and dreamlessly, sure that their wishes will be fulfilled) a plague strikes Thebes. The presence of the king's murderer in the land has caused the pollution; and Oedipus, in zealous search of the truth, discovers his origins, blinds himself, and goes voluntarily into exile.

1

Freud's Oedipal Model

Out of these bare bones of a story much has been made. Actually the flesh and fat of later interpretations have accreted around a bit more of a structure than here outlined, but it will do for now. This is what Freud, in *The Interpretation of Dreams* (1900), made of one version of the myth:

> If *Oedipus Rex* moves a modern audience no less than it did the contemporary Greek one, the explanation can only be that its effect does not lie in the contrast between destiny and human will, but is to be looked for in the particular nature of the material on which that contrast is exemplified. There must be something which makes a voice within us ready to recognize the compelling force of destiny in the *Oedipus*, while we can dismiss as merely arbitrary such dispositions as are laid down in (Grillparzer's) *Die Ahnfrau* or other modern tragedies of destiny. And a factor of this kind is in fact involved in the story of King Oedipus. His destiny moves us only because it might have been ours—because the oracle laid the same curse upon us before our birth as upon him. It is the fate of all of us, perhaps, to direct our first sexual impulse towards our mother and our first hatred and our first murderous wish against our father.[1]

Freud adduced this interpretation of Sophocles' play (about 430 B.C.) by way of confirming his medical judgment that "Being in love with the one parent and hating the other are among the essential constituents of the stock of psychical impulses which is formed at that time [childhood] and which is of such importance in determining the symptoms of the later neurosis."[2] These feelings of love toward Mother and hatred toward Father are universal; neurotics merely exhibit our common emotional constitution on a magnified and distorted scale. Thus the Oedipus complex, as Freud found it useful to call the phenomenon, is fated for every human being, and Oedipus' physical destiny alludes to our own psychic one.

Freud based his hypothesis of this complex on his analysis of patients' dreams, fantasies, and telltale slips of the tongue or of memory. More important, he found he suffered such feelings himself, and on 15 October 1897 made the announcement to his most encouraging and sympathetic friend, Wilhelm Fliess:

> I have found love of the mother and jealousy of the father in my own case too, and now believe it to be a general phenomenon of early childhood. . . . If that is the case, the gripping power of *Oedipus Rex*, in spite of all

the rational objections to the inexorable fate that the story presupposes, becomes intelligible, and one can understand why later fate dramas were such failures. ... but the Greek myth seizes on a compulsion which everyone recognizes because he has felt traces of it in himself.[3]

While Freud constantly refined this psychical construct, he never deviated from the basic principles; quotations that do little more than repeat the above statements may be extracted from almost all his monographs and book-length lectures. Soon the hypothesis became a dogma, albeit one that bound together a group which the rest of the world, if it knew of them, regarded as a bunch of crackpots. And Freud spoke *ex cathedra* for the group:

It has justly been said that the Oedipus complex is the nuclear complex of the neuroses, and constitutes the essential part of their content. It represents the peak of infantile sexuality, which, through its after-effects, exercises a decisive influence on the sexuality of adults. Every new arrival on this planet is faced by the task of mastering the Oedipus complex; anyone who fails to do so falls a victim to neurosis. With the progress of psycho-analytic studies the importance of the Oedipus complex has become more and more clearly evident; its recognition has become the shibboleth that distinguishes the adherents of psycho-analysis from its opponents.[4]

He also pursued some of the implications of his doctrine. "The myth of King Oedipus," he observed in *Five Lectures on Psychoanalysis*, "reveals, with little modification, the infantile wish, which is later opposed and repudiated by the *barrier against incest*."[5] Oedipus did the bloody deeds, we do not—how come? Freud wrote *Totem and Taboo* (1913) as an answer to that question: In the beginning was the primal horde. Aboriginal man lived in small communities, each governed by the most powerful male, who claimed all the women for his pleasure. This male fought with and drove out his brethren when they came to threaten his supremacy; and they, if they could manage it, would then found hordes of their own. Thus was created the practice of exogamy, which (after the establishment of totemism) was promulgated as "No sexual relations within the tribe."[6]

If the totem animal is the father, then the two principal ordinances of totemism, the two taboo prohibitions which constitute its core—not to kill the totem and not to have sexual relations with a woman of the same totem—coincide in their content with the two crimes of Oedipus ... as well as with the two primal wishes of children, the insufficient repression or the awakening of which forms the nucleus of perhaps every psychoneurosis.[7]

But the totem animal or other sacrifical beast is periodically, ceremonially, slaughtered. Why? One day the exiled brothers united and killed and ate their father; by devouring him they felt they acquired some of his strength. "The totem meal, which is perhaps mankind's earliest festival, would thus be a repetition and a commemoration of this memorable and criminal deed, which was the beginning of so many things—of social organization, of moral restrictions and of religion." The brothers had hated their father for limiting their power and sexual activities, but they had also loved and admired him. After they had killed him and identified themselves with him, their hatred waned, their love grew, and they began to feel guilty. "They revoked their deed by forbidding the killing of the totem, the substitute for their father; and they renounced its fruits by resigning their claim to the women who had now been set free." Thus the two taboos of totemism correspond to the two wishes of the Oedipus complex. Ambivalent feelings, however, remained; remorse was balanced out by the eating of the totem meal, celebrating the brethren's triumph over their father.[8]

The prohibition of man's natural aggressive and sexual impulses had the advantage of promoting civilization. The social and fraternal feelings, which made possible the cooperation necessary to overthrow the powerful father, "continued to exercise a profound influence on the development of society. . . . To the religiously based prohibition against killing the totem was now added the socially based prohibition against fratricide." A complicity in crime became the basis of society.[9]

The social pact made agriculture possible, and thus the son had new opportunities to express his incestuous libido by cultivating Mother Earth. At this time there arose vegetation gods who committed incest with the goddesses in defiance of the father god: Adonis, who was cut down by a charging boar that is probably a metamorphosis of Venus' older lover Mars; Attis, who was driven mad and castrated himself in service to the goddess Cybele, whose own severed genitals in the form of an almond—she was once a he, and her severed parts grew into a nut tree—impregnated Attis' mother.[10] (Freud, despite his mention of Attis, ignores the possibility of a castrating woman and, as always, sees hostility and threats emanating only from the patriarchal side of the clan or pantheon.)

But where had the concept of god come from? Well, if the totem is the first, a theriomorphic form of the father surrogate, the god is a later form—one in which the father has regained his anthropomorphic shape, after the sons' animosity toward him has lessened, their longing increased. They have ideal-

god + beast

ized him into a figure embodying the unlimited power of the primal father
against whom they formerly raged but to whom they had for a while submitted.
Thus the original sin from which Christ redeemed mankind was murder. "And
if this sacrifice of a life brought about atonement with God the Father, the
crime to be expiated can only have been the murder of the father."[11]

Religion, Freud concludes in *The Future of an Illusion*, is the universal
obsessional neurosis of humanity. It arose out of the Oedipus complex, and so
with the growth of the individual and the progress of the human race a turning
away from religion will inevitably occur.[12] Not only religion but man's whole
"sense of guilt springs from the Oedipus complex and was acquired at the
killing of the father by the brothers banded together."[13] And in *The Ego and
the Id*, Freud's anatomy of the soul, he locates the sense of guilt in that organ
called the superego, which "according to our hypothesis, actually originated
from the experiences that lead to totemism." For the superego "retains the
character of the father, while the more powerful the Oedipus complex was and
the more rapidly it succumbed to repression, . . . the stricter will be the domination of the superego over the ego later on—in the form of conscience or
perhaps of an unconscious sense of guilt."[14] The guilt that leads to the sublimation of incestuous or patricidal impulses was the wellspring of civilization:
"the beginnings of religion, morals, society and art converge in the
Oedipus complex."[15]

> Religion, morality, and a social sense . . . were originally one and the same
> thing. . . . They were acquired out of the father-complex: religion and
> moral restraint through the process of mastering the Oedipus complex
> itself, and social feeling through the necessity for overcoming the rivalry
> that then remained between the members of the younger generation. The
> male sex seems to have taken the lead in all these moral acquisitions; and
> they seem to have then been transmitted to women by cross-inheritance.[16]

Freud found confirmation for his account of the revolt of the primal horde
and celebration of the totem feast in the structure of Greek tragedy, in which
the Chorus plays the band of brothers and the protagonist, or hero, plays the
primal father. The hero must suffer, but he suffers—and here's the twist—not
his own suffering but the burden of the Chorus's guilt. "The crime which was
thrown onto his shoulders, presumptuousness and rebelliousness against a great
authority, was precisely the crime for which the members of the Chorus, the
company of brothers, were responsible."[17] Some Freudians have reiterated this
position and pointed out that Oedipus in Sophocles' play functions as both the
revolutionary son and the overthrown father; the community has created a hero

development of individual organism

who can perform the forbidden deeds, which they themselves long to accomplish, and who then will bear the blame for them.[18]

Now all of this presumes too much: in the case of the Oedipus complex, a precise sequence of events in infancy, from first witnessing the parents at intercourse to enduring threats of castration if our exemplary tot does not stop fondling himself; in the case of the primal horde, a sequence of unverifiable events in the prehistory of religion and society. What if none of it is true? Freud wavers on that aspect of his argument.

"Oh, don't take that seriously," he once remarked about his theory of primal patricide, "I made that up on a rainy Sunday afternoon."[19] Maybe he wasn't joking. While his belief in the inheritance of acquired characteristics could be used to explain why modern man, especially modern neurotic man, behaves as though he actually killed and ate Father, Freud himself thought the mere desire to do the unspeakable sufficed to arouse primal guilt. "We find no deeds, but only impulses and emotions, set upon evil ends but held back from their achievement. What lie behind the sense of guilt of neurotics are always *psychical* realities and never *factual* ones." Neurotics prefer their fantasies to the world's facts.[20] Could not primitive man, too, only have wanted to commit these crimes? No, Freud counters, for in the beginning of our racial history, psychical reality *did* coincide with factual reality—as it would for children if their parents didn't sit on them occasionally. Ontogeny, to bring in another of Freud's evolutionary biases, recapitulates phylogeny. " 'In the beginning,' " he concludes *Totem and Taboo*, quoting Goethe's most un-Christian phrasing, " 'was the Deed.' " But in *An Outline of Psycho-Analysis* he returns from the irrelevant and murky past to the all too well-lit present and insists that the superego calls the ego to account not only for deeds but for intentions: "its excessive severity does not follow a real model but corresponds to the strength of the defense used against the temptation of the Oedipus complex."[21]

racial history

Bruno Bettleheim has drawn attention to the highly metaphorical nature of Freud's language and to the importance of not taking his metaphors as factual statements[22]—even when he meant them as such, we might add. For Freud was a master at retaining the essential truth of his metaphors even when forced to yield on points of evidential fact, and we should regard many of his constructs as works of fantastic literature—like all of metaphysics in Borges' invented cosmos, *Tlon, Uqbar, Orbis Tertius*—or even as new myths in their own right.

Metaphor relies on a congruence of one thing at least with another. In this case, since both myth and social institutions are products of the human mind or soul, Freud finds the structure discernible in one to be a confirmation of the structure provable (by his lights) in the other. Myth matches dream data, and prehistory matches myth. Myth may contain unconcealed materials which would be concealed in an individual's account of his family life. This is because the shocking events of myth are placed in the distant past, in the words of Freud's follower Karl Abraham, "from which every member of the people which created the myth feels himself far removed in consciousness." The primitive, infantile, instinctual, uncivilized impulses that were rife in the early stages of a people's development were at a later stage "suppressed by means of a process which we can compare with repression in the individual. They did not become completely extinct, but were preserved in the individual." Myth is the product of mass repression. The Oedipus myth is particularly instructive because it so slightly disguises its symbolic content.[23] For those haunted by the same family of family ghosts as Freud was, his reasoning seems brilliant and conclusive; for those who are not, it appears forced and circular.[24]

Freud came across other Greek myths that he thought fit his oedipal model. First of all, he accepts the year-king theory, as expounded by Sir James Frazer in *The Golden Bough*, according to which the king in prehistoric times, as the embodiment of transitory male potency, must—when spent—be sacrificed and replaced by a newer, more virile prince.[25] (This theory, we shall see, presupposes a most un-Freudian historical primacy of matriarchy over patriarchy.) The new king's murder of the old, of course, repeats the oedipal murder of the father. Second, according to an account attributed to the Orphics—an odd Greek sect of limited appeal for their ascetic practices to ensure the pure life—mankind sprang from the ashes of the Titans, whom the gods chastized for mobbing, murdering, and eating the boy-god Dionysus-Zagreus. This myth resembles the story of young Orpheus himself, patron saint of the cult, who was torn apart by an enraged band (but a band of women—a detail unaccounted for by Freud).[26] And in *The Interpretation of Dreams*, published thirteen years before *Totem and Taboo*, Freud touches on another myth about the Titans just before he launches into his analysis of *Oedipus the King*: Zeus, on behalf of his brother and sister gods, castrated his tyrannical father Cronus, who had been cannibilizing his offspring (just as Cronus had punished *his* tyrannical father Uranus).[27]

The family troubles of the gods involve all three of the generations: Ge and Uranus (personifications of sky and earth), Cronus and the other Titans (humanoid but savage), and Zeus and the other Olympians (divine idealizations of human form and fortune). These generations and the strife between them may reflect the stages of Hellenic civilization. The Greek myths took shape during the Bronze Age—an intermediate and transitional period of racial and social oppression between the anarchy of the Stone Age and the relatively equitable and democratic Iron Age (not to be confused with the mythical Ages of Man)—when the gap between the weak and the powerful, as in the Age of Titans, was almost institutionalized. The same pattern of alliance and rivalry in the Olympian family can be detected—although Freud never did so—in the average Greek family, ancient or modern. Typically, mother marries husband X, and together they have son Y, who grows up and very likely names *his* son X. As the mother uses her son Y against her oppressive husband X, so she displays some animus toward her grandson—who may bear the same name as her hated husband—when he overthrows his father, her son. Father-son rivalry promotes grandmother-grandson difficulties. And so, when Zeus has overthrown his father Cronus, his grandmother Ge brings forth several sets of monsters to do him in.

Jacob Burkhardt, in a letter dated 1855, suggested that the Oedipus myth appealed to a specific something in every Greek.[28] E. R. Dodds points to the growth in anxiety and dread in Greek imaginations, due perhaps to insecure social conditions during the Archaic Age (700–480, a time of migrations, political upheaval, and religious fervor) and to the concomitant emphasis on individual rights and responsibilities as constituting a social climate in which sons began to question their previously infallible and sacrosanct fathers. So Father Zeus, in this Archaic Age, seems a source of good and evil alike, a tyrant who learns justice. "The peculiar horror with which the Greeks viewed offenses against a father, and the peculiar religious sanctions to which the offender was thought to be exposed, are in themselves suggestive of strong repressions." After Oedipus' self-blinding, exile, and long term of wandering, he becomes a saintly figure whose presence and blessing are sought by his rivaling sons (in Sophocles' *Oedipus at Colonus*). Dodds sees such a theme as the concern of a period when the father's position was no longer unquestioned. The revolt of sons against their fathers, which reached a peak during the sophistic fifth century B.C., may go back "to the earliest stirrings of individualism in a society where family solidarity was still universally taken for granted." And even the myth of the birth of Aphrodite from the severed genitals of Uranus may symbolize the son's attainment of sexual freedom through the removal of his father-rival.[29]

Incestuous dreams seem to have been particularly common in later antiquity. Jocasta tells Sophocles' Oedipus to calm down, there have been many dreams and oracles before now about mother-son incest, and they have meant nothing (ll. 980–83); but Freud thought they meant a great deal—that he was right.[30] And in the fourth century Plato cites among the lawless pleasures that can be controlled in his utopia such desires as body forth in dreams—sleeping with one's mother, for example (*Republic* 9. 571B–C). Artemidorus, a dream-diviner of the second century A.D., lists many sorts of incest dreams. "The case of one's mother is both complex and manifold and admits of many different interpretations—a thing not all dream interpreters have realized" (1. 79).[31] The deposed tyrant Hippias, for example, thought his incestuous dream meant that he would recover his power at Athens, but it turned out to signify only his loss of a tooth on Attic soil (Herodotus 6. 107); and the soothsayers interpreted Julius Caesar's dream of raping his mother as portending his destiny to conquer the whole of mother earth (Suetonius, *Julius Caesar* 7; Plutarch, *Caesar* 32). E. R. Dodds, who is sympathetic to the Freudian case, explains that "the necessary disguising of forbidden impulses was accomplished, not within the dream itself, but by a subsequent process of interpretation, which gave it an innocuous symbolic meaning."[32]

The Ancient Evidence

So much for Freud's position on the Oedipus complex and for the ancient sources that support him. What classical material can we adduce against Freud, what can we find wrong with his methodology in explaining myth or with his application of myth to psychoanalytic concerns? For one thing, a myth *qua* myth is a late phenomenon. No such item survives from classical Greece. Certainly Greeks spoke of a *mythos* or a *logos*, sometimes using the words interchangeably, sometimes attending to the distinction between a made-up or at least highly elaborated story and a factual account. But the idea of a bare plot, such as one can look up in half a dozen popular handbooks, was one alien to a society that lacked any convenient reference works, any religious dogma, and anything like a modern concept of narrative consistency. All that survives from Archaic and Classical Greece are various "tellings"—a sense that inheres in the word *mythos* but is lacking in "myth." Of course there must have been many tellings of the myths that were of a low valence, compelling in their way but relatively free of poetry or of any significance except for a common sort of moralizing—bedtime and campfire stories, learned by rote and repeated by rote to charm the children to sleep or to pass long winter evenings. But these versions, written only on the night air, have not survived. What *have* survived are literary versions, highly allusive (because everyone knew the oral paraphrases), charged with meaning, and calculated to enlarge our sensibilities and bestow aesthetic satisfaction. These versions were created by poets and philosophers out of the campfire or hearth-fire stories or out of the variously charged versions of their predecessors and colleagues: Euripides' *Electra* (413 B.C.) was an answer to the recently revived *Oresteia* of Aeschylus; and Sophocles' *Electra* (410 B.C.) was probably meant to reaffirm older standards of conduct and of dramaturgy in contradistinction to Euripides' avant-garde subversiveness.

Only after the death of tragedy and of the city-state, the conquests of Alexander, and the retreat of poetry to personal, perhaps cosmic, but never political, themes, did librarians, grammarians, and the schoolmasters to the children of the prosperous urban classes find it profitable to collate all the known versions of the myths and attempt to reconcile them with one another. They produced handbooks that were models of erudition and monuments to scholarly nervousness before the chaos of conflicting accounts in the poems and the plays. The scholars were writing for an audience to whom the world of the myths now (by the third century B.C.) seemed distant and fanciful. And of course the schoolmasters needed these true and precise accounts to test their pupils on. By the first century A.D., the Roman emperor Tiberius, no mean antiquarian in his own right, could amuse himself by tormenting the professors he kept at his infamous retreat on Capri with such questions as "What song did the Sirens sing?" or "What name did Achilles go by when he hid among the women of Scyros?" (Suetonius, *Tiberius* 70).

The first mistake that Freud made with the myth of Oedipus in *The Interpretation of Dreams* was to treat Sophocles' play as *the* myth instead of as one manifestation of the myth. *The* myth never existed, unless perhaps in the hypothetical first telling of it—and we'll never hear *that*—until the handbooks were compiled. His second mistake was to treat the play as *his* myth, to appropriate it for his own use. The Oedipus of Sophocles' play is not a neurotic, but a king. The term "neurosis" has no historical validity when applied to his struggle (a point Aristotle makes for us when he describes the tragic hero as a man like any other, only of high station)—except insofar as neurosis is symptomatic of the human condition, particularly of the intelligent human's condition, and insofar as forgetting is symptomatic of neurosis. But Oedipus never forgot, because he never knew, what the Freudian neurotic is supposed to have suppressed. The eponymous hero of the Oedipus complex never had one himself.

Let us retrace a few steps of his career before the opening of *Oedipus the King*. Immediately after birth, and perhaps without even being viewed by the anything but proud parents, Oedipus was sent out in the arms of a trusted shepherd to be exposed on the slopes of Mt. Cithaeron, his ankles pierced with a nail or a thong to prevent the tot from creeping away. Exposure of children was a common practice in an overpopulated country with strict laws of inheritance. If the child was simply unwanted, it was placed in a pot and left at the city gates, the local adoption agency—rather like a litter of kittens in a cardboard box on a campus lawn. If, as is generally the case in the myths, the parents wanted to do away with the baby, he was abandoned on a mountainside (the wild country between cities, which were built on the fertile plains) for the weather or wolves to take care of. If the parents were noble, as is also the case in the myths, they would probably entrust the job to a shepherd, the only person likely to have much business in the mountains. Shepherds are not much for town society, and they associate mostly with fellow shepherds and with sheep. Even today, they may look for prospective apprentices at the orphanage. In Oedipus' case, shepherd A met shepherd B on the massif of Cithaeron, and shepherd B happened to know that the king and queen of Corinth wanted to adopt a baby, no matter if he would never win the two-hundred-yard dash.

The boy was raised by King Polybus and Queen Merope as their son, and at age eighteen or so he was taunted by some friends about being adopted. Not getting a straight answer about this from his supposed parents, he went to consult the oracle at Delphi. The priestess ignored his question and sent him away from the temple precinct, saying that he was sure to have intercourse with his mother and to murder his father (ll. 788–93). In flight from Delphi and from Polybus and Merope (forgetting his doubts about them), Oedipus came to a crossroads, had a dispute over the right of way with a stranger, and in anger killed him. He proceeded on his way, avoiding Corinth, wound up in Thebes, defeated the Spinx, and was given the kingdom and Queen Jocasta's hand.

If Oedipus had had an Oedipus complex he would have killed Polybus and married Merope, the only parents he ever knew. Even Freud at his murkiest would not have claimed that some old salmonoid instinct drove the young prince to retrace his infantile route, slay his biological father, and crawl back into the original womb. Moreover, Erich Fromm points out, a myth about incest would hardly omit the attraction of mother and son for each other: "there is no indication whatsoever that Oedipus is attracted by or falls in love with Jocasta. The only reason we are given for Oedipus' marriage to Jocasta is that she, as it were, goes with the throne."[33] This is an old formula in myth after myth: the suitors' wooing of Penelope, Jason and the Queen of Corinth, Aeneas and Lavinia. And myth even permeates history, or both reflect some archetype in the Indo-European mind; to gain the throne or some other political boon, the usurper must sleep with the queen: Cyrus and Cilissa in Xenophon's *Anabasis*; Caesar and Cleopatra; Gyges and the wife of King Candaules in Herodotus' *Histories*—although Gyges had merely seen the queen naked, she nevertheless forced him to kill her husband and assume the throne. But this stage of the myth has been accomplished by the time the plot of *Oedipus the King* begins.

To understand *Oedipus the King* we must ask what Oedipus did and who he was. For the Greeks the latter question could pretty well be answered with "His father's son." One's breeding determines what deeds one is capable of, and thus one's character. Many heroes, superhuman men, are therefore fathered by gods. (Immortality, however, is a recessive trait.) Genealogy is destiny. Freud, too, maintained a dogmatic belief in the inheritance of acquired characteristics—even in the face of evidence to the contrary.[34]

George Devereux insists that "fate was merely the personification of a man's character-structure, and of his need to act out those of his intra-psychic conflicts which determine the course of his life."[35] But this turns out to be little more than a jargon-ridden expansion of Heraclitus' apothegm, *ēthos anthropōi daimon*, "man's character is his fate," or "his genius" (fr. 114). Freud put it better when he said that a man pursued by a malignant fate usually turns out to have arranged the events himself.[36] The Sophoclean, and sometimes the Homeric, treatment of fate—*moira*, man's portion or lot—involves the same substantial identification of a man's personality with the details of his career: it is well to remember that the etymon of our word "personal" is the Latin *persona*, the mask a tragic actor wore on stage or the character one chooses to present to the world. In the plays of Aeschylus and the *Histories* of Herodotus, however, fate often appears in more Oriental trappings, as an externally determined kismet, the will of the gods or of something that lurks behind the gods, or as an almost Biblical curse that is passed on from generation to generation: "The fathers have eaten sour grapes, and the childrens' teeth are set on edge" (*Jeremiah*: 31.29; *Ezekiel*: 18.2). Aeschylus treated the working out of such a curse in a trilogy on the Theban saga, as he did in the *Oresteia*. (This is the Fate, in religious terms, which Freud seems to have had in mind in biological terms, for Oedipus and for us all—a notion that arises from man's helplessness to escape the human condition.[37]) Sophocles, on the other hand, with his greater interest in the essential identity of character and action, concentrated on single plays and deemphasized the matter of curses.

Two of the most reliable proofs that Sophocles' play is a tragedy of fate disappear upon close examination.[38] The Oracle of Apollo is supposed to have told Oedipus that he "was fated" to kill his father and marry his mother: "That I was fated to lie with my mother . . . and I was doomed to be murderer of the father that begot me" are the words used in the translation most widely read today, David Grene's (ll.791–93). And this in fact is how the lines have usually been interpreted, even by those who, like Grene, read the play in Greek. The terms used in the Greek for "fate," however, are colorless, everyday words— *khreie* and the future tense of the verb "to be"—used for anything one is going to do or has to do. The key word that might mean "fate," *moira*, is missing; and even that word could denote merely "lot in life." Apollo in his wisdom simply knows what is going to happen; he doesn't cause it.

Next, Apollo is commonly said (even in the latest edition of the *Oxford Classical Dictionary*) to have sent the plague, in order to force Oedipus' crime into the light. But the Greek text says otherwise: "Ares who burns us . . . " (ll.190–92, my literal translation). Ares is always portrayed as the butcher of men, the impersonal enemy of the Greek heroes and constant ally of their enemies, whoever these happen to be. And Ares also happens, for better or worse, to be a tutelary deity of Thebes—the logical source, therefore, of divine retribution when his city has gone awry. Besides, Apollo said only that Oedipus was going to do these horrible things, not that he had to have his nose rubbed in their residue afterward: this is a play (as we often hear but don't believe) about the discovery of the deed, not about the deed itself. Finally, Tiresias is supposed to tell Oedipus that he, a blind old prophet, will not harm him, since "Apollo is enough . . . to work this out." But all the manuscripts say the reverse—that Oedipus can't harm Tiresias, since Apollo is well able to protect his favorite (ll.376–77). An eighteenth-century editor, believing this to be a play of fate, altered the text, and nearly every subsequent reader and translator has believed his fabricated evidence.[39]

The arguments continue. One analyst maintains that although the formation of an Oedipus complex in Freud's sense depends on a series of bizarre events, which certainly cannot be detected in the case of Oedipus himself, still the plays and myth display the Biblical conception of fate in which sons suffer for the sins of their fathers—Oedipus for Laius: incest is thus the punishment, not the crime.[40] And one classical scholar argues against Dodds and Knox that, no matter what the text says, Apollo *must* have sent the plague. Greeks believed a god's foreknowledge involved a kind of control over the events predicted; and Oedipus himself—half a generation later in myth-time, a full generation in the writings of Sophocles—says he was innocent; and so he must be.[41]

Sophocles' Theban plays are usually referred to and printed as a trilogy. They are not: *Antigone* (last in the chronology of the myth) was written first, about 441 B.C.; then *Oedipus the King*, about 429; and *Oedipus at Colonus* last, in 407; and Creon is quite a different character in each play. The form of a single play encourages the treatment not of some cosmic scheme but of a single action or a short sequence of actions, an intense examination of a hero in conflict with the leveling forces of the *polis* and of human experience, his inevitable defeat, and the nevertheless glorious heroic temper (in Bernard Knox's phrase) that he personifies.

Oedipus is his father's son. The sort of man who would try to kill another in a dispute over right of way at a crossroads is the sort to get killed by someone just like himself, his son. *His* son, in turn, is the sort to have twin sons, Eteocles and Polyneices, who kill one another in a duel over the kingship of Thebes. The meeting at the crossroads made more immediate sense to the original audience than it does to us. Oedipus was travelling on foot; Laius was riding in a chariot, accompanied by an entourage and preceded by a herald (l.802)— obviously a royal personage. The road was probably a rutted one, like most ancient Greek roads; only the wheel ruts, cut for axles of a standard size, were leveled, rather like railroad tracks in reverse. If two vehicles met head on, one of them would have to back up to a siding; clearly a traveler on foot should yield to one in a wagon or chariot.[42] Oedipus did not. The murder of Laius, moreover, occurred where three roads meet. Oedipus wanted to flee from the oracle at

Delphi, indeed had been ordered out of the precinct. Common sense should have told him also to veer away from the road down which had come the important-looking man he just killed. He had, after all, a third choice, to go to Daulis. Instead he went to Thebes, as the plot dictated.

Late in his life, in the *Oedipus at Colonus*, he grasps at the explanation of a curse and claims he was innocent of any crime: an understandable position, but the Greek audience would not have accepted his excuse in the way a modern reader is likely to. Certainly the motive, if it could be ascertained, would have influenced the jury's assessment of a killing, but motive could not undo the deed. Oedipus killed his father, perhaps in self-defense; but even so, he had to take responsibility for the action, though it involved no moral depravity. In one famous oratorical exercise of the fifth century, an athlete defended himself for having killed a spectator with a javelin when the man left his seat and dashed suddenly across the field. Greek justice was as logical and implacable as that of the Queen of Hearts in *Alice:* the athlete could not claim it was simply an accident nor that it was the imbecile's own fault; someone was dead and someone had to answer for it. Instead, the accused pleaded that he was innocent and that the javelin itself, or the boy himself, was the guilty party. (Antiphon, *Second Tetralogy.*) So ingrained in the Greek mind was the fear of pollution— an automatic, invisible, corrosive stain that must be lifted from the individual lest his state suffer—that one court, the Prytaneion, sat on cases against animals and objects.[43] Oedipus must have appeared more responsible for the murder and more of a fool in general to an audience attuned to the cultural code Sophocles was working with than he does to most modern interpreters—some of whom might agree with Freud that the play absolves men from moral responsibility and exhibits the gods as promoters of evil.[44]

In this most heavily ironic of all Greek plays the punishment, of course, must fit the crime. Oedipus puts out his eyes which are the organs of his intellect. Since he could not see the truth that was plainly before him, he must ever after walk in darkness. Eyes would also convey the shame of his situation to him, and he cannot bear that. Jocasta commits suicide rather than live with the disgrace. There are other versions of the myth, however, in which Oedipus did not blind himself or did but remained in Thebes anyway. (And no reference to the myth was very popular among the Theban nobility, who wished to disclaim any taint of incest in their lineage.) Freud's interpretation of the act of self-blinding centers on the all-determining power of the incest taboo. Oedipus' eyes, far from being connected with his intellect, are symbols of his sexual organs, via the path of upward displacement: items above the waist are substituted for those similar but socially less acceptable ones below the waist.[45] Oedipus uses the brooches from his mother's dress to put his eyes out, and these pins are understood to be symbols of the mother's phallic power over the son. The detail of the "brooches," as they are usually translated, introduced into the Greek spectator's mind an even more poignant, albeit offstage, scene than Freud imagined. These pins held together a woman's dress at the shoulders; when they were removed, her dress would fall open to the waist. Though Jocasta's corpse lay on the ground as Oedipus snatched the brooches away, and thus her dress was not disturbed, the scene nevertheless evoked the conjugal experience of most of the audience.

When he has discovered who he is, Oedipus rushes into the palace with a sword that he seems to have intended to plunge up her vagina—"the field of double plowing whence I was born" (1.1257). But the queen has barred the double (labial?) doors to her chamber, and so Oedipus has to wrench the bolts out of their sockets. Now certainly much of the symbolism we have come to know as Freudian fits this scene, but the imagery does not add up to evidence that supports the hypothesis of the Oedipus complex. The king's sword thrust into his mother's vagina (from the Latin word for sheath or scabbard) is a natural symbol under the circumstances. And the plucked-out doorbolts poetically anticipate the blinding soon to come: the open doors reveal the last of the horrors that Oedipus sees; his self-blinding ends all revelation.

Incest is the crime this hero discovers, because incest is one of the most horrible acts a man can commit. Another such horrible act is cannibalism, especially of one's own children, and far more Greek myths are concerned with cannibalism than with incest. By the time that Sophocles was writing, the origins of the incest taboo were so far in the past that they provided only the occasion for disaster in this play, the metaphor for Oedipus' blunderings, not the central theme.

The Need for Classical Evidence

Why did Freud tamper with Greek myth? First, he thought that every human creation bore the imprint of its maker's mind and thus lay accessible to the investigations of psychoanalysis:

> Any estimate of psychoanalysis would be incomplete if it failed to make clear that, alone among the medical disciplines, it has the most extensive relations with the mental sciences, and that it is in a position to play a part of the same importance in the studies of religions and cultural history and in the sciences of mythology and literature as it is in psychiatry.[46]

In 1909, in a letter to his collaborator on *Dreams in Folklore*, the classicist D. E. Oppenheim, Freud expressed a similar view but admitted his own deficiencies in classics.

I have long been haunted by the idea that our studies on the content of the neuroses might be destined to solve the riddle of the formation of the myths, and that the nucleus of mythology is nothing other than what we speak of as "the nuclear complex of the neuroses" . . . But we are amateurs, and have every reason to be afraid of mistakes. We are lacking in academic training and familiarity with the material. Thus we are looking about for an enquirer whose development has been in the reverse direction, who possesses the specialized knowledge and is ready to apply to it the psychoanalytic armory that we will gladly put at his command—a native enquirer, as one might say, who will be able to achieve something quite other than we who are intruders of another species. [47]

Freud also expected that the investigations of properly trained classicists would elaborate on the practical data and substantiate the theories of psychoanalysis; the "cause," the psychoanalytic movement would thus be advanced. He remained innocent that his whole approach to myth involves two fallacies, one of logic and the other of attitude.

The first is a complicated case of the confusion of temporal priority with truth. The case history or pattern of the neurotic's symptoms is found to resemble the structure and incidents of a myth. Since the myth comes from that Greco-Roman schoolroom where Western Civilization got its first book learning (or perhaps from that even earlier Egyptian or Mesopotamian cradle in which the first schoolboys were originally rocked), by invoking the paternal influence of our cultural ancestors we feel closer to our origins in general and therefore somehow closer to the truth. (Similarly in the world of heroes, as Nestor in the *Iliad* is fond of telling anyone who will listen, sons are never the men their fathers were, yet their noble genealogies lend them a valuation and an aura of glory they could not attain by merit alone in their shame-bounded society.) Moreover, the *locus classicus* for the myth of Oedipus is one of the greatest and certainly the best known of all the Greek tragedies, the model play of the model playwright, the work chosen by Aristotle to illustrate his theory of tragedy—itself the model of literary criticism. Founders of new political orders or of new ideologies have commonly needed holy books to justify their lines of power or logic, have needed to appropriate historical authenticity, wherever they could find it, for what may have been only a practical hypothesis or an expedient disposition of civil disorder. Caesar Augustus commissioned Vergil to write the Roman holy book, the *Aeneid*, and thereby made his victory in the civil wars and assumption of the principate fated, albeit by an *ex post facto* fate. And Mussolini, that former Latin teacher, commissioned new editions of the *Aeneid* and other classical texts that could serve as propaganda for a new Roman Empire. Great men write their own holy books—Mohammed, Plato, Freud. But even their works draw on earlier texts in order to achieve a commanding tone: the *Koran* on the whole prophetic tradition of the Semites, the Platonic dialogues on the Pythagorean writings and the sagas, *The Interpretation of Dreams* and *Totem and Taboo* on *Oedipus the King*. Freud had a special need for corroborative evidence from the Greek myths. A classical education provided an entrance into the mainstream of European culture for the newly prosperous Jews of Middle Europe,[48] and Freud wanted non-Semitic support for the psychoanalytic movement.

In the field of psychoanalysis, the dependence on earlier and therefore validating texts leads the practicing theoretician into the second fallacy. When a psychiatrist or psychologist deals with a myth, confronts it, admits it into his mental sanctum and office, invites it to lie on the primal couch, he changes it. Freud was at the stage of an early botanist who studies only specimens and remains ignorant of the system those specimens were designed for. A myth, uprooted from its native context, washed clean of jungle dirt, and brought back barely alive to civilization in a Victorian vasculum, has little content and no context left except that which the collector imposes on it. Freud brought home from his reading in exotic places a text alien to turn-of-the-century Vienna and insisted that Sophocles' play substantiated his own myth. Surprisingly, his appropriation masquerades as a discovery of the myth's true meaning, instead of admitting to being the blatant imposition of meaning that it is. The corpus of Greek myth has seemed a fair-game preserve of documentation to many other theoreticians on safari from the consulting rooms, but the rare beasts at large in that ancient paradise do not breed in captivity and can be tracked to their lairs only with proper knowledge of their habitats, habits, and life cycles.

Unfortunately for the patient, the myth which the analyst chooses as an allegory of a diagnosable complex may turn out to be a model he feels compelled to accept, whether or not it fits his case. Freud imposed his version of the Oedipus myth with a heavy hand on colleagues and patients alike. Because of the authority of the doctor and because of both the academic authority of a classical text and the éclat to be gained from identifying one's career, for better or worse, with that of a mythological character (the fashion for which the likes of Neumann, Kerenyi, and Campbell are mostly responsible, in works like *The Great Mother*, *Eleusis*, and *Myths to Live By*), the analysand may accept the myth not only as a diagram of his past but also as a plan for his future. If he relates himself to the myth in this way, then he chooses imprisonment over liberation. The fated behavior of the hero or heroine—fated, if for no other reason than that tradition says it happened this way, and so it must happen, again and again in the retellings—ought to function, for the most part, as an anti-model in the process of analysis. Only examples chosen with due attention to the almost inevitable sufferings and excesses that accompany such heroic careers should serve as partial models for certain stages of the patient's future. Myth has far too often been used as self-congratulatory self-justification; thus the beginning of Arthur Symon's "Modern Beauty":

> I am the torch, she saith, and what to me
> If the moth die of me?

W. H. Auden has formulated a definition of psychoanalysis which could serve as a warning to avoid the worst of the mythical models, an encouragement to adopt the best:

> As a therapy, the goal of psychoanalysis is to free the patient from the slavery of impersonal behavior so that he may become capable of personal deeds. A deed is an act by which the doer voluntarily discloses himself to others: behavior is involuntary and discloses, not a unique self, but either those natural needs common to all men or those diagnosable complexes which the patient shares with other sufferers of the same kind. Thanks to psychoanalysis, it is now a matter of public knowledge that, frequently, when we imagine we are acting as ourselves, we are really only exhibiting behavior, and it is one of the analyst's tasks to unmask this illusion in his patients. [49]

As we shall see in Chapter 2, too many modern interpreters, by removing the myths from their original poetic and cultural contexts, have transmogrified the deeds of the ancient characters into the pale foreshadowings of modern behavior.

Psychoanalysis has happened upon no more dangerous tool than myth. The characters of the myths found in their careers new ways of adapting their pathologies to the service of Bronze Age courts and developing city-states. The real-life characters of analysis, in search of some compromising course between the voracious demands of society and the tempting models for their own halt-ingly emergent personalities, may sail too close to the Charybdis of heroical prototypes and never free themselves from that ancient vortex of self-perpetu-ating tragedy. The danger is increased by the habit of oversimplification. The contrary versions of a given myth are conflated, even bits of unrelated material are collated and juxtaposed, and then all are thrown together into some al-chemical retort—with no respect for the variety of incident and detail wrought by generations of poets and artists—to create any Ur-myth the writer fancies. Those versions which do not support the new myth's claims for legitimacy are dismissed as bowdlerized; the new myth is used to illuminate the clinical material that inspired its creation in the first place. The authority of its pro-

nouncements are bolstered by their supposed resemblance to those paradigms
of experience first conjugated by the Greeks. The patient or analyst in search
of a useful model should instead turn to a precise examination of each version
of each likely myth.

Examination of each ancient myth patronized by psychoanalysis can
prove a source of liberating knowledge for a patient, auto-analysand, or careful
reader when confronted by the explanations of the modern mythographers. Just
so, psychological interpretations can liberate one from the conforming effect of
the old cultural standards, as tyrannical a force (in the life of ancient and, until
recently, of modern man) in their way as the myths of analysis. What is rec-
ommended here is not a rejection of psychoanalysis' readings of classical myths
in favor of a return to the myths' "original" meanings, but rather a cultivation
of the knowledge of both sets of readings and, in Philip Rieff's phrase, a "rational
alienation from public enthusiasm" over either—a floating between two potentially despotic ideologies, and a conscious and constant playing off by the
skeptical reader of an archaeology of myth against theoretical speculation.

Inquiry as Therapy

As the founder of psychoanalysis Freud quite properly felt himself to be
a discoverer and explorer of new realms. And as a physician dealing with
traumas repressed by embarrassed patients he pursued his investigations under
many of the same constraints that beset the detective. The melding of the
psychological yarn and the thriller is a natural one: *Oedipus the King* is the
first mystery, as Freud noted in *The Interpretation of Dreams*, in which the
detective turns out to be the killer: "The action of the play consists in nothing
other than the process of revealing, with cunning delays and ever-mounting
excitement—a process that can be likened to the work of a psycho-analysis—
that Oedipus himself is the murderer of Laius, but further that he is the son
of the murdered man and Jocasta."[50] Freud is said to have been the only man
to have analyzed himself, because he was the first and there was no one else
to do it for him. But in point of fact, or point of myth, Oedipus beat him to
it. Tiresias, the prophet, functions as a kind of anti-analyst who says to the
patient, "Are you sure you want to go ahead with this? You may open up a can
of worms"; or like the knowledgeable old crony in a thriller, who warns the
detective that it's better not to know. But Oedipus the analysand, like the determined private detective, chooses knowledge over safety and himself both asks
and answers the most difficult of questions.

After locating the symptoms, the clues, the analyst then has to interpret them to his satisfaction and to that of his patient. Since Freud himself had not been analyzed, he tended to talk too much during an analytic session and to bully his patients;[51] when the patients claimed they couldn't think of anything more to tell him, he insisted there *was* more. Although he once claimed that insistence works only for a little while and then fails,[52] elsewhere he argues that strife—bad in scientific controversies—is useful and necessary in analysis: the analysand's critical faculty is not an independent function but "the tool of his emotional attitudes and is directed by his resistance. If there is something he does not like, he can put up a shrewd fight against it and appear highly critical." The analyst should, in fact, be dissatisfied if he cannot provoke resistances and point them out to the patient.[53] Picture again our cinematic "shamus" as he punches the truth out of an uncooperative witness; Oedipus, too, uses a little muscle on one of the shepherds when the chap claims he just can't seem to remember.

From the biographies by Jones and Clark and Max Shur, we know that the family situation into which Freud was born was fertile ground for the growth of an Oedipus complex. He was almost closer in age to his mother than was his father,[54] and he came to feel the relation between mother and son provided "the purest examples of an unchangeable affection unimpaired by any egoistic considerations."[55] Freud suffered from an Oedipus complex himself. Having discovered and analyzed it, he was the first to apply self-knowledge to psychology. "The amazing thing about this discovery is that it is directly accompanied by the conviction that this singular adventure is also a paradigm of destiny," Paul Ricoeur writes. "Being honest with oneself coincides with grasping a universal drama."[56] Self-knowledge stiffened into oracular dogma as the analysand stepped out of the shaky role of Oedipus the murderer and into that more secure one of Oedipus the mouthpiece of the gods. Certain of the nature of his own neurosis and enthralled by *Oedipus the King*, he never questioned whether the subject matters of the two were one and the same: they both evoked such powerful emotional responses that they simply had to be identical.

Having found "the truth" about himself to lie in his past, Freud remained fascinated with the Past of the race. He collected ancient *objets d'art*; enjoyed comparing the work of the analyst with the work of the archaeologist (the unearthing of buried bits and dusty pieces, the fitting together of forgotten fragments, the drawing of conclusions about the historical whole); and made the levels of Rome a model for the many-layered psyche.[57] Of course for Freud there was no other way. We all live too much in the past, because we have incompletely digested or suppressed it. The neurotic has cathected on some event to a debilitating degree, and can be rendered more functional again only by being led back to this trauma which refuses to be ignored; once he has learned to accept the past, to make a practical compromise with it, he can live relatively free in the present.

Freud's emphasis on the past makes the present of each Oedipus seem inevitable.

> So long as we trace the development [of a mental process] from its final stage backwards, the connection appears continuous, and we feel we have gained an insight which is completely satisfactory or even exhaustive. . . . [But we cannot follow up the premises to make a prediction.] The synthesis is thus not so satisfactory as the analysis; in other words, from a knowledge of the premises we could not have foretold the nature of the result. . . . But we never know beforehand which of the determining factors will prove the weaker or the stronger. [58]

Oddly enough, this comes close to a conception of fate common among the Greeks: after it's all over, you feel that it had to have turned out that way. Thus only the past is determined.

The past constitutes an obscure text. Who will come to interpret it? The myth of Oedipus not only lent its name to the complex that dominated Freud's life and thought, but it also provided a mythological model for the hermeneutic role that Freud expected the analyst to play in the modern world—interpreter no longer of entrails, but of dreams. With the task of interpretation Freud's real confusion of roles began: the psychoanalyst both as explorer, detective, poet (insofar as he expounds myth) and as priest or intermediary between the laity and the gods or demons that beset their souls. One role contaminated the other: Freud remained the detective (Oedipus) even as he became the prophet or priest: discovering, prophesying, but—unlike the ancient soothsayers—always the past, never the future.

Central to Freud's understanding of psychoanalysis and to the disputes that have swarmed about Sophocles' play are Oedipus' visit to the oracle and his encounters with Tiresias. The oracle told Oedipus his "destiny" (Freud's word, not Sophocles'); and twenty years later Tiresias told him his past. In the psychoanalytic myth, Freud has taken the place both of the oracle which is the ultimate expression of divine wisdom and of Tiresias, the human interpreter of that wisdom who has been blessed by the gods with the burden of explaining the oracle when its utterances are most obscure or frightening.

By replacing the oracle and the prophet with the analyst, Freud reversed the direction of ancient prophecies, examining only the entrails of the past and neglecting the flight of the future. The usual function of the major oracles and the local prophets was to give practical advice, not to solve enigmas: should we make war on our neighbors in Megara? what gods should the new colony to Pontus worship? will Nicostratus, son of Stephanus, make a good husband for my daughter? Even where the inquiry is directed toward the past, the real concern lies with the future: what must we do to get rid of this pollution or that curse, in order to restore health and prosperity to the land? Many Greek plays before *Oedipus the King* dealt with the seemingly endless troubles of a noble family, but usually those troubles were, in the course of the dramatic action, resolved into a new future for the polis. Oedipus, however, expends his heroic energies in unearthing his past, but with no comprehension of where any new knowledge will lead him or his city. It took Sophocles nearly twenty-five years to create a future for his protagonist in *Oedipus at Colonus*; for when *Oedipus the King* ended, a broken king went into exile, leaving behind a Thebes too shocked to realize that the plague had been exorcised, and the various contrary versions of the myth then current left the original audience far from certain what would happen to the hero.

Does psychoanalysis have anything at all to do with the future? Freud's method may suggest an answer. He looked always for the mechanism of a process, "which is of the same kind in all cases," while the factors favoring the process "are variable and not necessarily essential."[59] What about varying content? "Well, contraries are treated in the same way as conformities, and there is a special preference for expressing them by the same manifest element."[60] The interpreter, it would seem, cannot tie himself to the facts. One could take a dim view of this attitude, but Philip Rieff does not: "As an empirical worker, he looked not for evidence but for meaning."[61] Freud practiced, in a sense, the interpretative act as the aesthetic act. A sufficient number of sufficiently imaginative aesthetic acts can build a utopia, liberating us from the oppressiveness of what is actual. Nietzsche, for one, attributes world-making significance to the art of interpretation.

Somewhere the atelier of the psychoanalyst as artist must share a party wall with the board room of the lunatic fringe. The fact remains that Freud was building a world—and one that many have entered and taken as a way, the modern skeptical way. Behind its self-advertisement as an empirical science, Freudianism (Rieff claims) stands as the most influential heir of nineteenth-century rationalism. It tells us how to live and offers a new, secular pietism for the turning of Western man's attention inward.[62] It thus prepares the way for its own demise. For Freud, in bullying his patients and colleagues, aroused their resistances, taught them the sense of independence that comes with a pugnacious skepticism, and prepared them for a split with him.

Roland Barthes speaks of an ultimate dissatisfaction with all critical languages—psychoanalysis included—a desperate resistance to any reductive system. "It was better, once and for all, to make my protestation of singularity into a virtue—to try making what Nietzsche called the 'ego's ancient sovereignty' into an heuristic principle."[63] Interpretation of the past has shaded off into discovery of a future. One could, of course, lose the way on the way. As Auden notes, the psychoanalytic method, like the Socratic, presupposes on the part of the patient "a genuine passion for truth or health. When the passion for truth is lacking, dialectic becomes a technique for avoiding coming to any conclusion just as, when the passion for health is lacking, self-examination is used to justify neurosis."[64] Asking unanswerable questions of one's self could prove a more alluring vocation than simply "getting on with it." Nietzsche cathected on the question mark.[65]

Can such a rigorous inquiry as this truly be called a cure? Freud claimed to be interested first in the cure, by way of the inquiry. But elsewhere he makes it clear that analysis is more useful for the healthy than the sick, who are less able to withstand the rigors of the quest and bear the shock of discovery at the end. Rieff calls psychoanalysis "a therapy for the healthy, not a solution for the sick—except so far as the sick themselves become analysts and find in this therapeutic their personal solution, as Freud did."[66] Certainly the founder of psychoanalysis had a bias for curious, intelligent patients. But Freud eventually had to admit that a neurosis may in fact be the most viable course for a patient, given the realities of his life and the frailty of his psyche; Oedipus, on the other hand, concerns himself only with the inquiry, although Tiresias and Jocasta and his own premonitions all tell him that his sanity depends on ignorance.

Art and Analysis

If Freud in some sense behaved like an artist, claiming the poetic privilege that once went with the prophet's staff, how did he treat his fellows in literary craft? With inconsistently professional animus, as it turns out. Freud and his epigones have regarded the poet, playwright, and mythographer with ambivalence—on the one hand as their distinguished colleagues in probing the mysteries of the unconscious, on the other as simply the ignorant producers of raw data (like dreams or free associations) for analysis. The artist differs from the neurotic chiefly in the matter of success: he manages productively to sublimate the very fears and tensions that drive a neurotic to distraction. Freud's confidence in his rationalism leads him to ride down the aesthetic imagination of others; he presumes that the power of art depends on an appeal hidden both from the artist and from his audience.[67] The psychiatrist supposedly eschews the role of the poet who creates meaning—though in that act of creation the poet may feel like only the mouthpiece of forces prior to and greater than his own consciousness—and prefers to wear the persona of the physician-anthropologist who discovers the original and therefore true meaning of a text, explains it to the intelligentsia (the native mythmakers, even Greek ones, must unfortunately be left in darkest ignorance), and applies a poultice of its essences to the psyche of modern man. Like superstition, art is pretty much the product of "conscious ignorance and unconscious knowledge of the motivation of accidental psychical events." And much of the mythological view of the world "*is nothing but psychology projected into the external world.*"[68]

The analyst can fit his interpretations to dream, parapraxis, or play alike. That the Oedipus of Sophocles' play didn't know what he was doing is an inevitable deviation from the analytic facts, merely a poetic *distortion*. "The ignorance of Oedipus is a legitimate representation of the unconscious state into which, for adults, the whole experience has fallen; and the coercive power of the oracle, which makes or should make the hero innocent, is a recognition of the inevitability of the fate which has condemned every son to live through the Oedipus complex."[69]

Freud's methodology never distinguishes between art and dream. A dream, he insists, is not a coherent narrative. "On the contrary, it is as a rule like a piece of breccia, composed of various fragments of rock held together by a binding medium." The dream itself really doesn't count, but rather the memory and account of the dream. If our memory distorts the dream, the distortion is as important as the original.[70] The distorted account then constitutes the text for analysis. The analyst penetrates the text to explain what the dream images mean; he unveils the original, unconscious material behind the account and forces the patient to accept his interpretation. Ultimately the interpretation reigns supreme over the dream or the dream-text. Similarly, Freud makes art give testimony, in Rieff's words, "not for itself but in praise of his own insight."[71] Once the scientific juice has been squeezed out of the work of art, only the rhetorical pulp remains, and that can now safely be discarded.

Freud, the scientist, accepted the notion of a true fiction. Indeed, all anamnesis is a tissue, if not of lies, then of fabrications. What actually happened (*res gestae*), K. K. Ruthven muses, "is knowable only through an account of what happened (*historia rerum gestarum*)," and so the historian becomes a sort of mythmaker.[72] We remember stories, even stories *we* have told—if only to ourselves—as though they actually happened. Myth, in its most general sense, is merely memory distorted by narration; mythology, a form of communal solipsism.

The analyst, then, presuming that the end product of all these various distortions conceals one and the same brand of truth, treats the texts of dream and literature exactly the same way. It doesn't work. For one thing, in a work of art the author has selected his material and shaped and organized it in such a way as to have a calculated effect on his audience. The psychoanalyst, on the other hand, wants to hear everything a playwright had to leave out, and he would, if he could, riffle through the notebooks the writer gathered material in before calculation took over. More conscious design obtains in a work of art than in a dream, and this design is not identical with the "distortion" that inheres in any account of a dream—the emphasis in which originally fell on the images. In the myths, the emphasis falls on the narrative; in analysis, on themes.

For another thing, while the literary text may be said to be more a product of conscious effort than the dream, the artist himself, unlike the analysand, does not get a chance to appear before the doctor as a sentient being who can sit up, make eye contact with his interlocutor, and challenge the doctor's decrees. The work of art, as André Green points out, is mute, except for the discourse already and finally incorporated in it. The work cannot provide additional material through free association, give any indication of how it came about (though we can, of course, dig for clues in a biography of the author), go back on what it has said, nor dispute the analyst's interpretation with him. The analyst must therefore proceed with greater care, in a certain sense, in his examination of the work of art than with a living patient; he must stay close "to the lines of force that govern the architecture of his object."[73] Though more defenseless than a living analysand, the work of art does possess one great advantage over doctor and patient: longevity. And the work remains unmoved by analysis.

In fact, what further analysis the doctor or critic can properly perform upon poem or myth—themselves the products of long reflection—may be phenomenological, structural, rhetorical, or a kind of psychological *amplificatio*. Gérard de Nerval's epigrammatic reply to the question why he kept a pet lobster and walked it on a silver chain down the Champs Elysées—"because she doesn't bark and knows the secrets of the sea"—can be picked apart in many ways, but not psychoanalyzed unless our purpose is the trivial and probably pointless one of understanding Nerval's personality rather than his art. Shakespeare's Hamlet or Nabokov's Humbert Humbert are not dramatic embodiments of a psychoanalyst's dream data, but renderings of characters, solid readings on them, psychological interpretations of them. The violence that may be done to literature by psychoanalysis grows in proportion to the work's age and, paradoxically, to its literary qualities: less to the tale of Little Red Riding Hood (interpreted by Erich Fromm as an allegory of menarche and of male envy of pregnancy), greater to *Oedipus the King*.

A last problem in this matter of interpretation must be dealt with: Greek drama, for the most part, lacks a psychology in our sense. Façade is all. Deed is character, particularly in the ancient theaters where the actors relied on

stylized masks and broad gestures to convey emotion all the way to the back
rows. The very quality that seems to render, say, a Greek play malleable under
the blows of interpretation makes it, in fact, inflexible. The rigidity of the
characters is just that, a stiffness that ruins them for roles in the situational
analysis and ethics so dear to our twentieth-century hearts. Their situations are
not ours. Their visages denote both less and more than ours do.

   Prosōpon, the Greek for "mask," also means "face," "aspect," "stage-
figure," "person"—which last English word derives from the Latin *persona*,
or "mask." John Jones contends that the look of a man, for the Greeks, contained
the truth about him and that the mask isolated the essentials of a character
better than nature itself could: "unlike the modern face and the modern mask,
they [the ancient masks] did not owe their interest to the further realities lying
behind them, because they declared the whole man. They stated; they did not
hint or hide."[74] We, however, are dedicated to the proposition that truth is
recoverable not so much from the essentials of a character—he is a king, he
is the son of Laius, he has a quick temper—as from the inessentials: the walking
stick purchased in Delphi, the fondness for sheep cheese, a particular turn of
phrase or way of pausing before speaking an endearment. All sorts of things
that the myths omit.

   New interpretations may still today be imposed upon the old figures, but
often only at the price of such violence done to them that they will bear little
resemblance to the former inhabitants of Sophocles' mind and plays. Indeed,
the great advantage that the Greeks found in the myths was that they were fixed,
and thus might serve as prototypes of human experience and noble conduct—
standards notched into the doorposts of Western Civilization, against which
the distressing shortcomings of daily life might be measured, and in healthy
competition with which the race's and the individual's deficiencies might be
overcome. Subtle variations in the myths were permitted to the poets, and on
occasion some innovator might create a new meaning out of an old story; but
even radical changes were made with a view toward a gradual refinement of
laws, customs, and models of behavior within a quite restricted arena of invention. The avant-garde by Greek standards is pretty tame by ours—inured as
we have become to the whimsies of Dali, Warhol, and The Talking Heads.
Did the ancient audience practice a reading-into-the-myths such as psychoanalysis silently advocates? Yes, at times, but with an important difference: the
Greek readers-into-the-myths shared most of the same codes that the mythmakers employed in composing their tales. Tradition guided all.

Intellectual Blindness

"Many men, even in dreams, have lain with their mothers," Jocasta says to Oedipus, intending to comfort him (ll.981–82). Freud took these words as proof that he was on the track of the right complex. The fascination, however, which this play holds over analyst and patient, and over a patient turned analyst, is due to the perfect model it offers for the psychoanalytical task. But this is a formal model and not one for the content of the neurosis. Freud's reading of his own myth into *Oedipus the King* was right in a sense after all, for this is a most peculiar play. First of all this is the play most devoted to the discovery not simply of identities but to the significance of nearly forgotten deeds, just as the work of analysis often is. Then too, the protagonist—Oedipus, "Whom all men call great" (l.40)—has a reputation for intelligence, and we wonder how he got it. He solved the riddle of the Sphinx. But his ignorance of who he is or at least of the regicide he committed strains the elasticity of even the most willing suspension of disbelief. Aristotle thought he had solved the difficulty by calling this a play of discovery and prescribing that, if the plot requires implausible events, these should have transpired before the play opens. But Aristotle did not so much resolve our doubts about the play's credibility as avoid them. For there are really two plays here. One of them inheres in Sophocles' text, the play of discovery, the play that offers the conflict of manifest versus ironically latent meaning.

This is the play that almost everyone has seen, written about, and been satisfied with. Nevertheless one idiosyncratic critic, Philip Vellacott, has decided that Oedipus must have known all along that he was the regicide and that he nobly contrived the search for the murderer in such a way as to reveal his guilt, force his banishment, and save the people of Thebes, who had no other savior, from the plague.[75] A patently ridiculous interpretation, especially because of the effect that the revelation has on Oedipus; and yet Vellacott sensed something truly odd about this play, and he correctly described the common need of the criminal or the neurotic to be found out. Freud's interpretation, too, can easily be refuted from Sophocles' text. But Freud, like Vellacott, was interpreting the antitext of *Oedipus the King*, the play that Sophocles never wrote but which it is impossible for us to ignore as we read the one he did write. This antitext is a play not of discovery, but of repression. For no sensible man could kill a king (obvious from his entourage, herald, and chariot) old enough to be his father, marry a queen old enough to be his mother—doing both deeds after having received the terrifying prophecy from Delphi—and then ignore the implications of his actions for a decade and a half. Yet we are expected to regard Oedipus as a smart man. The implausible events that Aristotle says we can ignore because they happened before the opening of the play are the very premises of the play's whole action, the knowledge that sustains dramatic tension through scene after scene of interrogation. The text of discovery presumes the existence of the antitext of repression. And Oedipus accomplished this repression of the obvious so thoroughly that we cannot help but judge him guilty. Is his guilt, however, not of sexual but rather of an intellectual nature?

Freud thought he had discovered the essential identity of the two issues. Thus in *Three Essays on the Theory of Sexuality:*

> At about the same time as the sexual life of children reaches its first peak, between the ages of three and five, they also begin to show signs of the activity which may be ascribed to the instinct for knowledge or research. . . . We have learnt from psychoanalysis that the instinct for knowledge in children is attracted unexpectedly early and intensively to sexual problems and is in fact possibly first aroused by them.

In fact, the prepubescent question—where do babies come from?—is "the same riddle that was propounded by the Theban Sphinx."[76] The intellectual quest, for the wise Greek hero and the skeptical Viennese doctor, is the same as the quest for sexual enlightenment and liberation. (One Freudian scholar even thinks that eyes can be equated with genitals because of the importance of voyeurism in infantile sexuality—seeing is desiring and wanting to know more—and that knowledge in general, for adults, replaces the desire to view our mothers.[77])

Oedipus is a prototype for the neurotic because he forgets—but incompletely—his problems, traumas, and sins, until forced by circumstances to remember it all. The plot of *Oedipus the King* can serve as a model for a Platonic or Pythagorean rebirth through anamnesis; just so in *Three Essays on Infantile Sexuality* Freud uses the play as a model for the psychoanalytical experience.[78] The neurotic's forgetting and then remembering under decontrolled conditions, which constitute the process of analysis, is only a small part of the larger human condition of coming to self-knowledge.

> In general people experience their present naively, as it were, without being able to form an estimate of its contents; they have first to put themselves at a distance from it—the present, that is to say, must have become the past—before it can yield points of vantage from which to judge the future.[79]

But both the healthy man and the neurotic will fend off memories from the past that could cause pain. Freud compares the forgetting of such memories to the flight reflex of an organism in the presence of painful stimuli. The rules of

military service and romantic love both forbid the forgetting of anything connected with their duties. In this way they suggest that forgetting is deliberate.[80]
Oedipus has forgotten something terribly important, prides himself on his wisdom, and then fails, finally, to forget the past completely. In neurotics and
hysterics, Freud observes, "their repression of the idea to which the intolerable
wish is attached has been a failure."[81] In one sense, then, Oedipus does exemplify the fated human condition: he thinks he knows it all because he can't
remember the worst parts until the old story-telling instinct for the truth forces
it out of him and his associates. And so his story allows us to connect a wide
variety of nasty events in our own lives to some mythical pattern, for better
or worse.

The spellbinding effect that the play works on the reader or viewer depends
on the risks that Sophocles takes with irony; and this effect operates on two
levels. The one that is usually discussed is the level of dramatic irony, on which
the audience is gripped by a foreknowledge of what Oedipus is about to do and
by a helplessness before his headlong rush to understanding and so
to destruction.

The other irony, however, can claim responsibility for the success of the
first and for the theatrical success of the play in spite of Sophocles' violations
of the principles of dramatic structure. This irony might best be called "au-
thorial," for it arises from the audience's anticipation not of the actor's but of
the dramatist's next move with his plot, his next demand that they—familiar
with the myth, of course, but witnessing this structuring of it for the first time—
accept the growing strain each new coincidence places on their credibility.
Laius rewarded Shepherd A with a place in the royal retinue for his good services
in exposing the child. This man was the only one to escape alive from the fight
at the crossroads. He left the palace service when he saw Oedipus become king.
Now, Oedipus happens to be interrogating him when a messenger from Corinth
arrives to tell him that Polybus is dead. Oedipus mocks the oracle that told him
he would kill his father, but worries he might still marry Merope. The messenger
tells him to relax: Merope isn't his mother; in fact, the messenger himself
brought him as a baby to the king and queen and was rewarded for relieving
their childless state by being given a job in the palace at Corinth; he used to
be a shepherd and . . . why, there's his old friend, the other shepherd, the one
who gave him the crippled infant. This second irony strains the credibility of
all who read or view the play. The coincidences of the plot are too neat and too
numerous. But something strange happens in the mind of the reader, between
the entrance of the characters and the exit of the Chorus, and saves this play.
Gradually it dawns on us that we know what is coming in each scene, not
because of our vast experience with bad drama but because of our experience
with life. Daily life is this ludicrously coincidental. We, with our twentieth

century sensibilities, do not laugh at the unbelievable turns of this plot because
we know they could happen. Even a so-called intelligent man could be this
foolish; for intelligence often manifests itself as cleverness, not wisdom, and
cleverness loves to lead its glib practitioner into folly. The psychoanalytical
journals overflow with case histories this bizarre, as would the annals of every
Greek village and American small town, if annals were kept these days. The
best argument for the historicity of the sagas would be based on their lack of
realistic plots; only life could concoct such scenarios.

And so we come back to the theme of the play: intellectual blindness.
No matter how smart we are, the weight of mortal thought cannot out-maneuver
the gossamer twists of fate.

Unnatural Wisdom

On Sophocles' stage we view the consequences not so much of incest as
of the theft of the super-bestial knowledge that distinguishes man from the
monsters and makes him cut such a lonely figure in the universe. Oedipus,
like every Sophoclean hero, stands alone and isolated from his fellows, the last
man in the play to listen to advice, the only one who can never drop his regal
pose and accept the comfort of common emotions. Though high-soled buskins
were not worn by actors until late in the second century B.C., we still picture
Oedipus striding uncomfortably across the stage (on, to borrow a phrase from
Randall Jarrell, seven-league crutches), head and shoulders above all the other
characters. At the opening of the play, Oedipus' wisdom, real or imagined, has
already separated him from the citizens of Thebes. The members of the Chorus
in tragedy after tragedy, as here, sing their hopes that such distinction and glory
as the royal family has earned might never touch their lives—for disaster always
strikes the exalted.

In the *Birth of Tragedy* Nietzsche came closer to solving the enigma of
this hero than Freud did in *The Interpretation of Dreams*:

> How else can one compel nature to surrender her secrets if not by trium-
> phantly resisting her, that is, by means of something unnatural? It is this
> insight that I find expressed in that horrible triad of Oedipus' destinies; the
> same man who solves the riddle of nature—that Sphinx of two species—
> also must break the most sacred natural orders by murdering his father
> and marrying his mother. Indeed, the myth seems to whisper to us that
> wisdom, and particularly Dionysian wisdom, is an unnatural abomina-
> tion; that he who by means of his knowledge plunges nature into the abyss
> of destruction must also suffer the dissolution of nature in his own person. [82]

Oedipus, by his devotion to the search for the truth, was bound to be an exile. Incest provides the excuse why home can never be home to post-lapsarian man. He has asked questions which, whether or not he ever gets the answers, make it impossible for him to remain a member of any society, for stability requires ignorance, native or self-imposed. Schopenhauer, that arch-misanthrope, declared that the philosopher in seeking the truth must act like Oedipus, who pursues his inquiry even when he realizes the horror of the answer.[83] And Nietzsche, perched tipsily on his icy crag in the valley of the Engadine, observed that the superman's quest for knowledge, his struggle with self-overcoming, marked him as a rare beast, one set apart from the masses who dwell on the plains, content with their bread and sausages. Oedipus was doomed from his birth to wander across the rocky and chaotic intervals between the secure walls of the cities, the wild country that first received him. In a countryside ruled by the grudge and the vendetta, no act of murder could be more isolating and more dangerous than patricide.

In a letter to his fiancée Martha, Freud actually toyed with the idea of living more like the Gentiles and "not striving after discoveries and delving too deep."[84] His moment of weakness of course passed; but in contrast to Oedipus and Nietzsche, those twin mountaineers who dared to seek answers to the same terrible questions as psychoanalysis asks, Freud does take on the odd aspect of a city man, indeed almost a boulevardier. Odd, because wisdom or knowledge, which we of the Western tradition can gain only in cities, paradoxically renders one unfit to dwell there amid the din and press of human intercourse. Deep learning leads to the kind of neurasthenia that Attila the Hun might have suffered from. Jocasta clearly belongs in the city, for to be of the city means to be amenable to compromises. Freud, simultaneously urbane and outcast as only a Semite can be, saw compromise as essential to the healthy personality, or at least to the functional one—since sickness, neurosis, is part of the human condition and we simply have to learn to get along as conscious cripples in a society of unconscious cripples. Oedipus, however, refuses to temporize, to accept his handicap. Creon, Jocasta, and Tiresias beg him to give in, not to worry, to listen to reason, to live lightly; and none of these suave suggestions has any effect.

Nietzsche imagined that incest and knowledge follow from each other in the process of a philosopher's, a superman's, revolt against the commonality and leveling power of nature. But Freud's major contribution to the history of our understanding of the emotions, if not to the history of thought, was to assure each analysand that, outsider though he may be—due to his intelligence and to the social embarrassments of his neurosis—he is only one of a small legion of outsiders, all flocking to their psychiatrists with the same complex. Sophocles presents Oedipus as a singular man, Freud presents him as an everyman. The two myths are not antithetical, but compensatory.

In his playlet *Oedipe*, André Gide gives a bizarre twist to this theme of the outsider. Tiresias, portrayed very much like a French priest or an Anglican bishop, cannot rest until Oedipus—who regards himself as superior to the masses and beyond needing the gods (they would only hold him down)—comes into the fold, even if he must do so as a broken hero instead of as a healthy penitent. Tiresias and Creon conspire to force a crack in the king's happiness—for his own good of course, since such health as his and independence from the ways of his ancestors constitute blasphemy and must somehow be the cause of their own unhappiness. Even the Chorus declares that Oedipus should at least have the good sense and decency to disguise his individualism. Oedipus' resistance to the authorities of church, state, and tradition represents for Gide the noble isolation and eventual exile of the superior man surrounded by the captious masses. Gide's homosexuality and apostasy from Christianity color his treatment of the hero. Eteocles and Polyneices' desire for intercourse with their sisters cannot shock Oedipus, since even before he learns of his own crimes he regards this incest as just one more taboo erected to contain the spirit of man: perversion is the brand upon the brow of the outcast intellectual. Tiresias insists that no man is without stain; therefore a sin must be found for Oedipus. Our hero, however, far from bowing to his guilt, regards his deeds, once he discovers them, as crimes imposed upon him by God. No dignity remains for him, except in isolation; no nobility, except in renunciation. He blinds himself and departs, not in shame, but in pride.

The intellectual's severing of the bond between himself and his biological brethren is an act of metaphorical murder. Thus we find that many apparently harmless souls have a deep affinity for violent deeds. Conversely, the intellectual fantasizes about what the masses would do to him, if they only knew what he was thinking; Nietzsche often speaks of how he is the most dangerous man alive and how, if the people had any sense, they would murder him. Just so, the spy makes a far better existential hero than the knight or even the detective. The detective relies on a partner, or at least on a secretary; the spy can trust no one, kills without license, would be arrested at once if recognized, and works for the security of the establishment but himself operates *extra ecclesiam*: after all, he belongs to the intelligence branch of the service.

The intellectual fabric of the myth, then, almost demands that the hero whose forte is wisdom commit patricide and, for lack of a ready-made term (in standard English), matri-matrimony. The wisdom of the patriarch must either be stolen or defied, the love of the mother either rejected or perverted. Eventually the hero must recognize his mistakes, accept the limits of his intellect, and admit his ignorance before the mysteries of the coincidental cosmos. Socrates stands out as the mythical prototype, and maybe monotype, of the hero as a philosopher who does not need to commit incest or patricide, since from the time we first meet him—and seemingly from birth—he knows that he doesn't know. But Socrates, too, eventually proves the oedipal rule that knowledge is dangerous, one way or another, and that the jealous masses are murderously quick to respond to the threat of a superior mind. A hemlock bush grows on the horizon of every wise man.

Several times Freud suggests that the trouble with paranoids is that they are right.[85] He might have added that, though correct about the existence of danger, they seldom look for it in the right place. *Oedipus the King* is a study of a paranoiac's search for a murderer—poking behind every arras but the one that conceals himself.

2

The Afterbirth

Therefore I maintain that it is necessary for the interpreter of dreams to
have prepared himself from his own resources and to use his native intelligence rather than simply to rely upon manuals, since a man who thinks
that he will be perfect by theory without any natural talents will remain
imperfect and incomplete, all the more, the more he is set in this habit.
—Artemidorus,
The Interpretation of
Dreams (trans. Robert White)

CAST OUT from village after village, with no company but his daughter
Antigone, Oedipus wanders for years (according to Sophocles' last play) until
at last he comes to the suburbs of Athens, to a place called Colonus. When he
learns a grove of the Furies is close by, he recognizes from an old oracle of
Apollo's that this locale will be his final home. Here one of his twin sons,
Polyneices, finds him and seeks his blessing for civil war against the other son,
Eteocles, who had locked his brother out of Thebes when the first year of their
adulthood was over and it was time for Polyneices to take his turn on the throne.
Oedipus curses both sons who, unlike Antigone, have never done anything for
him all these lonely years of exile. His resolve to withhold himself from his city
and family now that they want him back—his presence has grown beatific
through suffering—is shaken but not overturned when his uncle/brother-in-
law Creon, who backs Eteocles, shows up to kidnap Antigone and hold her for
the ransom of Oedipus' support. But just in the nick of time the hero Theseus
gallops up, with the Athenian cavalry behind him, rescues both father and
daughter from their dastardly kinfolk, and offers them the hospitality of Attica
forever. Oedipus now dies, leaving his bones in a secret place known only to

Theseus; as a hero he will bring blessings on Athens in perpetuity. But the saga of Thebes goes on, so the earlier plays of Sophocles and Aeschylus have shown us.

Polyneices, six other heroes, and the armies they have raised attack Thebes. The seven generals charge the seven gates of the city and die in the assault. Polyneices and Eteocles, who seem to have learned their swordsmanship from the same opera coach, simultaneously do each other in. Creon—regent many times before, king now at last—forbids the burial of the attackers. Antigone, home after years in her father's service but still more loyal to her gods than to her city, buries her brother, and allows herself to be caught; she is sentenced to be buried alive but hangs herself in the rock chamber rather than suffer a slow death. Creon's son Haemon, her betrothed, kills himself; Eurydice, Creon's wife, kills herself. The sons of the slain generals, the Epigoni ("those born later," the next generation), muster new armies, attack, raze, and resettle Thebes.

Easy Equivalencies

"The bossiest of men," Jean-Paul Sartre, that self-styled Oedipus, observed, "commands in the name of another—his father—and transmits the abstract acts of violence which he puts up with."[1] Polyneices attacks not only his brother, but his father's town; he fails. A third generation of warriors attacks again and succeeds; but the town is destroyed. This last set of sons, called the Epigoni, managed to do what their fathers had not and demolished the Ur-father's polis; yet the derivative word in English, *epigone*, signifies the weak imitator of some sort of hero (usually a writer) of the recent past. What are we to make of Freud's epigones or imitators, particularly on the subject of the Oedipus complex? Did they accomplish more or less than the master? Did they strengthen or weaken the walled city he had ruled?

Alfred Kazin has noted how well Freud wrote, how his common sense tempered his intellectual zeal, how his literary skill could accommodate a "balanced and often rueful sense of the total image presented by the human person." But—"many of the analysts who turn to writing seem to me not so much writers as people clutching at a few ideas." Freud himself could reason out the whole of a system of interdependencies; the other psychoanalytic writers expand on one or a few of Freud's claims, insist they have fully explained the psyche, and expect the authority of Freud's entire opus to carry the case for them.[2]

laborious work

On the subject of myth, Freud got by with a minimum of homework; there is no sign that he bothered to dip into Carl Robert's monumental *Oidipus* (Berlin, 1915), and he relied for many of his classical references on the lucubrations of underlings. His successors, however, lacking his devotion to and nimbleness in handling major issues, have found the byways of the Oedipus saga productive of a book or an article or two. Freudianism's methodological ancestor in this endeavor is allegoresis: all is revelation, although the mouthpieces of the truth may not enjoy an understanding of that whereof they speak. All psychoanalytic interpretation relies on the allegorical proposition that the language of the text is symbolic: myth, in this case, is essentially a social fantasy reflective of repressed impulses.[3] Since intensity and association are the ruling categories in this language, the power of our feelings and the logic of our subconscious connections suffice to render the ancient text readable.[4] Meanwhile, the analysts' dabblings in source-criticism, as illuminated by their therapeutic experience, have muddled any notion of a text: various stages of a myth, as preserved in writers across a millennium and from two or three cultures, are said to constitute fragments from one and the same racial dream.

As Freud's investigations progressed, he refined his schema of the psyche in keeping with his still materialistic but progressively more philosophical thinking. His epigones, however, have for the most part busied themselves working out elaborations of his earlier, more mechanistic principles. They have been able to jury-rig confirmations of even their most far-fetched conclusions (just as the Ptolemaic astronomers preferred the idea of the Rube Goldberg universe they had created to abandonment of the master's geocentric dogma). Freud turns out to be right, often enough, even when he is wrong; or if he is simply wrong, he is worth continuing to read because he is so wise. "The errors of great men," Nietzsche declaimed, rather self-congratulatingly, "are venerable because they are more fruitful than the truths of little men."[5] Freud's successors have been lesser men than he. Still in all, some of the Freudians' pronouncements are in fact valuable, some are famous, and some hilarious.

In a way their mistakes are understandable. A gesture, quotidian or mythological, always means more than itself, although we may never discover that meaning. We must, of course, try to understand the full import, the hidden meaning of each gesture. But not all meanings will wholly reveal themselves to us at once; some will never do so. While remaining zealously curious, then, we must nevertheless fall back in humility before these eternal, perhaps trivial, mysteries—not push our interpretations too far lest effrontery lead us to substitute our own clear, but wrong, meaning for the gesture's concealed one.

First, a few principles of non-equivalency must be learned. Mythical characters are not real personalities; while they may possess personal histories in a sense—because one or another source contains earlier stages of their stories

than the events under analytic scrutiny—they do not possess pasts from which
we can reconstruct their motives.[6] The Oedipus of one author is not the very
same as the Oedipus of another, although there may be useful resemblances;
nor does one of Sophocles' Oedipuses necessarily inform us reliably about the
other; nor may the modern case of the oedipal patient have much to do with
the situation of a character in an ancient literary form.

Let us look at some examples of the Freudians' work before last warnings
are issued. According to Karl Abraham, one of Freud's original followers, the
charging horses of Laius, which Oedipus attempted to stop by blocking the
road, stand (judging from fantasy material collected from patients) for the parents' sex act which the boy-hero wishes to interfere with. The road symbolizes
the female genitalia, and thus Oedipus' struggle with Laius is a fight for Jocasta's
prize. This, however, is not simply a highway but a crossroads, a place of heavy
traffic—and so the mother is represented as a prostitute. The blows to Laius'
head are symbolic of castration in retaliation for Laius' symbolic castration of
Oedipus by piercing his ankles; the many followers of Laius are all father substitutes. The whole episode resembles dreams in which the subject finds his
way along the birth canal blocked by his father. Oedipus' journey to Thebes is
thus a second birth.[7]

"But do you faithfully believe," Rabelais inquired of his readers, "that
Homer, in writing his *Iliad* and *Odyssey*, ever had in mind the allegories
squeezed out of him?"[8] Time renders many interpretations risible: Michel
Bréal, a nineteenth-century scholar of the school of solar-philological myth
interpretation founded by Max Müller, interpreted Oedipus as the personification of light, his blinding as the sunset, the Sphinx as a stormcloud.[9] It was
a minor sport among hyper-intellectual English majors of the fifties to see who
could best practice on the telephone directory the same analysis of themes,
images, and sources as their professors performed on T. S. Eliot's *The Waste-
land*. The evidence, after all, was there—who could deny it? But evidence,
even an interpretation of evidence, means nothing for sure without checks and
corroborations. No many-leveled cultural context encloses and sustains the
telephone book (at least not the White Pages), as one did Eliot's poem, and
provides the same sort of response a speaker needs from his audience to know
he is making sense. Abraham's symbols are not Sophocles'.

Géza Roheim finds the Oedipus complex everywhere, in all myths,
among all cultures, the Navajo and the Australian aboriginal in particular. The
Platonic myth of the three original sexes, in Aristophanes' speech in the *Symposium*, for example, might represent the child caught in a primal scene between mother and father[10]—no matter that Aristophanes' sets of Siamese twins
(male-male, female-female, male-female) don't match the primal trio. And
since the answer to the Sphinx's riddle is revealed to Oedipus in a dream

(according to an ancient commentator on Euripides' *Phoenician Women*) we are justified in "regarding the *meeting with the Sphinx as an anxiety dream*."[11] The illogic of this logic speaks for itself. Roheim (continuing to rely for his discovery of the true meaning of the myth on the ancient commentaries to this corrupt text) accepts a reconstruction of the original myth in which Laius was sent by Tiresias to Cithaeron to sacrifice to Hera and it was on this errand that he met his death at Oedipus' hands. "Tiresias and Oedipus are two aspects of the same person." And when Tiresias saw the two snakes copulating, he too was really seeing his parents copulating.[12] Apollodorus, a scholar of the second century B.C., records three explanations of the blinding of Tiresias: for revealing the secrets of the gods to men, for having seen his mother's friend Athena naked, and for having seen the snakes copulating (3.6.7). Richard Caldwell, a writer with better scholarly equipment than Roheim, also finds in these versions a key point of similarity between Oedipus and Tiresias: they all express forms of oedipal sexual curiosity and incestuous wishes. Both Oedipus and Tiresias were blinded for having seen the primal scene; the secret that Tiresias told may have been that Zeus, the father of gods and men, had intercourse with a mortal woman (Apollodorus 2.4.8); and Tiresias was able to solve the sexual riddle Zeus put to him—concerning who, the man or the woman, got greater pleasure from sex—not because he had lived for a while as a woman (in some versions *this* was the punishment for having *struck* the copulating snakes), but because he both recognized his mother and realized the impossibility of his desire.[13] Some have even seen a connection between the possible etymology of Oedipus' name from *oida*, "know," with the similar-sounding *eidō*, "see."[14]

This set of interpretations suggests another warning, for it presupposes the easy possibility of another equivalency: Mr. X is not really X, but Y in another form—nothing as subtle and suggestive as a double, however, merely a symbol of a symbolic figure, another shade of a shadowy projection of the analyst's imagination.

If we know what we are looking for, we are sure to find it. Simone de Beauvoir argues that the symbolic values of certain actions are not dictated by the libido, but rather the libido colors the manner in which we become aware of those actions.[15] In the case of Freudian analysis, the interpretation, then, not the original actions, may be what is truly destined.

Such interpretations smack of more than a touch of paranoia. Freud noted two things about paranoiacs: they are right, and in their case it isn't worth it. The paranoiac "recognizes something that escapes the normal person: he sees more clearly than someone of normal intellectual capacity, but the displacement on to other people of the state of affairs which he recognizes renders his knowledge worthless."[16] And this, regarding Alfred Adler—"As a paranoiac, of course he is right about many things, though wrong about everything."[17]

Many of the Freudians suffer from a hermeneutic variety of paranoia, even as Freud himself described it. Typically, they attach the greatest significance to minor details of other people's behavior and draw far-reaching conclusions from their interpretations of these details.[18] Now an odd shift from paranoid subject to presumably neurotic object occurs in some of the analytic writings on Oedipus. Paranoia, Freud notes, "regularly arises from an attempt to fend off excessively strong homosexual impulses." And again: "*paranoia persecutoria* is the form of the disease in which a person is defending himself against a homosexual impulse which has become too powerful."[19] And sure enough, there was a line of the myth in which Laius doomed himself to death at the crossroads by kidnapping and raping the son of his longtime family friend and host Pelops (Euripides' lost *Chrysippus*; Hyginus, *Fables* 85; Apollodorus 3.5.5). And so George Devereux, working not from original sources but only from Otto Rank's mention of them, presumes that—like father, like son!—Oedipus suffered from the same tendency. He interprets the struggle at the *narrow passage* of the crossroads as an oedipal competition of father and son for anal violation of some other boy or as the struggle of a father sexually to dominate his son. Now none of this is found in Sophocles' play, but Devereux employs the later sources to get at what he claims are earlier stages of "the myth." By reconstructing the unexpurgated story he implies that Sophocles' version is expurgated.[20] (Edmund Leach, by way of explaining the methodology of Claude Lévi-Strauss, finds a structural connection between Laius' having taught his host's son Chrysippus to drive a chariot before he raped him and Oedipus' driving a chariot when he met Laius—although Leach never bothers to say in what accounts he found these mythical details or what they signify in context.[21])

Freud suggested something along these lines in "Some Psychological Consequences of the Anatomical Distinction Between the Sexes": "even in boys the Oedipus complex has a double orientation, active and passive, in accordance with their bisexual constitution; a boy also wants to take his *mother's* place as the love object of his *father*—a fact which we describe as the feminine attitude."[22] In 1899 Freud wrote to Wilhelm Fliess that he had recognized the key to much of human intercourse: "Now for bisexuality! I am sure you are right about it. And I am accustoming myself to the idea of regarding every sexual act as a process in which four persons are involved. We shall have a lot to discuss about that."[23] And in *The Ego and the Id* he remarks that the relative strength of the masculine and feminine sexual dispositions, in both sexes, determines the outcome of the oedipal situation as identification with the father or with the mother.[24]

Theodor Reik found the theme of bisexuality imaged in the sphinx: the Egyptian species was male, the Greek female. The bisexuality of the beast

imitation

signals a cultural transition from hetero- to homosexuality. The slaying of Laius resembles the slaying of *the* Spinx, for the monster is a late development of the totem animal, which of course stands for the father. Oedipus' combat with this diachronically bisexual Sphinx, then, combined the killing of his father in the past with the rape of his mother in the future.[25] No need, of course, for Reik to distinguish between his sources, because the racial past is replicated by the individual's unconscious, which is inherently too murky to need sorting out.

Freud suggested a way out of this mess—that the little boy's identification with his father allows some affection for the mother to be retained and the boy's masculinity to be consolidated.[26] A function, mimesis, can explain away a problem that only increases geometrically if viewed as morphological. René Girard expands on this and disputes Freud's insistence on the concomitant primeval desire for the mother:[27] The disciple (son) imitates the model (father) even to the point of desiring the model's choice. Thus, oedipal rivalry arises in a mimetic situation, not a basically sexual one. Only because Father wants Mother does the son want her too and decide to take on a rival. Freud, as a philosopher of consciousness, credits the child with too much discernment and cleverness in recognizing and achieving his desires; rather, the Oedipus complex derives from the simple predicament the child finds himself in—act like your model but don't act like him.[28]

Developments and Disagreements

Robert Graves, blending sociohistory with his own personal religion of the Goddess, thinks the possibility worth considering that Oedipus was an invader of Thebes in the thirteenth century B.C., who conquered, became king by marrying the queen (the only way to gain power under the old matriarchal system), tried to replace matrilineage with patrilineage, and got banished for his impudence (after Jocasta had committed suicide and Thebes was visited by a plague).[29] While some archaeological evidence exists for Graves's musings, their real scholarly antecedent (which Graves claimed not to have read) is J. J. Bachofen's *Das Mutterrecht (Mother-Right)*, a classic of Victorian research through intuition—so little archaeological evidence being available at that time or sorted out. Bachofen coined most of the connotations that *matriarchy* and *patriarchy* carry for us today.[30] Carl Robert, drawing on all available sources for his monumental *Oidipus*, extended Bachofen's line of feeling: Oedipus is a chthonian hero (all heroes, once they have been buried, are chthonians); his incest was originally with mother earth, whose son naturally becomes her

heroes etc.
dwelling under
the earth

husband; and Laius was an old year-god who had to be killed before the new year-god could ascend the throne.[31] Thus, the Freudian pattern of the son's overthrow of the father can be adapted to a bias for neo-pagan matriarchy.

Some later Freudians have worked to bring the sons of the matriarch back into the Viennese fold. George Devereux believes the Oedipus myth may have evolved in response to stresses arising from the first Greeks' imposition of patrilineal descent and inheritance on the pre-Greeks. Oedipus gains possession of the throne by a pre-Hellenic ritual: killing the king in order to leave the queen, through whom the kingdom is passed on, free for marriage. But patrilineage wins out in the end.[32]

Erich Fromm argues that Freud's is too rationalistic an approach to the Oedipus complex, one which in emphasizing the sexual aspect of the matter evades the real problem of the boy's emotional tie to the father. He accepts Bachofen's distinctions between matriarchal and patriarchal cultures—an emphasis in the one on ties of blood and a passive acceptance of all natural phenomena, an emphasis in the other on man-made laws, rational thought, and domination over nature. And so he challenges Freud on the Oedipus complex, asserting that the myth symbolizes not the incestuous love of the son for the mother, but the rebellion of the son against the patriarchal father—the marriage of Oedipus and Jocasta being only one of the son's privileges when he takes his kingly father's place. Father-son conflict is the issue of the whole trilogy: "In *King Oedipus*, Oedipus kills his father Laius who intended to take the infant's life. In *Oedipus at Colonus* Oedipus gives vent to his intense hatred against his sons, and in *Antigone* we find the same hate again between Creon and Haemon." Creon and Antigone stand, respectively, for patriarchal and matriarchal principles. Whether or not Freud's clinical description is correct, it doesn't deserve the name Oedipus complex—which, however, does fit the case of the son's revolt against paternal pressure and the authoritarian structure of a patriarchal society. Freud mistakenly gives the father the rôle that really belongs to the mother—the great object of our love—and he "degrades the mother into the object of sexual lust. The goddess is transformed into the prostitute, the father elevated to the central figure of the universe." Fromm identifies patriarchal principles with those avowed by the politicians and sophists to justify the Peloponnesian War, and he concludes that Sophocles promoted the democratic matriarchal principles to counter the spirit of the war party and of his whole age.[33] A conflict between generations was certainly seething within the fifth-century family, but it was probably fostered by, rather than a cause of, the imperialism and war-mongering of Pericles' Athens. And it was the sons, the mass of the people, and the democrats who tended to promote the war; the fathers and old oligarchs, who opposed it.

Harry Slochower sides with Freud against Fromm, pointing out that Oedipus feels as guilty over the incest as over the patricide. Like others who call that famous fork in the road, the Triodhos, a symbol of Jocasta's genitalia, Slochower extracts the same significance from the leafy grove of the Eumenides where our hero goes to die in *Oedipus at Colonus*.[34] The classicist Ivan Linforth, however, was unkind enough to point out that nowhere in that play is it said that Oedipus actually disappears into this grove and there meets his end, and that the whole company which followed him would hardly have violated a tabooed precinct; nor is any connection mentioned between Oedipus and the female powers who haunt the grove, the Eumenides, except to identify Oedipus' place of death.[35]

Oedipus' return to the powers of the Mother is also supposed to involve his reconciliation with the primal father in the person of Theseus.[36] Oedipus, by acknowledging Theseus as a ruler, undoes the crime of patricide, revives his father figure, and reconstitutes his relationship as a dutiful son; he accepts the laws of the community and achieves forgiveness for his rebellion.[37] One Jungian sees the move into Theseus' territory as a particularly therapeutic one because Theseus is the mythical founder of patriarchy.[38] Many identify the stages in Oedipus' career with the stages of childhood development or of an initiate's rite of passage, as in Mark Kanzer's summary: "Oedipus, Creon, and Theseus represent the same character, but with increasingly successful maturation as he seeks to solve the riddle of the Sphinx."[39] In his son Polyneices, Oedipus encounters the projected image of his former self, and in pouring hatred on him shows how far he himself has gone in becoming identified with his father. His failure earlier to work through the relationship with his father had kept him a child and stunted the formation of his superego; his lack of identification with his father had made him regard women as monsters. But unlike Bachofen, Kanzer thinks some women are, in fact, dangerous; and he takes Theseus' victory over a thuggish Creon in the *Oedipus at Colonus* as a proper triumph of patriarchy over matriarchy.[40]

Some have seen the Sphinx, herself the offspring of an incestuous union, as an embodiment of the bad mother. Since Oedipus has failed to come to terms with his oedipal emotions, since the boy cannot admit to desiring his mother, he splits her into the virgin and the whore. Jocasta receives the charge of love, the Sphinx that of hatred. The oracle, after all, said he would kill his parents, and his slaying of the Sphinx may be a disguised form of sadistic intercourse. As for the riddle of the Sphinx—the coital embrace of the parents involves four legs, and from this is born the child of two legs, who grows up to grow a third leg. Sophocles wrote the play in order to strengthen the barriers against incest; the audience's proud re-dedication of themselves to moral principles and their satisfaction at seeing punished those who violated those principles constitutes the catharsis that Aristotle specifies as the function of tragedy.[41]

The dangerous women of Greek mythology, often indistinguishable from monsters, are of much concern to the Jungians, and a treatment of them will take up much of the next chapter. Incest, at least metaphorical incest, as a motivating fear in the hero's rise to consciousness, is also a Jungian theme and will find its topical home in chapters 7 and 8. Robert Stein, however, has come up with an offbeat interpretation of Oedipus' meeting with the Incest Archetype. Oedipus commits incest of the real sort because he is spiritually sterile. He believed his substitute parents to be his real parents because he couldn't consciously distinguish between the personal and the archetypal parents. The incest taboo, by hindering real incest with the mother, promotes symbolic or spiritual incest with a mother-substitute. But Oedipus never managed a matrimony of the spirit, and so his Apollonian principle (reason) became inflated and his consciousness destroyed him. The exposure of Oedipus as a child, the presence of the Sphinx, and Oedipus' incest with Jocasta all indicate a cultural breakdown in Thebes due to "a neglect and devaluation of the feminine principle and the feminine mysteries." By blinding himself Oedipus submits to the darkness of the mother world. In addition to all of this, Stein finds he can confidently assert that Oedipus killed his father because of a deep unconscious resentment for having been exposed to die.[42] Now the matter of archetypes aside (see chapter 4), Stein defines culture in his own terms, and claims a breakdown of it in Thebes, without ever specifying when or how this breakdown occurred and without looking far for evidence of it. Nor can the confines of logic constrain him when he wishes to make Oedipus do something unconsciously that he never could have been conscious of in the first place. Or does coincidence equal fate, archetypally determined? To do something in utter ignorance is not the same as to do it unconsciously.

Otto Rank put a more dynamic interpretation on the Sphinx, while also coming close to the Jungian implication of the incest taboo with the rise of consciousness. The character of the Sphinx as strangler marks her as a clear reference to the birth anxiety. Her maternal character—*pace* Reik and his researches on Egyptian male sphinxes—is thus primary. She represents not only the wish to return to the mother as the danger of being swallowed, but also parturition itself and our struggle against it—insofar as "the human upper body grows out of the animal-like (maternal) lower body without finally being able to free itself from it."[43] The riddle of the Sphinx, then, asks the destiny and the origin of man; Oedipus strives to solve it, "not intellectually, but by actually returning to the mother's womb. This happens entirely in a symbolic form, for his blindness in the deepest sense represents a return into the darkness of the mother's womb," as does his final disappearance into the earth. Incestuous desires can profitably serve to help overcome fear of the mother's genitals by transforming them into an object of pleasure. [44]

Rank accepts Carl Robert's claim that Oedipus was originally a phallic vegetation god and that father and son were waxing and waning twins. But whereas Freud sees the myth as expressing an instinctual desire of the son for the mother, Rank finds that the mythical tradition reflects the transition— actually accomplished in Greek civilization—"from heroic self-perpetuation to man's reluctant acceptance of his biological rôle as father and his perpetuation through the generations." *Oedipus the King* is a drama of fatherhood, and the incest expresses the hero's desire to be his own successor. [45] The Oedipus conflict proves to be an heroic defense against assuming the role of father. Laius long ago rejected his sexual role; Oedipus wishes, through his incest, to beget his own self. The son rebels against being a successor, the father against being succeeded. The son wishes to grow up, not under parental control, but as a free man in the wilderness; the species coerces the individual to submit to marriage and fatherhood. The myth, thus, portrays the struggle between the individual ego and the racial ego; the oedipal strife between father and son represents the inner resistance of man against any kind of racial role, even preservation of the species. The Oedipus of the tragic poets, however, "represents a man already forced into the part of father." Oedipus struggles tragically to abandon fatherhood in order to regain personal immortality; he calculates the discovery of himself as a patricide in order to overthrow an undesirable, patriarchal cultural pattern. And the Oedipus complex of the present day may express a protest of the ego against every kind of family role; the analyst's emphasis on the power and universality of incestuous desire serves therapeutically to strengthen the patient's ego. But of course the revolt must end tragically. [46] Rank's emphasis falls, characteristically, on the righteous willfulness of the individual who refuses to effect a personal compromise with the demands of culture: the Oedipus complex is a kind of psychological spanner thrown under the bonnet of the social engine to prevent it from carrying the individual where he listeth not. Freud saw such a compromise as the only safe, nonneurotic way between the Charybdis of the desirous id and the Scylla of an authoritarian reality. Rank would prefer the pain of an heroic failure to the helplessness of treading the destined straight and narrow.

There are, finally, theories of a more original cast whose value is nevertheless no less dubious. And then there is Claude Lévi-Strauss. While the latter plots his formal graph across a pure geometry deduced from the various episodes in the Theban saga, the former issue their pronouncements with blithe abandon, projecting one or another syndrome onto the fixed persona of our hero:

—This is a story of a deprived and abused child.[47]

—No: "The manifest Oedipus myth is the case history of an adopted child."[48]

—Not quite. Oedipus has an Adlerian inferiority complex, due to organ inferiority. He has a physical handicap and lacks parental tenderness and social security; he is an unwanted child. He also lacks a proper place in the world and lives with foster parents. (No matter that the only mother and father he ever knew, his foster parents, wanted him.) As a result, he displays symptoms typical of those with feelings of inferiority, a quick temper among them. (No matter that every Sophoclean hero has a notoriously short fuse.) Oedipus has developed his wits to compensate for his inferiority, and seeks out his mother not for sex but for security.[49]

—No, Oedipus is a battered child, the victim of his parents' filicidal impulses. The part of the myth dramatized by Sophocles in *Oedipus the King* deals with the crisis of adolescence. The encounter with Laius at the crossroads "may be interpreted as a portrayal of the adolescent male at the crossroads of his life." The time is depicted as a place. "The toothed [?] goad may be regarded as symbolizing Oedipus' phallic-libidinal and aggressive strivings as well as the oral-sadistic contribution to these strivings derived from his relationship with the pregenital mother, projected onto the parental figure he meets at the crossroads." The encounter with the Sphinx, another form of parental aggression, is another rite of passage. And Oedipus' leaving Thebes or Corinth is like the patient's leaving the analytic situation or the analyst's leaving his own parent analyst.[50]

—Well, actually, the relationship of Oedipus with Jocasta, both as herself and as the Sphinx, parallels the fate and characters of patients seduced as children by their psychotic parents. Psychoanalysis can undo the damaging identification with the bad parent, and in this process the analyst acts like Tiresias. But despite analysis, the patient, like Oedipus, remains crippled and blind; Oedipus finds freedom at last only by remerging with the mother in the earth.[51]

—And last, but not quite least, a word for the mother's side—the complex of Jocasta, "the lonely, emotionally starved widow," whose problem Freud minimized: Jocasta mothering stems from a craving for children, the absence of a normal sex life, the death of a husband. These conditions were present in both the royal houses of Thebes and of Corinth. The child mothered by a Jocasta typically suffers from an unresolved Oedipus complex, a vague sense of guilt, masochistic and paranoid and homosexual tendencies, egocentricity, narcissism, and a crying need for fame. In short, Jocasta mothering tends to produce or nurture a budding genius—like Oedipus.[52]

Whatever the consulting-room truth of these interpretations, they mean nothing in terms of the myth—nor the myth, in terms of them—and their authors should not have attempted to apply a classical veneer to psychosociological chipboard. Lévi-Strauss, of whom more in chapter 4, cannot be dismissed quite so lightly. While hardly a Freudian, his structuralist approach to myth, which presumes the existence of underlying patterns in any product of the human mind, relies on Freud's revelation of the unconscious. Lévi-Strauss defines a myth "as consisting of all its versions; to put it otherwise, a myth remains the same as long as it is felt as such." (A subjective definition at best, particularly since the one whose feelings delimit the myth is, magesterially, only hinted at.) Narrative order has nothing to do with understanding the myth, since telling the myth requires a diachronic reading, through time, whereas analysing requires a synchronic reading, across time: the anthropologist sorts the various narrative details into columns, each containing items with one common feature. The common feature of Lévi-Strauss's third column for the Oedipus myth (containing much material from previous stages of the Theban saga) is "*the denial of the autochthonous origin of man.*" Thus the disordered walking that distinguishes all the items in the next column: "In mythology it is a universal character of men born from the earth that at the moment they emerge from the depth, they either cannot walk or do it clumsily." The myth of Oedipus, then, really deals with the problem, for a culture that believes mankind sprang from the earth, of finding a way to reconcile this mythical theory with the actual knowledge that man is born of a sexual union. The myth, once *understood*, becomes an equation: "the overrating of blood relations is to the underrating of blood relations as the attempt to escape autochthony is to the impossibility to succeed in it."[53] It turns out, however, that these columns do not contain all the details of every version—far from it—and that Lévi-Strauss has been just as selective of his material as Freud or any other theoretician. "Morsels of the raw evidence," K. K. Ruthven pronounces after finishing a plateful, "taste distinctly cooked."[54]

3

Electra and Other Monsters

HERE IS SOMETHING WITLESS in the way Oedipus, Jason, and others go about their tasks as heroes. A quest is proposed (the Golden Fleece, the Belt of Hippolyte), a monster is assigned to be slain (the Medusa, the Chimaera), a war must be fought (at Troy, at Thebes); and immediately our fair-haired boy hones his blade, laces up his sandals, and takes off across hill and dale or the wine-dark sea. Some conjunction, some transition, is almost always missing from the syntax of the hero's career, which might be read as a headlong rush to disaster rather than as a planned advance to immortal fame.

Why did Oedipus answer the Sphinx's questions? Why did he never ask himself what she was up to with her silly riddle? What *was* she up to? Marie-Louise von Franz, a student and later a colleague of Carl Jung, has made a brilliantly nasty suggestion: that Oedipus' real trouble began when he responded to the riddle of the Sphinx, fatuously believed her death scene, congratulated himself on his intelligence, and promptly put her out of his mind. What he should have done, von Franz says, was knock the monster down off her perch, beat her up, and demand to know what right she had to ask him such questions. *That* would have been the behavior of a hero. Instead, he proved himself a failure by submitting without a fight (while convinced that he was performing a great deed) to the authority of the destructive mother, that eternal *femme fatale*; and he proved himself a fool by trusting in his puerile cleverness to extemporize the right answer. The Sphinx, of course, never died; she only pretended to expire. Indeed, any answer from Oedipus would have sufficed for her to play the role of vanquished monster. Then she simply waited, ten or twenty years, to pounce on the boy-wonder from behind, when she reentered the myth in the person of his long lost mother.[1] Indeed, one Freudian believes that since the Sphinx and Jocasta both commit suicide after the solving of a riddle, they both must be the same female monster, who later becomes the city and earth of Thebes.[2]

49

Others might put the Jungian case in more technical terms: Oedipus was taken in by his female opponent's animus, her male side (see chapter 4), and looked for a victory according to the rules she had laid out; he should rather have attacked the very rationale of the contest she had arranged between them.[3] Von Franz, moreover, sees Oedipus' behavior as only a personal variation on the Greeks' attempt to escape the reality of the mother through philosophy; of course they could never put their ideas into practice, and as soon as they came up against a more masculine, more rooted, people, the Romans, they caved in.[4] Unlike Freud, von Franz makes no pretense of interpreting *Oedipus the King*. She is openly ransacking the language of Greek myth to give a historical shape to the theory of the *puer aeternus*—the archetype of the eternal boy. As Roland Barthes says, "Since myth robs language of something [in order to transform meaning into form], why not rob myth?"[5] Von Franz's advice-in-retrospect to Oedipus shocks us out of our complacency with the repetitiveness of myth, and forces us to admit that things might have gone a different way. The mythological paradigm of human behavior has been challenged.

By definition, a paradigm must be repeated; so too, the sum of one's habitual actions and quotidian gestures constitutes behavior. Roland Barthes, as a semiologist, finds richer material for analysis in the forms of various languages than in their contents: "This means that *quantitatively*, the concept is much poorer than the signifier, it often does nothing but represent itself. . . . This repetition of the concept through different forms is precious to the mythologist, it allows him to decipher the myth: it is the insistence of a kind of behavior which reveals its intention."[6] The repetition of a severely limited set of neuroses (limited by the banality of the patients' lives and the similarity of their psyches or by the orthodoxy of the analysts' techniques) is responsible for the boredom that settles upon us with the smothering weightlessness of a featherbed when we sit down to read a mass of case histories. The excitement such accounts *can* generate in the reader is due to the inventiveness of human expression. Quandry: should the analyst strive for a kind of second-order inventiveness in writing up his or her cases? Do Freud's case histories stand out as good reads because he fictionalized them somewhat, in order to protect his patients' identity or his own? Vladimir Nabokov's cavalier boast that even the dream he recounts to his wife across the breakfast table is only a first draft may more appropriately exemplify the attitude of the mythmaker than that of the scientist, whose passions require disinterestedly precise observation in order to generate trustworthy documents. But certainly something should be done to bring the case history closer to that literary form it most resembles, the novel—actually the science-fiction novel, of the sort in which the Creepy-Crawlies come to us instead of we to them.

A Wealth of Monsters

"Beyond this point," a common mid-Ocean legend on early maps of exploration reads, "are monsters." Nearly all the monsters of Greek mythology are female. And there is something monstrous about nearly all the many strong women of the Greek myths and even of Greek historiography; at least these women arouse the same fears in the men they have dealings with as the monsters do. Any powerful female might turn out to be the hero's enemy. Pausanias, for example, relates versions of the Oedipus myth in which the Sphinx was really a pirate or just an especially clever daughter of Laius who tried to do away with all her brothers in order to win the throne; in either case Oedipus vanquished her (9.26.2–4). More and more evidence has appeared or has been recognized that women in Ancient Greece, even in fifth-century Athens, did not in fact lead as restricted lives as has been commonly supposed. But social realities may be more (or less) benignant than mythic—that is to say, cultural—convictions. A man's self-protective attitude can easily seem oppressive to a woman; and any move on her part toward self-assertion might just as easily convince him that all his fears are justified. The Electra complex is in many ways the inverse not of the Oedipus complex but of the hero's drive to defeat the female, for woman's battle with man must always be a sexual one (see chapters 7 and 8). The daughter of Agamemnon and the offspring of the Echidna are blood sisters under the skin.

There are sphinxes and then there is *the* Sphinx. As a species, sphinxes enlarged their range northwest into Greece in the early seventh century B.C., travelling, along with a whole slew of Levantine and Mesopotamian monsters and motifs, on embroidered textiles and other *objets d'art* imported from the near East and Egypt. (Somewhere along the way the majority of them paused for a sex-change, for most Assyrian and Babylonian monsters are vividly male.[7]) Such barbaric, Oriental, composite beasts had been popular in Bronze Age iconography, but died out in Greece during the Dark Ages (1100–700) when the Mycenaean palaces were destroyed and living conditions, trade, and the arts all declined.

The Archaic period (700–480) that followed the Dark Ages must have been a confusing but exciting time for the Greeks. Political power was shifting from the aristocracy to the people. The usable, if not known, world was expanding—thanks to reopened trade routes and new colonies sent out to the northeast and the west in order to relieve the strain of overpopulation. Both a revived gaiety (as though from Minoan times) and a new dread manifest themselves in the nervous rhythms and contours, in the over-decorated textures of the poetry, sculpture, and vase-painting of the age. Everyone smiles all the time, or at least their statues (not yet portraits, but idealized visages and physiognomies) do. These compulsive smiles disguise a general uneasiness: temples on a much grander scale than ever before are constructed, a few new cults arise, many old ones are aggrandized, and oracles—especially Apollo's at Delphi— are thronged. Fear of pollution—perhaps occasioned by the loss of old, comfortable boundaries, the extension of landscape and inscape as the world suddenly grew larger—was the popular malaise of these centuries.[8] Finally, the Persian Wars, which brought the age to a close, proved the righteousness more than the might of the Greeks. God was on their side. The Persians, not the Hellenes, were the ones punished for exceeding the boundaries proper to man and exciting the envy of the gods. The Persians were blind and driven mad by hubris—that excessive pride which can lead a man or a nation to commit violent crimes—in order that they might more thoroughly be destroyed. In subsequent decades Greek artists represented this victory of civilization over barbarism, allegorically, in battle scenes of gods versus giants or Titans, or of Athenians versus Amazons, the forces of disorder being aptly symbolized both by monsters and by manly women. This self-congratulatory sense of superiority eventually deluded the Athenians, heroes of those wars, into new forms of hubris in the fifth century.

But meanwhile, in Archaic times, monsters of all sorts swarm about the temple precincts and across the papyrus rolls of verse. (Otto Rank thought their presence betrayed the failure of "Hellenization," the unsuccessful repression by the Greeks of the mother principle.[9]) The carnivorous, hybrid monster operates both as predator from another species and cannibal from our own. The rough conjunction of grinning human countenance and leonine or vulturine or serpentine body reveals, as no familiar shape can, the counterfeit of bliss, the utter refusal of thick globules of anxiety to be emulsified in a thin wash of joy. Nevertheless, these sphinxes and Chimaeras, these Tritons, Typhons, Harpies, Sirens, and Gorgons—this whole extended family of dangerous species—were a delightful group while they flourished, can still delight us now, frozen in limestone as they have been for twenty-five hundred years.

Statues of sphinxes, in particular, often sat on top of tombstones, their heads crowned by umbrella-frames of bronze to keep birds from defiling their faces. The stationing of the monsters here was probably apotropaic and euphemistic, rather than honorific: a fearful beast will more successfully ward off evil spirits from the departed's grave, and may even ward off the revenant relative himself, than will a statue of a faithful hound stretched across his chest (certainly a sphinx looks more enigmatically vigilant than a dog—even Cerberus is a simpleton); and by placing the monster here and putting a smile on her face, one ensures that *she* does not trouble the dead man, or us, in the night.

It is a commonplace that death is the twin of sleep, and commonplaces are myths in miniature, abstracted from all the exotic details that adhere to

intended to ward off evil

them from alien cultures. So it is by an easy step in the language of platitudes that we pass from the sphinx as guardian of the tomb to the sphinx as incubus. Marie Delcourt has collected representations of sphinxes in this role of ravisher of a dreaming youth, and she has commented on the passivity of the man in every scene.[10] The sphinx often seems to be reaching for his throat as she gazes at this still sleeping face or into his just opened eyes. Her gesture may bespeak the erotic tenderness of a caress or the threat of strangulation (not, we are learning, inconsistent with the moment of ecstasy), or her preoccupation with that fetish spot: the edge, smooth in man, rough in monster, where the head joins the trunk. Her wings, which are always open and never folded, suggest, as Delcourt says, both a soul in pain and a destructive demon. More of this agonized soul later; for now, the demon concerns us.

The Sphinx has a long genealogy; the best account of it is in Hesiod's *Theogony*. Ge (Earth) gave birth to Pontus (Sea), then coupled with him and gave birth to the sea monster Ketos, who coupled with her brother Phorcys and gave birth to the Gorgons, the Graeae (crones from birth), Echidna, and a hundred-headed snake named Ladon. Echidna, a monster in her own right (half nymph, half spotted snake) coupled with Typhon (or with Orthus—it doesn't matter: both were monsters) and bore the Chimaera, the Hydra, the Sphinx, the Nemean lion, and the Crommyonian sow. Doubtless there were other versions of the family tree.

How the Sphinx came to Thebes is left rather vague. We are told that either Hera or some other god sent her, but never why (Apollodorus 3.5.7). We could supply some reasonable motive for Hera—outrage over the barely consummated marriage of Laius and Jocasta; delayed vengeance for Laius' rape of Chrysippus; punishment in advance for the union of Oedipus and Jocasta; a fit of pique at the city where her husband once kept his mistress Semele—but it would be sheer invention. The texts, like the Sphinx when she wasn't singing riddles, are silent. Only Oedipus' route from cradle to Thebes can be traced, not the monster's.

As Delcourt points out, the exposure of Oedipus is both the elimination of a potentially dangerous creature and the initiation or testing of a youth.[11] Of course Oedipus survived that test and grew almost up. It is in the nature of heroes, just before reaching manhood, to seek and find or to create a quest to embark upon. To overcome forces greater than his youthful self the apprentice-hero requires divine aid, usually from Athena, occasionally from Hera, Aphrodite, or some other goddess. He never knew he could do such great deeds, and in fact he cannot perform them alone. Commonly, too, there is some last, great battle in which he and his divine patroness vanquish all their mortal enemies. Oedipus' career is quite different. No goddess whispers in his ear—goddesses seldom give advice on Sophocles' stage. Only an oracle, a king, a sphinx, a prophet, and at last a wife oppose him. His quest is not for glory, but for knowledge. A feminine presence may follow him all the way home, but his very ignorance of this demon that hovers beside him causes his demise.

Otto Rank, relying on the meaning in Greek of *sphinx*, "strangler," thought *the* Sphinx showed herself to Oedipus to advise him and all Greeks of that male-fixated world that they had to overcome the birth anxiety and come to terms with the mother.[12] Carl Jung and his disciple Erich Neumann have written in much the same vein about Oedipus' encounter with the monster and his marriage to Jocasta. Here is Neumann:

> The hero's incest and the conquering of the Sphinx are identical. . . . By conquering his terror of the female, by entering into the womb, the abyss, the peril of the unconscious, he weds himself triumphantly with the Great Mother who castrates the young men and with the Sphinx who destroys them. His heroism transforms him into a fully grown male. . . . [15]

There are, it turns out, two forms of incest: uroboric incest, a cosmic experience, in which the germinal ego is extinguished; and matriarchal incest, a more personal event, in which the son is seduced by the mother, and *this* incest ends when she castrates him. The hero's fight with the dragon—in Oedipus' case, with the Sphinx—is really with uroboros ("the primal dragon of the beginning that bites its own tail") and thus is a fight with our First Parents, not with our real parents. In such a ritualistic duel to the death, the murders of both mother and father have their prescribed places.

This somewhat arcane thesis was inspired by the following passages from Jung's lengthy *Symbols of Transformation:*

> Incest is the urge to get back to childhood. For the child, of course, this cannot be called incest; it is only for an adult with a fully developed sexuality that this backward striving becomes incest, because he is no longer a child but possesses a sexuality which cannot be allowed a regressive outlet.

And:

> When the regressing libido is introverted for internal or external reasons it always reactivates the parental imagos and thus apparently reestablishes the infantile relationship. But this relationship cannot be reestablished, because the libido is an adult libido which is already bound to sexuality and inevitably imports an incompatible, incestuous character into the reacti-

vated relationship to the parents. It is this sexual character that now gives rise to the incest symbolism. . . . the result is either the death of the son-lover or his self-castration as punishment for the incest he has committed.[14]

Jung attempts to refute the classic Freudian analysis of the Oedipus complex, whereby the cause of the neurosis, which bears an ineluctably sexual content, is located in the past (i.e., in traumas). Actually the neurosis is manufactured anew every day; every day one suffers the strain of consciousness and longs for the lost ease of unconsciousness in the infantile past. One should not take the neurotic's exaggeratedly carnal mode of expression too seriously. When we subject it to a more penetrating scrutiny, the sexual language of the regression changes into metaphors of eating, the incestuous tendency into a Jonah-and-the-whale complex and into fear of being devoured by the mother. The adult male, then, far from actually wanting to sleep with his mother, wants to insert his whole lonesome and frightened self back into the warmth of the nourishing and protective womb.

As to why the healthy male should fear intercourse with his mother—well, the incest prohibition hygienically blocks the infantile longing for the mother, for a return to the state of unconsciousness, and "forces the libido along the path of life's biological aim." It was, in fact, only the power of the incest prohibition "that created the self-conscious individual, who before had been mindlessly one with the tribe; and it was only then [at the moment of separation of man from mass] that the idea of the final death of the individual became possible. Thus, through Adam's sin, which lay precisely in his becoming conscious, death came into the world."[15] Jung neatly reverses Freudian anthropology: the incest taboo, far from being the precondition of the tribe's continued existence or of its unchallenged governance by the elders, turns out to be some natural law that has been promulgated—apparently by the great Collective Unconscious—to destroy primitive man's infantile relationship to the uterine tribe. Erich Fromm makes much the same point in *The Sane Society*: the incest taboo enables man to sever the emotional umbilical cord, for incestuous desire takes its strength not from sexual attraction to the mother, but from our craving to return to the womb.[16]

So why do we still have monsters? Because man has never lost both his longing for and fear of a return to the belly of the whale. Lesser men stray into Behemoth's precincts. "But what distinguishes the hero"—this is Neumann again—"is an active incest, the deliberate, conscious exposure of himself to the dangerous influence of the female, and the overcoming of man's immemorial fear of woman. To overcome fear of castration is to overcome fear of the mother's power."[17] The hero's fight with a monster plays an essential part in his overcoming the inertia of the libido. And his incestuous flirtation with his mother in the person of that monster is a regenerative stage—like Odysseus' descent into Hades—in his career. His successful passage through this danger makes the ephebe into a hero. "The treasure which the hero fetches from the dark cavern is *life:* it is himself, new-born from the dark maternal cave of the unconscious where he was stranded by the introversion or regression of libido."[18]

Too often, however, when he confronts his monster the hero behaves like a boy—places too much confidence, in typically male fashion, in his intellect or in some other supposedly masculine strength. The Sphinx spins her riddle as a trap for the unwary wanderer, but the real riddle turns out to be the terrible mother-imago, disguised as a beast. Oedipus' failure to evade the monster is a failure of consciousness, of which the eye is a symbol, and so his self-blinding is a form of uroboric castration. But since castration signifies loss of consciousness, we have merely been led in a very wide circle back to where Sophocles left us in the first place.

The Ambivalence of Monsters

What sort of wisdom would save the hero from destruction in the standard oedipal confrontation with the mother figure? What sort of wisdom or power does she possess? Let us examine more of the monsters. Before the transition from goddess- to god-worship (a religious and mythological event parallelling the sky-god-worshipping Greeks' historical conquest of the earth-goddess-worshipping pre-Greeks) preternatural wisdom was the perquisite of the oldest goddesses. Later, Apollo and Athena took over these oracular roles, speaking for their father Zeus—who seldom spoke for himself, not only in order to preserve an aura of inscrutability, but because his rise to power had something of the aspect of a gang war about it and so his forensic pronouncements were better left for his unsullied children to deliver. But this tradition of the wise crone survives in a few figures: The Graeae who possess only one tooth and one eye, both shared, between them, but who know the location of the weapons Perseus needs to slay Medusa; Ge the Earth-Mother herself, who once held the oracle at Delphi, as did the Titaness Themis and the great Python whom Apollo slew; the Pythoness or priestess of Delphi, a widowed old peasant woman; and the Furies or Erinyes.

The Furies, dog-faced, snake-haired, foul-breathed, buck-toothed females, have quite a struggle on their hands in Aeschylus' trilogy, the *Oresteia*, trying simultaneously to punish the matricide Orestes and to maintain their ancestral prerogatives against infringement by the upstarts Apollo and Athena. These divine bloodhounds are finally transformed by the theological legerdemain of the dramatist into Eumenides, gentle-minded agrarian spirits whose privilege it is to bring fertility back to the land and bless the polis; they are not particularly bright. In Sophocles' last play, however, *Oedipus at Colonus*, his swan song to the hero, to dramaturgy, to Athens, and to life, some of the associations of a kind of wisdom older and greater than the male kind are once again evoked. The blind old son of Laius finally comes to rest near a grove of the Erinyes—never named except as Eumenides, for to name them might be to summon them up from the earth. Through his years of suffering, Oedipus has achieved a kind of *sophia* more profound, less cerebral, than that expressed in the predictions of Apollo and Tiresias which he thought he could evade. Heroes are tied to the land; with the exception of Heracles, they never make it to Olympus, but leave their bones and spirits in shaft graves or huge beehive tombs, whence they ectoplasmically come forth to bring victory or prosperity to their regions. And so Oedipus appropriately finds, by this precinct of the fierce-eyed, all-seeing, underworldly goddesses, the only secure home he has ever had.

According to another version of the Theban saga, preserved by several scholiasts (ancient scribblers who packed the margins of papyrus rolls with as much scholarly information as learning and lamp oil could recover), Oedipus never went into exile. After losing Jocasta he married Astymedusa, an otherwise unknown lady, who falsely accused her stepsons of attempting her virtue. "Astymedusa" means "Medusa of the city"—not the city as body politic but the topography enclosed by walls and distinguished by marble edifices and mud-brick dwellings. Oedipus, then, is said to have married the namesake of the most famous monster of antiquity, a woman who behaved like the archetypal harridan, scold, murderous stepmother, and sexually threatening female of nightmare and case history—and a woman, moreover, who posed as great a threat to young men as the actual Gorgon did.

Medusa herself was once a lovely girl who was loved by Poseidon. Either she escaped from him when she turned herself into a horse, or else she eventually accepted his equine advances. In any case, Medusa made an enemy of the virgin goddess. Athena not only arranged her horrible metamorphosis from the girl who could make Poseidon play stallion into the face that turns anything living to stone, but also backed Perseus in his trophy-hunt after her monstrous head: a snaky-haired, pig-tusked, long-tongued, wide-eyed visage that could petrify the viewer. Athena, as eternal virgin, resented the girl's sensuality and condemned her to a fearsome celibacy; eventually the goddess mounted the Gorgon's face on her aegis, a goatskin cloak that she used to ward off enemies from Athens and suitors from herself.

In 1922 Freud laid the groundwork for subsequent psychoanalytical interpretations of the Medusa: fear of gazing upon the Medusa's head is really fear of castration—replaced in the myth by decapitation—which is linked to the sight of something: namely, of the mother's genitals surrounded by snaky hair. (Some classical evidence indicates the sight of the Gorgon's head had no effect on women.) The snakes, however, are also phallic symbols and reassure the spectator that, stiffened though he may be by the Gorgon's glance, he still possesses a penis. The display of genitals, male or female, also has an apotropaic effect, driving the spectator away.[19] Others have emphasized that Perseus' beheading of the Medusa was an act of castration, and he did, in fact, do the deed with the same sort of sickle or curved knife that Zeus used to castrate his father Cronus and that Cronus used on Uranus. Even Perseus' theft of an eye and tooth from the Graeae has been called a castration. One analyst interprets these interpretations as overthrows of the father;[20] but another sees it as the son's attempt to eliminate his mother as a polyphallic female, while simultaneously rendering himself rigid with fear of her genitals, i.e., impotent, so that he suppresses his oedipal desires.[21]

The most extensive treatment of the Greek attitude toward the mother has been Philip Slater's in *The Glory of Hera*, a psychosociological study of Greek mythology and the Greek family. Slater's thesis bears summarizing.[22] The Greek mother, frustrated by what is, despite increasing evidence to the contrary, still admitted by historians to have been a male-dominated society, took out much of her resentment on the only male within reach in her life, her son. Because the typical Greek marriage was between a man in his early thirties and girl of about sixteen and involved a relationship more like that between brother and sister than like our concept of what a marriage should be, the son became a husband substitute for the mother and served as an appropriate object for her vengeance against her master, since the perpetuation of his father's property and lineage rested on his narrow shoulders. Thus the menacing aspect of women in Greek myth. But the mother also believed that her little man would grow up to be a perfect hero and take care of her forever; conversely, he found he needed her to achieve his goals. (Greek women still today expand their power through mothering and console themselves for their lot in life with the thought of men's weakness and dependence on them.[23]) Even Athena turns out to be a phallic mother in disguise;[24] as a historical relic of the Mediterranean goddess who was suppressed by the Greek gods and maliciously left a virgin, she finds satisfaction in backing her surrogate sons, the heroes, in their quest for glory. The male child became both a scapegoat for and an antidote to his mother's penis envy. Her ambivalent attitude developed a narcissistic attitude in him, one which was fostered by the mother's own narcissism (since she had been deprived of normal object-love by her husband and by the society which excluded and secluded her) and by the unstable self-concept she had created in him. The male came to despise women at the same time that he feared them as a superior race. Such an environment obviously encouraged homosexuality as well as physical vanity and boastfulness. In fact, the competitiveness that marks every aspect of Greek behavior, the insatiable striving for honor and prestige, the obsession with fame and honor, all arose from a hypertrophy of narcissism, from the Greek's typical overvaluation of every aspect of his maleness. This homosexual *machismo* motivated the great individual efforts of artists and politicians, but also sabotaged all cooperative ventures and even led to the loss of the Sicilian expedition and finally to the decline of the city states. George Devereux differs from Slater on the mechanisms of Athenian family life which led to the idealization by an entire society of the beautiful boy and of homosexual behavior—emphasizing the son's relationships rather with the father and with the *erastes*, or lover. He concludes that the prolonged immaturity of the males resulted in a kind of pseudo-homosexuality, an essentially adolescent psychology with a genius for applying the creative potential of youth.[25]

Slater, following the lead of psychoanalysis, argues that the mother's ambivalence toward her son led also to schizophrenia, which generally originates in such a double-bind as she placed him. The family constellations, in fact, of schizophrenic and homosexual males are quite similar. And so we find a high incidence of madness in the myths—sent by goddesses or by that most effeminate god, Dionysus—upon parents and often causing them to destroy their children.

Fear of the mad mother-goddess, fear of her hairy genitals—which Bruno Bettleheim relates to the *vagina dentata*[26]—resulted in the Greek preference for pubic depilitation of women and for immature females as wives. Courtesans, who were obviously more mature and experienced than the average bride of sixteen, often assumed the sobriquet of some female bogey—Mormo, Lamia, Empusa, Charybdis, Phryne. "You can call every prostitute a Theban Sphinx," Athenaeus asserted, "they babble not simply but in riddles." The man who understands these riddles may depart unharmed, like Oedipus (13. 558d). One of the most famous brothels in Paris was operated under the sign of the Sphinx.[27] *Gorgona* can refer to a harlot in Modern Greek as well as to a lecherous marine monster, and the folklore preserves recipes for how to behead her instead of being seduced by her.[28]

The Athenian imagination slid easily from uterine monsters to chthonian ones, and most of our famous female beasties have strong connections with the earth, either because they are the children of Ge or because of their more or less serpentine nature. The symbolism of the serpent constitutes a mare's nest of conflicting but superficially complementary interpretations. Obviously, anything long, skinny, and squiggly can be a phallic symbol. But the serpent motif appears in myth in the form more often of a devouring female than a penetrating male: as a beast whose posture in fantasy—either poised with jaws agape and fangs dripping, or recumbent and with the just-consumed prey still outlined against its belly, or coiled around the akimbo limbs and sword of a young hero—aptly expresses mankind's eternal fear of envelopment and emasculation. (In Greek art, however, serpentine opponents are more often male than female—Triton, Achelous, Typhon—and many nameless bearded snakes twine themselves around sanctuaries in Archaic sculpture and painting.) The serpent cannot simply be written off as fell beast, for—like woman herself—it is the source as well as the symbol of life as well as of death. It crawls out of the crannies of the earth in the springtime, periodically renews its skin, and thus seems to embody the knowledge of cyclical health and eternal youth; yet no beast is more deadly, even in death when it can deliver its venom in a reflexive strike.

Today, every Greek from peasant to professor suffers from advanced herpetophobia. Cretan boots are cut knee-high to protect the shepherds from a viper six or seven inches long. In vain does the American passenger shout at a Spartan bus driver to swerve around a grass snake crossing the road. All serpents are deadly, or at least so wild *(agrios)* as to affront the sensibilities of a civilized man, and they deserve killing. To spare them bespeaks idiocy in the old sense, a violation of that pact of mutual protection which is the basis of civilization. Yet in ancient times many households harbored a pet snake who protected the *oikos* by its benevolent genius and guarded the storeroom against rodents, since domestic cats seldom found their way outside Egypt. On the other hand, Herodotus relates the savage natural history of the small flying snakes of Arabia: during copulation the female seizes the male by the throat and doesn't let go until she has chewed him through; but the young, while still in her belly, avenge their murdered father by devouring her womb and eating their way out to daylight—as does the single cub a lioness is supposed to bear (3.108–9). Thus the population of predators is kept low.

A great snake supposedly lived on the Athenian Acropolis, although no one except the priests ever caught a glimpse of it, and was associated with Athena in her role as guardian of the citadel. When it abandoned the site, leaving its ration of honey-cake untouched, the Athenians knew that the Persians would sack their city (Herodotus 8.41). Pausanias identifies this snake with Erichthonius, an early king of Athens who was born from the union of Hephaestus' premature ejaculate with the earth when he attempted to rape Athena, and who himself was half snake (1.24.7 and 1.18.2).

Athena's aegis bears a snakey fringe around its border and the Medusa's head in its center. In the psychoanalytic writings and in Greek literature the aegis is usually called a dreadful weapon. But just what harm does it do? Athena shakes it at her enemies, those who try to assault her or to attack her city, and they run away in terror; on an old temple on the Acropolis she was shown wielding one of the snakes against a giant. So far as I know she never actually

turns anyone to stone with the aegis. The aegis, then, only wards off danger—
a fairly benign deterrent except on the battlefield where a slaughter could result
from the panic it causes. Slater might argue that only a virgin goddess is
sufficiently un-threatening as to be allowed to wear the aegis and live in the
city as its protectress. But other goddesses, cruel ones like Hera, Aphrodite, and
Artemis, brooded over their own cities (Samos, Corinth, Ephesus).

Do the Gorgons have any other benevolent aspects? They are far too
common to be entirely fearsome. Whatever the original reason for such creatures being stationed on the pediments or roof peaks of temples, they multiplied
out of proportion to any magical use man could make of them and served as
specimens in the children's zoo of myth, if initially frightening to the child,
charming to the adult. They stare out at us not only from the narrative contexts
of painted vases—Perseus running like the dickens with the still sleeping although now decapitated head of Medusa just visible in his wallet, her sister
Gorgons in hot pursuit, Athena and Hermes standing casually by to lend moral
support—but they also decorate, fantastically but frivolously, all sorts of neutral
objects, plates for example. True, her face often appears on shields, grim-visaged
to fright the souls of fearful adversaries. But so do crabs, cocks, scorpions, bulls,
rams, lions, and other beasts. True, sphinxes guard the dead, perched on the
tops of tombstones, as do lions; but both eventually are replaced by simple
palmette ornaments and then by architectonic frames enclosing family scenes
depicted in relief. True, griffons are rapacious beasts—eagle-headed and be-
winged lions that once symbolized the power of the Mycenaean kings—but
seventh-century symposiasts invited them to their feasts, permitted them to
roost, cast in bronze, on the lips of their cauldrons and tripods. True, the
Medusa has an absolutely horrible face, in the beginning, but by the late
Classical and Hellenistic periods she has become a beautiful young woman,
terror-stricken herself rather than striking terror in others, or a dreaming damsel
pathetically awaiting death; she often graces mirror backs, cameos, and other
jewelry, perhaps to remind milady that all is vanity. And soon her hair, instead
of writhing with snakes, merely frizzes in the damp climate of later antiquity,
and nymphs and even emperors adopted her tousled coiffure as a mark of
authentic emotionality.[29]

The Devouring Mother

In Archaic times beards usually grow around the porcine mouths of
Medusa and the other Gorgons. The Elder Pliny called the Gorgons a very
hairy race, but his information was probably based on sightings of chimpanzees
(*Natural History* 6. 36). This male attribute by itself could signify merely the

eo = early

sexual repulsiveness of the Gorgons. And pigs were commonly associated both with women's genitals—*khoiros*, "little pig," was a slang term for vulva—and with the underworld. At the Thesmophoria, a festival in honor of Demeter, women carried pork and pastry images of pigs down into a cave beneath the Acropolis; and every initiate into the Eleusinian mysteries sacrificed a piglet to Demeter, the corn goddess who loses her daughter Persephone to Hades for a few months each year. One need not go as far as Slater, who insists that Perseus' beheading of Medusa represents at the very least a conquest of the Evil Mother through castration, or "unsexing."[30] The broad, collective images of myth seldom remain still long enough for such surgically precise elucidation. Nevertheless, the association of woman both with fertility and with death seems inescapable. Some might find in the conflict of hero with monster an allegory of man's rise from unconsciousness to consciousness, a victory over his desire to sink back into the eobiotic stew, and an affirmation of his separate nature free from the primal waters of chaos and the narcissistic concern over self-maintenance. For Slater the decapitation of the Gorgon and the slaying of the dragon at Delphi were severings of the umbilicus that binds man to the nourishing but dominating navel of the earth. Greek family life encouraged the child to idealize the always absent father, to look for a substitute outside the home in the fantasy world of the myths. And so the hero must go out to fight the demons who terrify the child, and an older man (the stepfather or his equivalent) unleashes the feminine forces on the yet untested youth: Pelias sent Jason to fetch back the golden fleece from a sanctuary guarded by the dragon of Ares; Polydectes and Poseidon let loose the Medusa and Ketos (a sea-monster) on Perseus; Iobates sent Bellerophon against the Chimaera.[31]

In Jason's myth his father (Aeson), uncle (Pelias), and future father-in-law (Aeetes) figure prominently. In order to restore the kingdom of Iolcus to Aeson, Jason accepted Pelias' challenge to bring home the golden fleece from Colchis. King Aeetes of Colchis believed that his life or power somehow depended on this treasure, and so he plotted to kill Jason after the hero had arrived at the capital on the ship *Argo* and innocently made known his quest. But with the help of Aeetes' daughter Medea, who drugged the guardian serpent, Jason made off with the fleece. Leon Balter finds the young hero's defeat of the old king to be an oedipal victory and claims not only that the dragon represents the father-figure and the fleece the mother's pubic hair but also that the famous clashing rocks through which the Argonauts had to sail are the jaws of the vagina dentata.[32] More likely, if any such symbolism is operating here, the dragon plays the role of the mother-monster, pretending to be dead but surviving in the guise of Medea to strike down the hero later in his career when he carelessly abandons her for a Corinthian princess.

Bellerophon is mythological cousin to Perseus. Perseus was asked to bring home the Gorgon's head as a wedding present for his father-in-law to be, and then (amid echoes from Oedipus' career) saved his mother and prevented the wedding by petrifying the old man; and he slew Poseidon's monster to save the rockbound damsel Andromeda and make her his wife. Bellerophon fended off a seduction by Sthenoboea, the wife of his host Proetus; in vengeance for being spurned she cried attempted rape. Her husband could not kill a guest, so he sent Bellerophon to his father-in-law Iobates, in Lycia. By the time his new host got around to opening the sealed death warrant which the hero had been asked to deliver, the sacred bond of hospitality *(xenia)* had once again been established. So Iobates sent him out, ostensibly to slay the Chimaera (a fire-breathing lion with a tail that ended in a viper's head and with a billy goat growing out of its back), but actually to get himself killed. Bellerophon, however, succeeded in killing the beast, then had to fight a neighboring tribe, and then the Amazons, and then the king's own Lycians. And when he had won every battle he was given Iobates' daughter in marriage. Now Athena patronized both heroes; she backed Perseus all the way, and she gave Bellerophon the golden bridle he needed to tame Pegasus, a winged horse that sprang from the bloody neck of the headless Medusa and had been sired on her by Poseidon's rape. Mounted on this stallion he hovered in the air above the Chimaera and hurled down a lead-tipped spear that promptly melted in her mouth and throttled her. The monster's death rattle was that gurgling noise which, in Greek, onomatopoetically names the Gorgon.

The ancient tenor of the myth emphasized the contrast between the glorious, early part of the hero's career and his later fall from divine grace, when, relying on the friendship of the gods, he tried to ride his mount to heaven. Pegasus made it, but bucked Bellerophon off when a gadfly from Zeus stung it on the haunch.

The two monsters, however, have much in common; the Chimaera simply has more features to explain. The depiction of Medusa's beheading decorates many fine black- and red-figure vases; Bellerophon and his monster are popular rather in statuettes and votive plaques which were hung up in temples as prayers of request or thanksgiving. The Chimaera's gaping lion's jaws and the clotted mane surrounding them bear a family resemblance to the Medusa's mouth and to her hair, which in Archaic art, when not full of snakes, has the same thick, unkempt look. The Chimaera's tail clearly marks her as the sort of opponent liable to strike one dead after she seems safely past. The goat, the placement of which every artist had to work out for himself, may be a sport of the imagination. It is the lion's body that arrests our gaze: as often as not it has two rows of milk-full breasts which distinguish it as a creature, like Medusa, both male and female—the queenly king of beasts. Her mane can be construed as a kind of beard as well as the attribute of the male of the species; the billy goat was renowned for his potency; the snake is ambi-sexual. And Bellerophon's swoop down upon the Chimaera is, in Freudian symbology, a sexual conquest. But a conquest over what?

The hero, before he can serve the cause of man's rise to consciousness out of somnolent oneness with Mother Earth, must create his own sexuality. That act of creation involves combat with both male and female forces, particularly in the hermetic context of the Greek family where a boy's natural androgyny was unnaturally protracted by his mother, aunts, and sisters and by his admirers in the gymnasium. When he set out to become a hero, the ephebe was a male only by birth and not by deed. Mother had to be killed. But he also needed to make his male mark in the world of his fathers, to fight for his status in the pecking-order jealously contested by kings, athletes, warriors, and bandits. The ambiguity of his initiatory conquest matches the ambiguity of the situation it delivers him from.

Lions and leopards were popular in Greek art. But leopards, having no distinguishing sex characteristics, came to be linked with Dionysus, and will be taken up in chapter 5. In the Archaic period the sex characteristics of lions are often confused; they can have, like the Chimaera, both manes and breasts. As with so many stylistic turns of ancient phrase, we may never know if intention or ignorance is operating here. The zoological question of whether lions ever inhabited Greece, and, if they did, then when they died out, has never been satisfactorily answered. Homer, apparently, never saw one in the flesh, for his lions do not roar. Herotodus brings in *Panthera leo* to attack Xerxes' pack-camels in Thrace and claims they are common in a small part of that region (7. 126). Aristotle and Pausanias attest to their presence in northern Greece, though they may only be repeating Herodotus' information (*History of Animals* 6.31.; Pausanias 6.5.4–5). But few Athenians could ever have seen a lion. It seems to have been known chiefly as an exotic beast depicted on Oriental textiles—a figure, then, conveniently located in the Greek imagination somewhere between fantasy and reality, one whose image in art might slip because of a simple mistake over manes or upon whose iconography the mark of some subtle, perhaps subconscious intention might be embroidered.

Action, not appearance, embodies their essence, which lies in rapaciousness. In art, they spring upon their prey, usually from behind, and bite the man or the animal in the throat, at the base of the neck, or less commonly on the flank. The deer or bullock bends its head backward in agony. The weight of the predator bears down on the dying animal; its fangs and claws are displayed to the viewer, seemingly wrapped around the flesh about to be consumed. The locks of the lion's mane radiate from the bite like lines of electrical force.

In poetry and prose, lions are almost always said to be *mountain* lions, who attack the baggage animals of those crossing through their alpine retreats, or who come down from the hills to raid the sheepfold or corral and are bespattered with the blood and gore of their victims. Here natural history lets us down. Plains are the usual habitat of lions, but of man as well. Under the pressure of a growing, secure population of Greeks, lions, like Oedipus, may have retreated to the maquis-clad slopes and bare crags (African lions often linger on the kopjes that dot the veldt). But whether Balkan ecology or the Greek imagination (locating the wildest beast in the wild heights between city-states) has created this aspect of the mythology of lions, an almost aquiline swoop upon the unwary conveys their nature. Only Heracles can reverse the advantage to establish a man-superior pose in his wrestling scenes with the Nemean Lion.

Like the Sphinx, then, lions attack from above. We may remember that to kill Medusa Perseus needed winged sandals, to speed him out of reach of her vengeful sisters. But these sandals also enabled him in his encounter with Ketos, their mother, to make a diving attack. To have a chance against the Chimaera Bellerophon needed a winged horse—the perfect Freudian symbol, since riding as well as flying stands for coitus and orgasm in the interpretation of dreams. The most common position for heterosexual intercourse among the Greeks seems to have been from behind, but face to face for homosexual couplings between an older man and a boy.[33] We might locate a clue to the terrible gaze of monsters in this emphasis on positions and heights: the Greek husband turns his wife or courtesan away from him for copulation, while the Greek hero gains altitude on monsters and perhaps employs a mirror to avoid the female's eyes—the bright glance that freezes a warrior, a helpless fawn or hare, a husband in his tracks. The verb *derkomai*, "to look," signifies the gleam that darts from the eyes to strike some living object, usually a victim. And the succubus holds her sleeping lover in her power as much with her gaze as by her position over him and her talons pinioning his arms.

The Scylla, Harpies, and the Sirens all maintain a literal superiority over their victims. Scylla, once a beautiful maiden who preferred the company of sea-nymphs to that of men or the sea-god Glaucus who loved her, was changed by a jealous Circe into a monster with six terrible heads, each with three rows of fangs, on long necks, and her lower body was hidden in a cave high above the water (*Odyssey* 12.80–110, 201–59); Ovid, perhaps drawing on contemporary Medusas, says that she kept her beautiful face but is all snarling canine jaws about the waist, loins, and legs (*Metamorphoses* 13.730–41, 13.898–14. 74). She leans out of her lair and snatches up fish or sailors from ships that are forced to sail in close to her ledge to avoid the nearby whirlpool Charybdis, which is also construed as a female monster. The images of engorgement could not be more obvious. Poor Scylla wished only to lead an idyllic, pastoral life with her girlfriends. But a beautiful girl cannot avoid love for long without causing men grief and without offending the great love goddess, here represented by Circe. And the hero or simple wanderer across the sea cannot avoid the twin risks, of being swallowed or being snatched away, which lie between him and his goal. Circe, tamed by Odysseus' guile and sexual allure, warned him against fighting with Scylla. But in keeping with his constant testing of himself, particularly against dangerous women, he donned his armor, tried to fight, and lost one of his men to each of her heads.

Odysseus also exposed himself to the Sirens' song, whose lure to shipwreck and death no man had ever before resisted. They do not snatch, tear or devour sailors; rather, the shores of their island are piled with the bones and rotting bodies of willing victims. More horrible than vultures, Sirens do not even clean away the carrion they create. Odysseus stuffed his companions' ears with wax as a defense against their singing, and had himself tied to the mast. He had to hear the words of their song, not only as another nearly destructive but ultimately strengthening encounter with Woman, but because it tempted him—the hero whose forte was cleverness, whose flaw was curiosity—more than any other man who had yet tried to row past their fatal rookery (no wind blows in their vicinity): "For we know all that has happened on the nourishing earth" (*Odyssey* 12.191).

Their song "enchants" *(thelgo)*, a word used three times for Circe's magical power to change men into beasts, and often meant to convey the horrible power of love or of some other form of madness to becloud a man's judgment and lead him to destruction. Plato describes the charm *(thelxis)* of speech, which his form of dialectic is calculated to interrupt, so that a sober philosopher can keep his logical wits about him in the midst of a stunning rhetorical display. Such a spell as Circe's or the Sirens' or the Sphinx's must be "chanted" to achieve its effect. The Sphinx chants her riddle, *ainigma*, or carries off those caught by her song (*Oedipus the King* 391; Euripides, *Phoenician Women* 806–07, 1500–05, *Electra* 471–72; Pausanias 9.26.2); the Sirens of course sing or play a flute and a lyre (in the *Argonautica* of Apollonius of Rhodes only the even more powerful song of the androgynous poet and mystic Orpheus drowns out theirs and saves Jason and his crew); and Odysseus' companions find Circe singing as she works at her loom.

Men as well as women can use words put to music to work their spells, as we shall see in the myths of Odysseus, Orpheus, and the sophists. But women alone can weave and cook, both activities mysterious to men in the simple world of the Greeks. So the weaving of Helen in *Odyssey* 4 and her knowledge of sleeping draughts and poisons, the weaving of Circe and her spells and pharmacopeia are not unconnected; Ovid has Circe neglect her loom but at work sorting herbs when Odysseus comes upon her (*Met.* 14.264–67). As in English, to weave can have the metaphorical sense of to scheme or devise: *griphos*, the Greek word for a woven basket, also means "riddle." Women, out of necessity, have been far better schemers than men throughout history.

Penelope, the epitome of good wife, weaves the great schemes of the *Odyssey*—the web or shroud that delays the suitors for several years and the contest of the bow, by which her husband and a few faithful servants are enabled to destroy an overwhelming number of opponents. Clytemnestra, the model of an unfaithful wife in Aeschylus' *Oresteia*, murders her husband and tries to murder her son. She has planned for years to kill Agamemnon upon his homecoming. To accomplish this, she first bends his will to hers as though he were a beast that must go willingly to the sacrifice, and persuades him to walk on a crimson tapestry from his chariot into the palace. Then, after he has snuggled down into a warm bath, she throws a hunting net over the tub, to hold him helpless, and with the aid of her lover Aegisthus slaughters him with an axe or a sword. Images of predation and weaving abound throughout the trilogy, and Aeschylus ensures that connotations of vileness accrue to Clytemnestra's reputation by having her and her vigilante Furies ranked among the menagerie of monsters and predators. In the *Eumenides* the priestess of Apollo fails to identify these Erinyes but can only compare them to Gorgons and Harpies. Cassandra, the helpless prophetess, calls Clytemnestra an amphisbaena and a Scylla and a lioness who beds with a wolf (*Agamemnon* 1233, 1258). Faint evocations of Helen and Circe are sounded when Cassandra compares Clytemnestra's preparations to murder her husband and his mistress to those of a wife mixing drugs (1260). The Chorus in the *Libation Bearers* exhorts Orestes to have the heart of Perseus in his breast (831–32) and later tells how he, by killing Clytemnestra and Aegisthus, lopped off the heads of two snakes (1047). And earlier in this second play of the trilogy, the murder of Agamemnon makes the Chorus think of the women of Lemnos who murdered their husbands.

These women of Lemnos forgot once to sacrifice to Aphrodite and were punished with a terrible body odor that drove their husbands to take barbarian mistresses. For this insult the wives murdered them all and were ever after reviled—for agitating a primal fear in the minds of Greek men. Only revenge, through seduction, impregnation, and abandonment, could arrest that fear. And so Jason and his crew stopped off at Lemnos and put the women in their place, once the odor had worn off.

Twice the Chorus of old men in the Agamemnon lament over their dead king caught in a spider's web (Clytemnestra's hunting net—1492, 1516). Spiders and other stinging insects and beasts commonly play character roles in dreams and fantasies, as images of the deadly female or sometimes as the fascinating but testy unconscious. (Karl Abraham thought the spider a symbol of the wicked mother formed like a man, with her single phallic thread emerging from the pubic web.[34]) In his *Memorabilia*, Xenophon recounts Socrates' advice to the courtesan Theodota that, though she has better equipment for catching her prey than a spider's web or a huntsman's nets, she could learn much from his contrivances for engaging disciples (3.11.5–18). The passage shows that the conjunction of voracious female with devouring beast and with the lures and machines of entrapment was a commonplace of calculative thinking in ancient Greece. Certainly the spider's web is a natural symbol for the enmeshed death of Agamemnon and the tangled claims of justice that complicate the issue of his murder. The aptness of the image, however, may be far more precise than the Chorus or their creator imagined.

Now, female insects and spiders of many species make postcoital meals of their spent mates. Did Aeschylus know this? Does the neurotic caught in the arms of a nightmarish arachnid somehow know this? Where art fails, natural science may offer psychology a solution to the threat of the devouring female.

The male of a certain kind of spider, indigenous to Greece, is said to have developed an efficient ploy to avoid the fate we all—according to the psychoanalysts—fear. He first kills a fly and presents it to the spideress of his choice as an amorous hors d'oeuvre. Then, while she is busy sucking the morsel dry, he sneaks around behind her, reaches under her belly with one leg, and tickles her to sleep. Wiser than Oedipus, he doesn't rely on his enemy's repose, but quickly ties her up with his own silk and gets what he was after. The rape wakens her, of course, but by the time she can untie herself the lover has safely made his escape.[35]

Electra

Clytemnestra, the human summation of all the composite bestial fears of the Greeks, is the greatest of the monsters but not quite the last. She has defeated the hero who thought he could ignore her dangerous aspect, and now awaits execution at the hands of her son and daughter. Electra, in killing her mother, will become the ultimate monster of the ancient world and the emblematic one of twentieth-century womanhood. She will achieve victory, but at the price of that powerful sensuality she has inherited from her mother and learned from her mother's familiars.

What sort of a girl does such a culture breed, where every strong woman risks classification among the endangered and dangerous brood of wide earth; where every good father absents himself from the home for much of the day with his cronies if he is merely a citizen, for much of the year with his faithful companions if he is a hero; where the husband may make a mistress of any slave-girl, spear-won or store-bought, but adultery or display of backbone in a wife is thought to deserve severe punishment? The dramatists differ in their answers.

Aeschylus gives us little more than a canvas cut-out of a girl, who once she has performed the womanly office of singing a dirge for her father sinks back into the scenery—though musty odors of witchcraft do get mixed in with the incense during that lament, when she and Orestes stand above the grave and summon Agamemnons's ghost to their aid. Sophocles' Electra bears the scars of her virtual imprisonment and of the various family atrocities she has witnessed, but despite her emotional instability does yeoman's work as the hero of the play. Euripides' girl is a different case entirely. His Electra manages subtly to align herself with her brother Orestes in taking a man's view, albeit a mite unsteadily, of women and sexuality in general. Euripides thereby takes another one of his giant steps toward the invention of psychological insight, as we understand it, and continues his attack on all traditional values. In his deft administration of a dose of psychological and moral nihilism, Euripides is Ovid's precursor.

First the ideals and the images that support them. Orestes arrives on the scene as the heroic son of legend, under orders from Apollo to assassinate the murderers of his father. Electra is eager to help. In one of his supposedly irrelevant odes Euripides has the Chorus sing about the weapons Achilles wore when he went to Troy to punish Helen, a veritable rogues' gallery of monsters in bronze—the shield with Perseus lifting the Gorgon's head on it, the helmet on which sphinxes hold enchanted prey in their talons, the greaves decorated with the Chimaera fleeing from Pegasus (*Electra* 464–75). Later the Chorus tell Electra that Orestes is coming, bringing not the Gorgon's but Aegisthus' head. And Orestes says that he threw his cloak across his eyes (like Perseus) and blindly struck at his mother (1221).[36] After the murders, a remorse that arises from their own souls and not from some deity whispering in their ears propels brother and sister into a catatonic stupor. The heroes Castor and Pollux land on stage to declare, perhaps for the first time in Western literature, that the characters' feelings indicate the correct moral stance: Apollo's orders were wrong. And by the way, they add, Helen never went to Troy—Zeus sent a phantom in her place when she refused to be unfaithful. Even our old friends, the monsters, seem somehow rehabilitated once the murder of Clytemnestra has been discredited. Euripides elicits the sympathy of the audience and the ethical judgment of his characters and then betrays both trusts to the ambiguities of life and of myth treated realistically. He begins by upholding the old ideals and ends by shattering them.

At last the young girl's complex can be told. Until now woman was either stupid and submissive (Iphigeneia, Chrysothemis, Ismene), masculine and potentially threatening (Athena, Artemis, Antigone), or powerful and seductive but voracious (Clytemnestra, Scylla, the courtesans). In the last play of the

Oresteia we experience the irony of the most manly of goddesses, Athena, condemning a woman of manly counsel, Clytemnestra. It was not possible in Clytemnestra's day or in fifth-century Athens for a woman with her gifts to exploit them to her own satisfaction *and* to the good of the community.[37] In such a world of fighting lions and lionesses, of active heroes and passive heroines, of the overvaluation of man at the expense of woman, a young woman had few models to follow except her father or the heroes of saga. If her father happened to be one of those heroes, then so much the worse.

The Electra complex has never gotten quite the press as has Freud's more famous invention, but in fact it designates a phenomenon perhaps more commonly verifiable and one that preoccupied Carl Jung, though he seldom names it, far more than it did his Viennese colleague. Freud devoted himself to discovering the mechanisms and needs of the psyche and then to reconciling each individual to an uneasy peace within the tyrannous but ineluctable confines of culture. Jung on the contrary pursued an Other—first an outer something, the girl, and then an inner woman, his anima, and finally an inner voice, a spiritual attunement to the directions and guidance emanating from the various images and symbols that rise up out of the archetypes of the collective unconscious and cut across all cultural lines (see chapter 4). For a man on such a quest, the temptations of the dangerous woman never cease to be fascinating, since he flatters himself that he could not have penetrated as far as he has into alien realms if he had not withstood her blandishments: many monsters are beautiful.

In Freud's earliest years as an analyst, most of his women patients claimed to have been seduced by their fathers. Eventually he discovered these lurid accounts were merely fantasies, from which in fact were derived the women's hysterical symptoms. He handled their cases with strict professionalism. "The majority of hysterical women are among the attractive and even beautiful representatives of their sex," Freud remarks in his study of narcissism,[38] but he seems to have remained immune to their allure. He comments coolly on their skill in manipulating to their advantage the erotic aspects of the analytical transference;[39] he even took their fantasized accounts of father-daughter incest as evidence for his theory of the Oedipus complex, which accounts mainly for the incestuous desires of sons for mothers. One of his biographers attributes Freud's ignorance of women and their ways, his lack of an explanation of love besides sex, to his own low sex-drive.[40]

In his *Introductory Lectures on Psychoanalysis* (1920), Freud takes the Electra complex to be simply the female version of an Oedipus complex—the mechanism working as smoothly in reverse as it does forward.

> Things happen in just the same way with little girls, with the necessary
> changes: an affectionate attachment to her father, a need to get rid of her

mother as superfluous and to take her place, a coquetry which already
employs the methods of later womanhood—these offer a charming picture,
especially in small girls, which makes us forget the possibly grave consequences lying behind this infantile situation.[41]

By 1925 he had begun to modify his thinking, although he generally
resisted Jung's neologism, Electra complex, and preferred the term Oedipus
complex for any constellation of childish erotic impulses. In "Some Psychological Consequences of the Anatomical Distinction between the Sexes" he presumes that the little girl, as well as the little boy, originally takes her mother as
the object of her complex (here far removed from neurosis) while she concentrates on the potency of the vestigial penis, her clitoris. But once she discovers
her anatomical deficiency, her lack of a real penis, and admits her envy of the
boy's far superior appendage, she shifts her hold from her mother as a love-
object to her father. At the same time, she pretty much abandons clitoral masturbation for vaginal eroticism.[42] In "Female Sexuality" (1931) he indicates that
a woman with a strong father attachment need not be neurotic, but he does
find such a bond always preceded by an equally strong and passionate attachment to the mother. In this pre-oedipal stage, the child plays a masculine role,
corresponding to her reliance on her vestigial phallus. But when it suddenly
strikes her how powerless her clitoris really is, the girl doesn't turn to hatred of
her mother—as a boy turns to hatred of his father when threatened with castration—but, if she is healthy, glides over to vaginal genitality and temporary
fixation on her father.

> If she pursues the second line, she clings in obstinate self-assertion to her
> threatened masculinity; the hope of getting a penis sometime is cherished
> to an incredibly late age and becomes the aim of her life, whilst the fantasy
> of really being a man, in spite of everything, often dominates long periods
> of her life.[43]

The castration fear then in the case of a boy operates as the long arm of
culture, forcing him to obey the taboos of the tribe; while in the case of a girl
this . . . shock, perhaps, rather than fear, delivers the command of nature—"it
is time to seek a man." The feminine form of the Oedipus complex is the
lengthy and circuitous result of a castration complex. Girl learns to cleave to
man only after woman as castrated creature has been discredited in her eyes:
"The girl is driven out of her attachment to her mother through the influence
of her envy for the penis and she enters the Oedipus situation as though into a
haven of refuge."[44] Finally and most simply, in An Outline of Psychoanalysis
(1938, published 1940), Freud argues that "identification with her mother can

take the place for a girl of attachment to her mother," and the wish for a baby take "the place of wish for a penis."[45] Something nineteenth-centuryish is creaking in the joints of this complex, some naive and rusty presumption that if psychic work is being done then there must be a mechanism operating. Nevertheless, the Electra complex may account for more of the facts than does the Oedipus complex.

Freud thought the Electra complex a less efficient mechanism than the Oedipus complex; he claimed that girls remain in it "for an indeterminate length of time; they demolish it late and, even so, incompletely."[46] To this phenomenon he ascribed the weak development of the superego in women and their shaky sense of morality.[47] He never explained the difference between a normal or healthy female Oedipus complex and one that leads to neurosis— presumably because the mechanisms of the two cases are the same; they differ only in intensity. And he abbreviated his treatment of the issue of penis-envying girl, with a few remarks on her unwillingness to accept her castration and vaginal genitality, her identification with her phallic mother or father, and her refusal to submit to her own passive femininity and to male aggressiveness; in extreme cases she becomes a homosexual. But what about all those cases that are not so extreme? All those hordes of women attempting to find some less rigid model than meek mother or swaggering bluestocking?

Jung, intentionally or not, picked up where Freud left off. He may have invented the term "Electra complex," but his interest lay in complexions of adult failure and success and in antidotes for future mistakes, not in tracking tiny tot monsters back to their lairs. Freud tried to explain Electra; Jung only described her, but the description proves more useful than an explanation. In "The Theory of Psychoanalysis" (1913) Jung admits the existence of a female Oedipus complex, in which little girls court their mothers, and attributes its existence to the sexually undifferentiated nature of the libido in early childhood. Girls soon move on to the Electra complex.[48] At this same stage of his thinking, he asserted that psychoanalysis should be freed from a purely sexual standpoint and introduced his view of the libido as a well of more generalized psychic energy.[49]

Much of *Aion* and of the second half of *Two Essays on Analytical Psychology* is directed at Electra herself or at the layman or analyst who must deal with an Electra grown up. For the animus-ridden woman of Jung's analysis usually has a father-fixation, as Euripides' Electra certainly does. The male aspect of her psyche, her animus, has become her inner father (the sum of conventional opinions) and plays a great role in her arguments with men.

> No matter how friendly and obliging a woman's Eros may be, no logic on earth can shake her if she is ridden by the animus. Often the man has the

feeling—and he is not altogether wrong—that only seduction or a beating or rape would have the necessary power of persuasion. He is unaware that this highly dramatic situation would instantly come to a banal and unexciting end if he were to quit the field and let a second woman carry on the battle. . . . [50]

And:

In intellectual women the animus encourages a critical disputatiousness and would-be highbrowism. . . . Without knowing it, such women are solely intent upon exasperating the man and are, in consequence, the more completely at the mercy of the animus. . . . A woman possessed by the animus is always in danger of losing her femininity, her adapted feminine persona, just as a man in like circumstances runs the risk of effeminacy. [51]

This "woman with a man's will" (*Agamemnon* 11) is the true daughter of Clytemnestra—the wife who was a match for her heroic husband, the daughter who waits only for the brother to arrive before taking on her father's assassins. But Jung here abandons all reference to the mythical prototype, and with as good reason as he neglects Freud's elaborate construct. The myth does not fit the psychoanalytical case—although Jung's analysis does throw light on the mythical figure.

Not much about the emotional history of a character can be revealed on the Greek stage. Electra, in fact, was never a child, except in the brief glimpse the myth gives us of a young girl helping her brother to escape from the palace after the murder of their father. Euripides' *Electra*, the most psychologically fertile of the three surviving plays, displays the girl now past her prime, fixated on her dead father, praying for the return of her vengeful brother, obsessed by the thought of her mother's sex life with Aegisthus, and herself balanced unsteadily between misandry (her close-cropped hair and filthy clothes) and nymphomania ("Don't touch what you shouldn't touch. . . . I am utterly yours, for you are stronger." *El.* 223, 227). A believable figure has walked across the stage, but one whose present suffers the lack of a context for her past. And this myth, even in Euripides' version, lacks the depth a psychoanalyst needs for his model; thus Jung recognized for once that he should not lean too heavily on the classics. Euripides can give his characters life, but he cannot give us causes for the effects he presents on stage. Set motive and fixed motifs—not yet character development—were still the order of the dramatic day.

Freud's elaborate mechanism, as brilliant in its way as it may be, seems out of place when set next to our mythical heroine and far too elaborate for her simple needs—like a trash-compactor among the Masai. The apparatus doesn't even work: our father-fixated girl is not supposed to hate the hero who cheated her out of a penis, and our oedipal boy is supposed to want to kill the father who threatens to mutilate him. But Oedipus never *wanted* to kill Laius, and Electra has been planning Clytemnestra's murder for years.

Monsters are doomed to lead frustrated lives and come to bloody ends. Electra, last of the monsters, was portrayed third time around with a sympathy worthy of being called psychological insight but without a full-blown psychology. Although she may represent modern woman's predicament, Electra lacks depth—an emblem being, by definition, two-dimensional. She has no past, for allusions to the earlier stages of a myth do not constitute that series of clues to one's secrets that Freud called a past and which Oedipus possessed. And she has no future—the orders of Castor and Pollux, her semi-divine uncles, at the end of Euripides' play for her to marry Pylades hardly amount to the archetype's advice to the soul, which Jung strained his ears to catch. She is simply a fine figure of a girl, alive for a few hours that have been stage-managed out of the wealth of the sagas, as profound a character as we care to make her, but only for the moment.

The real issue here, which psychoanalysis has found it useful to explore, the matter of the female monsters, was never resolved in classical Greek literature. By Hellenistic times the images of those creatures had been sufficiently domesticated and glamorized that they could pose languorously across a silver makeup case or transport a god or goddess through the tesselated waves of a floor mosaic. At the end of the millennium Ovid, a Roman inheritor of the Greek mythological corpus, introduced a new sense of mystery to our experience of monsters and a new stage in the history of thought.

Ovid's interest in myth, albeit one whose lines of inquiry were laid down far from the high road to the eternal verities, led him to a new portrayal of the psychology of change, of the transition from man to monster, of human to bestial, of animate to inanimate, and thus by an emphasis on dynamics to the beginning of psychology as we understand it. In his epic poem on changes, the *Metamorphoses*, we see portrayed, for the first time in literature, the difference between essence and appearance; what it feels like to turn into a laurel tree or a heifer or a spider but still retain the sensibilities of a young girl. In this he was anticipated by Euripides, who gave us a parade of double-dealing characters; and before Euripides, Homer gave us a self-sufficient hero who could retain his wily essence through the indignity of disguise as a beggar. But Ovid took a giant step backward when he reinvigorated all of nature, art, and now psychology with a breath of animism. The world of the *Metamorphoses*, like the magical world of Lucius Apuleius after him, and the modern world of our daimon-ridden psyches, is always other and more than it seems.

4

Daimon and Archetype

NOBODY has ever met an archetype—at least not an archetype as Jung eventually came to define it—and lived to tell of the experience. Nor has anyone outside of Plato's dialogues or Charles Williams' apocalyptic novels ever achieved a face-to-face encounter with one of the Forms or Ideas. But tales of meetings with daimons, nymphs, satyrs, genii, and other such intermediary demi-gods and spirits abound, from Homer to E. M. Forster and later. In their roles as messengers between gods and men, translators of the robust ineffable to our delicate sensibilities, some of these creatures resemble the archetypal images that, Jung said, arise out of the collective unconscious to assail our constellated neuroses or to lead our souls into the salvation of individuation. Like the archetypes, a daimon can sometimes be dangerous.

Nymphs in particular are said to survive still, here and there in isolated pockets of the countryside where the internal combustion engine, urban pop-culture, and the suburban building-boom have not yet overwhelmed the old beliefs. (One old man recently told a couple of anthropologists that the *exotika*, the pagan supernaturals, no longer exist; with modernization, the old powers to see them have gone but "we have become the demons ourselves."[1]) Now they are called nereids, which originally meant only nymphs of the sea—just as trees, mountains, and rivers were long ago allotted to dryads, oreads, and po-tamiads respectively. Today the nereids are renowned for their beauty and charm, their lovely voices and skill at cooking and weaving. They have acquired some of the nasty habits of Lamia, Gello, Charon, the centaurs, and other demons who also survive in altered forms. Nereids may lust for handsome shepherds and lonely travelers foolish enough to nap in the cicada-loud heat of the day by one of their springs or under one of their trees.

The sleeping youth carried off by a company of nymphs is used and abused by them and finally returned to society spent and dazed. Thereafter he

rows ferry across styx
to Hades

forest gods

can nevermore keep his mind on his work or find mortal women attractive. He drags out his life in melancholy daydreaming. A brief taste of semi-divine flesh has left him no appetite for the merely terrestrial.[2] Vladimir Nabokov's Humbert Humbert is the most famous character in modern fiction to be caught by the nymphs. For him, the budding charm of Lolita is preferable to the plump carnality of her mother, Charlotte Haze. Only a heart attack can put an end to his longing for the not quite eternal girl. Nymphs live a few hundred or a few thousand years: Aphrodite, in the Homeric *Hymn* to her, tells her lover Anchises about the mountain nymphs who mate with sileni and with Hermes, and at their birth pines and oaks spring up, and then their trees die and they die too (156–72).

Less famous than Humbert, but more to the point, is Rosario La Ciura, retired classical philologist and hero of Giuseppe di Lampedusa's story, "The Professor and the Mermaid."[3] The old, curmudgeonly professor tells the rakish first-person narrator, Paolo Corbera, a tale about the summer of 1887, when as a stripling of only twenty-four he was studying himself to distraction in order to prepare for the university chair he hoped to win. He retreated to a cottage on a remote bay in Sicily, to find peace for his scholarly labors and to preserve what shreds of sanity he had left. Each day he would row himself a little way out from the shore and start plodding through his Greek texts, often reciting the poetry aloud. One morning a mermaid, attracted by the sounds of the familiar language, swung herself over the rotting gunwale, chatted with the youth in her native tongue—ancient Greek, pronounced correctly!—and offered herself to him. They spent three whole weeks together, when she wasn't off fishing or exploring, and the experience of her love was as indescribable as the taste of sea urchins. She was free of all culture but possessed a certain raw wisdom. The autumn weather arrived early that year; her companions of the sea called her for the storm festival. She left La Ciura with only the memory of this brief participation in a kind of Dionysian bliss, of union with a creature in whom the divine and the bestial are conjoined. But she promised that he could come to her whenever he liked. Three years later he got the chair of classics at Pavia, and now, an old distinguished professor of seventy or so, he chooses at last to tell his story and explain to his friend why mortal women hold no attraction for him and modern scholarship cannot earn his respect. A day later, on his way to a congress in Portugal, he is reported lost at sea; he had finally accepted the invitation of Lighea the undine, daughter of Calliope.

Such a story could easily be told badly; this one is exquisite. So thoroughly does the otherworldly girl captivate La Ciura that neither the pallid learning nor the pale flesh of simple mortals can do more than provoke fits of expectoration from him. The charm of this one embodiment of the feminine ultimately draws the lover to her through the medium of a watery grave. "None ever escapes

the Sirens," the professor said. In modern terms, the archetypal feminine is
brought to life in the person of, to use an ancient term, the nymph. Certainly
no case history could more accurately record the phenomenon of a *coup de
foudre*, of the creation or projection of the ideal woman (tinged with a Nietzschean dash of paganism), and subsequent possession by her to the point of
rejecting all normal human relationships. Significantly, this most barbaric
event—despite the trappings of Grecian antiquities—takes place in a wild and
lonely setting.

Archetypes

Nature retains her mysteries, which in the city are transmuted into exciting but comprehensible events. Just as Freud became the urbane philosopher
and uneasy proponent of the demands of culture, Jung assumed the role of
prophet in the countryside, where he could be surrounded by echoes and
rustlings of the primitive. "People who know nothing about nature," he wrote
in his autobiography, *Memories, Dreams, Reflections*, "are of course neurotic,
for they are not adapted to reality. They are too naive, like children."[4] As a man
of the city, Freud presumed that the contents of the unconscious consist of
material that has been suppressed; Jung, like an explorer in an unmapped
jungle, that these contents have never been conscious and rather constitute a
set of *a priori* forms or modes or potentials for experience, which he
called *archetypes*.

The connotations and etymology of this word are as important as its
denotations. From 1912 until 1919 Jung relied on a couple of terms usually
translated as "primordial image." But shortly after World War I he introduced
archetype from the *Corpus Hermeticum* (Scott, *Hermetica* I,140,12b, where
God is called "the archetypal light") and from Dionysius the Areopagite (*Concerning Divine Names* 2.6) who suggests that God is like an archetypal sealstone which makes slightly different impressions in different substances.[5]

The *arch* base can mean first or ruling and also old; *tupos* designates a
well-aimed blow or the effect of such—the mark a seal leaves in clay, or a foot
in wet sand, then any form beaten out of metal or released from stone by an
artificer, and finally a general form or model. Jung changed his terminology to
support two developments in his theorizing and to gain, I believe, a rhetorical
advantage. The *arch* base pleasingly conveys associations of arcane and long-
lost wisdom, and *tupos* indicates (in his later writings) not an image, but what
creates that image.

But *arch* also means not simply the first as a rough prototype for an evolving series of products, but the ideal, governing, controlling pattern for generations to come. This innate pattern must be sought by us if we are to learn the hidden order of our lives. The archetype both provides us with a goal and, as an intelligence or something like an intelligence, directs us toward that goal. *Archetype* implies the impossibility of invention; one cannot create, but only discover, a means of expression for what was there potentially all along. Yet for every current archetype there must have been a *prototype*, a first instance struck from a pristine die in the cosmic mint. Hesitating to call anything a first, which can we say leads a more shadowy existence, the archetype or the prototype? We cannot deny that at times our pens shrink from writing *arche-* and inscribe *proto-*; and at other times, vice-versa. What archetype controls this process of selection?

By the invention of one term, Jung joined the forces of psychoanalytic and scientific and scholarly investigation with those of religious faith. Faith may come suddenly, but investigation requires prolonged effort and a sense of where to do one's looking. In primitive man—and here most anthropologists, philosophers, and psychologists would agree with Jung—the main body of psychic life was projected.[6] Previous ages and cultures, some of them far from primitive, possessed living symbols—often, as in the case of monsters, much too alive for comfort. Our culture has not inherited any viable symbols, and so we must talk of psychology and the unconscious.[7] But we cannot describe the psyche directly—Edward Whitmont, a Jungian analyst and interpreter, allows—only indirectly, by describing human behavior "*as if* it expressed aspects of a hypothetical pattern of meaning, *as if* a potential, encompassing wholeness were ordering the parts."[8] By implication, we must also search out the dormant symbols of previous ages, in books where they have lain quietly where the operations of the collective unconscious left them. Jung felt it was his calling in life to restore the vital force of "primitive" religion to the enervated soul of modern man, and he attempted to do this as much through scholarship as by psychotherapy. Myths are evidence of the image-making power of the unconscious on the minds of men of the past, and they contain the same archetypal patterns as dreams do, but in forms that have been refined by the care of centuries and freed from the more personal associations that adhere to our dreams. "The old teachers knew what they were saying," Joseph Campbell assures us: "Once we have learned to read again their symbolic language, it requires no more than the talent of an anthologist to let their teaching be heard." As a key to the grammar of mythological symbols, Campbell recommends psychoanalysis.[9]

Clearly, little room has been left in this approach for the peculiar suggestions or interpretations which a classical poet or playwright intentionally or unintentionally placed in his version of a myth, and cultural and linguistic differences between mythologies are ignored in the search for universal themes. Indeed, Jung and his followers pay even less attention than Freudians to the problem of versions, but accept contributions to "the myth" from any and all sources—since these are all part of one myth anyway or expressions of a single archetype.

Just what are these archetypes we are looking for? Jung defined them differently each time he wrote about them. This does not bespeak a cavalier approach to truth so much as it does the development both of his thought and method. At first he talked about the archetypes as though they were images, but gradually he made them into the sources of those images.

> The archetypal representations (images and ideas) mediated to us by the unconscious should not be confused with the archetypes as such. They are very varied structures which all point back to one essentially "irrepresentable" basic form. . . . The archetype as such is a psychoid factor that belongs, as it were, to the invisible, ultra-violet end of the psychic spectrum.[10]

But this still does not tell us what the archetypes are. Jolande Jacobi explains what Jung, frankly, has failed to make clear.

> The archetypes make up the actual content of the collective unconscious; their number is relatively limited, for it corresponds to "the number of typical and fundamental experiences" incurred by man since primordial times. Their meaning for us lies precisely in the "primordial experience" which is based on them and which they represent and communicate.[11]

Freud himself had thought of something like this. In *Moses and Monotheism* he commits himself to the Lamarkian opinion that "the archaic heritage of mankind includes not only dispositions, but also ideational contents, memory traces of the experiences of former generations."[12] In *Introductory Lectures on Psychoanalysis* he comments that "symbolic connections, which the individual has never acquired by learning, may justly claim to be regarded as a phylogenetic heritage." On the family tree of neurosis, prehistoric experience and infantile experience are kissing cousins; some primal fantasies may be a phylogenetic endowment.[13] And in *An Outline of Psycho-Analysis* he refers to the archaic material in dreams, which as children we bring with us into the world, and which is paralleled by the content of many myths and primitive customs.[14] But he made little use of this material, for he related it only to our racial past, not to our individual futures.

For Jung, however, archetypes compose the sum of latent psychic potentialities, a store of ancestral knowledge about the relations between God, man,
and cosmos. Discovering and opening this store in one's psyche can "save the
individual from his isolation and gather him into the eternal cosmic process."
The archetype also "by its enhanced energic charge (or numinous effect) pro-
vokes in the individual who experiences it the increased emotionality or partial
abaissement du niveau mental [relaxing of ego boundaries] which is indis-
pensable if synchronistic phenomena of this kind [forebodings, prophetic
dreams, hunches] are to occur and to be perceived." The specific form this
energy takes in the psyche is the image.[15]

We are left once again with the images Jung started with, the definite
motifs that are repeated in dream after dream and in myth after myth. If the
archetype itself is empty and formal, an *a priori* possibility of representation,
what can be said about it?—"it seems to me probable that the real nature of
the archetype is not capable of being made conscious, that is, it is transcendent,
on which account I call it psychoid."[16] And again—"archetypes are not determined as regards their content, but only as regards their form and then only to
a very limited degree."[17] Can we talk about what we can't talk about? Wittgenstein said no, but it seems that in our need for transcendent goals, our very
physical brains insist on generating metaphysical schemes replete with their
own impressive, albeit imprecise, terminologies.

Jung complained that his ideas aroused unwarranted resistance in the
scientific community, that the existence of the instincts—to carry the fight back
to Freud's camp—was no more provable than the existence of the archetypes.[18]
But an advocate of instinctual man can rarely find a way to serve the cause of
religion, and an advocate of archetypal man seems committed by his teleological
view to a quasi-religious stance. Jung sought an uneasy mode of inquiry between
the confines of the scientific method and the freedom of metaphysical speculation. No wonder he had enemies. He offered his followers little proof but their
own faith. Jung presumed—reasonably, he would say; rashly, Freud would
say—that the truth must make us happy, and so if some discovery makes us
truly happy then it must be the truth. The inchoate nature of the so-called
science of mythology tempts an analyst to decorate his theories with any gods
and heroes he chooses and to call it a verification of his articles of faith. Jung
for the most part did not even analyze the myths; he simply listed them, over
and over again, to illustrate a point—often a different point, often the same
point, each time.

Jung should have confined himself to talking about images and specific
archetypes—matters where the referents of his terms have a fairly visible existence. Perhaps the most useful characters he created for the drama of life are
those twin antagonists, animus and anima—the dream goddess of each man

and the dream lover of each woman, personifications of the unconscious feminine in man and the unconscious masculine in woman. He took the terms from Latin, but his use of them has little precedent in ancient texts. *Anima* has much the same history in Latin as *psyche* at first does in Greek, and means air, breath, and then the breath of life. *Animus* was a far more complicated and common word, designating the soul as the seat of reason, memory, will, consciousness, and emotion—all of those things which psyche eventually came to mean.

Jung's anima is an amalgam of all the women a man has ever known and all the images of woman he has inherited. She embodies the inferior side of man: feeling, emotion, intuition, helplessness, and all that is dark and mysterious. When he falls passionately in love, a man projects this image onto his beloved. At first a woman may accept the role, because she doesn't want to lose the man; but often she rudely surprises him when, under the strain of living together, she throws the image off and becomes herself again. If we men fail to bring the anima into the realm of consciousness, where it can be controlled, adapted to real women, and put to use in the development of our individualities, we suffer the fate of being at the mercy of the archetype and behaving like textbook cases: "Whenever a man acts in identity with his anima—unconscious to the moods that 'pull' him—he acts like a second-rate woman. . . . When an emotion-charged situation arises and he attempts to react with reason, without *first* or at least *also* realizing his emotional response, he is likely to suffer an anima attack."[19] Loss of control of this aspect of the unconscious often manifests itself late in life, in effeminacy for men and masculinity for women.

The inferior side of woman which the animus represents consists of her intellectual side—logic, opinion, dialectic: "The unconscious world of the woman's animus contains a formidable array of undifferentiated convictions, stereotyped manners, and inflexible morals (the animus is a great moralizer). We find here the source of feminine dogmatism, rigidity, self-righteousness, inflation, aggressiveness, and possessiveness." Animus-possession may express itself "in the pattern of the woman who sits at the feet of some great master, as the only one who understands him. . . . Or she herself may go out and preach the ultimate, unalterable, final truth; at least she will be having the last word."[20] Sean O'Faolain reminisces about the women he met with the IRA in Dublin, who were "driven by that unfeminine animus which seems always to make the male constituent in women behave like the worse side of the feminine element in men. They were . . . ruthless, abstract in discussion, and full of a terrifying sentimentality."[21] Like Maud Gonne who darkened Yeats's thoughts for half his life.

The ancient Greek world provided little opportunity for the tantrums of such a woman. The phenomenon of animus-possession occurs in myth mainly in the form of downtrodden wives, daughters, and sisters who wait for the returns of lovers, fathers, or brothers to execute their intentions and give indirect but concrete expression to the masculine side of their natures: Clytemnestra needs Aegisthus; Electra, Orestes; Penelope, Odysseus; only Antigone dares to operate alone, and then because she has no lord to do her will: Creon is her *kurios*, or protector, but he also happens to be her enemy. In the myth of the philosopher-hero we find the nearest thing to an assertive woman: Xanthippe, probably a pretty typical representation of a harridan, tries but of course fails to bully her husband Socrates into taking care of his family.

In the world of the myths, if not within the walls of the actual Greek *oikos*, women often take a physically passive role and that is the end of that. Men take an active role, in which they need to cultivate the feminine side of their natures after the masculine side has failed them in the midst of dangers; and so the anima will turn up as the good aspect of the monstrous female— the divine patroness whom a hero usually needs to succeed in his tasks. When the hero actually suffers defeat or delay or is forced to drag out the last years of his life as an ordinary mortal once again, the anima seems to have tricked him into helplessness. Odysseus on Calypso's island, Heracles enslaved to Omphale, Jason sitting on the beach at Corinth—all are men forced into effeminacy by their loss of control over the feminine.

Jungian Myth

The most characteristic feature of an archetype is said to be its ambivalence.[22] The ambivalence of a force, however, does not excuse an ambiguous description of it. A great artist may be able to suggest powerful contrarities without causing the least confusion. Jung and his followers have respected the almost direct line an artist seems to have into the unconscious, but they have neglected to tender as much respect to his skill at controlling whatever slippery medium he has chosen in order precisely to render what lies just beyond the perceptions of the rest of us. Without such skill Picasso would be no better a painter than one of Jung's patients. Rhetoric is the art of persuasion, and Socrates criticized its practitioners and their admirers for depending on vague terms to win the assent of their audiences. The matter of style, then, cannot be divorced from the search for truth as though it were an affectation beneath the concern of those out for more important quarry. Jung, however, took an antiintellectual and anti-artistic stance toward the critical faculty, upon which style—whether in writing, painting, music, or whatever—depends:

> A symbol loses its magical or, if you prefer, its redeeming power as soon as its liability to dissolve is recognized. To be effective, a symbol must be by its very nature unassailable.

And:

> The protean mythologem and the shimmering symbol express the processes of the psyche far more trenchantly and, in the end, far more clearly than the clearest concept; for the symbol not only conveys a visualization of the process but . . . it also brings a re-experiencing of it, of that twilight which we can learn to understand only through inoffensive empathy, but which too much clarity only dispels.[23]

Many things in great literature stand for more than themselves, and refuse to explain themselves for fear of destroying themselves. Freud downgraded these symbols into symptoms and insisted on explanations; Jung elevated them to vessels of psychic experiences that cannot be contained by the more rational categories of understanding. Instead of penetrating an object or symbol and risking its destruction, Jung recommends being penetrated by it—permitting its mystical emanations to wash over us. Symbols, according to Jung, break through the boundaries that normally separate different sectors of reality, whereas concepts categorize and separate things.[24] Jung treats life like literature, for he finds as many symbols in daily life as he does in literary or mythological texts. Just as the literature takes us out of ourselves, so the more vividly manifested symbols from the collective unconscious can transport us out of our usual lives and into some transcendent realm. But this is to confuse life with literature, and ecstasy with understanding.

The application of archetypal criticism to literature and to psychotherapy has aroused considerable hostility from the intellectual community. Jacques Lacan, a French psychoanalyst and *philosophe*, expresses his bitterness in mandarin prose: "It is of the utmost importance to realize in the experience of the unconscious Other in which Freud guides us that the question does not find its lineaments in protomorphic proliferations of the image, in vegetative intumescences, in animic halos irradiating from the palpitations of life."[25] And K. K. Ruthven asks how we can approach the universal except by way of the particulars. The stock use of *archetype*, full of disdain for the particular, is often a euphemism for *cliché*; archetypal images "are not intrinsically valuable, and may pop up in a toothpaste advertisement as readily as in an epic poem."[26]

Plato, too, understood the virtues of myth—its ability to handle material not comprehensible by *logos*. Not being a poet by profession, he always found it wise to interrupt the dangerous charm of whatever myth he was telling with a sobering blast of dialectic. Style, and the analysis of style, is finally the only weapon the ego—by definition, a gyroscopic little solipsist within us—possesses to maintain its identity against the collective and collectivizing forces of the unconscious. Speech, logos with some flair, brings the ego into firm and conscious connection with the perceptions.[27] One cannot achieve great clarity of understanding by avoiding clarity of expression. Jung actually preaches the virtues of the imitative fallacy as an investigative and stylistic principle. But the ineffable cannot be made more intelligible by opaque language; and although the numinous may impose its presence on us in a compelling but also an obscure manner, it cannot serve as a model for good, expository prose. Jung took it as such.

Jung's anti-intellectual tendency must be blamed for depth psychology's refusal to look closely at any myth and respect its historical, social, and artistic context and content. Jung read widely, but also lightly and intuitively—although not as frivolously as many of his disciples. Seldom in his works do we find a penetrating analysis of any one version. Nervously he flits from myth to myth, flipping through the pages of his notebooks with one hand and composing with the other. He directed his energies more to collating the literary and artistic motifs, the symbols and sacred texts of the world than to investigation of the psyche *in vivo*. Like earlier prophets and learned apologists, he left men's souls in the care of his followers and to the guidance of his new scriptures.

He was basically a polytheist born into a rigorously monotheistic (or dytheistic—money and Christ) Switzerland, who tried to reconcile his inner compulsion to keep religious open house with the scholastic demand for synthesis. Thus his confusion over definitions: how can you define something that changes each time you read a new book and discover a new set of gods? True polytheism may offer a better explanation of the variety of human experience than monotheism, and it discourages fanaticism. But a polytheist cannot organize his deities and beliefs very thoroughly without pushing some unknown god out from behind a cloud and into conflict with tradition—as Xenophanes, Aeschylus, and Plato learned. Freud owed much of the clarity of his arguments to his monotheism. We may not like the god he chose—sex—but at least we know what that god stands for.

The reader of Jung, tired and dizzy from the interminable comparison of one image to another, yearns for some hard-headed distinctions. But the intensity of his writings is an emotional one, not well suited to discriminations. The intensity of Freud's prose—whether or not emotional drives may have motivated it—is rather intellectual. One can argue with an intellectual's statements; one can only assent to or dissent from the teachings of a divine.

In his autobiography, *Memories, Dreams, Reflections,* Jung describes Freud's authoritarian stance and paternal insistence that his chosen psychoanalytic heir, Jung, carry on the cause of the sexual theory as a bulwark against the "black tide of mud . . . of occultism."

> One thing was clear: Freud, who had always made much of his irreligiosity, had now constructed a dogma; or rather, in the place of a jealous God whom he had lost, he had substituted another compelling image, that of sexuality. . . . A dogma is set up only when the aim is to suppress doubts once and for all. But that no longer has anything to do with scientific judgment; only with a personal power drive. [28]

Jung rejected the new religion of his intellectual stepfather, just as he rejected the old religion of his natural father. Johann Paul Achilles Jung was a minister who suffered depressions as great as those of his heroic namesake. In the last years of his life he went mad, and Carl associated this loss of sanity with the failure of Christianity any longer to offer viable myths to live by. It seems he also took Freud's moroseness as a sign of an incipient derangement that stemmed from the frigidity of his sexual "religion."

Because of his emotional myth- and god-making, Jung in fact was just as dogmatic as Freud. Freud's dogmatism, however, was not as dangerous as Jung's, for it comprehended the means of its own refutation—skepticism. Freudian man, the great doubter, distrusts his declared motives for doing anything and regards his every action as symptomatic—of what he isn't sure, but it's more than likely to prove embarrassing if he can discover it. Jung, the great believer, saw his and Freud's careers as complementary: the nihilist Freud tore down the old beliefs so that the new prophet Jung could raise up others in their place. Jung's theories would be hypothetical only in the sense that, like any mythology or religion, they would have a natural life-span, after which it would be some new theorist's turn. Now, the two approaches do constitute a complementarity, but a synchronic, not a diachronic one. The debate must continue or the critical faculty, the ego, loses the central place Jung claimed it had in the psyche and one becomes a fanatic—identifies one's self with the archetype and is possessed by it. If the critical faculty operates alone, as it obviously did not do in Freud's case, then of course the creative impulse dies; a catatonic or autistic bitterness sets in.

Jung warns constantly against the danger of fanaticism but gives his reader no equipment to fight it: "We must, therefore, no longer succumb to anything at all, not even to good. . . . Every form of addiction is bad, no matter whether the narcotic be alcohol or morphine or idealism."[29] While disclaiming any dogmatic stance or mantic pose, he acted otherwise—so that his students behave like followers, call him a prophet, and refer to his writings as teachings. No leader more subtly threatens the integrity of the souls attracted to him than the leader who claims not to be one. "Why are you following me?" Christ asked, and they followed all the more persistently. Jung of course had an excuse: he had a calling—to rescue men from the loneliness of modern life and show them the way to individuation through a better connection to the collective unconscious. He advertised this endeavor, however, with the fervor of a missionary decrying the godless evolutionists.

> What we are to our inward vision, and what man appears to be *sub specie aeternitatis*, can only be expressed by way of myth. Myth is more individual and expresses life more precisely than does science. Science works with concepts of averages which are far too general to do justice to the subjective variety of an individual life.[30]

By "myth" he meant a personal myth—collated from world mythology, personal dreams, and fantasies.

On the other hand: the Jungian investigator—analyst and analysand are more nearly equal than in Freudian psychotherapy, since both are about the same business of improving the relationship between the unconscious and the ego—has relatively little fear that the scholarly or analytic quest will reveal shameful evidence about his secret life. Freud presumed that we are all more or less ill because we are all more or less repressed and dealing inadequately with the conflicting demands of instinct and culture. Jung, on the contrary, insisted that "suffering is not an illness; it is the normal counterpole to happiness. A complex becomes pathological only *when we think we have not got it.*"[31] Since symbolic and redemptive meaning can be found in even the filthiest contents of the unconscious, the investigator is relieved of the need, if not the fact, of his shame. Because evil is the necessary counterpart to good, the analysand can proceed with the attitude of an optimistic Zoroastrian.

This loss of shame parallels the suppression of the critical faculty. Jung replaced the Christian and Freudian examination of conscience with the "adapted attitude." Disaster and what used to be called sin are now embraced for the good which can come out of them. "What doesn't destroy me makes me stronger," Nietzsche proclaimed, and "The mark of a truly strong man is the ability to turn absolutely everything to his own use." Unlike Nietzsche and Freud, Jung presumed that every culture and every psyche must have a god-term built in and that, particularly as one grows older, a new religious attitude must be found in order for the patient to adapt his inner needs to reality. As Philip Rieff observes, "the object of therapy, in the Jungian sense, is, therefore, to reconcile the individual to whatever authority he carries within himself. Such an authority is inescapable; the wise man adapts himself to it."[32] The psyche thus comes into harmony with the collective unconscious. Not a little of this doctrine originates in the belief in the absolute value of sublime accord; democracy requires the individual to bow to the authority of the body politic. Jung has managed to argue that, properly understood, the personal and the great collective authorities are one and the same; conflict can thus be valued for the synthesis it produces. Nietzsche, siding with nature, and Freud, siding finally with culture, long ago abandoned all hope of such a peaceful union. Obviously the Jungian reconciliation of the microcosmic with the macrocosmic will take place not in the real world, which remains quite resistant to human efforts at peacemaking, but in one's fantasy life, where personal dreams can be infused with meaning from the world's impersonal myths.

Structuralism

As a schoolboy in Basel, Jung found himself unable to work out problems in algebra without substituting real values for the abstract symbols. Just so, he overcharges myth with meaning and imposes his superfluous valuations on alien texts. Structuralism, on the other hand, with its spooky diagrams, recondite jargon, and meta-intellectual bias, deploys myth in a way antithetical to the archetypal approach. For Claude Lévi-Strauss emptied myth of its content and reduced it to mere forms that can be expressed by standard algebraic signs. Every myth is said to be a mediator between polarities, and so these signs form an equation separated into twin antitheses by an equal sign. (See chapter 2 for his analysis of the Oedipus Myth.) Arguing that only the structure of a myth should claim our attention since only the structure persists through the various tellings in various cultures, Lévi-Strauss denies all meaning to that empty shape he has recovered from the world of primitive man. Algebra suffices to expound the vagaries of myth, because myth has been defined algebraically. It does not, however, have to be so. Jung insists that religious meaning, and often the same meaning inhere in wildly different mythomorphs, because he has defined myth in religious terms. Nothing more shapeless than an archetype has ever challenged a philosopher's ability to refine his terms. Nothing more exact than one of *those* formulae has ever begged the humanistic question: what difference does it make? Structuralism aspires to the precisions of the natural sciences; but since nothing in nature is being described, it cannot benefit from the inspiration of beauty that gives the older sciences their passion, nor will it ever attain the aesthetic symmetry of pure mathematics.

Jung and Lévi-Strauss have much in common. Both search for the fundamental and universal properties of human nature, supposedly in order that we might improve ourselves. And both probe "the unconscious nature of collective phenomena."[33] Both the psychoanalysts and the structuralists presume the existence of a code of the unconscious, and both attempt to crack its messages in myth. But Lévi-Strauss has no explanation for the code's existence and no humanistic or humanitarian reason for cracking it. In Edmund Leach's words, for Lévi-Strauss "the universals of human culture exist only at the level of structure, never at the level of manifest fact. ... [He] seems to be more interested in an algebra of possibilities than in empirical facts."[34] The significant, the Freudian or novelistic, detail must be eschewed in favor of the pattern formed by the sum of circumjacent details.

For Jung, however, the real world teems with manifestations of the collective unconscious, all of which can easily be fitted into the grand archetypal scheme. And that scheme has deliberately revealed itself to us—like some *deus absconditus* bored with remaining hidden—so that we can change our ways and become that which we were meant to be. Jung raided the world's libraries, but only as a preparation for his return, at least in spirit, as a native son to the primitive and archaic world we left behind us at the beginning of the Renaissance. Structuralism—colonial despite its Marxist pretensions—exploits the primitive world, whose inhabitants will never benefit from the white man's development of their territory: the theory of myth's mediation between polarities generates the axiom that the primitive mythmaker is ignorant of his story's "true" meaning. Nor will the anthropologist ever journey back to the clearing in the jungle and enlighten him. More urbane than even orthodox Freudianism, structuralism depends on a Hippodamian grid, and on a Métro of the unconscious complete with subterranean transfers of meaning.

Like Freud, Lévi-Strauss is an intellectual child of nineteenth-century materialism. But the anthropologist chooses as his model of the psyche that cool algebraic machine, the computer, rather than the hot invention of an earlier civilization, the steam engine—powered by an over-strained boiler of the libido. Lévi-Strauss seems to have developed his binary program of yes/no, thesis/antithesis, synchronic/diachronic with reference to the methods of Univac's progenitors and to the historical determinism of Marx, but he preferred musical metaphors to information theory. The computer is too practical a gadget, while music preserves a sublime inutility. What counts in music is not the individual sounds, but their relation to other sounds. An orchestral score contains both harmony (the notes read synchronically) and melody (the notes read diachronically). So too both the themes (events taken together) and the narrative (events as a series) of a myth require attention. Finally, however, the anthropologist returns to practical matters: since all the details of all of the versions of each myth are equally valuable, they must be recorded and sorted out in a sort of pigeon-holed affair, eventually to be replaced by IBM equipment and punched cards.[35]

Where does this leave us? Still without any semblance of meaning, it would seem. For after a myth suffers de-structuring or deconstruction, it undergoes restructuring into a language more comprehensible by machine than by man, to whom the resulting equation now signifies little more than its own symmetry. Musical sounds have no intrinsic value, but words and events do. And a musical score remains a set text; but for a myth, in Lévi-Strauss's sense, there is no fixed text—since he treats all tellings, literary or not, as the fluid products of an oral culture—nor can we ever know if we have all the versions. And even if we did have them all, they would never coexist in one time or in one place, except in the anthropologist's mind or on his desk. Lévi-Strauss made an attempt to bring meaning in the back door by alleging that the patterns we can discover in the myths must reflect the structure of the psyche, just as the syntax of a language does. But never is the import of any of these patterns evaluated for us against those of, say, linoleum. As with Jung, the pattern may work itself out through man—"think itself" through man[36]—just as the archetype may possess someone. But what does the structuralist thought think? What is the logos of this austere logic? The armchair, alas, is silent.

The real focus and point of interest in the structuralist writings may be not what man fabricates, as it is in literature, nor his fabricating in itself, as it is in psychoanalysis, but the fabrications of the critic's mind at work on man fabricating his fabrications. The structuralist's pugnacious approach to myth or fiction treats the poet or novelist as a Freudian father-figure; the anthropologist-turned-critic then becomes the son-murderer, sitting cockily at the crossroads of interpretation, on top of the corpse of the text. Having dealt his opponent a deathblow, our structuralist can claim the battlefield of letters for his own and marry the recently widowed Muse.

Inevitably we must ask if anyone has ever found or even looked for some neurological basis for archetypal or structuralist patterns. Well, yes, Carl Sagan, Julian Jaynes, and others have looked—but not with Jung or Lévi-Strauss in mind. In the *Dragons of Eden* Sagan suggests that some of our primordial fears—of falling, of snakes—stem from the Mesozoic war between the mammals and the reptiles, during which the mammals may have slept in the trees by day and preyed by night on the dinosaurs immobilized by the chill, or at least on their eggs. Reptiles do not dream, but mammals do and so do birds (much closer to the reptiles than we breast-fed vertebrates), although only episodically. Does this mean that animals descended from reptiles have to dream because the reptilian brain is still functioning? Indeed, dreams do seem to develop in the brain's R-complex, which we have in common with the reptiles, and in the limbic cortex, which we have in common with the other mammals, but not in our very own, rational, neocortex. As the night wears on we seem to dream progressively earlier (perhaps archetypal) material. We dream of falling and of snakes, because we once hid from the reptiles in the trees; of being pursued, because we were once the prey rather than the predators of larger, if slower-witted species; and of repeatedly and unsuccessfully performing new tasks, because that was in fact the experience of early hominids. [37]

From his psychiatric practice and his travels in Africa and the American Southwest, Jung learned that primitive man is not aware of thinking but rather believes that something thinks in him or through him, and so the main body of his psychic life is projected. [38] Both E. R. Dodds in *The Greeks and the Irrational* and Bruno Snell in *The Discovery of the Mind* have examined the psychological fragmentation of Homeric man, and Julian Jaynes in *The Origin of Consciousness in the Breakdown of the Bicameral Mind* has enlarged on their conclusions with a few speculations of his own in the light of modern neurology. [39] Snell points out that Homeric man has no sense of a unified physical or mental self. (The Greek word which by the seventh or sixth century B.C. came to mean body, *sōma*, in Homer means only corpse; and the later word for soul, *psychē*, in Homer means only the force of breath that keeps a human being alive.) Rather than comprehensive terms, Homer uses words for the various parts of the body and for the various mental and emotional functions subsumed by the word soul. The fragmentation of man appears also in the Geometric art of the period: a man or an animal has no unity, no compact center, but is all in parts which have been reduced to their basic, angular shapes and then stuck together. When one hero spears another in the *Iliad*, the location of the wound and the damage done are precisely described. When the speared man dies, his limbs are loosened and his *psychē* departs through the wound or through his mouth.

This primitive entity, the epic hero, does not understand the causes of his behavior and so suffers from mental instability. "Homer's man," remarks Snell, "does not yet regard himself as the source of his own decisions."[40] His mood and intentions change without warning and seemingly without reflection. All outstanding successes, victories, disasters, defeats, and even decisions are projected onto the operations of the gods—deities either benign or malign, either unknown or named, who in many cases are the specific patrons of this or that warrior or city. Arguing from the invisibility of Athena when she appears to Achilles and restrains him from killing Agamemnon (1.188–222), E. R. Dodds suggests "that in general the inward monition, or the sudden unaccountable loss of judgment, is the germ out of which the divine machinery

inspiration

developed.[41] And, we might add, it is also the afflatus by which psychological man is inspired to create, slowly and tentatively, a sense of himself.

Julian Jaynes calls these gods hallucinations. After all, they make themselves visible at moments of great stress for their favorites or their enemies—to Achilles sulking before his tent, to Hector fleeing around the walls of Troy from certain death, to Odysseus waking up on the beach at Ithaca—and are usually invisible to everyone else. Homer and Hesiod, under the strain of beginning an epic recitation or a judicial pleading, claim to hear the voices of the Muses, authoring their poems for them. Schizophrenics commonly hear voices, as does a small percentage of the world's supposedly sane population, particularly in moments of depression or emotional crisis—like St. Paul's experience on the way to Damascus. Jaynes argues nothing less than that the normal primitive man was schizophrenic, possessed of and possessed by a bicameral mind; or, physiologically speaking, when the left or rational hemisphere of his brain had done its best to solve a problem, the right or intuitive hemisphere stepped in, spoke to it, actually made itself heard as a voice from the outside. "The language of men was involved with only one hemisphere in order to leave the other free for the language of gods."[42] Jaynes—a respected if somewhat unorthodox psychologist at Princeton—locates the bridge across which these divine directions passed in the brain's anterior commissure which stretches between Wernicke's area, which is necessary for normal speech, and a complementary portion of the right hemisphere. *joint, seam*

In the bicameral period, an individual was divided into the human and his god. "Each person had a part of his nervous system which was divine, by which he was ordered about like any slave, a voice or voices which indeed were what we call volition . . . and were related to the voices of others in a carefully established hierarchy."[43] Neither was everyone free to follow his own private admonitions and society to break apart: the peons hallucinated the voices of their lords, and the lords heard the voice of the king, and the king listened only to the gods. Inevitably then, the ancient kingdoms were theocracies. When the king died, his subject continued to hallucinate his voice from the tomb, and so he actually became a god. When the epic hero Gilgamesh, king of Uruk, addressed the statue of Ishtar, the Mesopotamian love-goddess, he actually heard her reply.

The presence of voices that had to be obeyed was a necessary stage in the development of consciousness—that refined sense of multifarious integrity in which the self debates with itself before directing itself. As Kierkegaard agonized: "Man is spirit. But what is spirit? Spirit is the self. But what is the self? The self is a relation which relates itself to its own self."[44] And so on. In a sense we have become our own gods. But since the god-hero relationship was the forerunner of and similar to the Freudian superego-ego relationship, we might

daemon = ancient demi-god

2900–1100 B.C.

argue with Jaynes that in another sense we have never left off being servants who now have got uppity and may or may not choose to obey the master's orders.

Toward the end of the second millenium B.C., Jaynes somewhat unclearly explains, the social chaos resulting from natural and political disasters (which a classicist or archaeologist can amplify—the Trojan War, the migrations of the sea peoples, trouble in Egypt, the eruption of Santorini 70 miles north of Crete, change in climate and subsequent famine) contributed to the breakdown of the bicameral mind and the emergence of consciousness. Among the various causes he adduces is the weakening of the auditory sphere of perception by the advent of writing. But syllabic writing in fact died out in Greece, after having been used for centuries by only the palace scribes. Jaynes also suggests that prototypical angels and demons emerged in Mesopotamia at this period because the forlorn followers of the now vanished gods desperately needed intermediaries to carry their messages. The psychological devastation of transitional man matched the destruction of his civilizations. Nice as this hypothesis sounds, it cannot stand against the evidence. Nature daimons of a sort can be seen on Middle Minoan seals and early Late Helladic frescoes. And more importantly, the projected deities of the Homeric heroes begat the ethical daimons of Socrates and Plato, who in their turn begat the aesthetic demons of Nietzsche and Kierkegaard. (I use *daimon* for the ancient demi-god and *demon* for the medieval or modern unclean spirit.)

A student of Marshall McLuhan might suggest that it was rather the introduction and relatively widespread use of the more abstract system of alphabetic writing about 800 B.C. in Greece that led to a final flowering of the epic tradition and of the bicameral mind in the poems of Homer—and to the subsequent destruction of that mentality, which can already be seen deteriorating in the moral and psychological self-consciousness of the *Odyssey*. The gods, as King Alcinous of the Phaeacians says, have always appeared among us and sat at our feasts (*Od.* 7.201–206). But by the late eighth century Phaeacia had disappeared.

Writing, once its effect was widely felt, transformed man's understanding of himself and thus his use of myth. Minds matured without benefit of literacy tend to notice action more than appearance and to attribute a man's essence to his deeds rather than to his character.[45] An oral culture enshrines its customs, what it regards as wisdom, in narrative, not in general, abstract statement: through experience, and the passage of time, wisdom was acquired; through a story, that wisdom shall live forever. Since both the wisdom and its vehicle, the narrative, are traditional, the notion of creativity lacks any currency in an oral culture.[46] Individuality—apart from an exceptional performance, at singing, orating, or spear-chucking—is hard to come by. So too is the past: oral cultures conveniently forget inconvenient parts of the past. What is valued must be preserved in the medium available, in versified clichés, rhythmic and therefore memorable formulas. Oral memory works best with heavy characters.[47] The early systems of writing, pictographs and syllabaries, did not improve things. Eric Havelock has suggested that if it is easy for us to find archetypal characters in the myths, that may be because the transcribers of them—for the sake of readability and understanding—recorded the archetypical.[48] Mythological characters must, for technical reasons, be flat. Writing, and later print, made possible the mnemonic retention of characters with such—in the sense of oral memory—unmemorable traits as those of an Emma Bovary or a Leopold Bloom. It is rounded, novelistic characters like these which psychoanalysis regards as its subjects,[49] but oddly enough the mythological flat ones which it takes as behavioral models.

Writing also separates the knower from the known, makes the known into less of an event and more of a thing, kills and stuffs it, freeze-frames it. Thus introspection becomes possible—stepping out of the flow of your own life and regarding yourself, for the moment, as an Other. Traditional wisdom can now be left to a text to remember, and so the mind is set free from mindless labors to roam the halls of speculation at will.[50] It may even dare to transfer certain alien forces, and their voices, into the privacy of the soul. At the same time as the mind begins to enjoy its freedom from the immediate, the tribal, past, it also becomes aware of the depth and factuality of history, whose true father (Havelock notes) was not Herodotus but the alphabet itself. Writing, in short, raises consciousness a few pegs[51]—was beginning to do so by the time of the final composition of the *Odyssey*, was well on its way to doing so by Plato's day, had achieved much more in the way of noetic elevation by Freud's.

The Socratic Daimon

The divine patroness of the epics evolves, with the growth of consciousness, into the personal Socratic daimon whose Italian cousin is the Roman *genius*. Socrates' "voice" always or almost always (there is some debate over which) acts to restrain him from wrong action. Similarly, while a goddess may send *thumos*, the organ or force of emotion and volition, into the breast of a Homeric hero, she generally appears to the hero to restrain him from action arising from anger or the impulses of that *thumos*. The archetype often does the same duty. "The archetype is spirit or anti-spirit. . . . Archetype and instinct are the most polar opposites imaginable." Man's turning away from instinct— and here Jung transmutes Nietzsche's description of consciousness as a crime against nature into an almost Christian duty—creates consciousness: "Instinct is nature and seeks to perpetuate nature, whereas consciousness can only seek culture or its denial."[52]

T. Wolff gives us a clue as to how this Jungian principle might be applied to Homer: "Everything unconscious is projected; i.e., it appears as a property or activity of an object. Only by an act of self-knowledge are these contents integrated with the subject, detached from the object and recognized as psychic phenomena."[53] But precisely what is Homeric man projecting? Jaynes has called it little more than intuition. Jung more ambitiously declares: "In so far as the archetypes do not represent mere functional relationships, they manifest themselves as *daimones*, as personal agencies. In this form they are felt as actual experiences, and are not 'figments of the imagination,' as rationalism would have us believe." And from such encounters with quasi-personal archetypes man learns to derive "consciousness of himself as a personality."[54]

Significantly, most of the apparitions of deities in the *Iliad*, *Odyssey*, and in those later works that draw heavily on the epic tradition are of goddesses, and most of those are of Athena. When in distress, the hero converses with the feminine portion of his soul. Soul itself is grammatically feminine in Greek (*hē psychē*) and later comes to be personified as a young woman in need of instruction (see also chapter 9). What does the goddess do and how does her behavior constitute an allegory of the hero's relationship with his soul? For one thing, she laments; Thetis knows that her son, Achilles, is doomed, that the masculine code of the warrior by which he lives reduces his labors to a quest for glory and ironically abbreviates his mortal life at the same time as the glory bestows immortal fame. Similarly in the code of the Samurai, cherry blossoms symbolized the essence of the swordsman—a brilliant efflorescence for two or three days and then the delicacy of petals trampled in the spring mud. Woman exists only for the warrior's pleasure, as an honorific decoration during his brief time on earth, and then to sing the dirge over his corpse.

For another thing, the apparition of the goddess advises the hero against the masculine impulses of his *thumos*, which usually amount to wanting to cut off his opponent's head or to rush alone into a hall full of enemies. She is the soul-wife who counsels: "Now dear, think again. Do you really want to do that?" For masculine action she substitutes woman's age-old weapons, words and guile. Hera inspires Achilles to call the assembly of the Achaeans, in the middle of which Athena appears, stops Achilles from killing Agamemnon, and suggests he use abusive language instead of his sword (1.55 and 1.188–222). In Jason's case the goddess (Hera) enlists Aphrodite's help in rendering him irresistible to women: he then can employ the masculine side of his bride Medea to destroy his enemies. In the *Odyssey*, Athena suggests to Telemachus that he go look for his father and to Nausicaa that she go down to the river (where she will meet Odysseus) and do her laundry, and so her role is not entirely dissuasive. On the beach at Ithaca she admonishes Odysseus to go to his palace in disguise, and alters his appearance to that of a beggar. But the most useful inspiration comes to our hero not from the goddess but from his wife Penelope, when she proposes the contest of the bow to her still unidentified husband and he approves it.

Odysseus is probably the first hero who would rather talk to women than to men. He depends not so much on his charm but on his developing sympathy with all sorts of women and goddesses to bring him safely home. While the art of public speaking, at which he excels, is a masculine one, the Muses or some other daimon supply the words. His other forte, cleverness, was thought decidedly effete until he popularized it. His physical relationship with women proceeds from connections with minor goddesses in his travels on his way back to the real world and to his true love, the mortal Penelope. He never has closer physical contact with his divine Athena than sitting side by side with her under an olive tree to plot the destruction of the suitors. On a metope from Olympia, Heracles, Athena's other great favorite, actually touches her foot with his accidentally, as he sweeps the Augean stables under her direction. Athena makes the ideal patroness not only because she speaks the wisdom of her father Zeus, but because she persists as the eternal virgin, arousing the hero's libido and then channeling it into public service. Nevertheless, while she may function as a personal friend from on high, she remains too socially determined, too much of a canonical deity to serve as the individual "voice" that Socrates heard. Before such oftentimes apparently anti-social voices flex their vocal cords, consciousness must take a few more steps up the evolutionary ladder.

I am arguing that the archetypes, or their manifestations, are evolving as consciousness evolves, and that we can perceive a prototype of the anima in Athena and occasionally in other goddesses; that this prototype developed into Socrates' daimon or voice, who restrained, and into Platonic Eros, which impelled, and eventually into the Jungian anima; and that the philosophical tradition of eudaimonism—how to lead the happy life—proceeded from a primitive concept of glory in the *Iliad*, through a more developed and ethical sense of a spiritually integral man in the *Odyssey*, to the Platonic and Socratic obligation to lead the virtuous life, and finally to the concept of individuation in all its various modern forms—Kierkegaard's, Nietzsche's, Jung's, and Freud's.

The Rise of Consciousness

How do we get from Athena to Socrates' famous daimon? According to McLuhan, print culture gives rise to individualism, because it sets man free from the confining, unquestioned oral traditions of his tribe. The technoculture of electronics restores us to tribalism via its pan-global reach. Now the first scratchings on sheepskin or papyrus of a new scribal craft may not seem like much, but if writing could have altered the sensibilities of poets at large— in a tradition that honored poetry as much as it did athletics—those poets could have influenced the emergence of consciousness. At any rate, Odysseus— who was conceived by a poet called Homer perhaps a generation further into the eighth century and into the alphabetic tradition than Achilles, who was conceived by the poet's previous serial self, also called Homer—displays advances in awareness of himself as a whole man.

Proof: he is capable of deceit, and to deceive (as contrasted with to bluster, at which Achilles, Agamemnon, and others of that kidney are adept) requires a recognition of one's persona (the mask, not the "true" self, that one chooses to present to the rest of the world) as contrasted to one's essence. Odysseus agrees to enter his own home, as he entered Troy long ago—in rags—and that other who knows him best, Penelope, recognizes the stamp of his personal lie: "I was born in Crete," said the Cretan liar (*Od*. 19.172ff.).[55] A hero from the *Iliad* would never have deigned to play such scenes, nor to use a bow. Hector's and Paris' and Agamemnon's attempts to play false deceive even themselves.

It has been argued that the author of the *Odyssey* by complicating his or her[56] narrative line was trying to destroy the epic mode or at least to prevent the poem from assimilation into the impersonal oral tradition, where poets might be honored for their abilities as performers but only the Muses are credited with invention.

At the same time that writing may have made the writer (or dictating composer) aware of himself as creator of a universe all his own, it also enabled him to compose metrical tours de force and accomplish, in lyric and choral poetry, associational shifts of thought too complicated for spontaneous invention and execution. The choral material bears witness to an increased sense of professional worth among the bards, and the lyric poetry provides the first exercise ground in Europe for the private hopes, fears, and self-mockeries of itinerant and resident minstrels.

> Let me only glance where you are, the voice dies,
>   I can say nothing,
> but my lips are stricken to silence, under-
> neath my skin the tenuous flame suffuses. . . .
>   (Sappho, Diehl 2, trans. Lattimore)

The lyric tradition also reduces the epic grandeur of the warrior through humorous or self-centered pragmatism.

> Some barbarian is waving my shield, since I was obliged to
>   leave that perfectly good piece of equipment behind
> under a bush. But I got away, so what does it matter?
>   Let the shield go; I can buy another one equally good.
>
> (Archilochus, Diehl 6, trans. Lattimore)

Complex private emotion that is shared slowly replaces public exhibition of practical skills as the arena in which a man truly comes alive.

Man set free to explore his spiritual landscape is man confronted with choices. Because he projected his psychic apparatus, Homeric man experienced himself as chosen rather than choosing. But the characters—not yet individuals—who stride across the tragic stage of fifth century Athens must make choices, indeed are defined for us as characters by the double-binds they find themselves in, rather than by the collections of peculiarities which today constitute fictional and dramatic characters. The gods may appear on stage from time to time, but only to state the case for one of the alternatives, not to make up the protagonist's mind for him. Sophocles' gods rarely do even that much. Euripides delights in the apparitions of gods, but only so that he may exploit their contrarieties and amoralities to the fullest; they are, in the long run as well as the short, no help at all. In Aeschylus' *Oresteia*, it is true, Athena and Apollo act as spokesmen for their father and contrive to resolve the issue of justice and vengeance to the satisfaction of all concerned, except the dead. The god behind the resolution preserves an enigmatic anonymity:

> Zeus: whatever he may be, if this name
> pleases him in invocation,
> thus I call upon him.
>
> (*Agamemnon* 160–62, trans. Lattimore)

Which is an old formula in prayers and is intended to pin down a definite but slippery deity who may prefer to keep his real name a secret. The formula, however, may also denote an essentially inscrutable personage, whose ways are mysterious but who eventually will lead man and the city-state into a better future as he himself learns wisdom and civility.

Ignorance, not magical compulsion, lies behind the use of *daimon* to mean simply a god whose name is unknown: "Doubtless some daimon caused this," heroes commonly assert. Here we have only the old divine patron or enemy, but without an identity card. He could be Zeus, or he could be some lesser, perhaps only semi-divine being just one step removed from the vague forces of animism and pantheism. *Daimon* is also used for chance *(tychē)*, for

guardian

the power controlling one's fortune, the good or evil genius of an individual or a family, the personification of irrational impulses which tempts us to destruction, the bogey who avenges a murder, the souls of men of the Golden Age who now are tutelary deities (like saints), ghosts in general, a faceless Good Genius (*agathos daimon*) who was toasted after drinking parties, the spirit of a place (especially a river), or guardian of a person.[57] The range is considerable.

The term came naturally to Plato's pen when he wished to refer to that extra-rational voice which will guide a man—should he choose to listen to it—to right action. Doubtless Socrates really heard a voice; as Goethe said to Eckermann, "The higher a man is, the more he is under the influence of the demons. . . . " And Paul Friedländer intones: "What ordinary people experience only in the relaxation of sleep is given to human beings with a pure, serene soul—whom we then call holy or demonic—in their waking lives. Such a human being, free from disharmony and turmoil, was Socrates."[58] We can never know whether Plato really believed in the daimon; he claimed to have communicated his real beliefs only orally (Letter VII, 341 C–E). Daimons partake of that mythical realm which he ransacked whenever he had pushed reason, logos, to the limit and whenever he found that it needed to be grounded once again in the emotional life of man. The Greeks, moreover, had no sense of a personal unconscious. If character and virtue are knowledge in the intellectualist, Greek, view of man (the verb *oida*, "to know," is often used to comprehend feelings or features of a man's character—such as, "he knows evilness"), then what one doesn't know must come from the outside.[59] What we would call the ego must still decide whether to accept or reject this outside interference.

In Plato's repertoire of mythic images, the daemonic commonly occupies a level intermediate between the divine and the human. The daemonic man is ascending to a higher realm of existence, that of divine wisdom, and leaving behind banausic man (common, utilitarian, base).[60] We read in the *Timaeus* that god has given to each of us as a daimon that kind of soul which raises us up toward our heavenly kin (90 A); and when a good man dies, Socrates explains in the *Cratylus*, he becomes a daimon, a "knowing" man (398 B–C). Notice the similarity between Plato's myth and Jung's, and the same disdain for those who have never heard the call or block their ears to its summons. On this ascent to the divine the daimon serves to protect one's vocation—seen in modern terms as an actualization of one's potential self. The daimon limits the personality to itself. "Subjectivity is stopped in its outward flow," as Kierkegaard puts it, "it terminates itself in a particular personality."[61] On the other hand, Eros—often conceived of as a daimon in his own right, though not a personal guardian—leads man out of himself and impels him to the abstract higher good, while the personal voice turns him away from concrete evil. In his role of

practical

cosmic matchmaker, Eros actually ties the universe together. This greatest of the daimons operates first like the Freudian and then, if we are virtuous, like the Jungian libido.

Plato's treatment of Eros in the *Symposium* simultaneously elaborates the myth of Socrates and offers a solution to man's problem of being in the world but not of it. The nature of Eros presupposes the lack of that which one desires: the beloved, or not exactly the beloved but his beauty and all his good qualities, or not exactly those but the Good and the Beautiful (almost identical concepts in Greek) as manifested in him. By definition then, Love cannot be beautiful since it cannot possess what it desires. Socrates' ugly face was known all over Athens. The surviving portraits of him and accounts of his appearance refer to a pug-nosed, high-browed, sharp-eared countenance, a rolling gait, and an apparently huge set of genitals. Zopyros, the first physiognomist, read lust in his every feature.[62] In short, he looked like a satyr or silenus, a horse-man (not a goat-man)—and we all have witnessed or heard about the dream-appearances of horses as embodiments of the libido.

The daimons as halfway beings—Indian scouts, in buckskin trousers and denim shirts, riding point for the great wagon train of life—led men to the gods. So too, Eros and Socrates advance beyond the rest of mortals and lead them to the Ideas or Forms of beauty. On the way to Beauty, one must start with individual beauties and gradually move from the realm of physical particularities to the more intense realm of the spirit. Unlike his puritanical followers, Plato until his last years did not lose respect for the sensual element of human nature as a necessary and constant guide to more etherial possibilities; and Socrates certainly remained an erotic creature throughout most of his career.

Self-transcendence—the following and fulfillment of a personal myth—goes back to a notion common in Greek literature from Hesiod to Plato: of the virtuous life as the happy life, and therefore of virtue as a good outside of one's self and sometimes quite distant, beyond the cypress-hedge of death. Man works at first to possess that good within his nature and finally, it would seem, to lose the carnal part of himself in the interest of the Good. While the critical ability of man is necessary to find the Good, we must, it would again seem, eventually abandon the individual logos that separates us from knowledge of the divine. The body contains as well as imprisons us, and when the soul departs, the self loses much of its discreteness. This, for Plato, must happen, because there is only one Truth, one Mind *(nous)*, and if you and I have both attained the vision of it then we are conceptually identical although formally distinct. Plato is very vague on all of this. He stops just short of having consciousness dissolve as we rejoin nature—higher Nature—but certainly his thought indicated the way to such monopsychic mysticism.

For Jung on the other hand, no dissolution is desired. Nature reaches its acme and goal in consciousness, and that means we must constantly be coming to terms with the always restless elements of the unconscious. Those elements, the archetypes, can prove dangerous or even fatal to the man who goes after them without his wits about him. For Plato, nothing can harm the virtuous man because he realizes himself by disembodying himself—like Socrates standing frozen in thought and a million miles away while the world swirls around his vacant body. For Jung, man has been set in the world for a purpose and must give an account for his incarnate nature.

Both Plato and Jung presume that the forces which drive us toward "self-improvement" are innate—inherited, in the modern way of thinking; remembered from a previous life, in the ancient. Since much of the same potentialities and archetypes are common to all of us, self-realization is a social action that benefits the race as a whole. For Jung, this process takes place in and through the physical world and thus, if universally pursued, would theoretically result in the greatest variety of personalities, whereas the frustration of individuation (neurosis) results in the sameness of textbook cases. For Plato, the general pursuit of virtue would demand and result in similar personalities for those who are capable of following the rigorous course—the philosophers—or rather would result in the abolition of personality, since we cannot retain our masks before the divine ineffable. Ironically, the model for the pursuit of virtue, Socrates, appears the greatest eccentric because the rest of the world is not living the virtuous life. Yet by his example and annoying questions the philosopher confers the greatest benefit on the community at the same time as he offends it by refusing to adapt himself to his fellow-citizens' unreflective ways (*Apology* 30A).

The problem of a conflict between self-realization and the demands of society never came up for most of the Romans. They managed these things better than the Greeks did, of course: each man had his individual genius; each family its collective genius; the state had its personal goddess, Roma, and its impersonal genius; and each place its vague numen. A perfect pyramid of spiritual power—organized by a bureaucracy of efficient freedmen, directed by fate, overseen by the official pantheon of gods, and ruled by the emperor.

Ovid and the Daimonic

With the conquests of Philip and Alexander of Macedon in the fourth century B.C., control of the visible world at large passed out of the hands of the gods and citizens and into the more capable ones of kings and their bureaucracies. Religion kept pace with politics and, outside of emperor cults and mercantile or military gods, concerned itself mostly with the fate and hopes of private man (no longer public since he had nothing left to do with the running of the state). One's sphere of interest was now more likely to be circumscribed by house walls than city walls; personal poetry, rather than epic, helped to pass private time; the romance novel was born and along with it that cultural glory of small towns, the lending library. Philosophers and theologians constructed elaborate models of the universe so that the prosperous urban classes could calculate their chances in the great knucklebones game of life. Old mystery religions struggled to keep afloat against the competition from new, mostly Oriental, cults which likewise promised through initiation and instruction to ensure an individual's salvation in the afterlife. These new mystery rites cost a great deal and prepared the way for that bargain-basement cult, Christianity.

Political power shifted to Rome, and the world now seemed much larger than before, stretching from Britain to Persia and beyond. Elaborate schemes for the workings of fate or fortune had to be interposed between man and chaos to make him feel as secure as he had in the fifth century, when on a general scale of things he had seemed to himself pretty large indeed—"Man is the measure of all things," Protagoras had said, and few had felt a need to challenge the audacity of this aphorism. The daimons were called on to do yeoman's work in justifying the ways of the old gods to post-city-state man. They provided the late pagan theologians—working to save Greco-Roman religion from the assaults of philosophical reason and Christian faith—with an explanation of the bad deeds or dastardly exploits of the gods: the little daimons did it, not the great Olympians.[63] And they carried out all sorts of menial work that would otherwise have gone wanting for theological explanation. Lucius Apuleius, a Neo-Platonic rhetorician and novelist of about 200 A.D. lectures a potentially Christian world on the daimons: "It is not a task for the gods of heaven to descend to things here below. This lot befalls the intermediate gods, who abide in those regions of the air that are adjacent to the earth and so on the borders of heaven, just as in every part of the world there are animals peculiar to that part."[64] This Platonic concept of a Great Chain of Being led in later Neo-Platonism to theurgy: a collection of magical practices to set in motion a concatenation of sympathies stretching up to the deity one was trying to reach, in order to produce a divine apparition and attain communion with the godhead.

After many years of civil war, during which the original, city-state constitution of Rome was accommodating itself to the requirements of governing an empire, Augustus (grand-nephew of Julius Caesar) emerged as the nominal first citizen but de facto emperor. The Pax Augustana (peace) now obtained throughout the civilized world. The Golden Age, before strife and pain existed, had returned. Or so the propaganda went, and after so many years of troubles the average Roman felt it his civic duty to believe in this vision. Ovid could not quite manage to believe in anything.

Paradoxically for such an urbane wit, Ovid is a great poet of landscape and has furnished centuries of European painters with leafy backgrounds for their canvases, as well as mythological foregrounds. For these natural settings he drew on the tradition of pastoral poetry in which the fields, hillsides, and copses, where shepherds take their graceful ease, make exquisite love, play the rustic flute, and compose flawless verse, represent not the interurban wildness (as in Sophocles' plays) but an extra-urban retreat. To the harried masses of the Hellenistic cities (Alexandria, Pergamum, Athens) and of Imperial Rome itself, the countryside seemed a *locus amoenus*, a pleasant setting, for all those cultural activities they were too busy to pursue and for those now charming labors of the simpler world they had lost.

Ovid transformed the pastoral scenery, which symbolized for his audience the peaceable kingdom that Augustus had restored to them, from a comfortable world where pillowy swards, private nooks, and spreading, benevolent trees abound along cool, gently bending brooks into a world full of unpredictable danger and insecure souls. "The very mysteriousness of these Ovidian landscapes," Charles Segal observes, "befits the arbitrariness and incomprehensibility of a world in which the human individual has little or no power to protect his person."[65]

What has this to do with psychoanalysis? Well, analysts and psychologicians should be aware of the spirit in which the mythological texts were composed: it may coincide with our own attitudes or it may refute their premises. Philip Rieff explains a subtle aim of depth psychology: "The Jungian theory proposes to every disaffected humanist his 'personal myth,' as a sanctuary against the modern world."[66] Jung advised us to decorate our sanctuaries with souvenirs from the ancient myths. We may be guilty of misappropriation of meaning if we ignorantly take comfort in what was meant as a warning. Ovid shows us that no retreat from danger is possible: that sanctuary which appears safest contains, in fact, the greatest danger for the weary wanderer.

A typical scene: the tired, sunburnt hunter seeks rest from his exertions in the fields and across the rocky hills; he comes upon a grove, untouched by man or beast (no dung on the ground), hidden deep in a little valley and nourished by a gelid spring; the spreading boughs of a plane tree offer protection from the glare of noontide; the soft turf invites rest. Our hunter dozes in safety. By a sudden but slight shift the landscape alters. A nymph of the place emerges from the bushes, her cheeks reddened, her breasts tingling, her loins aflame with passion for the limp youth. The isolated spot now seems fraught with danger. (The first grotesques were enacted in grottoes.) The cool water suggests an icy death rather than refreshment. The trees lean menacingly over the sleeping intruder. A struggle, seduction, pain, and metamorphosis ensue—into a flower, a tree, a hermaphrodite, a deer that is torn apart by the hunter's own hounds. Or, in just such a haven, Hera chooses to take vengeance on one of Zeus's hapless mistresses.

Ovid has an almost Irish sense of faerie. While not all of the metamorphoses occur in the woods and not all involve nymphs, a sense of magical place and magical beings nevertheless pervades the whole text. Secluded corners of nature, not the city, encourage the fantastic. The world that is usually too much with us recedes when we leave pavement and walls behind. Now anything can happen. The virginal landscape is charged with sexuality. Nymphs, by virtue of their beauty and the eroticism their name connotes, are likely to attract the lusty attention of Zeus and suffer the consequences (Zeus is immune to consequences) or to pounce upon young men who stray into their lairs. And most of Ovid's metamorphoses are precipitated by lust or love—those halfway states of being in which we are transported dangerously out of our usual selves. Nymphs, living permanently in such a halfway state, constantly tempt us and the gods to quick and easy ecstasies.

Again and again characters in Ovid engage in apparently harmless pursuits, perform neutral or even noble deeds, and excite the envy, wrath, spite, and vengeance of the gods or goddesses. Perhaps their intuitions could have warned them of trouble. Synchronicity, that phenomenon in which inner perceptions (forebodings, visions, dreams) "show a meaningful simultaneity with outward experiences,"[67] determines the sequence in which patterns of landscape are linked with patterns of danger. Just as surely as the television-scripted private detective should know that if he leaves the door of the strange apartment open behind him then someone will come through it and knock him on the head, Ovidian man and woman should know enough to avoid: affairs with Zeus, ominous oases of greenery in the sere middle distance, dewy nymphs, catalogues of the gods' misdeeds, neglect of any popular cult, etc. But even if these poor characters knew what threatened them, the outcome would be the same.

The heroes and heroines of the *Metamorphoses* are inevitable victims of personified but arbitrary forces that strike them suddenly, often in most peaceful circumstances. Out of the quiet of nature burst demonic powers that shatter the pastoral bliss of the characters and the aesthetic bliss of the poem's readers. The resemblance between this kind of bolt from the Olympian blue and the abrupt manifestations of the dangerous aspects of the unconscious, like maggots emerging from a healthy limb, goes far to explain the dream-like quality of Ovid's episodes. Only the poet's skill restrains the mood of fantasy and supplies a controlling self-consciousness to check the development of the scenes. Before the horror of each metamorphosis has sunk in, we are whisked by remarkably varied and elegant segues into the next pleasant setting for the next horror.

Jung has instructed us about the real dragons a too-careless probing into the cave-dark unconscious can release. Ovid performed a similar admonitory service for turn-of-the-millennium Romans and he can do as much for us. No more subversive a poem than the *Metamorphoses* was ever written. Despite his pretense that the endless shifts of form in an amoral universe came finally and securely to rest in the comfortable world Caesar Augustus had molded out of the chaos of the Civil Wars—a pretense undercut by the speech of Pythagoras in Book 15: there is *no* permanence—the careful readers of his poem learn enough by the end of it to take him seriously, but never at his word. Augustus himself, unfortunately for Ovid, was among those careful readers: the shores of the Black Sea, near Costanza in Rumania, made a quiet albeit lonely refuge for an exiled poet to draw out his last years on earth.

Ovidian man grows aware of himself only as he loses himself and turns into a bestial, vegetable, or petrified other. Only after he has undergone metamorphosis can he look back and contemplate that object which was his previous self. His appearance has changed utterly, but not his essence, which has only been enlarged by the experience and pain of coming to know the pre-human. Through this pain, Ovid's heroes also come to grips with that other face of the universe—not the benevolent persona it at first presents to the naive wanderer and which Augustus, too, wanted to show to his senate and people—but that perverted, amoral, utterly wasteful face of nature which could gaze calmly, disinterestedly, on the agony of a girl in a bear's shape or on the consequences of a volcanic eruption or oversee the proscription of thousands of old enemies from the Civil Wars (Cicero's head was one of the first to roll).

Before Ovid's imagination had its say, man, the universe, and the poet himself may have been fragmented but never consistently self-opposed—as his Medea and his Althaea oppose themselves over the murders of their children. The poet of all these doublings had to maintain in his verses a constant, witty, self-consciousness of his role as narrator of the bizarre. For wit, as well as grotesquerie, demands a sense of contrast—between the pretended intent and the intended pretense. But Ovid and his age could not go beyond this clever de-structuring of the person, of the cosmos, and of the vatic role itself into endless doublings.

If the Greeks had discovered the operations of the psyche, they wouldn't have known what to do with this new machinery any more than they knew what to do with the steam engine after Heron of Alexandria invented it. The Romans probably would have suppressed psychological wisdom as a threat to law and order, just as Tiberius executed the man who invented tempered glass—

re a prophet

for fear the new material would devalue gold (Petronius, *Satyricon* 51; Pliny, *N.H.*36.198).

Ovid had no better apparatus with which to run his characters than an outmoded social order of projected gods and goddesses in a universe that seemed to mirror the bilateral asymmetry of man and of the poet's craft. In this superannuated world, the oldest gods, the eternally young nymphs, satyrs, and other daimons, persisted and still persist in preserving that link across the rungs of the evolutionary ladder between man and the archetypal inhabitants of his dream world.

5

Dionysus

The fullness of life and the violence of death both are equally terrible in Dionysus.
                              —Walter F. Otto, *Dionysus*, trans. Robert Palmer

The force that through the green fuse drives the flower
Drives my green age; that blasts the roots of trees
Is my destroyer.
                              —Dylan Thomas

N O GOD CAN EMPTY THE WOODWORK like Dionysus. That, after all, is his function. The documents of his myth and cult have fed the flames of more controversies—scholarly, theological, philosophical, and psychological—than those of any other pagan divinity or hero. Some of the contenders in these academic imbroglios have themselves produced documents of their adoration before or resistance to his terrible magnificence.[1] Dionysus has a way of taking possession of those who would write about him soberly or otherwise— Nietzsche, Jung, Otto, Kerenyi, and many others. If Lévi-Strauss had cared to attempt a proof of his contention that even the modern analyses of a myth are all part of *the myth*, he would have found plenty of evidence in the career of this polymorphous troublemaker.

At the risk of losing our own levelheadedness, we must begin with what we do in fact know about the god who was also called Bacchus, Liber, Zagreus, Bromius, and Iacchus: a necessary conflation of his myths, a brief history of his worship in Greece and rise to power, a description of a few of his most important cults, and some notes on his appearance in ancient art. As little as all this is, it will take some time in the telling; and then we can move on to Dionysus as god of the modern unconscious and libido.

107

The Myth of Dionysus

Zeus fell in love with a mortal girl, as Olympian gods commonly did in the days when Greek religion mirrored the social structure of Mycenaean feudalism, where the lords undoubtedly exercised seigneurial rights over the peasant maids—which structure itself reflected the conquest, early in the second millennium B.C., of the earth-goddess–worshipping pre-Greeks (sometimes called Pelasgians) by the sky-god–worshipping Greeks. This time (and there were many times) the object of Zeus's attentions was Semele, one of the four daughters of Cadmus—the founder of Thebes and great-great-great-great grandfather of Oedipus. Zeus came down to earth in mortal form, told the girl who he was, had his way with her, and of course made her pregnant. His wife Hera couldn't punish Zeus, so she harmed his mistresses instead. In disguise as a skeptical nurse, she advised Semele to ask her lover to promise her a boon—any boon—and then to specify that he prove his divinity by showing himself to her in all his glory. He did as requested, and she was burnt to a crisp by his blazing appearance. But Zeus managed to snatch the fetus from her still crackling womb and sewed it up in his thigh. (For general accounts of this and what follows see Ovid, *Metamorphoses* 3.259–315, 3.510–4.41, 11.67–145; Euripides, *Bacchae*; *Homeric Hymn to Dionysus*; Apollodorus, 3.4.2–5.3, and elsewhere; Pausanias, *passim*; and many, many other sources.)

When the child was born, Zeus gave it either to Semele's sister Ino or else to the nymphs of Mt. Nysa (location unknown), perhaps with orders the boy be raised as a girl so that Hera wouldn't find him. But find him she did, in his late adolescence, and drove him mad. In his madness, he wandered through Greece and Asia and eventually came to Phrygia (north-central Turkey), where the Great Mother, Cybele, finally cured him. He continued his wanderings, but now with a new purpose—conquest. At some time, it could have been when he was made sane again, he became a god (perhaps at the same time he was cured of his madness)—not yet an Olympian, but nevertheless divine although he had been born a mortal like most children with only one parent a god. In any case, he now began to spread the new religion of himself and to aggrandize his godhead. He seems to have continued east, acquiring new lands and new worshippers on his way, until he won a great victory at the Ganges and came to a halt. (Alexander the Great, who also claimed Zeus as a father, in this one respect may have thought he was imitating the holy blitzkrieg of his half-brother when he headed his armies across Asia.)

Next, Dionysus turned his attention back to Greece. On his first excursion into the Aeagean, he appeared alone, still youthful and beardless, on the shores of Chios, where he asked for passage on a Lydian ship to Naxos. The sailors or pirates—the distinction was once a pretty thin one—agreed to take him; but since he was so pretty and seemed so helpless (still drunk or drugged from his Asiatic revels) and would fetch a good price, they sailed instead for the nearest slave market. The god, however, was only toying with them, waiting until they had committed themselves to committing a crime. He sent his vines shooting up the mast to produce clusters of grapes in an instant; wine streamed across the deck; ivy tendrils bound the oars; real or phantom leopards, lynxes, and other dappled beasts filled the ship. The pirates leapt overboard in fear, became dolphins, and hereafter do penance for their sacrilege by befriending sailors.

Joined by a train of Asiatic maenads (literally, "mad women," who were probably his original nurses, the nymphs) and satyrs or sileni (nature demons in the shape of men with equine ears, tails, and penises), and employing all sorts of barbaric paraphernalia—drums, castanets, brightly embroidered dresses, thyrsi (fennel wands wreathed with ivy and tipped with phallic pine cones), tame snakes, and an endless supply of wine—he imposed himself on one Greek city after another. He appealed mostly to the townswomen—seducing them from the boredom of their daily tasks in the home and from the confines of the polis to become maenads themselves and join in his nocturnal, though not necessarily lewd, orgies. He invited them to worship him with their bodies, to dance and wander over the mountains (oreibasia), to hunt down spotted creatures and eat them raw (ōmophagia) as though they were consuming the god himself, and to allow him to enter their blood with the drafts of wine.

He started in northern Greece and worked his way down the peninsula, meeting with resistance almost everywhere. King Lycurgus of Thrace attacked him with an ox-goad, and Dionysus, a divine but still effete ephebe, fled to an undersea grotto, where he was comforted by the goddess Thetis, a surrogate mother. But he soon managed to establish himself as the god who is gentlest of all when accepted and cruelest of all when opposed: his self-confidence restored, he returned to shore and drove Lycurgus mad, as he himself had once been maddened. The king, thinking that he was destroying the god's budding grapevines, cut down his daughters with an ax. After this reversal of power, Dionysus became the one who sends madness and panic on others; never again is he himself moved by irrational forces: that mania which was once outside him and inflicted upon him has become part of his essential nature.

Next stop, Orchomenos in Boeotia: the daughters of King Minyas refused to leave their looms for the orgies on the local mountainside and were turned into bats as a punishment. And, after them, the men of Athens rejected this new religion and were rendered impotent: Dionysus believes in letting his vengeance fit the crime. The women of Athens eventually complained about the situation, an image of the god was brought in a phallic procession from a nearby village and virile stiffness was restored. Now only Thebes remained to be won over.

Old Cadmus had handed over the kingship to Pentheus, child of Agave and Echion (one of the earth-born Sparti who sprang up from the scattered teeth of the dragon that originally guarded the site of Thebes). Pentheus, too, resisted Dionysus. He was convinced the new god was a charlatan who used wine and exotic, barbarian rhythms to drive the women wild with passion up on Mt. Cithaeron. In this case, the revelling band *(thiasos)* was composed of Pentheus' mother and aunts, and a few other Theban ladies, who had slandered the god by claiming Semele had slept with a mere mortal: divine madness comes as both a gift to those who accept Dionysus and a punishment on those who reject him. Pentheus, then, despite his spies' reports to the contrary, believed that sexual license was the essence and the point of the orgies.

He tried to imprison Dionysus, whom he captured masquerading as a priest of his own religion. But ignorant of his prisoner's identity, Pentheus allowed his cousin to lead him up in maenadic costume to see the rites. Dionysus placed him in the top of a pine tree, supposedly for a better view, but actually to present the maenads with a sacrificial beast. The mad women, led by his mother Agave, pulled him down and tore him apart—a ritual *sparagmos*. The ancient accounts stop short of reporting an actual ōmophagia, the eating of the raw flesh of the dismembered victim, but Euripides adds a touch just as grisly: in the *Bacchae* his Dionysus appears to Agave and all concerned, once they have regained their sanity, tells them they got what they deserved, and actually gloats over their suffering.

The Dionysus who appears throughout much of this play in disguise as a priest actually looks the part of the post-adolescent, still beardless, sometimes drunken, and effeminate or even androgynous god of wine. But the god who appears at the end of the play and pronounces the doom of the various characters is (if the actor who played him changed masks, as he almost certainly did) the older, bearded, sober, and utterly masculine Dionysus. In his youthful form the god often appears (in later Greek art) as the victim of his own intoxicating powers, very much as he was once the victim of Hera's anger; but, in his more mature aspect, he has achieved a status unbound by terrestrial vicissitudes and become the unmoved mover of men. Coincident with, but not dependent on, this development in his appearance and life cycle (the artistic development has to do mostly with a general loosening up of restraints in the representations of gods), Dionysus has become an Olympian.

Hera threw her son Hephaestus out of heaven because he was born lame. Being a splendid blacksmith and cabinetmaker, he contrived a magical chair and sent it to her; it trapped her as soon as she sat down. The gods had to ask

Dionysus for help; he got Hephaestus so drunk the outcast didn't care where he went and allowed himself to be returned to Olympus, with a full Bacchic procession. By acting as celestial kidnapper, Dionysus seems to have made up his quarrel with Hera and been formally admitted to the exclusive pantheon of Olympian gods. But as the only one of them with a mortal mother he never really fit in and always retained a quite un-Olympian interest in the lot of the common man.

About this time he also acquired a wife. For a god of the irrational impulses—indeed for any god—he had conducted relatively few affairs before coming to the rescue of Ariadne, the daughter of Minos and Pasiphae and the seduced and abandoned mistress of Theseus. Theseus—after charming her into helping him kill her half brother the Minotaur, escape from the labyrinth of her father's palace at Knossos, rescue the Athenian youths and maidens sent there as sacrificial tribute, and get away from Crete—dropped Ariadne off at Naxos on his way back home to a kingship and a declining career as a hero. There, just outside the main harbor, on the islet of Palatia where today stand the scanty remains of an Archaic temple and the substantial bulk of a modern discotheque, Dionysus came for her and took her as his bride. They made a perfect marriage and had a number of children named after various phases of wine-making and drinking; and he finally set Ariadne among the stars as the Corona Borealis or Northern Crown. He may also have raised his mother from the grave and made her another constellation.

The Cults of Dionysus

While in Hades, Odysseus sees the ghosts of various heroines—among them Ariadne, whom Artemis killed because of the witness of Dionysus (Odyssey 11.321–25). Why would Dionysus arrange the execution of his bride? Some other ancient sources suggest that Dionysus was really Ariadne's original rustic lover, whom she abandoned for the attractive newcomer, Theseus.[2] Scholars used to think that Dionysus was a later immigrant to Greece, appearing on the mainland just before the time of Homer, who barely mentions him, and coming from either Thrace or Asia Minor where he had ties with various Thraco-Phrygian deities. But recently his name was found on the Linear B tablet from Mycenaean Greece and Crete (PY Xa 102, Xb 1419, X 1501), once in association with the word for wine. And bits of archaeological evidence have been juxtaposed to form a hypothetical picture of this god in Bronze-Age Greek and pre-Greek times.

Two seal rings from roughly 1400 B.C. are carved with scenes that may refer to the meeting and flight of Theseus and Ariadne from Crete and the rescue of Ariadne from Naxos by Dionysus; dolphins accompany the ships in both cases. The female figure resembles the dancing goddesses on other contemporary seal rings where the contexts are almost certainly religious. The scenes, that is, represent cult-practices that generated myths, rather than myths themselves. The earth-goddess, in the person of her priestess, may have gone away over the sea after the death of her consort. The Island of Dia, just off the coast of Crete north of Knossos, is a likely site for her hibernation. The fields, of course, became barren after her departure; but, with the opening of the new sailing season and the greening of the earth under the late winter rains, the goddess returned and a new consort guided her.³

Many islands were called Dia (probably a feminine form of Zeus's name and the Greek way of referring to, and linguistically appropriating and subjugating, the pre-Greek goddess), and were said by their inhabitants to be the true location, rather than Naxos, of Ariadne's abandonment and rescue. One of these Dias was a peninsula of Keos, a Cycladic island on which the archaeologist John Caskey recently excavated one of the few Bronze Age temples so far discovered in Greece. Large statues of the goddess or her priestesses were set up in the cult room. Caskey also found a model ship and dolphin and a bronze consort or "adorant" figure in the vicinity. In the early Archaic Age the temple attendants rescued a head of one of the female figures and set it up again on a low platform; and by the late Archaic Age the temple received dedications to Dionysus.⁴

A reasonable conclusion would be that the cult of the pre-Greek goddess, in her various aspects, was once strong throughout the Minoan and Cycladic regions. As the first Greeks, a herding people, came to dominate the area, they suppressed the goddess and her diminutive lover as religious forces connected with the mysteries of nature and of agriculture—a murky realm and a set of abstruse techniques which they slighted as antithetical to the clear, sunny world of the Olympian hierarchy. But just as the earlier peoples did not die out but were more or less absorbed, enslaved, or pushed into remote districts like Arcadia by the invaders, so too the old goddess and god lived on—in a spiritual fastness set up and maintained by the peasants who continued to find the fertility couple worth worshipping. As mythology reflects the historical events and social structures of a region, so too political and religious history recapitulate psychic mechanisms: new and advanced powers temporarily conquer the indigenous ones, only to suffer an uprising of the primitive forces later.

The old gods would out. After the difficult centuries of the Dorian invasions and the Dark Ages, they once again allowed themselves to be viewed and worshipped. The Greeks of the fifth century thought Dionysus was a relative newcomer to their land, having arrived sometime in the eighth century. In fact, he was there all the time, hiding in the bush, though his revived cult gained fresh impetus from the recently renewed contact with his relatives in Thrace and the Near East. (These northern and Oriental connections of Dionysus show up only in later Greek art.[5]) The suppression of the earth-goddess and Greek emphasis on the superiority of the male had substantially altered Dionysus' cult: the great goddess had been reduced to a mere heroine, and he—once upon a time merely her annual consort—had grown to a full divinity.

In the sixth century, the age of tyrants, the popularity of Dionysus increased. As god of the common man, he lightened the burden of daily toil with his care-dissolving gift of wine and the license to revel; as a god of mysteries, he held out the hope of an afterlife to those whose earthly lives were devoid of hope. The Olympian gods might patronize city-states, but very few individuals were worth their notice: Zeus and his brethren existed rather as objects of smug contemplation for aristocrats already leading godlike lives.

Pisistratus, tyrant of Athens in the second half of the sixth century, elaborated the rural festivals of Dionysus into the City Dionysia—an affair lasting several days, inaugurated by a procession commemorating the introduction of the god's cult and the restoration of Athenian virility and embellished with a new form of literary performance—tragedy. Much has been written about the essential connection between Dionysus and tragedy. No one has come close to proving the contention that the tragic hero was offered up as sacrifice to the god whose sufferings he was repeating in his own heroic way. The proper literary milieu, political patronage, and the individual genius of Thespis, the first tragedian, account for the invention of this dramatic form.[6] And the need to decorate a festival with the kind of performance that could draw and hold crowds, make the city more famous, and please the god—who, being Greek and made in the image of man, enjoyed the same sorts of entertainment as we do—accounts for the presence of tragedy at the City Dionysia. Although many of the gods preferred athletic games at their festivals, Dionysus was an androgynous type and went in for the arts. *Tragedy* means "billy-goat song," and a goat was probably both the prize and the sacrifice, because it eats the god's vine shoots and thus is his enemy—but also because it embodies great sexual potency as he does and expresses the same brand of madness in its mask-like face: its grey, vertiginous eyes seem to radiate a vinous insanity and capricious panic. There is room in each herd for only one billy. When the nanny goats were safely pregnant, by early spring, and it was thought he was too worn out for another season of tupping, he would be sacrificed. Thus the Dionysia commemorate the waning and waxing of the vegetation god's powers.[7]

As Dionysus frees man from the bonds of hard labor—which, as Freud and Herbert Marcuse argue, is opposed to and restrains Eros—so he also loosens the social restraints which have for so long managed to contain our sexual activities within the normal limits of civilized behavior. Satyrs and mae-nads, or satyrs and satyrs, copulate to the point of exhaustion along the painted bands of black-figure cups and wine pots. In red-figure painting a century later, genre scenes replace many mythological ones, and so we find drunken sym-posiasts taking their pleasure with courtesans and wine boys on the same sorts of pots. Satyrs at all periods are likely to follow too closely behind the mules and asses of Bacchic processions and obscenely prod the beasts on their merry way. The animals themselves display massive erections. Asses do so because they are renowned for lustiness; mules, because the potency of Dionysus can inspire even sterile beasts. Of course the Greek attitude toward the perversions was far more casual than ours.

The god who periodically enfranchised such permissiveness must have aroused much opposition among the stiff-necked and jack-booted Dorian Greeks, when they first encountered him on their way into Greece in the eleventh century—as well as among the upright citizens of the newly developing city-states of the eighth century, when he began to emerge from his temporary retirement as a mere folk-deity into greater prominence than ever before in the Hellenic world at large. So the myths of resistance to his cult and to the intoxicating powers of the grape proliferated in an age of increasing puritanism. He would not be defeated, but neither did he completely succeed in winning over the tight little city-states. His cults, nationalized or polis-ized at the same time as Apollo's rise to pan-Hellenic prominence, testify as much to his un-popularity among the aristocrats, especially the men, as they do to his popularity among the peasants and the women. If you can't wipe it out, the next best thing is to legalize it, make it an official matter, write up rules for it, and pull its teeth.

The works of scholars like Farnell, Nilsson, and Parke (not to mention those of the antique antiquarian Pausanias) are full of information on these cults.[8] We can't attend to all of it, but we should try to keep two festivals in the middle distance of our consciousness. At the Anthesteria, in early spring, the jars of new wine were broached and vague but powerful spirits set free—volatile spirits who had been noisily fomenting plots against the family while the grape juice had been fermenting into new wine in huge resonant amphoras leaning against every wall. The sailing season was inaugurated with a parade led by Dionysus in a ship-cart, and the religious leader of Athens, the King Archon, impersonated Dionysus in a ritual copulation with his wife who probably took the role of Ariadne. There was also a meatless sacrifice to Hermes on behalf of the dead, which is a matter we shall take up shortly. The connection of Dionysus with sailing goes back to the coincident arrival of fair weather with the landing of the eternal goddess and the year-god who came from over the sea to re-green the land. And the holy marriage recapitulates the original annual union of this native couple, as well as hygienically epitomizing the unsanitary peasant festivals.

At Delphi, the greatest sanctuary of Apollo, the god of reason and boundaries made a pact with the lord of unreason and breachings. Every other winter, women from a number of city-states took part in a mountain-wandering (oreibasia)—raging and revelling from crag to snowy crag, worshipping the god or awakening him from his deep sleep beneath the drifts, and as often as not getting themselves lost and in dire need of rescue by some Delphiots of the opposite sex.

The festival at Delphi was only the best known and most prestigious of the oreibasiai. Local, simpler, but still powerful cults found their way into the civic calendar. After the god of the old Aegean chthonian religion was revived, his cults and myths crossed and at times fused with those of other deities. The fate of the sacrificial animal, in early versions of his myth, was probably once the fate of Dionysus himself and was connected with the concept of inherited guilt and some original sin of mankind. In the sixth century, Onomacritus called this Dionysus who was slain "Zagreus," an otherwise obscure figure, and embellished his story with features that promoted the tenets of Orphism. At the instigation of Hera, so it was said, the Titans tore apart and ate the child of Zeus and Persephone (mistress of the underworld), namely Zagreus. Zeus struck the Titans with a thunderbolt, saved and ate the boy's heart, and re-sired the child, now to be called Dionysus, on Semele. Man, born from the Titans' ashes, contains a divine element from the flesh of Zagreus which must be cultivated and a Titanic element which must be purged. This myth helps to bridge the gulf between Dionysus and Apollo the god of purifications, whose missionary work Orpheus probably did.[9]

Dionysus' myth also shows the influence of the story of Cretan Zeus, itself probably an attempt to Hellenize true-Cretan (eteo-Cretan, i.e., old Minoan) beliefs. Cretan Zeus was born in a cave and saved from his murderous father Kronos, by the distracting, ecstatic dances of his mother Rhea's young men, the Curetes. Similarly, the Phrygian goddess Cybele was accompanied by revelling Corybantes, who had much in common with the satyrs of Dionysus. The heavy influence of various oriental deities at Athens during the later years of the PeloponnesianWar—especially of Sabazius, the son of the Great Mother, who was identified by the Greeks in their syncretic way with Dionysus—probably inspired much of Euripides' portrayal of the Bacchic invasion.[10] Non-Greek and pre-Greek divine figures, in other words, took the name of Zeus but preserved characteristics of Mediterranean fertility spirits utterly alien to the manner of the Greek sky-gods. And the separate divine youths tended to coalesce finally into one, many-faceted, many-named god. We find an expres-

eating of raw flesh

sion of this theological flux in a fragment surviving from Euripides' *Cretans*, where the chorus of worshippers of Cretan Zeus tell Minos: "I have lived a pure life from when I became an initiate of Idaean Zeus and herdsman of night-wandering Zagreus; I performed ōmophagia, held up torches to the Mountain Mother, torches of Curetes, was raised to a holy level and named Bacchus."[11] And in a chorus of the *Bacchae* (119–34) the Corybantes invent the drum in the cave of the Curetes and bring it in a Bacchic rout, complete with satyrs, to Rhea, the mother of Zeus. All for one and one is all: the essence of the Dionysiac experience, anyway, is the loss of the personality, collective death, collective rebirth, and universal joy. The death of the young god was commemorated in a sacrifice on Tenedos in which a calf was first dressed in the booties of baby Dionysus and then poleaxed. The slayer had to flee from the ritually angry onlookers (Aelian, *On the Nature of Animals* 12.34).

Dionysus always plays the outlander, crossing borders, breaking down walls, dismembering the resister as he himself was once dismembered. He is the only integral being in whatever scene he graces with his presence, either rupturing or occupying all would-be sovereignties that he encounters. In this Sherman-like march through the ego he behaves like the autochthonous god Pan, the onset of whose enthusiasm (panic) is even more sudden than the god of wine's epiphany.

All the immortals rejoiced at the birth of Pan, it says in *Homeric Hymn* XIX, but especially Dionysus (45–46). If Dionysus combines the ecstatic creativity of youth with the eventual sobriety of maturity, Pan summarized these polarities at his parturition. He was born with a full beard and wears a spotted lynx skin (39, 23–24); and all dappled creatures are of special concern to Dionysus: the lynx, the leopard, the fawn, and maybe the *Amanita muscaria* mushroom—the closest approximation in the vegetable world to a spotted epidermis in the bestial—if Robert Graves is correct that the maenad's rage and superhuman strength came from eating the cottage-cheese-dotted red and yellow caps of this fungus.[12]

The vocabulary of Greek and the conventions of ancient art do not clearly distinguish leopard from cheetah from serval or even from lynx. Like patterns of shadow and sunlight on the floor of a leafy glade, one spotted beast shifts and blends into another in the image-repertoire of classical zoo-mythology. Leopards (or panthers—they are the same animal) naturally emit sweet odors and are themselves drawn to the heady vapors of wine; once drunk, they may easily be captured (Theophrastus, *De causis plantarum* 6.17.9; *Natural History* 8.62 and 21.39; Oppian, *Cynegetica* 4.320–53).[13] To ride upon the back of a leopard or cheetah, as the god or his favorite may do, is to be transported by the rippling muscles of sensual rapture—very much as in the ride upon a Ketos. The sidesaddle posture of the momentary debauchee never varies, for thus are the androgynous contours of male hips and female shoulders silhouetted against a staid and heterosexual background. The dynamic eroticism of the leopard deteriorates into a stale symbol of lust in the Middle Ages, but no such codification of signs threatens our untamed predators in the Archaic and Golden Ages.

The spotted skin worn by the maenad or by Dionysus himself suggests by its broken patterning the dismembered or dismembering personality it was meant to conceal. In the Archaic Age, E. R. Dodds writes, "the individual, as the modern world knows him, began to emerge for the first time from the old solidarity of the family and found the unfamiliar burden of individual responsibility hard to bear. Dionysus could lift it from him."[14] In this age of the reorganization of the state and of the constitution of the individual, Apollo appealed to the few who sought stability through knowledge; Dionysus, to the many who needed release through action from the burden of their new selves— offering a kind of athletic mental healing and preparing the participant for renewed efforts at living in an ever more lonely-making world.

Drunkenness, as it melts down the discrete wills of the participants into general good cheer, also, as William James says, "brings its votary from the chill periphery of things to the radiant core; it makes him for the moment one with truth."[15] A quick, if not a safe, road to conviction. Now, Dionysus does not preside over vegetation in general but over moist and flowing nature, including wine. The theological lecture that Tiresias gives Pentheus in the *Bacchae*, in which this theme is developed, has been dismissed as no more than the rationalizings of an old priest trying to keep his shoddy religion in fashion with modernist thought (lines 266–327, with Dodds' commentary at 274–85). But only the rhetoric and the diction of the speech are sophistically tendentious; the content is entirely traditional. As Plutarch summarized it many centuries later, Dionysus is lord and bearer of all moist nature (*On Isis and Osiris* 364 D). His epithet *dendritēs*, god of the tree, indicates that his power drives the sap up the trunk; and in the *Bacchae* his maenads can make all of nature spurt with nutritive juices at their will. The ecstatic cult is part of or the same as the vegetation cult; for the growth of vegetation inspires the revelry and the revelry promotes the growth through a kind of magic: as the goddess Demeter lay with Iasion and as farmers lie with their wives, in a thrice-ploughed field to make the grain grow, so the sexual fervor of the Bacchants inspires the sap to rise throughout the land. The old truth which Dionysus brings mankind back to is a sympathy, on one, pre-conscious, level of existence, with organic nature's drive to life, growth, and reproduction.

The whole Bacchic *mise en scène* is an illusion, of course. And, Nietzsche aside for the moment, Dionysus in his own way stage-manages more special effects than does Apollo. The god's ability to make grape vines and ivy

orgies of eating or drinking

twine through his scenes in red- and black-figure painting, to send vegetation shooting across the deck of the pirates' ship and up the mast or about the looms of the daughters of Minyas, to pull the fir tree down to the ground for Pentheus—all of these stunts constitute a conspiracy to convince the Bacchant not that the world has suddenly been bewitched, but that it was always so, only she or he had been too obtuse to perceive the circumambient marvels. Finally, of course, the sense of power and freedom Dionysus brings turns out to have been imaginary, or at least only temporary. Slowly, with the first blood-shot glimmerings of a crapulous dawn, reality creeps back.

The wonder of Dionysus is that he comes so suddenly, when all had seemed lost, dead, or at least boring. So too, his grapevine awakens in an instant from a dead stump to send out its green tendrils across the landscape. His other plant, ivy, pursues a cycle counter to the grape's—blooming in the fall, remaining alive through the winter, and fruiting in the spring. These are the fastest growing plants in the Greek world, and both, appearing suddenly around the corner of a wall, can take over and impose their forms upon a previously secure plant or building. In the greatest mystery cult of the ancient world, at Eleusis near Athens, the moment when the whole secret was revealed supposedly involved the display of a sacred ear of wheat. Walter Otto has suggested that the grain may have somehow been made to grow up with vine-like, hallucinogenic swiftness during the actual night of the mysteries and right before the participants' eyes. [16]

As goddess of all dry nature, especially cereal, Demeter offered her humid counterpart a place at her shrine. We know of two divine children at Eleusis: Iacchus—the son of Demeter, or else her young lover, or maybe Persephone's child (and identical with Zagreus)—and Triptolemus—missionary of the cultivation of wheat and son of the local queen whose other child Demeter nursed. Dionysus became identified with Iacchus, but some of the agriculture-hero characteristics of Triptolemus also adhere to him. The innocently obscene fertility rites of the Haloa were celebrated in honor of Demeter and Dionysus. [17] And Pindar, probably referring to the Eleusinian cult, says that Dionysus was enthroned beside Demeter (*Isthmian Ode* 7.3–5). The old earth-goddess and her consort manage to continue their affair even in the cold, clear daylight of classical Attica. But the Elusinian mysteries go way, way back.

Initiation into them brought the promise of a paradisiacal afterlife to "him who had seen." Demeter, then, not only rules the life of the fields, but her realm also extends beneath the fertile few inches of topsoil to the true underworld where, in the person of her daughter, she will welcome the initiand back to the beatific vision he had glimpsed only for an instant one October night but had preserved in his memory as an earnest of his salvation.

Demeter could enjoy a joke as well as her nephew, and Dionysus, too, was master of souls. With the opening of the jars of new wine at the Anthesteria, the spirits of the dead were set free or summoned up to wander at large for a few days. And on a Linear B tablet from Pylos (Fr 1231) the dead are called *di-pi-si-jo-i*, "the thirsty ones."[18] Dried vine-clippings were a common fuel for funeral pyres; and the grave stelae represented on white-ground *lekythoi* (oil jars given to the dead) often have a phallic shape; and the shape of wine jars is not so different from that of burial jars. "If they were not making a procession for Dionysus and singing a hymn to the shameful parts," Heraclitus intones, "most shameless would be their actions. But Hades and Dionysus are the same" (Fr. 15, Diehls).

The Greek language is particularly suited to such antitheses and paradoxes as Heraclitus loves; "on the one hand ... on the other ... " is a standard, maybe *the* standard, sentence pattern: the good, the bad; the noble, the shameful; the body, the soul; death, life. And Dionysus is a god who does not glibly mediate between these last two polarities so much as he raucously embodies and maintains the tension they generate. He is the shadow-side of Hades, and vice versa. Dionysus' purview includes both death and life, the god and the sacrificial beast (who himself is both an enemy and a substitute), both gentleness and cruelty, both the Kore and the Ariadne of the upper world and the Persephone and the sleeping heroine of the lower, the seed that is buried and the grain that springs up, the plantings on graves, and the soul-fragmenting but revivifying experiences of the *thiasos* and of the Eleusinian mysteries.

irregular Greek chorus

Nietzsche

For us, heirs to the rich and burdensome legacy of nineteenth-century German thought and soul-searching, Apollo stands as a familiar antithesis to Dionysus and even as his enemy. Nietzsche, although he had predecessors and colleagues in his dithyrambic revival of the spirit of Greek tragedy and cult, for us declaims the first and, for better or worse, almost the ultimate word on what he imagined was an ancient antagonism between the two gods. In fact, this theological dichotomy was mostly a projection of his own personality onto the texts. The nature of his genius, which he well understood, was his ability to distill in the retort of his own soul the philosophical conflicts ("religious crises" might be more accurate) that were soon to constitute the dilemma of modern, psychological man. Nietzsche prophesied the creation of a new system of categories with which to think about man; Freud carried out the prophecy. Freud, however, began his theorizing as a shaky monist and wound up as a shaky dualist, whereas Nietzsche developed from a rabid dualist into an equally rabid monist. It is his dualism which first concerns us as psychologists and mythologists.

> In contrast to all those who are intent on deriving the arts from one exclusive principle, as the necessary vital source of every work of art, I shall keep my eyes fixed on the two artistic deities of the Greeks, Apollo and Dionysus, and recognize in them the living and conspicuous representatives of *two* worlds of art differing in their intrinsic essence and in their highest aims. I see Apollo as the transfiguring genius of the *principium individuationis* through which alone the redemption in illusion is truly to be obtained; while by the mystical triumphant cry of Dionysus the spell of individuation is broken, and the way lies open to the Mothers of Being, to the innermost heart of things.[19]

The spirit of Dionysus cannot be sustained for long without great danger to the human organism; the blind will of the god, the utter abandonment that music inspires, and the drunken frenzy of his service threaten to destroy all forms and codes and to dissolve the individual into the primal chaos that energetically swirls about us and from which we draw power. We need the illusion of which Apollo is master, for illusion shields us from too much reality and enables us to go on living. The god at Delphi gives artistic form to what in fact is shapeless—sculpting, as it were, the physiognomies of heroes and divinities out of a rude mass of Parian marble. "We possess *art* lest we *perish of the truth.*"[20] And again, "Here, when the danger to his will is greatest, *art* approaches as a saving sorceress, expert at healing. She alone knows how to turn these nauseous thoughts about the horror or absurdity of existence into notions with which one can live: these are the *sublime* as the artistic taming of the horrible, and the *comic* as the artistic discharge of the nausea of absurdity."[21] The *mere appearances* of art have a nocturnal parallel in the beautiful illusions of dreams, which like art encourage us to somnambulate on through the horrors of existence. Nietzsche has transmuted Schopenhauer's Idea and Will into Apollo and Dionysus and invented the concept of the dream as wish-fulfillment.

Nietzsche values aesthetics over ethics and epistemology. Showing more common sense than many of his epigones, he comes down firmly on the side of Apollo rather than of Dionysus.

> An ascetic, will-negating mood is the fruit of these [Dionysiac] states. In this sense the Dionysian man resembles Hamlet: both have once looked truly into the essence of things, they have *gained knowledge*, and nausea

inhibits action; for their action could not change anything in the eternal nature of things; they feel it to be ridiculous or humiliating that they should be asked to set right a world that is out of joint.[22]

He insists that Greek culture has all along been misunderstood as only Apollinian (Nietzsche's spelling), whereas it actually arose from the same sort of conflict that the Greeks immortalized in their games, poems, and history. What Slater interprets psycho-sociologically and reductively, Nietzsche interprets metaphysically—or, as he himself would insist, physiologically: "It seems impossible to be an artist and not to be sick."[23] In a few, albeit widely spaced, strokes he has outlined the Freudian concept of sublimation.

But the art of Greek tragedy is more than self-delusion; man conquers the horrible through the art of the drama. He responds with a resounding affirmation to the destructive turmoil of life, as epitomized by the sufferings of the tragic hero. Unlike the Buddhist who wanly seeks resignation and a vegetable will before life's unfathomable ironies, or Schopenhauer who dyspeptically argued for the negation of the animal will before the sordidness of conflict, the Greeks found virtue (in the old sense of "excellence") in the *agon*, the contest, the struggle against defeat and death and dissolution. Schopenhauer, prophet of *Thanatos*, the Freudian death-wish, saw tragedy as a confirmation of his pessimism; Nietzsche's view of it was quite the contrary. "At the same time I grasped that my instinct went into the opposite direction from Schopenhauer's: toward a *justification of life*, even at its most terrible, ambiguous, and mendacious: for this I had the formula 'Dionysian.' "[24] Artistic production might transcend Freudian sublimation in that it both inspires and constitutes the noble response of the healthy man to the challenge of life's diseases. "In truth, however, the hero is the suffering Dionysus of the Mysteries, the god experiencing in himself the agonies of individuation. . . . "[25]

But life itself is not a disease; one does not draw strength from the fly-ridden atmosphere of the charnel house nor from the antiseptic vapors of the hospital. Nietzsche held it against Socrates that he rationalized away all suffering ("Nothing can harm the virtuous man.") and considered the body a prison and life itself a sickness ("I owe a cock to Asclepius"—his last words in the *Phaedo* and his last words ever, which Nietzsche took to mean that as death released Socrates from the disease of living he owed a sacrifice for his new found health to the god of medicine).

Nietzsche anticipates Freud yet again: Life may be a struggle, but not one of us is ever completely victorious; sickness has found a purchase on every soul. And so we are all neurotics. Those who are heading toward health—and no one can do more than head in that direction, since the fight that must be fought inevitably continues—have at least recognized their predicament. A difference in temperaments accounts for Nietzsche the cheerful warrior in contrast to Freud the dour camp physician. There are, Nietzsche maintained, such things as neuroses of health.

It might be inferred, even from only the above quotations from *The Birth of Tragedy*, that Nietzsche's yea-saying to life must eventually have led him to combine Apollo and Dionysus into a new Dionysus who, through dismemberment and rebirth, has become the fully formed divine precursor of the human hero, of the individuated Zarathustra. Nietzsche claims, anyway, that the Greeks mitigate the original barbarisms of Dionysianism in order to suit their more temperate, Apollinian, character: "the bravery of the Greek consists in his struggle with his Asiaticism."[26] His own youthful, easy slide from romanticism into Dionysianism soon came to make Nietzsche himself cringe in embarrassment. He had found his way into the sticky abyss of soul-searching and soul-creating and soul-losing that usually strikes the intelligent in adolescence and again early in middle age, but never ceases to plague the sensitive German. Thomas Mann's Aschenbach, of *Death in Venice*, spends *all* his early and middle years in forging a literary success story and so behaves most un-typically, like an Englishman or a French industrialist, in succumbing only at the end of his long career to the imberbic blandishments of eternal youth. These are much more dangerous and potent when they tempt one at 55 than at 28.

The Puer

Jung by contrast saw himself as a *senex* type, a variety of wise old man, the dangerous shadow-side of which ("personality no. 2," as he liked to call it) was the Zarathustrian *puer*, the eternal boy wonder.[27] Jung's precept of compensation, *enantiodromia* or the reversal and complementarity of opposites that Heraclitus talks about, was not enough to convince the psychoanalyst that the philosopher's abyss could be safely vaulted across.

In a chapter in *Psychological Types*, "The Apollinian and the Dionysian," he does not question Nietzsche's interpretation of Dionysus but rather his positive evaluation of the god's influence:

> The creative dynamism, libido in instinctive form, takes possession of the individual as though he were an object and uses him as a tool or as an expression of himself. ... Thus in the Dionysian state the Greek was anything but a "work of Art"; on the contrary, he was gripped by his own barbarian nature, robbed of his individuality, dissolved into his collective

components, made one with the collective unconscious (through the surrender of his individual aims). . . . Aestheticism is a modern bias that shows
the psychological mysteries of the Dionysus cult in a light in which they
were assuredly never seen or experienced by the ancients. [28]

Jung, then, does not make the intellectual's common error of romanti-
cizing violence; consequently he does not put Dionysus on a pedestal or a
magic-mountaintop. Rather, he overestimates the mayhem actually committed
by the *thiasos*, and both he and Nietzsche exaggerate the rift between Apollo
and Dionysus. Jung cannot conceive of a religion with any vitality left whose
participants do not commit themselves body and soul to its practice. Life is
lived from brink to brink—a thought that would have intrigued Kierkegaard:

> The aesthetic approach immediately converts the problem into a picture
> which the spectator can contemplate at his ease, admiring both its beauty
> and its ugliness, merely reexperiencing its passions at a safe distance, with
> no danger of becoming involved in them. The aesthetic attitude guards
> against any real participation, prevents one from being personally impli-
> cated, which is what a religious understanding of the problem
> would mean. [29]

While Dionysus embodies an expansiveness associated with the extroverted and intuitive type of character, Apollo counsels the self-withdrawal and
conservation of energy typical of the introverted and thinking type. It is to Jung's
credit that he refused to exalt this kind of aestheticism, but to his discredit that
he declined the safe release the Dionysian experience was meant to offer to
introverts and extroverts alike. "The more deeply Jung entered into Nietzsche,"
James Hillman explains, without meaning to suggest a backwards metempsy-
chosis, "the more he was dissuaded from the Dionysian."[30] But, Hillman insists, Jung recognized that Nietzsche was really talking about Wotan, not about
Dionysus. Similarly in Mann's *Death in Venice*, the images of Dionysianism
turn out to be really Wotanic, Wagnerian, Nietzschean ice-demons in Bacchic
disguise, presaging *Götterdämmerung*, or the twilight of the idols and of us
too, rather than announcing Dionysian rebirth. Although Jung saw through to
the Wotanic shadow behind this pseudo-Dionysus, he nevertheless thought the
two gods were cousins. Perhaps, Hillman suggests, we should defend ourselves
against the cold cruelty of Wotan, but not against the sunny warmth of Dionysus, who brings about a spiritual, not physical, dismemberment, and *abaissement du niveau mental*, necessary for the distribution of consciousness through
all of the body's parts. [31] Hillman continues, attempting to elucidate the Puer-
perplex that Dionysus embodies:

> So the puer personifies that moist spark [sic] within any complex of attitude
> that is the original dynamic seed of spirit. . . . The puer offers direct
> connection with spirit. Break this vertical connection and it falls with
> broken wings. . . . When it falls we lose the urgent burning purpose and
> instead commence the long processional march through the halls of power
> towards the heart-hardened old king who is often cloaked and indistin-
> guishable from the sick wise old man. [32]

Jungian psychology, based primarily on the creative instinct, is thus a
creative psychology. Hillman leaves no doubt that the "notion of the creative is
the self-perception of the instinct through the image of the *puer aeternus* and
the archetype of the divine child."[33] And it seems that any activity, provided it
involves inventive problem-solving, can be creative and any creative activity
can produce a more nearly fulfilled soul. The "ordering-process" of creativity,
moreover, requires *hard work*, and such work can close the gap between the
genius and the common man. [34] Without ever forswearing the work of his prede-
cessor, Hillman outlines a thesis which pursues certain of Jung's premises to
their logical conclusions. On the way to these conclusions, however, he misses
much evidence that could support his case.

Just as Hillman adopts the persona of the god he is writing about, Dionysus, and thereby incarnates the fallacy of imitative form, Jung also assumed
a role which stood for what he was describing. He abandoned the god of his
fathers, and of his own father, and taught that men could become gods of a
sort; for his model deities he retreated to the "pagans." Not that he was ever
such a grand poseur as consciously to put himself in a god's buskins, but surely
the character of Zeus suits him better than any other. Olympian Zeus is the
senex in spades; Dionysus (his child) or Cretan Zeus (Zeus himself as a child)
is the puer. By this connection with Zeus, Dionysus breaks out of his restrictive
cycle and acquires a future with status: he grows a beard and the other Olympians set a place by his empty chair at high table. And so Zeus too has found
a way to preserve a link with eternal youth. Other mythological parallels between the analyst and the god—such as Jung's many spiritual wives—it would
be unfair to elaborate on.

Hillman reveals the grounds for his championing of Dionysus only toward
the end of *The Myth of Analysis*, when he equates the Apollinian with the
Adamic and with the scientific world-view. Psychology, Greek mythology, the
Judaeo-Christian tradition, and Western thought as a whole, upon only cursory
research, reveal an irrational prejudice against the feminine, an elevation of
the masculine: sky vs. earth; above vs. below; male vs. female; Adam as first
vs. Eve as derived; and Apollo vs. the Furies in Aeschylus' *Eumenides* (on the
subject of whether the father or mother is the true parent of the child). Since

Freud, like Apollo, takes the morphology of the male as a prototype, the inferiority of the female must follow: " 'Anatomy is Destiny,' to vary a saying of
Napoleon's."[35] But, Hillman points out, Freud never analyzed a little girl and
he saw little Hans only for one interview. "Freud's fantasy *of* the little girl's
mind becomes a Freudian fantasy *in* the little girl's mind." And this fantasy
"resulted in the need for psychotherapy to develop the inferior and feeble femininity."[36] The Apollonic method of most therapies in fact works against the
Dionysian substance of them. The ultimate aim of analysis would be to cure
even the malaise that afflicts this method: the "end of analysis coincides with
the acceptance of femininity. . . . " And this means "the incarnation of durable
weakness and unheroic strength that we find in the image of Dionysus."[37]

Hillman quite rightly sees the Dionysian force as closely akin to Eros,
and he does indicate what aspect of Dionysian Eros he thinks we must at last
confront—the bisexuality of the god, for Dionysus represents *zoē*, pure libido,
in which the two sexes as well as life and death are intermixed. The low view
of Dionysus in early classical scholarship, Hillman contends, grew out of a low
view of women in nineteenth-century Europe, and, before that, in classical
Greece.[38] Greek men, Slater claims, could not tolerate mature women nor
could Greek women abide mature men. So the men converted Artemis and
Athena—real females, once upon a time—into *virgin* goddesses and the
women rejected Zeus for Dionysus.[39]

This whole thesis, however, is far from new. In *Eros and Civilization*
Herbert Marcuse writes:

> Whatever the implications of the original Greek conception of Logos as
> the essence of being, since the canonization of the Aristotelian logic the
> term merges with the idea of ordering, classifying, mastering reason. And
> this idea of reason becomes increasingly antagonistic to those faculties and
> attitudes which are receptive rather than productive [Marcuse is speaking
> as a Marxist, against the capitalist attitude.], which . . . remain strongly
> committed to the pleasure principle.[40]

Norman O. Brown offers a similar hypothesis: "that formal logic and the
law of contradiction are the rules whereby the mind submits to operate under
the general conditions of repression. . . . What the world needs, of course, is a
little more Eros and less strife; but the intellectual world needs it just
as much."[41]

Regrettably, Hillman completely ignores the dangers of the Dionysian
experience, which Jung admittedly overemphasized—or which Hillman claims
Jung overemphasized. Freud, the most level-headed of all the analysts, indicates
the nature of those dangers: "*Protection against* stimuli is an almost more

important function for the living organism than *reception of* stimuli."[42] The cortical shield of an organism endeavors to preserve it against the enormous energies of the external world which assault it and tend to destroy it through a levelling out of energy. Hillman makes the same clinical mistake Jung often makes, which is to advise our hypothetical analysand to give up the self-defenses provided by his critical faculty—his ego as bulwark against the unconscious (Nietzsche's reality). Freud, despite his patriarchal authority, never ceased to regard the ego-ism of his colleagues as more important than any potential personalities they were missing.

Dionysus and the Pleasure Principle

Freud, as Garfield Tourney has shown, sometimes begins what appears to be a discursive work with a myth which he promptly connects to a psychoanalytic hypothesis, the significance of which he finally broadens into a new myth: the Oedipus complex and totemism as the basis, through sublimation, of civilization, art, and all creative endeavors. In the case of Eros and Thanatos (formerly, sex and aggression; later, the life instinct and the death drive), "Freud again begins with a mythical concept, molds it into a scientific hypothesis, and then extends the meaning of the hypothesis until once again it has mythical significance in its divergent and extensive explanations of cultural phenomena." In contrast with his treatment of the Oedipus complex, he could muster very little clinical data to support this even grander scheme. "Freud can thus be viewed not only as a physician, psychologist and scientist, but like the Ancient Greeks, a creator of myths, many of which have been assimilated into the intellectual atmosphere of our time. . . . Where science fails, myth supports."[43]

For Plato, that other mythmaker in spite of himself, science (that is, the *logos*) failed most obviously in matters of natural science and ancient history; for Freud, it failed in the area of the irrational *(mania)* composed of the id and the superego. Freud realized the sudd of impreciseness which his attempts to generalize his thinking often led him into; like Plato, he regarded the realm of ultimate psychological concepts not as a comfortably vague reference point to orient himself by whenever his mind refused to work clearly, but as a *terra incognita* posing a constant challenge to his abilities as mapmaker of the soul: "The theory of the instincts is so to say our mythology. Instincts are mythical entities, magnificent in their indefiniteness. In our work we can never for a moment disregard them, yet we are never sure that we are seeing them clearly."[44] As Jung fell back at times for an explanation of compensation on the Heraclitean concept of pairs of opposites endlessly giving and taking, Freud found classical antecedents for his own brand of dualism in the never-ending tension of Love and Strife described by Empedocles.[45]

If Freud had had the time to pay more attention to Greek literature he might have found in the *Bacchae* of Euripides the perfect myth and the perfect play to help carry the weight of the dualistic and meta-psychological conclusions of his later work. I am not proposing yet another structuralist reading of a primary, literary text through a secondary, theoretical one, or vice versa. I propose simply this: that both Euripides and Freud were developing many of the same ideas—although one was writing drama in the mythological tradition of the Athenian stage and the philosophical tradition of the sophists and Socrates, and the other was, finally, writing psycho-philosophy in the tradition of European thinkers since Descartes and Diderot, after long clinical experience with neurotics. And we readers, if not the amused ghosts of analyst and playwright, can benefit from the posthumous meeting of their minds.

Most writers analyzing the *Bacchae* from a psychoanalytic point of view trace the mechanism of Pentheus' psyche which generated his neurosis. For example, we are told by William Sale that Pentheus is a victim of castration fears: the pine tree he perches in is really his erection; the uprooting of the tree is his castration by the one who gave him the fear in the first place, his mother; and he gives in to transvestitism because in this way he can please her by looking like a woman.[46] But none of the easy equivalencies of which such analysts are so fond obtain in a great work of literature. Otherwise Sale would be as fine an artist as Euripides.

Some, however, of the orthodox Freudian and Jungian insights into the oedipal situation certainly hold true for the play: the son gets to bully, well, not his father but at least his grandfather; to watch his mother in what he imagines to be some primal scene; and to return at last to the comfort of her embrace.[47] In fact, the issues of the play, to which the elements of Pentheus' abnormality contribute only their fair dramatic share, come close to constituting a dramatic restatement of Freud's meta-psychology—his macrocosmic interpretation of the microcosmic psychic apparatus. Rieff points out that for Freud the unconscious functions, in Kenneth Burke's phrase, as "a god-term."[48] For Euripides, Dionysus in the *Bacchae* does the same duty.

The topography of the myth as told by Euripides reflects the topography of the soul. The countryside matches the id; the city, the super-ego; the individual, caught between the two, the ego. Dionysus, great god of the id, storms the walls of the city and rouses the forces of the superego against himself. If the individual gives in to the god and accepts a temporary and refreshing opening up of his psychic gates and fragmentation of his soul, then Dionysus is most gentle; if he resists, then Dionysus turns into "he-who-must-be-obeyed," and the recusant suffers dismemberment.

refusing to comply

But Euripides produces no church-players' allegory of simple choices between right ways and wrong ways. The individual, particularly the ancient Greek, is part of a group, and our playwright, an anti-social intellectual in his own time, dramatizes for us the dangers of living the natural life, of succumbing to the dehumanizing ways of the Dionysiac group and to the drugged peace that alternates with the furiousness of undiscriminating emotionality. While the Theban bacchants (Pentheus' relatives) suffer from having suppressed their emotions, the Asian bacchants (the Chorus) participate not in some moderate cult, like the historic festivals of mountain-wandering, but in a violent, merciless incursion of Bacchism: Dionysus weaves a black as well as a white spell. [49] And Pentheus, who fancies himself a clever fellow (sophos), would, as Dodds says, measure everything by the canon of reason and vulgar experience, not by the wisdom which is part of the order of things and marks man's place in that order. [50] Only with difficulty can a few manage to come by the sophia that would enable a Pentheus to tend to the urges of his soul, satisfy the security of the polis, and lead what Euripides, if he had read Freud or Philip Rieff, might call a rationally alienated life.

How could a fifth-century playwright avoid being caught in the very predicament he seems to have set himself to dramatize? One way: Euripides adopted old-fashioned forms for the Bacchae (of diction, meter, plot, and involvement of the Chorus), but he stood the original content of those forms on its ear: now, the consequences of the sins of the fathers are no longer visited on the heads of the children, but, instead, the grandfather must pay for the sins of Pentheus; now, the tragic effect is not catharsis, nor a strengthening of social conformity, but a pollution of the viewers' religious sensibilities and an erosion of the foundations of their community; now, no choice entertainment is produced for the spectators and for the god who, in the person of his priest, witnessed the first performance of the play, but rather a riot of nihilism stage-strikes away all that the Greeks thought constituted their Greekness and leaves them with nothing to take home but emptied souls. Euripides discovered he could do two things at once with his mythological argument: devitalize the religious tradition by presenting the old stories clearly and simply, but in a modern dress that emphasized all the absurdities and immoralities obscured for so long by the rhetoric of respect; and charge myth with a new force by making the Homeric and Sophoclean double-motivation (god wills what man wants to do anyway) a metaphor for the psychological processes. It was a generation or two after his death before an audience was prepared to keep up with this.

What forces of psychic energy did Euripides allow to run amok and bring his characters to disaster? In The Ego and the Id Freud writes: "The ego represents what may be called reason and common sense, in contrast to the id, which contains the passions. . . . Often a rider, if he is not to be parted from his horse, is obliged to guide it where it wants to go; so in the same way the ego is in the habit of transforming the id's will into action as if it were its own."[51] The ego has many devices whereby to gain a semblance of control over irrational forces. One way is through projection—the tendency to treat too-vigorous internal stimuli as though they were coming from the outside, so that the psychic skin might act as a shield against their presumed assault.[52] Not all of the ego's devices to defend itself, however, are self-delusory:

> The relation to the external world has become the decisive factor for the ego; it has taken on the task of representing the external world to the id— fortunately for the id . . . [which could not otherwise escape destruction]. In accomplishing this function, the ego must observe the external world, must lay down an accurate picture of it in the memory-traces of its perceptions, and by its exercise of the function of "reality-testing" must put aside whatever in this picture of the external world is an addition derived from internal sources of excitation.[53]

Under the ego's instincts of self-preservation, the pleasure principle is replaced by the reality principle. If the ego retains control and the organism manages to insure its own survival—a scenario to which there are many exceptions— the reality principle replaces the pleasure principle.[54]

The superego manifests itself as a sense of guilt or of self-criticism, or even as a feeling of being watched, "for the sense of guilt is the perception in the ego answering to this criticism."[55] This superego, or ego-ideal, originates in a need to modify the ego in order to repress the Oedipus complex; thus, "the super-ego retains the character of the father." But, since this ego-ideal is in fact the descendant of the Oedipus complex, "it is also the expression of the most powerful impulses and most important libidinal vicissitudes of the id."[56]

Before we can understand the essential relationship between the superego and the id, we need not accept the origins of the superego in the repression of the Oedipus complex by the patriarch of the primal horde. The ego-ideal "is partly a reaction-formation against the instinctual processes of the id. Psychoanalysis is an instrument to enable the ego to achieve a progressive conquest of the id." Thus, the superego "is always close to the id and can act as its representative vis-à-vis the ego. It reaches deep down into the id and for that reason is farther from consciousness than the ego is."[57] The psychological flip, then, which Pentheus and his kind make—from holding an authoritarian position to being held hostage by a dictatorial unconscious—goes not from reason to unreason but simply from the one kind of irrationality to the other. This flip may be precipitated by a moral factor, a sense of guilt that finds its satisfaction in illness and suffering. [58]

As a child needs love from its mother and father, so the psyche needs love from its parent-part. "To the ego, therefore, living means the same as being loved—being loved by the super-ego, which here again appears as the representative of the id." [59] When an individual loses a sexual object, an erotic object-choice, he or she ensures the continuity of being loved by setting up that object inside the ego; these abandoned object-cathexes transform the ego, but they also give it control over the id and deepen its relations with the id, "at the cost, it is true, of acquiescing to a large extent in the id's experiences." Just so, particularly in manic-depressives, the ego-ideal might be "temporarily resolved into the ego after having ruled it with especial strictness . . . so that the person in a mood of triumph and self-satisfaction, disturbed by no self-criticism, can enjoy the abolition of his inhibitions, his feelings of consideration for others, and his self-reproaches." [60] But on the melancholiac side of the psychic swing the super-ego becomes a gathering place for the death instincts.

Freud once believed that all activities of an organism either lead it to pleasure or help it to avoid pain (un-pleasure). Clinical experience with the repetition compulsion, negative therapeutic reaction (irrational attachment of a patient to his disease), and sado-masochistic behavior led Freud to formulate his theory of a death instinct. He explained sadism as the death instinct turned outwards, masochism as the same instinct turned inwards because of impediments to its expression in the outside world, and certain forms of compulsively repetitious behavior as satisfying a need for self-punishment. He named the pleasure principle Eros and the death instinct Thanatos. Eros, which resides principally in the ego, aims at complicating life as well as preserving it; like Plato's *erōs*, it binds together the disparate parts of the universe. Eros is the impersonal, immutable life force, whereas the libido is personal and mutable. [61] Although the libido belongs to an individual, its energy never acquires a heterosexual quality but remains undifferentiated, bisexual or even pan-sexual.

The destructive instinct, on the other hand, undoes connections. While it operates internally, as a death instinct, it remains silent, only coming to our notice when it is diverted outward. This diversion must occur for the preservation of the organism. "When the super-ego is established," Freud maintained, "considerable amounts of the aggressive instinct are fixated in the interior of the ego and operate there self-destructively. This is one of the dangers to health by which human beings are faced on their path to cultural development." [62] Freud, quite understandably, kept fiddling with his models of the psychic mechanism. In an earlier formulation of many of these same ideas, he located the destructive component in the superego, where it can turn against the ego: "What is holding sway in the super-ego is, as it were, a pure culture of the death instinct, and in fact often succeeds in driving the ego into death, if the latter does not fend off its tyrant in time by the change round into mania." Eros impinges on the ego from the territory of the id; the death instinct does the same from the newer realm of the superego—even though, as we shall see, Thanatos is in a sense more archaic than Eros. "Helpless in both directions, the ego defends itself vainly, alike against the instigations of the murderous id and against the reproaches of the punishing conscience." The defense doesn't always succeed, "since the ego's work of sublimation results in . . . a liberation of the aggressive instincts in the super-ego, its struggle against the libido exposes it to the danger of maltreatment and death." In melancholia, the superego actually becomes a mustering ground for the death instincts: when the superego gets on its super-moral high horse, it becomes "cruel as only the id can be. . . . The more a man controls his aggressiveness, the more intense becomes his ideal's inclination to aggressiveness against his ego."[63]

An instinct, then, or its manifestations, may easily turn around into its opposite—as love can turn into hate, with the intensity of the original emotion remaining unchanged.[64] So Pentheus turns from a sadist into a masochist in the sense that he goes to his slaughter as a willing victim; and so too he adds more than a touch of exhibitionism (the maenad's costume, his perch high in the pine tree) to his voyeurism. Some of the lower animals even die after or in the act of copulation, or allow themselves to be killed, "because after Eros has been eliminated through the process of satisfaction, the death instinct has a free hand for accomplishing its purposes."[65] These purposes differ only in intensity from the fugitive side of the pleasure principle: to avoid all pain is to achieve a state of freedom from all irritability, which is to be dead. Freud has transformed the monism of sexuality into the monism of death. Or, as Marcuse puts it, "The death instinct is destructive not for its own sake, but for the relief of tension."[66]

In an attempt to refine his definition of "instinct" at the same time that he was complicating the role of the instincts in his formulation, Freud insisted, in Beyond the Pleasure Principle, on the conservative nature of all the organic instincts: they tend to bring about the restoration of an earlier state of things. The goal of life, then, cannot be a state that has never before been attained— the creation of consciousness for Jung, the transvaluation of all values and the birth of the superman for Nietzsche, the attainment of immortality and the beatific vision for Christianity—but must rather be the return to an inanimate state. "The aim of life is death." Everything dies for an internal reason, from the tension created by previously inanimate matter striving to abolish itself. The instincts, however, ensure that the organism follows its own path to death and wards off the temptation to follow lethal ways other than those inherent in its makeup: " . . . the organism wishes to die only in its own fashion." The life of the organism moves with a peculiar, vacillating rhythm: one set of instincts rushes it forward, another jerks it back to prolong the individual's journey to the goal of life.[67]

Never content without an explanation for his explanation, Freud thought he found a clue to the biological origins of the death instinct in the writings of A. Weismann, who argued that unicellular organisms are potentially immortal and that death appears only with the development of multicellular metazoa. Freud concluded that once the body was divided into soma and germplasm an unlimited duration of life was pointless. The germ cells retain the original structure of living matter, separate themselves from the rest of the organism, and work for a kind of immortality through the generations of a species. The sex instincts are thus the true life instincts.

An infusorian, if left to itself, dies from incomplete voidance of its metabolic products; but the coalescence of two individual cells, which separate soon afterwards without sexual reproduction, rejuvenates both of them. Union with another living substance increases the chemical tension within, and introduces fresh vital differences into, an old organism, which then shows renewed resistance to the degenerative effects of its own metabolism. When two cells take each other as the objects of their sexual instincts, they neutralize their respective death instincts and thus preserve their lives. On the other hand, when they retain their discrete libidos, they behave like malignant tumors, in a narcissistic fashion.[68]

The self must seek union with another, or suffer dissolution into the otherness of death. Dionysus, the loosener *(lusios)*, relieves us from the toils of daily life and liberates us from the burden of our personalities—either through Eros or, if you prefer, then through dismemberment and annihilation. The fear of death, Lou Andreas-Salomé wrote in her diary, "is our punishment for insufficient love of life."[69] Pentheus, having rejected Eros, must accept the alternative. Karl Kerenyi even sees in the trieteric or two-year period of many of the festivals of Dionysus an analogy with Hegel's dialectic, and in both a reflection of the life drive and death drive—as though the rising and falling cycle of a single year does not suffice to contain the flood and subsequent drought of the Dionysiac experience.[70] The year-god cycle makes a wholeness of the Eros-Thanatos dichotomy and renders it emotionally acceptable.

The cycle begins again every year, or every two years on a grander scale. We are compelled to repeat both the playful gestures of lovemaking and the neurotic twitches of our little deaths, as if some daemonic power were forcing us on for better or worse. Repetition also has a starring role in each of the four kinds of divine madness distinguished by Plato, which differ from merely human diseases: the ritual madness of Dionysus, the prophetic of Apollo, the poetic madness of the Muses, and the erotic of Aphrodite and Eros (*Phaedrus* 265 A–B). Dionysus is both the cause of the repetition compulsion (*mania*) and the seasonal liberator from it; similarly Apollo's responses rarely strayed beyond the old homilies and homely ambiguities; the Muses were more active in earlier ages, when, through the mouths of their poets, they repeated the pebble-smooth syllables of formulaic verse; and one of Eros' many arrows stings pretty much like any other. Plato insists that great blessings have come to mankind through madness, but the loss of control that accompanies its attack rouses our fears of unholy possession by the demons of the unconscious. Among the Greeks, these demons were at first thought to beset the soul from without; but in Plato's *Republic*, as Dodds points out, "the soul's dialogue with 'the passions of the body' becomes an internal dialogue between the two 'parts' of the soul; the passions are no longer seen as an infection of extraneous origin, but as a necessary part of the life of the mind as we know it, and even as a source of energy, like Freud's *libido* ... " (*Republic* 441 B–C; *Phaedo* 94 D–E).[71] Things were so much simpler when the gods came from "out there."

Aristotle in his *Politics* says that the man who forms no part of the polis must be either a beast or a god (*thērion ē theos*, 1.1253 A)—or, we might add, a bit of both. The great hero of a land, like its great enemy, typically was born there but raised somewhere else—thereby mediating, a structuralist might say, between exogamy and endogamy. Dionysus enters Thebes as a barbarian, a stranger from an even stranger land. Charles Segal points out that the god "both repeats and reverses the good work of the original culture-hero," Cadmus.[72] He comes as a founder of a new religion, and as a destroyer of both the ego of the individual and the mega-ego of the city, the enemy of all who would resist him. He has at times been hunted and in turn has learned how to hunt while retaining as a persona his former helpless attitude: *Zagreus*, one of his many names, probably means "zealous hunter."[73] In the *Bacchae*, he comes to Thebes to honor his mother and be honored himself; to be sacrificed himself and to find a willing victim. He is the killer, but it is the innocent townspeople who are driven out after the slaughter of the scapegoat.

Dionysus is young, attractive, exotic, lion-tressed; an intolerant grandson of Cadmus, new at the game of ruling others and being worshipped by them. Pentheus, his cousin, is about the same age, but Hellenic (the only character on stage, aside from a few messengers, to wear Greek dress) and possessed of remarkably similar hair; a tyrannical relative and sworn enemy of the god: in short, a suitable sacrifice. As the new king, he stands for the forces of law and order, of what we might prefer to call the superego; Dionysus, as the invader from wildest Asia with his band of slavish maenads, rules the antipodal realm of the id. Pentheus, utterly inexperienced in sexual matters, thinks he can

repress the irrational forces that his mother and aunts have been driven moun-
tainwards to worship. He never understands that his rigid persona restrains a
nature akin to the god's and one that can break out in a parody of that other's
if it is not permitted an occasional stretch outside the prison-yard of his soul.
He and Dionysus differ on the location of Paradise. The word *paradise*, from
the Old Iranian *pairidaeza*, means a "wall around," and is close enough to its
cognates in Greek (*paradeisos*, from *para* or *peri* and *teikhos*) to be etymo-
logically transparent to a bright fifth-century Athenian. The real paradises that
we know about in Persia were irrigated hunting preserves, planted with trees
and bounded by long walls which kept the dry barren desert and the peasants
out, the greenery and dorcas gazelles in. Nearly all Greek cities were contained
and protected by similar walls, and Greek mythology and social psychology
show a strong sense of the contrast between the worlds of the in-here and of the
out-there, albeit a subtler sense and one more elaborately worked out in drama
and the other arts than that manifested in the clearing-in-the-forest myths of
Lévi-Strauss's Indians.

Now, boundaries may be broken from the inside, and walls may be built
to protect or to cage. The security of walls, buildings, and boundaries fascinates
Pentheus: he cannot tolerate the violation of civic order or personal security,
nor allow what he thinks should be contained to escape from its container.
Pentheus polices the polis; he even tries to chain and cage the god of freedom.
And so, the *sparagmos* he feared for the city turns out to be his own fate too.
Having deluded himself that he is the only man left in Thebes strong enough
to oppose the women and their effeminate favorite, he will go down to Hades
dressed as a maenad for eternity. There are no changing-rooms on the farther
shores of the Styx.

Dionysus, like Demeter and Persephone, presides over life and death.
One stage of life's cycle must eventually turn around and become the other but
not necessarily before its time. At an age when he should be getting out into
the world and discovering women, Pentheus chooses to abide in himself. A soul
poisoned by its fantasies and a loss of any self to abide in are the penalties he
suffers. Where does the third way lie?

Cadmus and Tiresias are rational individuals in Freud's sense: they know
how to make the proper social investments: to revel is theologically politic,
necessary anyway, and fun in the first place. R. P. Winnington-Ingram thinks
they represent the solution Greece ultimately found to the problem of Dionysianism.[74] "Sublimation," Philip Rieff writes, "is the successful adaptation of a
given instinct . . . to the repressive social process." (In the case of the theatrical
Dionysus of the *Bacchae*, however—thanks partly to Euripides' perversity and
partly to the losses the fertility cult had suffered during the Dark Ages—we
witness a society's attempt to adapt itself to a repressive instinct, and failing.)

But once it is adapted to society, the instinct always threatens to break out, with its original fierceness untamed, and to renew the original conflict; as we see in this play, instinctual forces can destroy even the best-intentioned compromiser along with the despot. "By their very existence," Rieff adds, "the instincts serve notice of the inadequacies of all social arrangements." The hard core of human nature does not easily accommodate itself to social experience.[75]

The instincts may make the individual their agent, but they also serve as his chief mode of defense against the world. In a similar way, the unconscious defends him against a repressive culture. Not only society but the ambivalent structure of the instinct itself makes an individual's response to any situation inadequate and sets up new conflicts. If dammed up, an instinct will burst out and send a man screaming back to the savagery whence he arose; but mere animal expressiveness cannot solve the conflict nor satisfy the psyche. Freud finally became a dualist, like Jung, but a pessimistic one, since for him the unconscious is no promised land of fulfillment but all that consciousness is not, can never be, and would not want to be even if it could.[76]

Dionysus offers instinctual man the chance to respond to him as a human animal should, through worship in a group. But that involves a danger in itself. While in a group, Freud writes in *Group Psychology and the Analysis of the Ego*, "the individual is brought under conditions which allow him to throw off the repressions of his unconscious instinctual impulses." Each group has a leader, who—we may argue, developing Freud's remarks on being in love—replaces or consumes the separate egos of the members, becomes their ego-ideal, and draws to himself all the narcissistic libido each would have lavished on himself or herself. Harking back to *Totem and Taboo*, Freud contends that "the group appears to us like a revival of the primal horde." The patriarchal father, chief, or leader of this original group "was the 'superman' whom Nietzsche only expected from the future. . . . His sexual jealousy and intolerance became in the last resort the causes of group psychology."[77] Some late classical sources claim that men as well as women could join the thiasos; but it seems more likely that a priest of the god was the only man present at the orgies—leading the women, keeping other men away, and perhaps participating in some of the revels.[78] Since the priest was probably old and the women actually maidens, his participation may have been merely a matter of presence, as it seems to have been at the Athenian festival of the Haloa.

The group experience can produce a power-struggle: on Euripides' stage one event revealed the tyrannical nature of the leader to the audience. After the earthquake shakes the palace and releases the "stranger" from prison, the Chorus prostrate themselves in adoration of Dionysus. Greeks, however, stood up straight, even when addressing their gods. The Spartan envoys to Sardis refused to crawl into the presence of the great king, as Persian protocol required; only barbarians groveled before the powerful, who, be they despots or deities, still put their sandals on one at a time like the rest of mankind. (Consequently, in the Greek view of these matters, it was quite in character for the Persians to ban homosexuality, since love between men implied a love of freedom and encouraged courageous resistance to tyranny. In a footnote to some of his remarks quoted above, Freud assumes that "the sons, when they were driven out and separated from their father, advanced from identification with one another to homosexual object-love, and in this way won freedom to kill their father."[79]

The old men, Cadmus and Tiresias, no threat to the turgid young god, do their best to join in the revels. But from Euripides' point of view, they behave foolishly, since they act without much real belief: two old men in fawnskins and brandishing thyrsi as they head up the mountain are not behaving rationally; they also look silly. Freud would have disapproved of the whole Dionysian folderol. Dionysianism is the social alternative to the heroic pursuit of excellence. Human beings, Freud claimed, have no instinct toward perfection. What appears as such in a few individuals can be understood as a result of instinctual repression, upon which is based all that is precious in human civilization; "the backward path [e.g., Dionysianism] . . . is as a rule obstructed by the resistances which maintain the repressions."[80] The resolve "always to excel" would then express a neurotic compulsion arising from the repressions and sublimations that Greek family life necessitated.

Euripides destroyed the legitimacy of the Greek way (Pentheus' rationalism), disgusted his audience with the excesses of the Asiatic or Pelasgian way (Dionysian irrationalism), and showed the ineffectiveness and absurdity of a third way (the rational commitment of Cadmus and Tiresias to the revels). No, the playwright presents no simple indictment of the god (Winnington-Ingram's judgment of the play) nor explication of the experience complete with a recommendation of a moderate approach (Dodds's view). For Freud there *was* a third way—rational alienation, along with a small but necessary social investment—but that is a modernist solution, not one available to many ancient Greeks. Euripides himself more or less followed this way. Not many others could afford to retreat from society as he did—eventually to faraway Macedonia, where, instead of realizing a sense of commonality with the common man, as Dodds suggests,[81] he may have felt safe enough to analyze and dramatize more vigorously than ever before the complementary predicaments of the mass man and the individual.

When the productions of art, religion, and philosophy, in the words of Rieff, "are not social enough or when wear and tear have rendered them no longer usable, as in the case of Christianity, they fall away and leave man with the terrible choice of neurosis or health."[82] For Nietzsche, to choose religion was the healthy or at least the expedient move; to choose the truth, the neurotic and nobler one. Formation of the ego-ideal favors repression; sublimation is a way to meet the claims of the ego without arousing the censure of that ideal. It works, Freud tells us—but only temporarily:

> A man who has exchanged his narcissism for the worship of a high ego-ideal has not necessarily on that account succeeded in sublimating his libidinal instincts. It is true that the ego-ideal requires such sublimation, but it cannot enforce it . . . and in general it is far harder to convince the idealist of the inexpediency of the hiding-place found by his libido than the plain man whose demands in this respect are only moderate.[83]

The common man found his salvation in Dionysus, who offered him instantaneous happiness and freedom from toil, pain, and eventually from life itself, as well as a chance to lose his differentiating identity along with the rest of the group before the great Will of their leader. In an age of anxiety, Apollo supposedly administered a balm to the more intellectual soul of the uncommon man who possessed the time, money, and curiosity necessary to consult the Delphic oracle and receive an enigmatic response—which Dodds construed as meaning "Do as the Father tells you; and you will be safe tomorrow."[84]

Apollo's solution, however, for the mythological heroes who approach him, turns out to be—like the analytical solution—only an invitation to ask further questions of oneself, not of the god. Not everyone, even in Plato's ideal republic, is up to asking questions all the time; and so Apollo makes a show of giving answers to some, and Dionysus a show of bestowing happiness on others. The one god hides himself from us behind his priests, priestess (the Pythoness), and mantic abracadabra; the other remains inscrutable behind his mask—even, or especially, in the midst of revelry.

Dionysus loves masks: in the city, where at the dramatic festival the stylized features which the players assumed insisted on the flatness of the play's characters; and in the countryside, where at local Dionysia a tree trunk was dressed up as the god, given his mask, and then was made to witness the ensuing ritual. According to John Jones in his *On Aristotle and Greek Tragedy*, Euripides deliberately challenged the ancient conventions with mask-piercing and mask-exploiting effects.[85] And Walter Otto, in Nietzschean tones, proclaimed that the mask indicates the actual epiphany of Dionysus would prove too violent an assault on the senses.

In what too horrible image of man is this god made? Dionysus, as a man, suffers dismemberment at the meaty hands of Titanic nature; as a god, he has subtler ways to inflict that *sparagmos* on his victim in turn. And so the poor bacchants must be protected—from too much reality, from the unconscious, bestial side of themselves, and from the god's blissful countenance—by a linen and gypsum veil. But that mask also protects the god himself from any responsibility to mankind. Behind the benignly smiling mask that Euripides gives to the god of the *Bacchae*, an amoral brute, the spotted, feline Dionysus, gazes out on the panorama of life and from time to time disinterestedly destroys what he sees. "To the god," Heraclitus said, "all things are fair and good and just, but men have taken some as unjust and others as just" (Diehls, fr. 102). And: "The lord whose oracle is in Delphi neither declares nor conceals, but gives a sign" (Diehls, fr. 93, trans. Kahn). and—Heraclitus might have added—he shakes hands with Dionysus.

6

Apollo and His Boys

Finally, carrying my notion to its conclusion, I said that Culture, born of
life, ultimately kills life.
　　　　　　—André Gide, *The Immoralist* (trans. Richard Howard)

APOLLO DOES NOT EXCITE the imagination. Though he brought civilizing
order to the chaos of the savage land around Delphi and, with his Muses,
presides over poetry and other creative endeavors, and, through his oracle and
prophets, clarifies the narrow ways leading out of our perplexities, no dervish
horde of theories and images—the like of which twirls around the primitive
statue of Dionysus—seeks inspiration and protection at *his* sanctuary.

Nietzsche, and those who have interpreted him, wrote the modern definition of Apollo. For Nietzsche, Apollo creates those illusions that make it
possible for us to go on living. Sculpture symbolizes his function, for it is the
art of bringing form out of a raw conglomerate, while the Dionysian art of
music melts those forms back down into their original incoherence. We must
attend to the eruptions of Dionysus, without which life could not continue,
but must ultimately choose the saving sorcery of Apollo—"for it is only as an
aesthetic phenomenon that existence and the world are eternally justified."[1]
By this construction, Dionysus—not Apollo—opens up the abyss of knowledge
for us; Apollo, however, prophylactically interprets and refines that knowledge
in the retort of art lest frail humanity expire from reality-poisoning. Eventually
Nietzsche's concepts of Apollo and Dionysus fused, so that a now perfect pagan
deity could be set against Christ. Like Freud, Nietzsche was not deprecating
the controls of reason and glorifying the freedom of the irrational, but rather
arguing that only when Apollinian restraints clashed with and held Dionysian
forces in check did a constant creative tension ensue and generate Greek civi-

139

lization. Or, as Freud puts it in *New Introductory Lectures on Psychoanalysis*,
"Where id was, there ego shall be. It is a work of culture—not unlike the
draining of the Zuider Zee."[2] And, elsewhere—"Our civilization is, generally
speaking, founded on the suppression of the instincts."[3]

Socrates, as the wholly theoretical man (according to Nietzsche) who is
convinced that the nature of things can be fathomed by human reason cheer-
fully working its way down the thread of causality, rejected Dionysus and the
instincts. (But Apollo, knowing how much he himself needs Dionysus to define
his Hellenism for him, rejected Socrates.) Without Dionysus and man's acceptance of the annihilation of his self, tragedy is impossible. Nietzsche thought
he would become the new Socrates who, by practicing a kind of philosophical
music-making, would (along with Richard Wagner) restore the spirit of tragedy
and the ancient tragic view of life to Germany. For a tragic *mise en scène*, he
argued, is a precondition for the creation of the Superman.

Our understanding of Apollo seems derived not from a sound reading of
The Birth of Tragedy, but from a confusion of the Greek god with Nietzsche's
Socrates. Thus, Apollo becomes the lord of pure reason, science, and calculation, relying on his slide-rule instead of on intuition—the very antithesis of
slyly winking Dionysus. Like many such confusions, this attempt to oversim-
plify the two divine figures has a basis in more than the bipolar structure of
the human mind. Not only were Apollo and Dionysus in a sense opposite types,
but Apollo himself embodies certain contradictions.

Zeus loved the Titaness Leto, who—after suffering many torments from
a jealous Hera—managed to bear the twins Apollo and Artemis. When only
a few days old Apollo travelled to Delphi, on the southern slope of Mt. Parnassus, slew the Python or guardian-dragon of the sanctuary, and either he
seized the oracle from the ancient female powers who had held it before him
or else they willingly handed it over to him. There, after he had done penance
for killing the Python, he became the god of prophecy, speaking the will of his
father Zeus through the mouth of a babbling priestess (the pythoness), whose
nonsense syllables were interpreted in extemporaneous verse by a skilled priest.
Apollo practiced his own brand of mantic irrationality before Dionysus came
to Delphi. Originally he was probably consulted, as a killer who had managed
to cleanse his own self, by homicides and even by whole cities in need of
purification; and thus he remains connected with primitive fears of pollution
that seem far from his nature as the god of reason.[4] From murder and blood-
guilt, he expanded his jurisdiction, in later, more rational and thus more anx-
ious ages, over justice and regulation and guilt of all sorts. He could send
plagues and cure them, destroy herds and build them up again, tell a new
colony what gods to worship, advise a city to go to war or a merchant to make
an investment. As god of the lyre he presided over the more "classical" forms

of music and led the Muses in song. He is always represented as a youth, a *kouros* of, say, 18—having just reached a man's estate but not yet sporting a beard on his girlish cheeks (Callimachus, *Hymns* 2.36–37)—with a youth's expressionless, Olympian self-absorption. Only Leto may stroke his adolescent locks, which are never to be shorn in initiation into manhood (Apollonius of Rhodes 2.707–10).

Despite his patronage of golden lads and his privilege of sending the winds of inspiration whistling down Parnassus and into the poet's study, Apollo remains a god of frustrated creative endeavor. He is not a *senex* figure, like Zeus or Jehovah, but the archetype of ever-youthful sterility. He operates not so much as a master of the afflatus, but as a purifier of the soul who prepares us for the quick spark of inspired madness, who reassures us that we may accept those alien influences which galvanize us into creative action—influences that he himself cannot act upon. He is a narcissist.

Failure in Love

Pausanias claims that Narcissus fell in love, not with himself, but with his twin sister and that when she died he knew he would find the image he longed for reflected by the surface of a pool of water: the siblings looked alike, dressed alike, their hair was the same, and they used to go hunting together (9.31.7–9). Apollo's twin sister, Artemis, has never grown out of her tomboyish ways nor been with a man; and he, although he has had a number of girls, prefers boys and himself retains the epicene cheeks of Greek adolescence.

Why does the narcissist need a twin or a lover? He—or she—doesn't. But it makes for a more interesting scenario. The finest analyses of narcissism are Freud's and Norman Mailer's. Here is an orienting quotation from Mailer (writing about Henry Miller):

> The same dialectic of love and hate that mates feel for one another is experienced within the self. . . . So two narcissists in love are the opposite of two mates who may feel a bond powerful as the valence holding the atoms of a molecule together. Narcissists, in contrast, are linked up into themselves. . . . They have a passionate affair to the degree each allows the other to resonate more fully than when alone.[5]

Can Apollo and Artemis be construed as such mirror-imaged siblings? Not only do they form a matched pair, but each of them in turn pairs up with a double; in others, they love only their own traits. And both are always frustrated in love—Artemis by choice, Apollo in spite of what he thinks are his best efforts. (And yet, just as Apollo protects the creative spirit which he himself cannot command, the maidenly Artemis is also a goddess of childbirth, the inspiratrix of fertility.) Both chose mates who cannot ever pull them out of themselves: Apollo, a long series of lovely females; Artemis, Hippolytus the son of the Amazon queen and himself a virgin. In vase-paintings brother and sister look alike—distant, divine, unattached. She is always narrow-hipped, small-breasted, the boyish girl Greek men preferred; Apollo never turns into a man. They both shoot bows, an uncommon weapon in the Greek world—one that permits the cruel assassins to operate at a distance, far from the sweaty embrace of spear-thrust or sword-play. Often, in red-figure art, they draw their bows far around the opposite side of the vase from their victims. They fear pollution—of blood or semen or a man's gaze. Artemis hides behind her nymphs, deep in a copse, untouchable even when she is naked; Apollo remains abstracted from human emotions—high up on Mt. Parnassus, deep within his temple at Delphi, behind a lapidary list of maxims inscribed on the marble lintel:

> Abstain from inauspicious words
> Fear authority
> Do not glory in strength
> Make obeisance to the divine
> Hate hubris
> Govern your spirit
> Observe the limit
> Nothing in excess
> Know yourself
> Rule women[6]

All of these insist on an intellectual self-sufficiency, a containment of the spirit, a self-restraint and suppression of the limitless irrational: "boundaries are best" Apollo seems to tell us. But boundaries isolate as well as secure the individual. "Nothing in excess" could mean "nothing outside of yourself."

The last maxim on the list does not seem to have helped Apollo much, for he himself could not rule women. The Sibyl, for example, agreed to sleep with him in return for the boon of immensely great age. Once she had received the promise of longevity, she went back on *her* promise to cooperate—knowing that the god was, in any case, bound to his word. Even when Apollo pointed out that she had forgotten to ask for long youth and thus had only the wizening centuries to look forward to, she resisted his advances. Petronius claims she eventually grew so small that she lived in a bottle; Apollo, ever faithful to his contracts, continued to inspire her squeaky prophecies.

Cassandra received from Apollo the ability to see past, present, and future as the bribe for her favors, but also reneged on her part of the deal and suffered the punishment of never being believed by anybody—not by the Trojans to whom she explained the ruse of the wooden horse, not by the Argives to whom she prophesied the death of Agamemnon. Narcissism—and Apollo's curse was to turn Cassandra into a kind of narcissist in spite of herself—leads to solipsism in the sense of one's knowing more than the self but being unable to communicate anything beyond the self.

Daphne, Apollo's first love, had played the tomboy for too long and refused to follow a man. So Cupid—a small but effective matchmaker—when insulted by Apollo for playing with a hero's weapons, responded by shooting the god with the golden arrow of pursuit and desire, the nymph with the leaden one of repulsion and flight. Apollo chased. She ran faster than the wind, but, growing weaker, slowed. Daphne begged her father for a saving transformation, and was turned, at last gasp, into a laurel tree. Even so Apollo, a sentimental egotist if ever there was one, continued to love her and made her arboreal form his emblem (Ovid, *Metamorphoses* 1.452–567).

Apollo loved the princess Coronis, but while pregnant with his son Asclepius she betrayed him for a mortal lover. When the god heard the news he killed her but saved the child, who grew up to become a great healer. Coronis' story is another version of Ariadne's original myth—a woman betrays her god-lover for a mortal—but without the cyclical happy ending, and thus with no mating and renewal of fertility; and Asclepius was destroyed by Zeus for violating the limits of mortal life when he raised a dead man. With few of his loves does Apollo succeed in procreating, in establishing his line, in finding a productive expression for his eros (he sired Aristaeus on the huntress Cyrene, and the prophet Iamos on Evadne). Gods cannot die, but they may lead very lonely, isolated lives. Apollo embodies ageless male beauty; but mortal beauty does age, and where the years take a boy Apollo cannot follow.

The God as Narcissist

At first, Freud says, all the libido is stored up in the ego—this is the state of primary narcissism. "It lasts till the ego begins to cathect the ideas of objects with libido, to transform narcissistic libido into object-libido. Throughout the whole of life the ego remains the great reservoir from which libidinal cathexes are sent out to objects and into which they are also once more withdrawn. . . . "[7] That is, when the libido is restrained by the ego, then the previously beloved object or person is established and cherished within the ego and made a permanent part of it.

Apollo made his various near-mistresses prophets and Daphne's laurel his tree, and he established festivals ostensibly in honor of lost boy-loves, but actually to glorify himself through them. Is this true, manly love? Not in Freud's sense:

> Complete object-love of the anaclitic type is, properly speaking, charac-teristic of the man. It displays the marked sexual over-estimation which is doubtless derived from the original narcissism of the child, now transferred to the sexual object. This sexual over-estimation is the origin of the peculiar state of being in love, a state suggestive of a neurotic compulsion, which is thus traceable to an impoverishment of the ego in respect of libido in favor of the love object.

The purest and truest feminine type, on the other hand, with maturity becomes more intensely narcissistic—just as, conversely, the boy grows out of his nar-cissism and into manhood. Freud continues—

> Such women love only themselves with an intensity comparable to that of the man's love for them. Nor does their need lie in the direction of loving but of being loved; and that man finds favor with them who fulfills this condition. . . . Such women have the greatest fascination for men. . . . It seems very evident that one person's narcissism has a great attraction for those others who have renounced part of their own narcissism and are seeking after object love. . . . "[8]

Thus we find children, cats, and beasts of prey charming, and we fantasize that some day they will return our love. Consider the falcon—perched for all to see, as though at a solitary café table. She (properly only the female is a falcon, one third larger than her mate the tiercel) acknowledges no protocol of give and take. Only take. Much time is spent in the sun, self-consciously grooming, doing stretching exercises preparatory to the quick stoop on a lark or a mouse. But even the tatterdemalion jackdaws seem to admire such ruthless beauty, giving her a wide berth while they afford one another no respect.

For a man, then, the woman he loves may become a kind of external superego. In the normal adult, Freud insists, childhood megalomania and ego-libido are displaced onto this ego-ideal: "To the ego-ideal is now directed the self-love which the real ego enjoyed in childhood." And this ideal is now thought to possess all perfections. "That which he projects ahead of him as his ideal is merely his substitute for the lost narcissism of his childhood—the time when he was his own ideal."[9] Both Western tradition since the Middle Ages and his own family life prejudiced Freud toward an emotional over-valuation of woman as beloved, just as they convinced him of the morphological inferiority of women as possessors of defective penises. Certainly aggressiveness and extroversion are well-established characteristics of the males of most of the world's mammals, a certain passivity and introversion of the females. But Freud—spiritual father of the structuralists—finds the antitheses of man/woman, lover/beloved, object-lover/narcissist as theoretically satisfying as he does the id/superego and Eros/Thanatos dichotomies. He thereby makes the psyche a bit too bilaterally symmetrical. Nietzsche finds the same satisfaction in setting Dionysus against Apollo.

At the risk of exaggerating the tension between male and female psychologies, we must refer again to Slater's analysis of the Greek family in mythology. The Greek mother regularly found emotional satisfaction through her son's heroic deeds; and her son was constantly trying to slay maternal monsters, and thus to win her favor as he escaped from her domination. Apollo also slew the twelve children of Niobe who had made fun of his mother Leto's infertility, and he and Artemis shot down the earth-giant Tityus who had tried to rape Leto. But he is best known for killing the python; and later he holds the Furies at bay: "Apollo's attacks on chthonic monsters thus incorporate the brittle narcissism of the Greek male in constant struggle against inundation by oral dependent longings and the dread of women. . . . Apollo's characteristics display themselves most vividly in his support of his matricidal protégés, Orestes and Alcmaeon."[10] Apollo's description in the *Eumenides* of the place where the Furies live epitomizes the male fear of castration at the hands of aggressive-females: " . . . where, by judgment given, heads are lopped and eyes gouged out, throats cut, and by the spoil of sex the glory of young boys is defeated, where mutilation lives, and stoning, and the long moan of tortured men spiked underneath the spine and stuck on pales" (185–90, trans. Lattimore).

Apollo serves his mother and then, when he gets the chance, murders mother-substitutes. Like his mother, he has no personality, no self, except in action—often through surrogates, the heroes or common citizens whom he advises. Nothing but being known by another can solidify one's sense of a self; autonomous knowledge alone cannot fabricate an autonomous identity: the narcissist therefore has the most shaky identity of all. He is particularly afraid of change, of losing his youth, of absorption (as he would put it) into another. And so he imagines he is threatened by fearsome snakes, voracious monsters, and murderous older women (like the women of Lemnos, who not only developed an overpowering body odor but murdered their husbands in bed). The narcissistic Greek god or hero finds he must after all wrestle with the snaky coils of Triton and Typhon and survive the serpentine transformations of Thetis and Proteus. Typhon, in fact, was the child of Hera and was raised by the

Python (*Homeric Hymn to Pythian Apollo* 300 ff.); in this story Hera reassumes her role as generic mother goddess and breeds a monster to oppose Zeus, because he had demonstrated his male self-sufficiency by giving birth to Athena without benefit of woman. (Hera, too, tried to produce a god by herself, Hephaestus, but he came out lame; so she resorted to what a woman can do better than a man—making monsters.) But Zeus crushed the Typhon, and Apollo came to Delphi where, after slaying the gentle nymph Telphusa for directing him away from her spring and grove, he shot the Python with an arrow—and the male strength of Helios the sun-god (sometimes identified with Apollo himself) rotted away her corpse (*Hymn to Apollo* 370–75).

Greek Homosexuality

It is time for a brief discussion of Greek homosexuality—a phenomenon that bears on Apollo's myths and on psychology's use of his myths. We can presume that the Greeks found certain sexual practices ludicrous or uncouth (masturbation, sodomy) but no such action morally repugnant in itself. The religious obstacles or socially conditioned aversions to homosexual practices which circumscribe our behavior did not, for worse or for better, obtain among them. But they were nevertheless constrained by the natural instinct to protect their sons from molestation, and they made sure their daughters enjoyed a greater or lesser degree of seclusion wherever possible—greater in fifth-century Athens, especially among the wealthy, less in seventh- or sixth-century Ionia or in Sparta at any period. Since girls were held back from the arena of daily sexual competition, boys took their place as objects of indiscreet desire, especially among the privileged leisure class. The boys were expected, as a matter of course, to flee; their would-be lovers, to pursue. A boy might encourage a worthy lover to continue his advances, in the hope of learning virtue from him and gaining prestige from his attentions. The lover, on the other hand, was expected to offer his beloved a higher education, of sorts. If all went well, the boy might grant his lover the boon of copulating with him (between his legs, K. J. Dover claims, but not penetrating him). The youth, then, may not have been expected to enjoy the sex for the sake of sex but to agree to it for the sake of promoting the didactic relationship, which was supposed eventually to mature into a desexualized friendship.[11]

The conduct of both parties was undoubtedly encouraged by the relationship between Greek mother and son (as described by Slater and referred to here and in chapter 3). And clearly such flirtatious behavior was implicated with what we call narcissistic tendencies. (An exclusive closeness with the mother is common to the background of most male narcissists.[12]) Freud recognized the narcissistic component of homosexuality:

> The boy represses his love for his mother: he puts himself in her place, identifies with her [who loves him—his ego-ideal], and takes his own person as the model in whose likeness he chooses the new objects of his love. In this way he has become a homosexual. . . . The boys whom he now loves . . . are only revivals of himself in childhood—boys whom he loves in the way in which his mother loved *him* when he was a child. He finds the objects of his love along the path of *narcissism*, as we say.[13]

Apollo seems to have played the role of the patron god of homosexuality. His statue, along with Hermes', presided over every Greek gymnasium. And in the gymnasium a youth's narcissistic preoccupation with the appearance of his body and the development of its musculature and mechanisms was promoted, prolonged, and admired. The ancient gym's lack of floor-length mirrors was more than made up for by the glittering eyes of its older patrons.

That most youthful Apollo of all those to come down to us—a Roman copy of Praxiteles' statue of the god as *sauroktonos* or "lizard slayer"—shows just such a boy as once must have broken the hearts of the elderly pederasts of Athens. Instead of the dragon of Delphi whom Apollo must slay before he takes that mountain village for the site of his oracle, we have a polka-dotted gekko lizard, such as any tourist today can spot doing open-mouthed push-ups among the ruins. And instead of a powerful athlete manfully drawing his recurve bow, Praxiteles gives us a slender, sinuous and sinew-less youth about to impale the little reptile with a hand-held arrow. *Lizard (saura)*, it turns out, can mean penis (*Palatine Anthology*, 12.3, 207, 242). Praxiteles shows us the god as he once, for a brief moment, was—luscious and cruel—before he became the unhappy, frustrated lover we know from the myths.[14] As he tormented the lizards who adored him, so, when he becomes the adorant, will he be tormented in his turn. Apollo, it seems, would have it no other way.

Orpheus

Apollo, then, loves boys and boyish women, prefers narrow and unvoracious hips. Orpheus, the legendary Thracian poet and preacher, who supposedly introduced homosexuality into Greece, may have been a priest of Apollo or of Dionysus or have attempted a reconciliation of the two cults. As a priestly or sacrificial surrogate he possesses features of both gods. Like Dionysus, he suffered dismemberment; like Apollo, he founded (or was said to have founded) a cult-practice of purification, played the lyre, loved boys, and endured a frustrating love-life. Much has been written about Orpheus and Orphism, but this is to the point here: although he mediates between Dionysus and Apollo, the Apollinian dominates his whole aspect—clean, clear-noted, long-haired, exclusionist, solipsistic. And, since he loses the one great love of his life, Eurydice, through a hamartia—a stupid mistake, his own fault—one cannot shake the impression that Orpheus too, like Apollo, is responsible for his own bad luck in love. The repetition compulsion is always the repeater's own fault; the unconscious mind has many and devious ways of exercising its will. After re-losing his lost love (snake-bitten bride) because he just *had* to look back—Hades and the other dead had warned him not to—as he led her up from the Underworld, Orpheus turned away from women and began to pursue boys. And so the women tore him apart. His is the fate that would await Apollo—if gods had fates waiting for them. Orpheus' lopped head sang a warning to all, as it floated down the river Hebrus and across the Aegean to a cave on Lesbos—that Apollo's lonely way is not for a mere mortal to follow (Apollodorus 1.3.2; Pausanias 9.30.5; Vergil, *Georgics* 4.520 ff.; and elsewhere).

Which brings us to the matter of the detachable self. When the lands around the Black Sea opened up to trade and colonization in the seventh century, the Greeks encountered cultures influenced by, if not actually based on, shamanism. The shamanistic religious experience is individual, not collective, "but it appealed," E. R. Dodds says, "to the growing individualism of an age for which the collective ecstasies of Dionysus were no longer wholly sufficient."[15] For some Greeks, then, travel proved not only broadening but psychologically deepening. The name of Apollo's mountain, Parnassos, is a pre-Greek, Asiatic word[16]; and Apollo himself came from the North or from the East or Near East—possibly from the amber country along the Baltic or from the depths of Siberia. (It behooves a sage, even a youthful one, to preserve a mysterious past.) In any case, he seems to have kept in close touch with the activities of Greek shaman-figures.

The shaman, a northern Eurasian medicine man, an uncommon and uncommonly labile individual, through a vigorous indulgence in mental and physical discipline and perhaps even a psychological change of sex, achieves the power of willingly dissociating his mind or soul from his body, traveling great distances, perhaps to several places at the same time, and returning with increased knowledge and creative powers as a poet and prophet. In short, he acquires the perquisites of a wise man.

Plato (as E. R. Dodds has shown)—drawing on examples of such semi-legendary figures as Empedocles (an old type of Greek shaman who combined the once undifferentiated functions of natural observer, creative thinker, magician, poet, philosopher, preacher, healer, and social commentator) and Orpheus—took the crucial step of identifying "the detachable 'occult' self which is the carrier of guilt-feelings and potentially divine with the rational Socratic *psyche* whose virtue is a kind of Knowledge." Plato, that is, cross-fertilized Greek rationalism with the magico-religious ideas of shamanism which he may have picked up from Pythagorean sects during his stay in Sicily.[17] For the shaman, *aretē*, virtue in the old sense of a special or almost supernatural quality or excellence, was power; but for Plato's Socrates it was knowledge that constituted *aretē*.

The ascetic life, physical discipline, psychic excursions from the body, an enhancement of one's mental skills—all contribute to a devaluation of the body and a disdain for the common life, to the development of a sense of guilt and a culture of puritanism, to the ego-idealism of the narcissist. The peers in a shame-culture who watched a warrior's performance on the battlefield have, in a guilt-culture, been transmogrified into the internal but still detached watcher whom we call conscience. But let me add that conscience, by the interposition of its commentary, puts internal thought processes into words. Style and that self-consciousness which produces style and that self-knowledge which is inseparable from self-consciousness have the same ancestor as conscience: the secret sharer who hovers over our dreaming bodies in bed. And the Greeks—Plato in particular—found the image of the shaman's soul traversing distant moonlit steppes, while his body remained sleepbound in some Siberian village or Cretan cave, a handy Ur-myth for the potential powers and immortality of the soul.

Although he is god of the ideal male body, Apollo also suffers from the shamanistic influence of puritanism, and thus all his desires are frustrated. He must present a flawless beauty to others but cannot enjoy beauty when he encounters it outside himself, in those very others whom he inspires. Indeed, one feels he made friends with Dionysus at Delphi as much for the vicarious ecstasy he might enjoy as for the sake of theological policy. So too, his metamorphosis into a dolphin and his shanghaiing of the Cretan sailors to Delphi to become his priests suggests an appropriation of the followers—human and animal—of Dionysus (*Homeric Hymn to Pythian Apollo* 388–544). In the lost Lycurgus trilogy of Aeschylus the followers of Dionysus may have clashed with the followers of Apollo, who were led by Orpheus (frr. 83, 71). And it was a satyr, Marsyas, a follower of Dionysus, whom Apollo had flayed alive for daring to compete with him on the pipes (*Metamorphoses* 6.382–400).

The Dionysian experience, which Apollo both opposes and longs for, compresses into a few moments of ecstasy a primitive and carnal form of knowledge that man, as he becomes more civilized and more intellectual, tends to forget. The Apollinian experience, on the other hand, severs man from the most basic connections with others and even destroys a relatedness to elements of himself. In need of love, but in fear of alien flesh, Apollo seeks out those who seem so much like him that no thought-disturbing adjustments are necessary; for the detached self leads a precarious existence which any too violent emotional shift might threaten. Such mirror-imaged loves as the narcissist contrives to maintain are of course doomed, for love requires the tension of daily adjustments and compromises to continue propagating itself. But Apollo, because he is a god, will survive the demise or metamorphosis of many boy- and girl-loves. Narcissus, on the contrary, will end up by destroying his very mortal self, as H. Spotnitz and P. Resnikoff put it, "because of his inability to withdraw his libidinal cathexis from the loved image to a sufficient degree so that he could seek new object relationships and survive."[18] Orpheus got himself killed for much the same reasons. All three characters are known for choosing epicene love-objects, and two of them for their prophetic and poetic gifts.

androgyny

Pale Youths

One of the trees that listened to Orpheus' song was the cypress—once upon a time not a tree, but a boy named Cyparissus, who loved a pet stag that was tame as a pampered goat, and who himself was beloved by Apollo. One summer's day at noon, that dangerous tide, Cyparissus accidentally transfixed the deer with his javelin. Having killed his love he resolved to die himself and Apollo could not dissuade him: because of the boy's weeping, the blood drained from his flesh, which then took on a greenish hue, and he became the tree that is planted around cemeteries and punctuates the buff Mediterranean landscape with its sharp black exclamation marks of grief (*Metamorphoses* 10.106–42)—the fast-growing, but short-lived, evergreen: *Cupressus sempervirens*. Apollo mourns him, while Cyparissus constantly mourns others. As in the cases of Narcissus and Orpheus, when Eros fails in its headlong rush to make new connections, to link up with another organism, Thanatos takes over and insures the individual's extinction through wasting grief or self-sought death at the hands of another.

Orpheus also sang about Hyacinthus, the next of Apollo's boys. The god and his beloved were passionately exercising one day, when Hyacinthus stepped into the way of his lover's discus throw and was hit edgewise in the face. He sank to the ground, Ovid says, like a violet or poppy or other flower, with stem broken and head drooping. As a memorial to his grief, Apollo turned the boy into a new kind of flower, one marked on its petals with the god's own lament— AI, AI (*Metamorphoses* 10.162–219).

Now, Ovid certainly enjoyed enriching his stories wherever he found too plain a narrative expanse, often with embellishments from earlier times. In Laconia the Hyakinthia were celebrated at high summer (Herodotus 9.7; Athenaeus 4.13 d–f). This festival of mourning for the withered blossoms must have originally been a pre-Greek vegetation cult (Hyakinthos is a pre-Greek name, as is Narkissos and probably Kyparessos), which Apollo took over.[19] Apollo seems to have appropriated from the earth goddess many of her cult sites and a number of her native lovers—dusky vegetation gods, all of them—whom he transformed into palely loitering eternal youths; and, in his morose way, he changed joyous peasant festivals of death and rebirth into wailing parties for noble athletes who died young.[20] (The middle day of the Hyakinthia retained the primitive features of a kermess.) The flower or tree that had once announced the young god's proud return now only memorializes the morbid grief of Apollo; the *huakinthos*, a species of iris, appears probably as a badge of the earth-goddess in Minoan-Mycenaean art.[21] A colossal statue of the god stood, for example, above the tomb of Hyakinthos aat Amyklai in Laconia (Pausanias 3.19. 1–5). Dionysus is the one vegetation god to escape this treatment, but not entirely: his grave was located and pointed out at Delphi (Philochorus, fr. 22), and a temple of Apollo's stood on the coast north of Mt. Pentelicon at a place now called Dionysus but in ancient times known as Ikaria—the site of Dionysus' first landing in Attica.

Artemis, too, had a boy-lover, albeit an anti-sexual boy. As portrayed in Euripides' play named after him, Hippolytus, son of Theseus and the Amazon queen Hippolyte, resents his illegitimacy, rejects women as the promiscuous sex (which was in fact the Greek popular belief), and seeks purity through solitary reading, vegetarianism, extreme cleanliness, and hunting with his companions in wild and unspoiled places—in other words, he tries to live like a male Artemis, which goddess he worships above all other deities. He also rejects Aphrodite—something that simply wasn't done in a polytheistic community where a man might, and should, have his favorite gods but never forget to tender some respect to all the Olympians and daimons. Hippolytus equates sex with uncleanliness and violence, since his father raped his mother; and he chooses the virgin Artemis as his surrogate mother. The uncut meadow that he fantasizes about as a place of retreat could signify a virgin's pudenda (lines 73–83). (*Leimōn* means a moist grassy place and is given a sexual twist in Euripides' *Cyclops*, at line 171.)[22]

Hippolytus' devotion to Artemis involves a kind of worship of himself as the perfect human, for whom she is the divine counterpart and mother-surrogate.[23] So too Apollo, the most Greek of the Greek gods, stands not for what his worshippers were like but for what they wanted to be like. The ego-ideal is not the self, but that against which the self judges itself. In obsessional neuroses and paranoia, Freud says, the neurotic separates himself from others by being especially clean and conscientious.[24] Apollo, the god of ritual purity, makes a fine ideal for Greeks or Europeans or Asiatics; but by identifying himself too closely with that ideal (or worse, with that ideal's sister) Hippolytus becomes a perfect narcissist.

For insulting her and neglecting her worship, Aphrodite arranged the destruction of Hippolytus. She made his step-mother Phaedra fall in love with him, make advances, commit suicide in shame when he rejected her, and, to protect her honor, leave behind a note in which she accused the boy of raping her. Theseus believed the note and called down the vengeance of his father Poseidon on Hippolytus. And so while driving along the coast road the young prince was assaulted by a bull from the sea (the same bull, perhaps, that had enjoyed Phaedra's mother Pasiphaë), who came out of the waves, startled the chariot horses, and caused the crash in which Hippolytus, as his name denotes, was "pulled apart by horses." Euripides has once again dramatized the psychic inversion, from the super-ego's supposedly rational control or even tyranny over the darker emotions to an absolute loss of power and helplessness before the seismic wave of mania that may destroy the individual from within or even rush upon him from the outside. This assault upon the protagonist from without, however, may be staged not only by dramatists but the narcissist himself, who delights—as Apollo's boys did—in his own death and finds a multitude of ways to make it seem natural.

Let us now examine the case of Narcissus, as retold by Ovid. One day in his sixteenth year, when he was out hunting, Narcissus was observed by the nymph Echo, who always repeated what she heard but could think of nothing to say on her own. When she echoed his words back to him, he called her: she called back again. Then she pursued him; but he scorned her and she withered away so that now only her flattering voice remains, which is all Narcissus wanted of her in the first place. He proceeded to torment his other admirers, both girls and boys, one of whom cursed him with the same fate that Cupid visited on Apollo (in disjunction with Daphne)—of falling in love but being unable to possess the loved one.

The heat of noontime, a clear spring hidden away and undisturbed by man or beast. Here Narcissus seeks refreshment and sees his reflection in the water: it is love at first sight, but love for the image of himself. He may as well be lusting for a picture of a statue. Longing for what he saw but could not possess, grieving and loving himself in grief, he wasted away. Even in the Underworld he continues to gaze at himself, wherever the waters of the Styx afford a smooth backwater. He, too, although never one of Apollo's boys, turned into a flower instead of a corpse (*Metamorphoses* 3.338–510).

Now Ovid was never known as a realist, but this particular episode has always seemed to depend on an excessively studied pose of the protagonist: surely

Narcissus understood the reflecting power of water? Indeed he did: "Alas! I am myself the boy I see. I know it: my own reflection does not deceive me. I am on fire for my own self. It is I who kindle the flames which I must endure. What should I do? Woo or be wooed? . . . What I desire, I have. My very plenty makes me poor." But just before dying he told himself that it wasn't so: "Where are you fleeing? Cruel creature, stay, do not desert the one who loves you. . . . " (3.463–66, 477–78, trans. Mary M. Inness). He made a daring attempt to learn something from himself, in the vain hope that the love-object which his self-love had generated might outlive himself—that he might never die but live on eternally young in the person of his image. "Know yourself" (gnōthi seauton), Apollo advised all who consulted him, but Tiresias warned Narcissus' mother that the boy would live to see old age only if he did not come to know himself (3.348: "si se non noverit"). It is though an onion were to peel itself, expecting to find at its center some determinative double-helix, but in fact exposing only a lachrymose void.

Echo-types may have been necessary in an oral culture, where most thinking was done out loud; similarly, narcissism—the adult, not the infant, variety—may be a necessary but critical stage in the development of consciousness. For most of us most of the time, Freud maintains, this organ that watches the real ego, claims to know it, measures it by the ego-ideal, and sees to it that narcissistic gratification is obtained from the ego-ideal, is conscience:[25] like Socrates' daimon it usually dissuades. Now and then it may impel one to realize his potentially greater self. But this rarefied other self which we occasionally contrive to bring into focus is for the narcissist a constant, nagging, accusing presence.

Narcissus' self-absorption strikes us as god-like—"Olympian," we call it. Indeed, Narcissus resembles Apollo in his disdain for normal connections. Although Apollo embodied the Hellenic ideal, he was still a god and the gods are all bored. Like immortal children on a perenially rainy day, they need us adults to amuse them. Divine narcissists can sit back and watch the show; from time to time they may take part, make their cameo appearances, tread on our lines, alter the scripts when the dialogue grows dull. The mortal narcissist, on the other hand, is a pure actor, never off camera. But where do the scripts come from when one plays at being god but without a god's resources of improvisation? Mailer describes the procedure: "So there are feverish and/or violent attempts to shift the given, to alter the context in which one self is forever regarding the other. It is the reason why narcissists are forever falling in and out of love, jobs, place, and addictions. Promiscuity is the happy opportunity to try out a new role. Vanity is the antidote to claustrophobia."[26] A dangerous career to pursue, particularly in the ancient world where relatively few of the universe's dangers had been legislated away and where the jealous or rejected populace had a far better chance than today to topple anyone who stood too tall. A narcissistic age does not comfortably tolerate eccentrics. The Greeks, as has been argued, were a nation of narcissists, and were even more ready to withdraw their support from whichever golden boy had claimed the spotlight than they had been to lend it. The right crowd eagerly projects its group narcissism onto a star, but finds just as much gratification in his fall from favor. The Greeks institutionalized this process and called it ostracism.

The safest route, then, for the battered narcissist, the only way finally and securely to control the external world is to fall in love with the proverbial soul-mate. Narcissus, alone by the pool except for Echo, at last sees someone who really appreciates him, the ideal other—and for whom he can therefore contrive the semblance of love. "The erotic defect of the narcissistic person," Lou Andreas-Salomé observes, "lies precisely in that his own love's outburst nearly suffices for him. It is contact enough for him with the world that he expresses his love."[27] He is grateful to his partner for providing an occasion for such expression. Thus Mailer:

> Narcissists, after all, do not hand emotion back and forth through their bodies so much as they induce emotion in one another through their minds. It is not their own flesh nor the other's which is felt so quickly as the vibrancy of their role. Their relations are at once . . . more perfect and more hollow. So it is possible that narcissism is a true disease, a biological displacement of the impulse to develop which could bear the same relation to love that . . . cancer [does] to the natural growth of tissue. . . . So to the narcissist there is always the unconscious terror that isolation, if unrelieved, must end in one arm or the other of the ultimate disease.[28]

Narcissus is little more than a shadow, and Echo the mere reflection of a voice. "Echo and Narcissus fit together perfectly," a child psychologist explains, "neither is able to initiate and sustain *dialogue*. Both are consequences. . . . Interaction proves fatal. The image dissolves."[29]

The situation that Ovid offers his Narcissus as a solution to his peculiar beauty and psychology turns out to be an ideal death. *Narcissus tazetta*, the poisonous plant into which he changed, is capable of both sexual and asexual reproduction. And, appropriately enough, the boy, when he attempted sexual connections, drove his partners to despair or suicide; but when he reproduced himself asexually, hydrophilically, he destroyed himself. The sadist changes into a masochist; the lover into a beloved other, who in turn becomes vegetable neither. Narcissus' fate, in the end, is not so different from Echo's—a case of too many possibilities, all become dead ends.

Alienation and Civilization

Narcissus can focus neither his eros nor his aggressiveness outwards. Instead he draws others into his circle of admirers and inspires them with the same self-destructive impulses that ultimately master him. In Conon's version of his story he even invited one of his suitors to commit suicide, and later killed himself in repentance.[30] Writing in *Civilization and Its Discontents* on the difference between normal object-relations and narcissism, Freud remarks that

> A portion of the [death] instinct is diverted towards the external world and comes to light as an instinct of aggressiveness and destructiveness. In this way the instinct itself could be pressed into the service of Eros, in that the organism was destroying some other thing, whether animate or inanimate, instead of destroying its own self. Conversely, any restriction of this aggressiveness directed outwards would be bound to increase the self-destruction, which is in any case proceeding.

What, in fact, happens to render the individual's primitive aggressiveness harmless to others?

> His aggressiveness is introjected, internalized; it is, in point of fact, sent back to where it came from—that is, it is directed toward his own ego. There it is taken over by a portion of the ego, which sets itself over against the rest of the ego as superego, and which now, in the form of "conscience," is ready to put into action against the ego the same harsh aggressiveness that the ego would have liked to satisfy upon other, extraneous individuals.[31]

This suppression of the individual's other instincts, carried out both by his superego and by civilization, directs his violent tendencies toward the only legitimate victim left in his sphere of influence—himself. The more advanced and civilized an individual, then, the sooner he is likely to return himself to that inanimate state whence we sprang.

The dilemma of modern man bears a resemblance to that of the Homeric hero, for whom the only worthwhile and everlasting possessions in an otherwise meaningless and transitory existence are honor in the camp or palace and glory on the battlefield—the pursuit of which is almost sure to end that brief but heroic life before its natural time. So, too, civilization—the modern, middle-class code—sets standards for the individual, the keeping of which may terminate his existence before his organism's own instinctual clock tells him that the time has come for Eros to fade, Thanatos to take over.[32] A narcissistic libido characterizes both the original state of the ego and that advanced state it might achieve under the pressures and directions of civilizations. Narcissus manages to retain his downy cheeks from the cradle to the senate chamber.

This second, or suicidal, stage of narcissism, in which Thanatos as much as Eros is aimed back at the ego, is brought about by a developed sense of guilt, which Freud related to the Oedipus complex. Whether or not one has killed or refused to kill one's father

> One is bound to feel guilty in either case, for the sense of guilt is an expression of the conflict due to ambivalence, of the eternal struggle between Eros and the instinct of destruction or death. This conflict is set going as soon as men are faced with the task of living together. So long as the community assumes no other form than that of the family, the conflict is bound to express itself in the Oedipus complex, to establish the conscience and create the first sense of guilt. ... What began in relation to the father is completed in relation to the group.[35]

This sense of guilt is the price we pay for our advances in culture—a loss of personal happiness because of our self-denial and abnegation of will before social responsibilities.

Some of us are more, some less, suited to adapting our original selves to civilization. Of those doomed to a series of petty failures in the attempt to measure up, Freud remarks: "Neurotics are that class of people naturally rebellious, with whom the pressure of cultural demands succeeds only in an apparent suppression of their instincts, one which becomes ever less and less effective. ... All who wish to reach a higher standard than their constitution will allow, fall victims to neurosis."[34] Freud insisted on incest as the root of all antisocial behavior, including murder. On the other hand, " 'Saintliness' is something based on the fact that, for the sake of the larger community, human beings have sacrificed some of their freedom to indulge in the sexual perversions. ... Thus incest is anti-social and civilization consists in a progressive renunciation of it. Contrariwise the 'superman.' "[35] While Freud's allusion to the Übermensch in connection with incest probably goes back, not to Zarathustra, but to the passages in The Birth of Tragedy discussed in connection with Oedipus in chapter 1, the matter of conscience and civilization is most fully treated by Nietzsche in The Genealogy of Morals: "I regard the bad conscience as the serious illness that man was bound to contract under the stress of that most fundamental change he ever experienced—that change which occurred when he found himself finally enclosed within the walls of society and of peace."[36]

"Custom is king," Herodotus said—by which he implied that men made social contracts in order more securely to survive the dangers that beset us all. The very rigidity and boredom which the Marxist solution programatically imposes on everyone turns out to be just as repressive of the individual in the all-too-short run as the uncertainties and dangers of the capitalist or pre-capitalist world. "Now the whole history of culture," Nietzsche notes in *The Will to Power*, "represents a diminution of this fear of chance, the uncertain, the sudden. For culture means learning to calculate, to think causally, to forestall, to believe in necessity."[37] But thinking causally imposes on us the burden of the past, as an explanation of the present. It means to have a conscience—to take a long and rational look at one's past and therefore to detach oneself from one's presently secured self. Apollo—the god of predictions, and therefore of causes; of the future, and therefore of the past—increased in importance as Greek civilization developed and as a sense of guilt became that civilization's malaise.

The old gods, the first-generation Olympians—Zeus and his brethren—and their Titanic forebears, behaved just as badly among themselves as the old Greeks did. The gods in those days were the gods that a warrior race (or, as they now appear to us since the decipherment of Linear B, a tribe of rapacious businessmen) could use. Trust Nietzsche to state the case for them with enthusiasm:

> The *Greek gods*, those reflections of noble and autocratic men, in whom *the animal* in man felt deified and did *not* lacerate, did *not* rage against itself! For the longest time these Greeks used their gods precisely so as to ward off the "bad conscience," so as to be able to rejoice in their freedom of soul. . . . In this way the gods served in those days to justify a man to a certain extent even in his wickedness, they served as the originators of evil—in those days they took upon themselves, not the punishment but, what is *nobler*, the guilt.[38]

But all that changed. With the fall of the Mycenaean palaces and, later, the rise of the city-states, the second generation of gods were taught to make themselves useful: Apollo and Athena eloquently convey to us the wise orders of their father—so we cannot confront Zeus directly and accuse him of imposing a higher standard on man than he himself met. These guiltless children of Zeus have returned the burden of guilt to man.

Apollo himself sinned against nature and acquired the guilt that comes with civilization. He took away the sanctuary of Delphi from Ge, Mother Earth (Aeschylus says she gave it to him willingly), murdered the great serpent, and changed a wilderness into a settled land (*Eumenides* 7–19). Even Apollo had to do penance for this crime against pre-conscious nature—a crime necessitated by the rise of civilization and the establishment of a secure society, and by the consciousness created when wisdom is passed from father-god to boy-god and then on to man. Nietzsche describes the process:

> All instincts that do not discharge themselves outwardly *turn inward*—this is what I call the *internalization* of man: thus it was that man first developed what was later called his 'soul.' . . . Those fearful bulwarks with which the political organization protected itself against the old instincts of freedom—punishment being among those bulwarks—brought it about that all those instincts of wild, free, prowling man turned backward against man himself. Hostility, cruelty, joy in persecuting, in attacking, in change, in destruction—all this turned against the possessors of such instincts: *that* is the origin of the 'bad conscience.'[39]

As the first to suffer the ill effects of civilization, Apollo gives advice on how to deal with them. He instructs a new or an old community how to live together and manage its collective guilt, now that divine license to prey upon our own kind has been withdrawn and nature substituted as a less than fully satisfactory victim. But while he, in one sense, represents the rise of individual consciousness through the getting of wisdom, his instructions—"worship the gods in the old ways and *restrain* yourself"—encourage the sublimation of the individual will in service to society, and ultimately lead to the death of the individual's Eros through solipsism. And he is the only Greek god I can think of who regularly communicated with his worshippers in writing; the incoherent oracular utterance of his priestess was translated into Greek verse and inscribed on a leaden tablet for the zealous inquisitor to puzzle over: thus one could contemplate one's self, or a hint about one's self, in isolated, alphabetic space. The Dionysian spirit giveth life, but the Apollinian letter killeth. Apollo becomes the god of Thanatos, of a cancerous turning of the cells back upon themselves in an attempt to avoid touching anything outside one's self.

"Repression, my crucial problem," Freud wrote to Wilhelm Fliess, "is only possible through reaction between two sexual impulses."[40] Which two impulses are at odds here in this war between the instincts and civilization? Dionysus, the god of pansexuality and the undiscriminating libido, versus Apollo, the god of less immodest impulses generated by a more fastidious Eros?

Perhaps the drive to culture, which Apollo spearheads, possesses an Eros of its own, does not simply press the separate libidos of its various members into service as an act of sublimation. Are there, to take another approach, natural restraints on both the flesh and the spirit? Might not Apollo have been there all along—*Paian*, "healer," one of his epithets, appears on the Linear B tablets—as god of innate human limits, just as each river and mountain had its proper daimon, while Hermes oversaw man-made boundaries? Jung, rather than Freud, trusted in an inborn ordering principle within each organism. Apollo worked in collusion with such a principle when he wiped the slate of each soul clean again, pulled back together the fragmented psyche of Orestes, for example, and restored his sense of skin. Typically, he prepared the way for a new wind of inspiration, after the previous season's scirocco had left the soul in tatters. But he could go only so far with this therapy.

In the last play of his *Oresteia*, the *Eumenides*, Aeschylus dramatized one solution to the problems of man's guilt and Apollo's clash with female powers. On the orders of Apollo, Orestes has killed his mother, in punishment for her murder of his father. Now the Furies, Erinyes—earth-demons with the faces of dogs and snakes for hair, who avenge the spilling of kindred blood—have come for him. Apollo has cleansed Orestes of the pollution acquired in the matricide, but, as a young male Olympian, he cannot alone oppose the wrath of ancient female powers; so he sends Orestes to Athena. Artemis really had started the trouble, by becalming Agamemnon's fleet on the way to Troy and demanding the sacrifice of Orestes' sister Iphigeneia: it was this murder that first angered Clytemnestra against her husband. Athena stands in now, as Apollo's other other-half and stops the feud. Artemis was Apollo's twin in narcissism and cruelty; but Athena matches and surpasses him in speaking the wisdom of their father Zeus. (Like Apollo and Artemis, she perseveres in an atypical sexuality: an eternal virgin, she acknowledges no mother, but sprang fully formed and armed from Zeus's forehead.)

Her solution to the crisis—for the Furies threaten to spread a cancer on the land if they are not appeased with the blood of Orestes—is to found a murder court—thereby breaking the back of the old chain of vendettas—and to placate the Furies for the loss of their prey by transforming them into Eumenides, gentle-minded ones, identified with the Semnai, fertility spirits who bless, not curse, the land and all its people's undertakings. Where the twin children of Leto could only cause trouble or fail to stop it, Athena invented a way out of the great complexions of guilt that beset Archaic man, who found his old ties to the earth and the Great Mother broken by the expansion of his inner and outer worlds, by a more sharply defined consciousness of himself as an individual, and by the new pressures of living with an emergent democracy.

The central psychological problem of civilization—faced by the Greeks in the persons of Apollo and his protégé Orestes—is how to promote communal life without stifling individual lives and all the instincts. The old answer—vengeance and the vendetta—was merely a version of the problem: the community (Troy, Argos) was always breaking down and individuals (Iphigeneia, Agamemnon, Clytemnestra) being crushed. The solution offered by Apollo at

Delphi and Athena in the trial of Orestes at Athens was to transmute personal vengeance into impersonal justice and to sublimate the old aggressive instincts (the Furies) in the promotion of fertility (the oldest expression of Eros), personified by the Semnai.

Acknowledging the female powers that be, finding a new home for them—in this case, a cave on the slopes of the Acropolis, directly above the theater where the play was being performed in the cool sunlight of a March afternoon—may not be a terribly elegant therapy, but it saved Orestes' life. The Apollinian isolation was broken and the audience was returned, via the Furies, to the care of the Mother, whence Apollo had led them several centuries before, when he took Delphi for his own.

7

The Great Mothers

The pure heaven longs to pierce the earth,
And desire seizes the earth to get her mating:
Rain, fallen from the brooding sky,
Quickens the land and she bears for us mortals
Pastures for our flocks and Demeter's life-gift—wheat.

—Aeschylus, *Danaids*

The Minoan Goddess

A MATRIARCHAL SOCIETY," C. G. Thomas explains, "can be defined as one in which women enjoy recognizable economic, social and religious privileges which, in sum, give them greater authority than men."[1] Religious icons, historical details, occasional hints of kinship bias—various aspects of female superiority—can certainly be documented, but that conclusive "in sum" eludes us for any prehistorical period. Some may find comfort in that, but all should beware of making too much of very little.[2] E. A. Butterworth claims that the women of royal houses in the Minoan-Mycenaean world were the ones who maintained the cults and dynastic connections. He sees the devotees of Ares—among whom he includes Orestes—as opponents of gynecocratic order, and concludes that as long as succession descended in the female line there was bound to be fierce rivalry for the kingship.[3] Some have even tried to connect the traces of matrilineage still to be found on islands of the Dodecanese with the society of Minoan Crete. On Leros, according to Stuart Rossiter in the *Blue Guide*, all real property descends in the female line; and on Simi all ships go to the men, all houses to the women. But, Simon Pembroke has concluded,

161

racial *individual*

"There is no single instance in which what the Greeks called the rule of women, in Greece or outside it, can be identified as a matrilineal system."[4] Minoan Crete nevertheless remains the place to look for the origins of Greek goddesses.

On the subject of every little girl's love and even worship of Mother before Father obtrudes his patriarchal presence, Freud observed "Our insight into this early pre-Oedipus phase in the little girl's development comes to us as a surprise, comparable in another field with the effect of the discovery of the Minoan-Mycenaean civilization behind that of Greece."[5] Although Freud did not develop this analogy between the phylogeny of religion and the ontogeny of the psyche, others have done so—and with good reason. Goddesses abound in the art of Minoan Crete; they appear alone or with priestesses, single or mated with a diminutive but erect and willing male consort. The first Greeks were so impressed by the dynamic beauty of these representations that they employed Minoan artisans and adopted Minoan iconography; until the decipherment of Linear B and the discovery of the names of various Greek gods on the tablets, it was even thought the Mycenaeans practiced the same goddess-oriented religion. Although the first Greeks did not give up their own gods so easily as that, the Minoan Mothers certainly influenced later Greek religion, and much of our knowledge of the early goddesses comes from an imaginative matching up of the traits of Artemis, Hera, Athena, Aphrodite, and the rest with the features of divinities represented on Cretan seal stones and frescoes and in a few pieces of jewelry and sculpture. We have hundreds of artifacts from Minoan Crete representing three main variations on the theme of goddesshood: the house goddess, the goddess of wild beasts, and the goddess of tamed nature. Their duties overlapped as did their contributions to later divinities.

The household goddess—probably the religious ancestor of Athena, mistress and protector of the citadel of Athens—is best known from a few statuettes a foot or less in height; monumental wooden goddesses may have been fashioned and worshipped, but have not survived. One, made of ivory, holds out two gold vipers, who twine down her arms and then turn back as if to nurse from her breasts. And a young lion perches birdlike on the head of a faience goddess from Knossos, who also holds up two snakes. Snakes protected the food supply from rodents in the days before Egypt shared her cats with the rest of the world; and the lion may represent the male power of the house, here reduced to suckling cubhood and dependency on the Mother of all things.

The Greek Artemis surely descends from the Minoan Mistress of beasts. Farnell describes Artemis in the earliest Greek religion as "an earth-goddess associated essentially and chiefly with the wild life and growth of the field, and with human birth." Indeed, Artemis was a kind of All-Mother. She presided over the safety of all young creatures, even human ones; a goddess of untamed places, she haunted the mountains (as opposed to the cultivated plains), both killing and conserving what was sacred to her. In Arcadia—the oldest center of her worship and an area that preserved many archaic customs and linguistic forms—her cults linked her with Demeter and Persephone. Aeschylus even called her the daughter of Demeter, that is, a double for Persephone (Herodotus 2. 156). Atlanta, huntress of the Calydonian boar, was her human counterpart.[6] (Doublings, twinnings, reversals of roles, and easy passages from divine to human status are all frequent in the fluid world of pre-dogmatic religion.)

One of the earliest types of Greek Artemis bore wings and held a lion helpless, head downwards, in each hand;[7] on a plate from Rhodes of about 600 B.C. a gorgon replaces Artemis as mistress of animals, the *potnia thērōn* who is the goddess most like a demon.[8] In just such a way did the Minoan Mistress of Animals love to pose for artists on the uberous mountaintops of Crete, where fertile plains creep far up the flanks of Dikte and Ida and their sister peaks. The goddess's affection for mountains may have to do with the prevalence of caves in Crete, in many of which crude fertility shrines were established and tended for centuries. This Minoan goddess is more Amazonian and less maternal than comparable Asiatic deities, who seem to have influenced rather the career of Aphrodite. Like the later Artemis, the Mistress of Beasts is often joined by rampant lions or huge birds; on a sealstone in the Heraklion Museum she holds her arms akimbo and permits two griffins to nurse from her breasts (no. 1657); sometimes a Master of Animals, her functional twin if not lover, takes her place; and sometimes only a pillar or tree trunk stands between the beasts, as on the triangular slab over the gateway at Mycenae.[9] Artemis' name turns up on one Linear B table (Pylos Es 605) and her brother Apollo may be *Paieon* on another (Knossos V 52).

Cults of historical times scarcely took notice of Artemis' virginity, and the oldest sense of *parthenos* was not "virginal" but "unmarried"—implying unusual fertility. Hierodules, "temple prostitutes," even served in some of her precincts. It is not difficult to connect Artemis with the later Mother of the Gods, whose cult was also popular in the religiously conservative villages of Arcadia where at a shrine by a ford of the river Alpheios two stone lions attended on her. In Crete, Farnell claims, the Greeks found a great mother goddess called Rhea, with whom they affiliated Zeus and some of the other Olympians: "in the Cretan great goddess we have the prototype of the Hellenic Mother of the Gods."[10] Apollonius of Rhodes tells of a sacrifice made by the Argonauts on Mt. Dindymum to the Mother—here, as often, identified with Rhea, the Titaness mother of Zeus: she makes the land fruit and flower, the springs to gush forth from dry rock faces, and her presence attracts the wild but wagging beasts (*Argonautica* 1.110–52). In her Phrygian form she is known as Cybele, rides across the mountains in a lion-drawn chariot, and once played nurse to the insane boy-god Dionysus. Aphrodite, too, can play Mother Nature: when she came for Anchises to Mt. Ida in the Troad, she was followed by wolves, lions, bears, and leopards; she put desire in their breasts and they mated (*Homeric Hymn to Aphrodite* 64–78).

The historical heirs to this aspect of the Minoan goddess are particularly prone to syncretism. A late example of this attracted Freud's attention. At Ephesus, Artemis took over the cult of the Asiatic mother goddess who may have been called Oupis. Artemis of the hundred breasts survived until the first century A.D. when Paul of Tarsus and the Christians suppressed her worship and ruined the trade of the pagan artisans in her service (*Acts* XIX). But John (of *Revelations*) established a cult of Mary in a basilica adjacent to the Artemision. "Now once again the city had its great goddess, and, apart from her name, there was little change."[11]

Artemis, goddess of all wild nature, retains her historical priority but yields in popularity to Demeter, whose prototype may be recognized on a series of Minoan sealstones: the goddess of tame nature who inspires worship of sacred trees and cultivated vegetation. Before a simple rustic shrine, priestesses are raptured into ecstatic choreography. Daimons carry water in elaborate libation vessels for a sacred tree growing up behind the altar or low wall. The goddess or her chief priestess pulls its fruit-laden branches toward her own generous breasts. Or else a ritual dance seems to be happening in a common field sprouting with a variety of plants. These representations of the return of life in spring must be connected with the scenes on a few other rings where the end of life, the departure of fertility, the burial of the seed, and the wilting of all *élan vital* seem to be commemorated.

The Demeter-figure has two functions: goddess of grain and goddess of birth. In later Greece Demeter and the cultivation of wheat were regarded as civilizing forces. Hunter-gatherers preserve an independence from ties and social obligations beyond the clan. In case of a dispute with their neighbors, they can always move on. But those who settle down and plough the fields and plant wheat and tend orchards must make peace with their neighbors, because crops and trees and villages constitute a permanent vulnerability. Agriculture encourages the making of treaties: according to Isocrates' *Panegyricus*, the gift of Demeter is the reason why men don't live like beasts, and thus Athens, which administers Demeter's mysteries at Eleusis, is the cradle of civilization. According to G. Zuntz, however, in his monograph on Persephone, there is little evidence outside Eleusis for the mother-goddess "as a concomitant of man's transition from hunting and food-gathering to agriculture."[12] Rather she is the divinity both of life and birthings and of death and dissolutions: with wide hips and large breasts, she is the universal Venus and the vulture-beaked or boar-tusked death-demon found in Neolithic shrines in Anatolia. (One statuette from

Çatal Hüyük shows the goddess in the act of giving birth while seated on a throne, with her feet resting on two human skulls.[13])

Zuntz exaggerates the differences between the vegetation- and the birth-goddess, both of whom promote life, both of whom need lovers who can play the role of child when the time comes. Guthrie, as always, puts it sensibly: "The same youthful, virile figure was often thought of as at once consort and son of the Mother." (These two, Mother and male, were often worshipped on mountaintops, not because they were proto-Olympians but because they were chthonians and lived in caves.[14]) Aphrodite and Eros constitute a similar set— the child lover and the mother-mistress. The divine youth, the *kouros* (and Artemis was known as *kourotrophos*, "youth-nurturer," and as "Hyakinthos-nurturer"[15]) was her child before he was her lover, and her lover before he was her twin.

The lover of the Minoan goddess is usually called an adorant, because of his salute—one hand to his breast or brow—and attentive posture. A penis-sheath or thick twist of cloth at the front of his loincloth alludes to his function in life, which seems to be a fairly simple and ancillary one rather than himself to play god of the land. But when the god becomes the goddess's twin instead of her lover, then he exercises power in his own right, as the Master of Animals. Apollo and Artemis may be the successors to this matched pair; Aphrodite and Eros to the unequal couple.[16] Traces of the prehistoric lover-adorant may survive in the figure of Pan, whom Pindar makes the companion of the Great Mother; and Dionysus sometimes sits enthroned beside Demeter (Pindar, *Pythian* 3.78; fr. 95; *Isthmian* 7.3–5).

The heroine of later myth, Ariadne, must have been in Minoan times the goddess herself or her earthly representative; her lover, then, was a Dionysus or a Theseus, or both in ritual turn. Ariadne's mother Pasiphaë is a more primitive figure; and her coupling with a bull—an action whose religious significance dropped back to lurk in the racial preconscious as the basic my-thological text was inscribed with various literary embellishments—was origi-nally a magic-ridden cult-drama, performed to promote fertility throughout Crete. Pasiphaë's other daughter, Phaedra, eventually ran off with Theseus, the same lover who had seduced and abandoned her sister; but Phaedra soon fell in love with his virile but virginal son by an Amazon queen, Hippolytus. Hippolytus never gave in to Phaedra, but she managed to ruin his reputation by claiming a rape that had never transpired: his father cursed him and the bull from the sea, left him broken, his life-force spent, his bones shattered, on the shore near Troezen. His fate is typical of those whom the goddess loves.

Her Lover

Wolfgang Helck had a theory that the paradigmatic myth of the Great Goddess is the story of her adoption of a young lover who dies prematurely because of her love. Walter Burkert suggests the source for this mythologem: Amazons who, in fact or fiction, would catch and use and then destroy young males. Amazons often served as the votaries of Cybele, Artemis, Ares, and even of Dionysus and Apollo Amazonius.[17] The dying youths whom Apollo loves and the dying lovers of the Goddess are almost indistinguishable in their epicenism and in their deaths. The mountain-mother held the cave-riddled sanctuary of Delphi until Apollo, her former lover and, as master of animals, her former twin, took it over. The lament for Linos may preserve a record of a clash between the two sets of lovers; Linos seems to have been the child-lover of the earth-goddess Urania or the embodiment of the sprouting wheat; Pausanias says Apollo murdered him out of envy of his beautiful voice (Pausanias 9.29.6–7; *Iliad* 18. 570; Herodotus 2.79).

Being the lover of the Goddess, while it required a more active libido than being Apollo's, could turn into just as dangerous a job. In one of the Homeric *Hymns*, Anchises confesses to Aphrodite that he is afraid of having slept with her (he didn't want to but she tricked him), for the man who lies with a goddess becomes no longer hale and hearty. Aphrodite tries to reassure him, but the example she cites—the love of the goddess Dawn and her consort Tithonus, whose mortality keeps him from following her down the road of eternal youth, so that now she keeps the old man locked in a room where he babbles away to himself—can hardly comfort Anchises. Then Aphrodite warns him not to mention their liaison, lest her reputation suffer (*Hymn to Aphrodite*). But of course Anchises does tell someone, and a punishing thunderbolt from Zeus cripples him for life. Compared to some others he was fortunate to escape with a limp.

Thanks mostly to Sir James Frazer's work comparing classical myths and cults with those of other archaic or primitive races, the Sumerian and Akkadian accounts of Inanna and Dumuzi (or Tammuz and Ishtar) came to provide the model myth of love-goddess and dying or damaged but eternally reborn god (Orpheus and Eurydice, Dionysus and Ariadne or Semele). They were brother and sister before they were goddess and lover. But in 1951 Frazerism received a shock when a missing section of the Sumerian account, the earliest version of the myth, was finally published and translated: Inanna, it turns out, does not go down to the nether world to bring the uxorious vegetation-god back to life; but rather, when she herself has returned from below, she kills the lively, prosperous, and unsubmissive Dumuzi by handing him over to the galla-demons as a substitute for herself.[18] The myth, then, may better explain the god's withdrawal from the land than his return. Perhaps, as the Mesopotamian people shifted from herding to agriculture, the relationship of goddess and lover changed to a more tender and mutually beneficial one: the lover, it was concluded, had to return each year if the crops were to sprout. The twice-double nature of woman—destructive or benevolent mother or mistress—manifests itself as the Sumerian myth shades into the later Akkadian version: an agricultural goddess must be kind to her lover, for she will need him again next year, and he must be just as strong as he was last sowing-season; but a goddess of war or herding or of sheer love, craving no tidy and responsible plainsman for her bed but some rough shepherd, fell hunter, or jaunty warrior, can afford to waste his life. One lover's potency quickly wanes, and she will soon find another.

The problem with the traditional, Frazerian, approach is that it presumes, as Jean-Pierre Vernant says, that every mythical figure can be defined as a discrete entity, who possesses some sort of essence, and that this essence corresponds to some reality in the natural world—and that the relationship between the figure and his appropriate part of nature is a symbolic one.[19] The relationship may, in fact, not exist at all, or else it may exist in the form of an elaborate code, not a single or simple equivalency. The myth of Tammuz and Ishtar clearly enjoys such intricacies and involutions as could drive a pious allegorist to doubt the existence of his deity or his theories. Moreover, this is not the whole story. For the full relationship of a dying god and his dangerous mother or mistress we shall have to turn to Aphrodite and Adonis and then to Cybele and Attis.

Adonis

"—Tender Adonis is dying. What is our task, Cytherea?"
"—Beat your breasts, Maidens, tear your frocks."

Thus Sappho; and thus

"O Adonis of the four-month span!"

They are not much, but these lines are Adonis' earliest appearance in Greek literature. His full story, unfortunately, was recorded only much later: Apollodorus tells us that while yet a boy Adonis fell afoul of Artemis and was killed by a boar. In another version, the Assyrian princess Smyrna fell in love with her own father; he tried to kill her before she consummated her passion, and she was mercifully metamorphosed into a myrrh tree. Ten months later the tree split open and Adonis was born. But Persephone got hold of him and wouldn't give his back. Zeus had to arbitrate: Persephone could enjoy the child for a third of the year; Aphrodite for a third; and for a third he could have himself to himself (Apollodorus 3.14.4; Hyginus, *Astronomica* 2. 6; scholiast to Theocritus, *Idyll* 3.48).

What has become the canonical account of Venus and Adonis is found in Ovid's *Metamorphoses*, where Myrrha managed anonymously to accomplish her incestuous passion but was forced into exile when her father found out whom he had slept with. After transforming into a myrrh tree, she bore the infant Adonis from her distended trunk. Venus, having accidentally scratched herself on an arrow protruding from Cupid's quiver, lusted for the youth, who without delay became her lover. She warned him to hunt only harmless beasts; he ignored the warning; a boar gored him in the groin. The spring anemones, their petals rhyming red with his blood, commemorate the death of Adonis (*Metamorphoses* 10.519–59, 708–27). Other suggest that Venus' lover Mars (Ares) sent the boar, or that Venus herself plotted Adonis' death after she had drained him. These late accounts may be calculated to bring Adonis' story into line with that of other dying gods who flourished as western civilization turned the corner from paganism to Christianity. Although the myth may be late, the cult is marked by the cyclical features of the old vegetation paradigm. Theocritus records or composes a dirge for Adonis at the yearly festival for him, held in Alexandria at the palace of Ptolemy II. The song describes the scene of the festival and how the statues of Adonis and Aphrodite were laid side by side in a marriage bed; it ends with a prediction of the actual dirge to be sung the next day, at the funeral of Adonis which will follow this wedding. And, the song paradoxically concludes, no one can return from death but Adonis *will* come again next year.

The Adonia was no mystery cult, initiation into which would bestow on the adept assurance of rebirth into the afterlife. Rather, the festival celebrated the cycle of mating and death and attested to the obvious: this cycle will be repeated in due time. Both the cult and the myth suggest that the temporal sequence—of mating with the love-goddess and death of the lover—is also a logical sequence: she deliberately or accidentally causes his death. The Adonia were celebrated at the hottest time of the year, when, as Jean-Pierre Vernant and Marcel Detienne claim, the erotic scents in herbs and spices were at their highest and the weather encouraged sexual license.[20] Hot summer days also encouraged our weary hunters of chapter 4 to seek a bosky sanctuary from the heat of noontime; where they too were rendered vulnerable to the dangers of sensuality, to the arrows of Artemis or the embraces of the nymphs, and where they suffered death or metamorphosis.

Cybele and Attis

In the story of Cybele and Attis, Zeus had a wet dream on Mt. Dindymus; from the damp earth and semen an hermaphrodite arose, whom the other gods castrated out of disgust. The mutilated creature grew to be Agdistis, Cybele; an almond tree sprouted from the severed genitals. A maiden, Nana, caught one of the almond nuts in her lap at harvest-time, got pregnant from it, and exposed the offspring, Attis, who was raised by a she-goat. When the boy grew up, Agdistis/Cybele, still his grandmother, fell in love with him, but by then he was betrothed to another. So she drove him mad and he castrated himself; in another version he was killed by a boar (Pausanias 7.17.9–12). After his mutilation he may have metamorphosed into a pine tree; and the cut pine came to be revered in the cult practices of Cybele late in the Roman period, when Attis himself tended to resemble another dying god, Mithras.

Edith Weigert-Vowinkel offers an orthodox Freudian interpretation of the story: "The mythology of Attis describes a manic-depressive individual, unable to free himself of his one-sided mother fixation. . . . Attis is a beautiful, narcissistic youth, who hardly attains the maturity of a genital love relationship. It is his fate to be one of those who 'die when they love.' He is the spoiled darling of the Great Mother. He himself does not love others, he only allows them to love him." Because he wants to remain a child, he fears the passion of a union and the subsequent separation; in fact, he hates his own procreative ability. In order to turn passionate womankind back into tender mother, Attis and his followers castrate themselves.[21] But Weigert-Vowinkel misses a major point: Attis, like many other figures we have met in the myths, must sever all connections because he cannot make the erotic connection; his castration is not the enactment of a primal fear but the next worst thing to suicide: Eros has once again submitted to Thanatos.

Jung, on the other hand, turns the Freudian interpretation inside-out. The self-castration of Attis is not a move in the grand strategy of keeping mother for himself and himself for mother, but rather inevitably occurs when the regression libido activates parental imagos and elects to reestablish the infantile relationship with the female instead of continuing to develop and mature. Since the former childish affection cannot be reconstituted—because of the presence

of the son's adult sexuality (a form of which Freud, unlike Jung, would claim
was present even in the infantile relationship)—the offending organs must be
removed, or else the son-lover must die. The son personifies the longing for
the mother which exists in the psyche of every individual who finds himself in
a similar situation. The mother personifies the (incestuous) love for the son.
The tree personifies the mother on the one hand and the phallus of the son on
the other. The phallus in its turn stands for the son's libido. The ritual felling
of a pine—castration—denotes the sacrifice of this libido, which seeks something that is as incongruous as it is impossible. The myth, therefore, depicts
through the arrangement and nature of the protagonists, the typical fate of a
libido regression that is played out mainly in the unconscious.[22] Indeed, Attis
wants to remain an eternal boy, a *puer aeternus*.

Marie-Louise von Franz thinks Attis tried but failed to escape from his
puerility:

> When Attis got interested in a nymph and was no longer interested in the
> mother-goddess, she jealously drove him into madness so that he castrated
> himself. . . . We could say that it was the aggressive animus of the mother
> goddess which killed or castrated the young god. . . . He has grown out of
> the tree; that is, his life comes only from his mother complex, or from his
> connectedness with the collective unconscious, and he is no living system
> in himself. . . . The *puer aeternus* and the tree symbol belong together.
> The tree fixates him, fastens him to earth, either in a coffin, or in life.[23]

Leon Balter, although a Freudian, finds a rather Jungian connection
between Attis and Oedipus: in both, the patriarchal forces revolt against the
matriarchal; after the matriarchal powers win, Oedipus resigns his kingship
and turns it over to a representative of matriarchy (Creon, the brother of Jocasta),
castrates himself (the self-blinding), and like the Galli, the priests of Cybele,
wanders the earth as a devotee of the Great Mother.[24]

Whereas Jung dragoons Attis into the numinous service of the archetypes,
the Roman poet Catullus encourages the myth to carry the weight of his own
passionate love for Clodia Pulcher, the "Lesbia" of his lyric cycle (poem 63).
Catullus' Attis, while showing traces of the syncretism that affected most deities
whose myths were not attenuated in the service of imperial propaganda, retains
the intensity of an earthly love. Catullus has written one of the fiercest ancient
poems to survive. Attis, driven mad, castrates himself and encourages *her*
Gallae (*his*, no longer) to revel in the worship of Cybele; then he sleeps the
sleep of the spent, and awakens to regret the actions of an alien self. Hearing
of his apostasy, Cybele looses one of her chariot lions to hunt out the skulking

to ward off evil

eunuch and drive him permanently mad. The lion catches him helpless on the shore and pursues him back into the woods; he will finish out his life as a slave of the goddess. Catullus ends the poem with an apotropaic prayer of his own—

> Dea, magna dea, Cybebe, dea domina Dindymi,
> procul a mea tuos sit furor omnis, era, domo:
> alios age incitatos, alios age rabidos.
>
> (Quinn's edition)
>
> Goddess, great goddess, Cybele, goddess mistress of Mt. Dindymus,
> Far from my house, Lady, may all your rage be;
> Drive others headlong, drive others raging mad.

Cybele here takes the emotional valence of *la belle dame sans merci* of romantic love, the heartless beloved relished by poetasters but here eschewed by the ironically cautious Roman.

consumptone

Robert Graves

To elude or foreswear the iridescent charms of the Goddess does not necessarily bespeak a costive nature, merely one that intends to live a little longer—his losses, not his genitals, cut. Robert Graves, however, has repeatedly asserted the opposite opinion.

> There is one story and one story only
> That will prove worth your telling,
> Whether as learned bard or gifted child. . . .

And he has put his logical prose where his poetic intuition is, arguing in *The White Goddess* and numerous essays that all *true* poetry (this is a *moral* matter) concerns itself with the career of the God of the Waning Year, his love for the White Goddess—she of the ice-blue eyes and flaxen hair, the hooked nose and rowanberry lips, whose brief love is bliss but whose embrace is death—and with his waning powers and doomed struggle with a "blood-brother, his other self, his weird," who will soon replace him in the arms of she who never changes, She-who-must-be-obeyed. This myth not only constitutes the only possible *gradus ad Parnassum*, according to Graves, but also (like a Jungian archetype) the ultimate ground of reality. Randall Jarrell's "Robert Graves and the White Goddess" is a sympathetic but still critical psychopoetical analysis of Graves' theories and his work in the light of his early family life and first marriage. Far from reducing Graves' world picture to a neurotic symptom— "an ordinary wish fantasy reinforced with extraordinary erudition"—Jarrell calls it "the fantastic theory that has accompanied a marvellous practice: some of the best poems of our time have been written as a result of this (I think it is fair to say) objectively grotesque account of reality."[25]

Fairly late in his career Graves discovered another character in his world myth and another stage in the true poet's life cycle: the Black Goddess, who has managed to combine the erotic *coup de foudre* of the White Goddess with a mother's enduring love, and her eventual theophany to the poet who has endured many deaths at the hands of her various sisters (all of them named Blanche). Whether this is another wish-fulfillment or Graves actually has encountered a lady who, having put aside her fickleness, still remains exciting for him, is not for us to speculate on. His Black Goddess, however, is *sui generis* in the world's mythologies: the best the classical myths have to offer—after the worst of Artemis and Cybele and Aphrodite—is Demeter.

Demeter

Demeter's story is preserved, in relatively consistent form, in the Homeric *Hymn* and in Ovid's *Metamorphoses* (5. 341–571), and in many other sources as well. Hades (also known as Pluto, or "Rich"—rich in souls and in fertile earth, since the chthonian powers command both the deep underground and the topsoil) carried off Persephone, the daughter of Demeter and Zeus, to be his bride and queen. But the aggrieved mother abandoned the rest of the gods and wandered among men. She blighted the earth and kept all seeds from sprouting. Zeus agreed to annul Persephone's marriage, but the naive girl had irreversibly consummated her move to the Underworld by eating a few pomegranate seeds. Even though she was restored to her mother and the upper world (where she is known as Kore, the eternal girl), she must return to Hades for a third of each year. There she becomes Persephone. (The abductions of Ariadne and Helen are variations of this mythologem.)

During her self-imposed exile from Olympus, Demeter came to the town of Eleusis, once the site of a Mycenaean great hall but a dependency of Athens in the fifth century and later. In disguise as an old woman, she was befriended by the daughters of the King and Queen. She told them a tale about how she was carried off from Crete by pirates, and she managed to get herself hired as a nurse to the baby, Prince Demophoön. Every night she would anoint him with ambrosia and lay him in the fire, burning away his mortality—until the Queen caught her in the act. ("Demeter," Kerenyi points out "treats Demophoön as though he were grain."[26]) But after the rescue of Kore-Persephone had been seen to, Demeter returned to Eleusis and established her mysteries as a gift to the people for their hospitality, and taught them agriculture.

Mysticism, according to Diodorus Siculus who probably relied on a prejudiced source, had its chief stronghold in Crete, whence the Eleusinian mysteries and other such rites were derived; on Crete these rites were performed openly, for everyone, and the gods there, especially Demeter, went out to the rest of the world as benefactors of mankind (5.77.3ff). We can identify Demeter or her prototype on a number of Minoan seal rings, illustrated in Axel Persson's *The Religion of Greece in Prehistoric Times*. Late in the Minoan period she manifests herself in the crude, blockish terracottas crowned by roosting doves or slit opium poppies. (Kerenyi suggests that as Minoan society decayed drugs became necessary to induce visions previously procurable by fasting alone.[27])

Demeter, formerly the Minoan goddess of cultivated nature, turned up at Eleusis. Her mysteries proved so successful that they remained mysterious from the mists of the Bronze Age, through the dry clear light of the classical enlightenment, until the Christian era when the cult was suppressed as undesirable competition for the new, official religion of the Roman Empire.

We do know a few details. Each initiand or *mystēs*, sacrificed a pig to Demeter, pigs being popular with the chthonian powers. Kerenyi suggests the animal stood in for the initiand when the knife fell and, by dying for him, enabled him (or her) to understand what lay beyond death. He also calls the pig a uterine animal of the earth, as the dolphin (*delphis*) is of the sea; a fragment of Epicharmus records the odd fact that a pig dedicated at the Elusinia was known as *delphax* (fr. 100);[28] Apollo's prophetic madness and Demeter's ritual madness both originate in womb-like sanctuaries. The man who emerged from Apollo's inner sanctum into the southern light of Delphi was intellectually renewed; the *mystēs* from Demeter's *telestērion* ("chamber of mysteries") found himself emotionally reborn.

Like the fertility aspect of Dionysus, Demeter's purview extends even into the tomb. Athenians sowed wheat over graves and called the dead *demetreioi* (Cicero, *De legibus* 2.63, from Demetrius of Phaleron; Plutarch, *De facie in orbe lunae* 943b). The jar (*pithos*) that might be used as a coffin also held grain. Demeter sustains and even embodies every man's hope of life after death, because her grain sprouts from parched seeds and because her daughter returned from Hades. A distinction should be noted between the descent of a god or goddess to the underworld and that of a human being; the divinity's job is the renewal of the earth's fertility, the man or woman's is the getting of a wisdom useful in confounding the Worm of Death. The Eleusinian descent of the initiands both commemorates the journey of Persephone (and thus magically ensures the actual fertility of the fields) and bestows a preternatural sagacity on the voyagers. [29]

Nilsson insisted that Kore's term as Persephone, the spell she spent below ground, stretched from the June threshing to the October planting, when the removal of the seed corn from underground silos was her *anodos*, or ascension to earth. The mysteries, which coincided with the planting, celebrated the joyful reunion of Corn Maiden with Corn Mother. The winter rains drew the Maiden further up out of the ground, helped her to mature into a mother herself, and the hot sun of June dried her into a crone, fit to be buried for three months as the last part of the cycle rolled around again: Kore, Demeter, and Hecate/ Persephone make up the three stages of womanhood. Others, like N. J. Richardson, are certain the absence of Kore corresponded to the winter, her return to the spring. [30]

In Vernant and Detienne's reconstruction of the Greek mythological-agrarian code, the cereals are situated in a realm midway between the two sorts of undomesticated and threatening vegetation: the antithetical territories dominated by the dank plants of death and those herbs and spices which exhale the hot breath of sensuality. Cereals, on the middle hand, require a proper, well-regulated society for their cultivation. So too marriage, a form of ploughing, mediates between wild sexual activity and death. The wife is the fertile field, and, when she marries, must rid herself of the wild character of the female— of both the coldness of Artemis and the excessive enthusiasm of Aphrodite. [31]

Whose job was it to plough this goddess of cultivated vegetation? And what was his connection with her daughter? Zeus lay with Demeter, and so did Poseidon, but neither was her mate—a complex role which shifted with the seasons. Nilsson insisted there were no Dionysiac elements in the Eleusinian mysteries until the fifth and fourth centuries when various cults got mixed up with one another. (Euripides hymns Demeter, Dionysus, and Cybele all in one long breath—*Helen* 1301–68.) But Iacchus, a kind of Dionysus figure, was included in the Eleusinian procession and acted as the leader of the *thiasos* of initiands and therefore as the mate of Demeter. [32]

Demeter the corn-goddess *(wheat-goddess)*, Persephone her daughter, and a boy Triptolemus (or Demophoön or Iasion or Iacchus or Plutus or Dionysus) make a trio that goes way back. Alan Wace suggested the ivory trio from Mycenae represent Demeter, Kore, and Iacchus; the somewhat later terracottas from Mycenaean tombs, also of two goddesses with a child, may commemorate the same trio. [33] And Demeter's name was found on one of the Pylos Linear B tablets (PY En 609). At Thelpusa, in Arcadia where cults of great antiquity were preserved, over-life-sized statues of Demeter, Kore, and Dionysus stood together (Pausanias 8.25.3).

The diminutive size of the adorant-lover on Minoan seal rings suggests the mixture of maternal with conjugal affection that characterizes Demeter's relationship with her males. Demeter bore a child by the hero Iasion, after they had lain together in a Cretan field, who was called Ploutos, or Plutus (Hesiod, *Theogony* 969–71). Hades, Persephone's lover, was also a Ploutos—the same one? On a late hydria found on Rhodes, Kore, Demeter, and Triptolemus (prince of Eleusis and the patron hero of agriculture) receive a male child seated in a cornucopia held by a woman partially emerged from the ground—is he the young Ploutos too? And on a cup in the British Museum Dionysus may appear as the ravisher of Kore.[34] What scholars have interpreted as syncretism—the melding of one deity into another with the passing of time and the shifting of religious needs and political borders—may in fact be an eternal set of changes rung across the centuries on the twinned themes of mother and daughter and their common son and lover. The destructive goddess of the wild, who took a herdsman or hunter to her bed, seldom had time or inclination to mother him or their offspring. But the goddess of the protected grainfield cannot separate the activities of mother and mistress—so quickly do the seasons change, so demanding is the subtle shift of her role. She inevitably marries her son, although sometimes, in the person of her daughter, she has to contrive an elopement. "At this level," Jung wrote in *Aion*, "the mother is both old and young, Demeter and Persephone, and the son is spouse and suckling rolled into one. . . . Every mother and every beloved is forced to become the carrier and embodiment of this omnipresent and ageless image, which corresponds to the deepest reality in a man. It belongs to him, this perilous image of Woman; she stands for the loyalty which in the interests of life he must sometimes forego."[35] By "the interest of life" Jung meant the development of the soul, of consciousness. No matter how good the Good Mother may be, the son must inevitably find her tendance smothering, and so he must vilify her image if not actually kill her.

Hatred of the Mother

What intellectual explanations have been given for this moral prejudice against women and a concomitant emotional excuse-making for them? In the *Generation of Animals* Aristotle claims that females were a natural deformity (*anapērian einai tēn thēlutēta phusikēn*), but he cleverly explains that more males happen to be born deformed because males move around more than females in the womb and thus get broken up (775 a). In the *Politics* he repeats this argument and elaborates on it: "the male is by nature superior and the female inferior, the male ruler and the female subject." This, he alleges, is because the soul and the intellect of the male have managed to tame the lower appetites more thoroughly than in the case of women (1254 b, trans. H. Rackam). Aristotle is not arguing a point the average Greek would have disagreed with.

Similarly for Nietzsche, woman is a more instinctual creature than man, more a victim of physiology and possessed of a lower order of consciousness. Women acquire and express what strength they have by making men feel guilty for women's weakness. Nietzsche shares with the Greeks the opinion that woman is less reliable, more labile than man. But, failing to notice that man is more romantic, more prone to project his illusions onto his personal landscape than woman is, he concludes that the difference between the sexes can only be attributed to the woman's potential for conception: "Everything about woman is a riddle, and everything about woman has one solution: it is called pregnancy." "The females find in their children satisfaction for their desire to dominate." "In a woman's love is injustice and blindness towards all that she does not love. And in the enlightened love of a woman, too, there is still the unexpected attack and lightning and night, along with the light. . . . Women are still cats and birds. Or, at best, cows."[36]

Freud, similarly, faced with the enigma of the complementarity but contrarity of the two sexes, was reduced to expressing himself in clichés: "For distinguishing between male and female in mental life we make use of what is obviously an inadequate empirical and conventional equation: we call everything that is strong and active male, and everything that is weak and passive female." From this presupposition it is only a short step for Freud to reach the same conclusion that Aristotle and Nietzsche drew: "I cannot escape the notion (though I hesitate to give it expression) that for women the level of what is ethically normal is different from what it is in men. Their super-ego is never so inexorable, so impersonal, so independent of its emotional origins as we require it to be in men." And in one of his last works, *New Introductory Lectures*, he insists that women have less ability to sublimate their instincts than men: "women must be regarded as having little sense of justice."[37] The intellectual excuse for this view of women was, in Freud's case, supplied by the Electra complex. One could, however, claim that all such prejudiced views of woman derive from man's conviction that women are the victims of their glands. Ignoring his own glands, Simone de Beauvoir argues, man thinks of woman's body as a hindrance, a prison, but his own "as a direct and normal connection with the world."[38]

Freud understood men better than he did women. He could explain the appearance of father-gods, whose priority he presumed on, but mother-goddesses seem hardly to have piqued his curiosity.[39] Our parents, he argued, are our first love-objects and they influence our later selection of love partners, for better or worse. Although marriage and child-bearing may revive a woman's identification of herself with her mother, the male in her life remains paramount. For Freud, as for the Greeks in Slater's reconstruction of their society, a daughter falls short of being a son. Indeed "A mother is only brought unlimited satisfaction by her relation to a son; this is altogether the most perfect, the most free from ambivalence of all human relationships. A mother can transfer to her son the ambition which she has been obliged to suppress in herself."[40]

Because he understood woman principally in terms of her feelings about and relations with men, she remained a benignly mysterious creature for Freud. When pressed to suggest what discoveries or inventions women have contributed to civilization, he specified the techniques of plaiting and weaving—the model for which Mother Nature herself supplies in the pubic hair concealing the female genitals. That anything dreadful or dangerous could be entwined in or lurk behind such a contrivance or natural screen—the Jungian fuss about monsters and their caves—seems not to have occurred to Freud. Indeed, he extended the love that obtains between mother and son to male-female relations in general. Although the son may wish to devour whole the mother who feeds him, he (and only he, never the daughter) fears being eaten by his father—as Zeus and his brethren were eaten by Cronus. This love of the son for his mother educes from him a devotion that inevitably brings him into conflict with his arch-rival, his father. While a woman may arouse a young man's fear of castration, it is always another (often older) man, his rival, who would carry out the mutilation—never the woman herself. This series of male-female attachments and male-male rivalries was intensified as civilization developed and is commemorated in classical mythology:

> The introduction of agriculture increased the son's importance in the patriarchal family. He ventured upon new demonstrations of his incestuous libido, which found symbolic satisfaction in his cultivation of Mother Earth. Divine figures such as Attis, Adonis and Tammuz emerged, spirits of vegetation and at the same time youthful divinities enjoying the favours of mother goddesses and committing incest with their mother in defiance of their father. But the sense of guilt, which was not allayed by these creations, found expression in myths which granted only short lives to these youthful favorites of the mother-goddesses and decreed their punishment by emasculation or by the wrath of the father in the form of an animal.[41]

A standard Freudian interpretation of Orestes' legend, then—such as Richard Caldwell has elaborated—makes him emulate Oedipus' career: the

four major episodes of the myth of the house of Atreus contain miniature
Oedipal dramas "in each of which the desired woman is won from her husband
or father by a hero who is then punished for his deed," by some form of castration. Caldwell's interpretation finds the desired paradigm, or erects it, everywhere. If incest, patricide, and castration are not apparent, we can claim
displacement, concealment, diachronic repetition, almost anything we want,
to conjure the desired motif. In support of his argumentation Caldwell cites
Derrida: "It is obvious that, if by *mother* one understands *real mother*, the
Oedipus complex no longer has any meaning."[42] Granted a few suggestions of
the incest theme can be detected in the ancient evidence. In the *Libation
Bearers*, for example, Clytemnestra begs Orestes not to kill her: "I raised you;
I want to grow old with you." But Orestes rejects this: "May such a woman not
become my housemate" (908, 1005–06). And in Sophocles' *Electra* the girl
seems to be fixated more on Orestes than on Agamemnon—she was, in fact,
her brother's nurse (*passim*, especially 1143 ff. and 1232); but does this constitute a case for an incest-wish displaced from the father onto the brother? In
the account of Orestes' trial inscribed on the *Marmor Parium* (a chronicle of
various historical, literary and mythological events), he is charged only with
killing the father of Erigone, the daughter of Aegisthus and Clytemnestra, the
girl he may eventually have married (Apollodorus 6.25–28); Caldwell claims
the patricide was displaced from Agamemnon to Aegisthus and the incest from
Clytemnestra to her daughter.[43] This is to read Aeschylus' trilogy through an
isolated inscription and to use the resultant interpretation to support
an ideology.

Slater goes further than Freud and Caldwell in this vein, even verging on
a Jungian interpretation of the myth of Orestes. He seems to suggest that castration is an attempt to deal with fear of the female by avoiding sexual conflict—
like getting out of the army by shooting oneself in the foot—and that this is
how we should interpret an account of Orestes' biting off a finger to placate the
Furies (Pausanias 8.34.1–3). But to kill one's mother is a far more serious and
guilt-producing business than to kill a monster: the monster represents only
the Bad Mother, or the oral-narcissistic conflict itself, but one's real mother
bodies forth the totality of Motherhood, even if she didn't nurse you: try to
burke her good side and the bad will be sure to haunt you, even to drive you
to self-castration. Orestes prefers the unproblematic company of virgins—Athena, Electra, Iphigeneia—to that of real women. Slater even argues that the
representation of Zeus as a dominant, sexually potent chief god is an attempt
to counteract Greek fears of the adult female by creating an impregnable male;
but Zeus's façade displays many cracks before the battering onslaught of the
maternal goddesses.[44] Perhaps even the Hesiodic portrait of the devouring
Kronos was meant, by displacement, to ease the fear of the devouring mother.

Orestes never actually castrated himself, but Attis did. Ernest Jones saw in the Attis myths a denial of procreative fatherhood and a tendency to avoid the father's rivalry in an oedipal conflict. (Freud and the original Freudians consistently downplay the fearfulness of the female.) And Reik describes the sufferings of the son-god as a penance for the murder of the father and claimed that initiation customs, by reenacting this murder and penance, free the child from his mother so that he can form homosexual ties with his coevals and thus become a useful member of the community.[45]

J. Friedman and S. Gassel have Orestes perform for the community a hygienic function similar to the one postulated by Reik. They more or less concentrate on Euripides' version but shift the Freudian values attributed to each of the players: Aegisthus is the one who has committed the same crimes as Oedipus—killing the father-king, sleeping with the queen mother; Electra is Orestes' good mother, Clytemnestra the bad mother; Orestes thus can direct his incestuous wishes toward his sister, and when Euripides betroths her to Pylades, the playwright achieves "a triangular relationship consummating Orestes' desired relationship with them both." By slaying the Oedipus figure (Aegisthus), Orestes denies his own oedipal wishes, and the community has created an Orestes to rid itself of its own mother attachment and throw off the guilt of its oedipal wishes.[46]

If Orestes submitted himself to any puberty rite, it was one that Apollo set for him. Sartre, in *The Flies*, suggests something like this by making the Argive hero almost a double for the Delphic god. Both, Sartre lets us know, have domineering, none-too-moral fathers; both kill their mothers (Apollo kills the dragon of Mother Earth); both have to be cleansed and do penance for the murders; both are about eighteen, or at least look eighteen; and Apollo's father, Zeus, plays father-substitute to Orestes (as Zeus said he did to Telemachus, by taking on the appearance of Mentor.)[47] The murder of the father-king, however, is the original sin of Sartre's Argives, the reason for their penitent, even craven attitude; whereas after the murder of his mother, his *rite de passage*, Orestes abrogates social responsibility—a share in the common pool of guilt—and elects to suffer the Furies' vengeance. Thus Sartre presents Orestes as a loner who rebels against Nature for the sake not so much of Nietzschean consciousness but of existentialist freedom. Sartre, I suppose, would have argued that freedom presupposes consciousness, even though some existentialist heroes wind up living out anesthetized lives.

Herbert Fingarette, in his analysis of the Orestes legend, creates a hero who sounds like Oedipus after therapy has curtailed his complexes.

Oedipus and Orestes represent, psychologically, one individual: Oedipus is the individual as he moves *into* the central growth crisis; Orestes is the individual as he moves out of it. Oedipus exhibits man's psychic bondage, the "acts" in which are the roots of his damnation; Orestes exhibits the man's liberation, the task whose fruits are salvation and harmony.

Clytemnestra is thus reduced to serving as a catalyst: she takes the role normally assumed by the father and threatens the boy with castration (either with her axe or through her Furies), and then she takes the boy's role and kills the father for him. "The father," in other words, "now speaks through the son, and the latter, in turn, becomes the legitimate heir. In psychoanalytic language: the son identifies with the father, his former rival, and the introjected image of the father becomes the love of the boy's superego." Although Fingarette shifts the Freudian furniture around considerably, he concurs with the orthodox devaluation of the mother, who in his construction becomes only an antagonist for the youth to test his psychic mettle on—not yet or no longer a character in her own soulful right.[48]

The Great Mother

Jung considered women, or at least a certain sort of woman, worth more attention than Freud gave them. Freud's world, his step-son insisted, was patriarchal; Jung approvingly noted that it was the Catholic Church—not the Jewish faith nor the Protestant churches—which finally made room in the divine bridal chamber for the Mother of God.[49]

The mother, begins Jung uncontroversially, always plays an active part in the origin of the neurotic disturbances, "especially in infantile neuroses or in neuroses whose aetiology undoubtedly dates back to early childhood." But unlike Freud, the archaeologist of the soul who turned his attention to unearthing the past because in its strata are to be found the fragmentary antecedents of our present behavior, Jung, rather like an astronomer of the soul, gazes into the galactic cloud of unknowing and contemplates the archetypes constellated there by our terrestrial neuroses. The disturbed instincts of the child arouse the archetypes, "which in their turn, produce fantasies that come between the child and its mother as an alien and frightening element." For a male, the mother-complex cannot appear in pure form, and so, "in every masculine mother-complex, side by side with the mother-archetype, a significant role is played by the image of the man's sexual counterpart, the anima."[50] Nietzsche puts it this way: "Everyone carries in himself an image of woman derived from the mother; by this he is determined to revere women generally, or to hold them in low esteem, or to be generally indifferent to them."[51]

In the daughter, however, Jung insists, "the mother-complex is clear and uncomplicated," for better or worse: it may lead "either to a hypertrophy of the feminine side or to its atrophy." The girl with an overdeveloped feminine side may become a baby-making machine or a carefree seductress, or she may identify herself so closely with her mother that she fails to understand men at all and any man becomes an abductor—"This was how Pluto abducted Persephone from the inconsolable Demeter. But of course Demeter got her daughter back for long visits each year."[52]

Jung not only used the myths as examples or illustrations of his analyses, but suggested that mythology itself constituted the language most appropriate for describing the archetypes: "Myth is the primordial language natural to these psychic processes, and no intellectual formulation comes anywhere *near* the richness and expressiveness of mythical imagery. Such processes deal with the primordial images, and these are best and most succinctly reproduced by figurative speech."[53] In *The Great Mother* Erich Neumann sets out "to describe the structure of the archetype of the Great Mother or the Feminine on the basis of numerous reproductions of art works. . . . However, the true object of our inquiry is the symbolic self-representation of the archetype that has passed through the medium of man."[54] While the structuralist asks what a thought thinks, Neumann asks how the Mother shows herself in the art, literature, myths, and dreams of mankind.

Neumann proceeds on the assumption that individual women are all occasional appearances of the essential Great One. Nor can we afford to neglect any features of those appearances: the Great Goddess is the symbol of creative life, so her display of her various aspects, in the mythic images of the ages, is a divine epiphany of herself. From a study of these appearances, of these parts, we see that the central but ambiguous symbol of the Feminine is the vessel. In contrast to the fertile womb or the protecting cave—

> . . . gapes the abyss of hell, the dark hole of the depths, the devouring womb of the grave and of death, of darkness without light, of nothingness. For this woman who generates life and all living things on earth is the same who takes them back into herself, who pursues her victims and captures them with snare and net. . . . This Terrible Mother is the hungry earth, which devours its own children . . . the tiger and the vulture . . . the flesh-eating sarcophagus.[55]

This, and very little more, is all the analysis Neumann offers us in 354 pages of text.

The problem with Neumann's approach in *The Great Mother* may have something to do with the passivity of his chosen subject. Most of what Neumann had to say on the subject of the archetypal feminine he put into his earlier *The Origins and History of Consciousness*, where he discusses the hero's relationship to the mother-principle and the mother's role in the hero's career. He returns to this subject briefly in *The Great Mother*: "the dialectical relation of consciousness to the unconscious takes the symbolic, mythological form of a struggle between the Maternal-Feminine and the male child, and here the growing strength of the male corresponds to the increasing power of consciousness in human development."[56] Jung had suggested this line of thought:

> There is no consciousness without discrimination of opposites. This is the paternal principle, the Logos, which eternally struggles to extricate itself from the primal warmth and primal darkness of the maternal womb; in a word, from unconsciousness. . . . Unconsciousness is the primal sin, evil itself, for the Logos. Therefore its first creative act of liberation is matricide.[57]

Or, as Neumann again puts it, "the hero is the man who overcomes the Terrible Mother, breaks the teeth out of her vagina, and so makes her into a woman."[58] Quite a task for an ordinary man particularly, according to Jung, when many women have developed powerful masculine sides and allowed their inferior sides to become voluptuously feminine, to slumber away in the unconscious,[59] where they wait for the right heroes to awaken them.

The good function of the bad mother, in Neumann's view, is to test the apprentice hero (unless she kills him outright) and thus challenge him to become the great man he really is:

> The numerous princesses who present riddles to be solved do indeed kill their unsuccessful suitors. But they do so only in order to give themselves willingly to the victor, whose superiority, shown by his solving of the riddle, redeems the princess herself, who is this riddle. In other words, even the seemingly "deadly" anima contains the positive potentiality of the transformative character.[60]

Just so, the nourishing and protective side of the mother, if one does not throw it off in time, can stifle the growth and transformation of the soul.

Woman's role in all this mythologizing is a relatively passive one. She—if she be a goddess or the Great Mother—throws down the glove. Unless the hero picks the glove up, the story will end here. If he does pick it up, the story will go on but it will be his story, not hers; she has none of her own. Goddesses, for the most part, maintain an arch silence. We come to understand them by understanding the actions and utterances of their devotees.

The changing of woman's destiny to a more active one is a task for women; the myths, however, and the men of the myths, certainly relished stereotypes of the "Second Sex": for man to write of what woman does is to write of what she makes him do, of how she makes him feel in her presence and in her absence. It is to write of woman as antagonist and ally and muse—as the Other.

Woman as Other

"The category of the *Other*," Simone de Beauvoir writes, "is as primordial as consciousness itself."[61] For consciousness, Nietzsche tells us emphatically, *"has developed only under the pressure of the need for communication."*[62] Consciousness, then, presupposes not only a sense of the self, but of another besides the self; the self, in fact, may know itself primarily through the opposition of another to its wishes and words—through dialogue and dialectic. De Beauvoir puts the antithesis neatly: "At the moment when man asserts himself as subject and free being, the idea of the Other arises. From that day the relation with the Other is dramatic: the existence of the Other is a threat. ... The Other—she is passivity confronting activity, diversity that destroys unity, matter as opposed to form, disorder against order. Woman is thus dedicated to evil."[63] Hegel's master-slave dialectic provides the model for de Beauvoir's analysis of the twoness of the sexes, for Hegel found "in consciousness itself a fundamental hostility toward every other consciousness; the subject can be posed only in being opposed." Consciousness thinks it is the essential one, any other the object. The Other may file a counter-claim; or it may submit to the secondary status which the one has imposed on it and may therefore choose not to try to gain or regain the status of the One. "Whence," de Beauvoir asks, "comes this submission of women?"[64]

She suggests various reasons for woman's acceptance of her slavish position; the most interesting is a modification of Freud's Electra complex. A little boy can view his penis as the Other, an *alter ego*; unequipped with such a material object from which to feel alienated, the little girl loses her integrity through accepting her whole self as the Other. And men do nothing to relieve women's sense of self-alienation:

> Men have failed to realize how much they need not just women's bodies but their whole other natures. Once the subject seeks to assert himself, the Other, who limits and denies him, is none the less a necessity to him: he attains himself only through that reality which he is not, which is something other than himself. ... In woman is incarnated in positive form the lack that the existent carries in his heart, and it is in seeking to be made whole through her that man hopes to attain self-realization.[65]

Man mates himself with his soul as he mates himself with another of the other
sex. Woman comes to man as a deliverer from the bondage of selfish unconsciousness. Through her, man may escape from the tyranny of his patterned
responses in the master-slave dialectic.

For the hero striking out into the alien world, woman is the "wished-for
intermediary between nature, the stranger to man, and the fellow being who
is too closely identical."[66] In the year-god cycle—to apply de Beauvoir's thesis
to mythology, something she herself did not attempt—the male was the Other,
but in the quest saga the roles have been switched and it is woman who must
play the Other. The hero, then, is he who—as civilization advances—himself
advances it and thereby excludes woman from the possibility of anything but a
passive life. By doing this he also excludes himself from what civilization is
supposed to have left behind; and that which he has excluded himself from he
inevitably regards as hostile territory. "Whereas," Neumann observes, "the male
god in myth, like the male hero, usually appears in opposition to the animal
that he fights and defeats, the Great Goddess, as Lady of the Beasts, dominates
them but seldom fights them. Between her and the animal world there is no
hostility or antagonism, although she deals with wild as well as gentle and
tame beasts."[67]

Woman's sympathy with nature makes her appear mysterious to man, an
object not to be understood but, like nature in the nineteenth century, only
conquered. And so, de Beauvoir says, man has perpetuated the negative relation
between man and woman, and "in the company of a living enigma man
remains alone."[68] Woman may remain indefinable even for herself—a sphinx—
because one can say little about essence, hers or anyone's, apart from action.[69]
De Beauvoir laments that so many women fail to make themselves anything,
but revel in self-indulgent maunderings about what they might have become
or really are—a vain question unless they are given more power with which
actually to do something.

An understandable lament, but one that doesn't much concern us as we
turn to the subject of the hero, for whom woman is both a motivating force
and a means to an end. On our quest for the hero's quest, however, we may
discover that an understanding of woman's essence can be distilled from an
understanding of man's deeds. And a woman may even appear along the way—
the hero's and ours, to whatever or wherever—who is the object of his search.

8

The Hero and the Quest

H EROES ARE KNOWN for their heavy tread; he who steps out lightly into the world leaves no mark on the earth. Some heroes and heroines have already offered us their sexual misadventures as illustrations of psychoanalytical models of the libido—characters like Oedipus, Electra, Orestes, and Clytemnestra— but now the more popular conception of a heroic personage concerns us: the great and noble man who undertakes a journey in quest of some treasured object or experience and who performs great deeds along the way. He may, through those very qualities that determine his greatness, bring destruction on himself. But whether disastrous or unblemished his career will ensure him a kind of immortality—enduring fame—in the legends about his life preserved and elaborated by the early poets and later mythographers. On this figure of the hero centers the issue of the use or abuse of classical mythology in psychoanalytical and psychological theorizing. Should an Odysseus at his adroit best, or a Heracles at his bumbling worst, serve as a paradigm or as an anti-paradigm for a modern soul under construction, or as neither—should they perhaps constitute a set of ideals only for contemplation but not for imitation? And how does the modern experience of the myths differ from the ancient one? Can the original audience's disposition toward the heroes of epic and tragedy be ascertained? Can a poet's intentions in the portrayal of a hero be guessed at?

We know that heroes or heroes in the making idolized and emulated other heroes, mythological or (a modern distinction) real. Plutarch preserves the antique anecdote that Theseus founded the Isthmian games in imitation of Heracles' foundation of the Olympic games; and he describes how admiration and envy for the achievements of Miltiades (general at Marathon) drove Themistocles (mastermind of the victory at Salamis) to excel in his own career in the very same way that Theseus dreamt of matching the feats of Heracles (*Theseus* 25.4, 6.7). This sort of patterning and competitiveness was typical of Greek thinking. Indeed after the Persian Wars the whole repertory of mythological victories of Greeks or gods over various outlaws was drawn upon for allegories of the victory of civilization over barbarism at Salamis and Plataea. The Parthenon metopes and the reliefs on the sandals and shield of Athena's great statue there constitute a compendium of such allusive scenes. Thomas Mann, in his essay on Freud, put it this way: "Life, then—at any rate, significant life—was in ancient times the reconstitution of the myth in flesh and blood; it referred to and appealed to the myth; only through it, through reference to the past, could it approve itself as genuine and significant. The myth is the legitimization of life; only through it and in it does life find self-awareness, sanction, consecration."[1] Who were these great men of the past who seem to have set a standard for the men of the classical present?

Hero Cults

To begin with, heroes (hēroēs) were the object of cult practices as well as the subject of myths. They were the ghosts of the dear but powerful departed of great families, who could help their living relatives or harm them if not conciliated. Like gods they enjoyed sacrifices, but not the same kind as those the Olympians savored. Sacrifices to the dead emphasized the underworld. The offerings were made at night, on simple low hearths, for the ancestors lurked nearby and there was no need to send the smoke rising up in broad daylight, as to the high gods. The dead preferred their ritual animal male and black, with head turned down when the knife severed the jugular; the blood had to soak deeply into the ground for the dry, ectoplasmic tongues to lap it up; and the fire consumed the victim utterly. "On special occasions," wrote Erwin Rohde (Nietzsche's friend) in Psyche, his lengthy work on ideas of immortality in ancient Greece, "a sacrificial meal was prepared to which the Hero was invited as a guest."[2]

With the passage of time and relatives, the ranks of the heroes swelled. Large numbers of their tombs were scattered about the countryside and the names of many of the inhabitants forgotten, so that they were referred to by anonymous titles like "the leader." Some of them became objects of fear to test the mettle of the best men around, perhaps future heroes themselves: the most beautiful virgin of the town had to be sacrificed every so often to the hero of Temesa until a famous boxer drove him out. And if you met Orestes in the dark he might beat you or tear off your clothes.[3] The hero cult, then, apotropaically appeased the mighty dead, who like the heroes of the Iliad and of Sophocles' plays had remarkably short tempers.

supernatural force

Apollo canonized the heroes—made it official that a dead man could lay claim to a cult from beyond his immediate family, indeed from all his fellow citizens, who made up a kind of politically extended family.[4] The city, in the legends that passed for history, developed from the clan, and the members of the clan are related by blood. Thus, some of the heroes became public ancestors who helped their civic kin and no one else, particularly in war. In the eighth and seventh centuries, when the city-states were founding colonies to the northeast and the west, heroes, arbitrarily plucked from the public corpus of mythology, had to be provided for those towns with no past. As soon as a colony's founder had died, he himself usually assumed the role of protective ancestor.

Sometimes a city would try to win the favor of its enemies' heroes or even to steal their bones, for the mana of heroes was bound to their tombs and their mortal remains, although arguments might arise as to which grave of several contenders was the real one. (Oedipus claimed four.) Before they could conquer Tegea, the Spartans had to recover the bones of Orestes, which turned out to be ten feet long (Herodotus 1.67–68). In Sophocles' *Oedipus at Colonus* each of the rivals for the throne of Thebes tries to get the old hero to come home with him, but Oedipus chooses instead to bless the hospitable Athenians with his posthumous presence. The Athenians even took the precaution of strewing the ashes of Solon, the sixth-century lawgiver, over Salamis so that he could never be stolen from them.[5]

Martin Nilsson traced the Greek sagas back to the citadels of Mycenaean power, Tiryns, Mycenae, Pylos, Thebes, Athens, and elsewhere.[6] Although these first Greeks may have brought their heroes with them when they wandered down from a migratory life on the Eurasian plains, the Bronze-Age culture that they developed in the Aegean basin and the socio-economic organization they imposed on the native Mediterranean stock constituted exactly the right environment to encourage the production of a complex mythology—one peopled by heroes who were not only better than the common run of men but almost of a different race, halfway to the gods whose favor they enjoyed and whose lives they imitated in their palace courts. (Greek mythology in general, and the hero myths in particular, preserves a masculine, aggressive bias—in contrast to the goddess-peaceful world of the Minoans; heroines, although common in fifth-century tragedy, remain anomalous protagonists.)

After the fall of the Bronze-Age citadels the plastic arts and architecture declined, and the traces of former greatness that survived fostered the hero cults. The rock-cut chamber tombs and prominent tholoi that the Mycenaeans had buried their best men in, complete with farewell banquets and gold and silver ceremonial objects for the afterlife, were naturally taken for the tombs of the heroes by the later, inferior Greeks of the poorer, less racially segregated Dark and Archaic Ages. But in poetry, an art less dependent on material conditions, the Mycenaean tradition carried on, flourished, and encouraged further mythmaking.

Epic poems—originally composed and recited to flatter and entertain nobles reclining after dinner in palace halls—were pretty much all the last Mycenaeans or their descendants took with them to Ionia when forced into exile by the newly arrived Dorian Greeks. These poems (that is, their plots and formulaic verses) now became the precious relics of a glorious past, a set of historical tales with which the Ionian Greeks could console themselves for lost wealth and prestige and which they could refine to contain an expression of the new age's hopes and fears. In Hesiod's *Theogony* (66) the Muses describe the subject of their singing as the customs and ancestral ways of the immortals. "Description here passes into prescription," Eric Havelock explains. "What is done becomes what ought to be done. It is the storage of such social directives *par excellence* which is entrusted to the enclave of contrived and memorized speech, and in particular to the epic."[7] The world of Odysseus, like the mythical world of rural England, may never have existed, but as a character in Isabel Colegate's *The Shooting Party* says, "That is why the idea is such a powerful one. It is a myth."[8]

At the end of the Dark Ages, in the eighth century B.C., when the world was widening once again and a modicum of prosperity returning, Homer (probably two different oral poets, working in competition, not cooperation) composed (probably with the aid of scribes) the *Iliad* and the *Odyssey*—the two longest and greatest and just about last epic poems in a tradition that went, as we have seen, way back. The characters of those poems have defined both for us and for the tragedians and philosophers of classical Athens the nature of heroic performance and appearance. Who were the Homeric heroes and what did they do?

Homeric Heroes

They were first of all the sons of their fathers: heroes are born, not made from scratch. In his analysis of the world of the *Odyssey* Moses Finley points out that the father's status, not the mother's, determined whether children were born enslaved or free, noble or base. And, while he insists that birth determined only superficial differences between men—the magnificence or the squalor of their households making the real difference—in truth the household was also inherited from the father as a birthright.[9] Although the son may fall short of the standard of excellence set by his father, he seldom exceeds it unless a god, along with a mortal man, took part in his siring (as Zeus did with Heracles and Poseidon with Theseus): one or two branches of his family tree may reach to heaven.

The hero stages his life on a level between that of the gods and that of mere men: like men, he dies, but the glorious manner of his death, recorded by poets in his family's service, ensures that he will live forever through his fame. In local cults, after his death the hero may go to the Isles of the Blessed, Elysium; in epic, however, all but the hero's fame effectively dies with him. The epic actually immortalizes the hero while reminding us of his and our own mortalities.[10]

The epic audience themselves had no chance of reaching the level of excellence attained by a mythical hero, for the age Homer sang about was, in Finley's words, "a time in which men exceeded subsequent standards with respect to a specified and severely limited group of qualities." That *many* men possessed heroic virtues, values, and capacities was what made it a distinct mythical age of heroes, between the bronze and iron ages of Hesiod's cosmogony. In the *Odyssey*, in fact, *hero* denotes any member of the aristocracy and perhaps even any free man.[11] In his mythical day, then, a hero was, at best, first among equals—not, as for Homer's audience and for us, of a different and matchless race. The Homeric heroes might imitate the even greater heroes of the generations before the Trojan War, but was such imitation and practical idealization meant to stop at the borders of the poems or to extend beyond the text? Was the audience challenged to compete with the heroes and to model their own lives on them?

No, argues Redfield the scholar: "The hero, after all, is not a model for imitation but rather a figure who cannot be ignored; his special excellence is not integration but potency." And so the might of Achilles is a more heroic quality than the craftiness of Odysseus.[12] Yes, writes W. H. Auden, voicing the popular opinion: "The warrior-hero of the Homeric epics (and his civilian counterpart, the athlete of the Pindaric odes) is an aristocratic ideal. He is what every member of the ruling class should try to imitate, what every member of the subject class should admire without envy and obey without resentment, the closest approximation to a god—the divine being conceived as the ideally strong—possible to man."[13]

Auden is right and Redfield partly so. The persona of the Iliadic hero utterly subsumes any idiosyncratic self. (The *Odyssey* makes a break with that tradition.) Even decisions to act do not well up from any private depths off limits to the onlookers, but are arrived at by debate between two dramatic parts of the man or between the man and his goddess. What you see in Achilles is what you get. The hero is public property and the scrutiny of his peers propels him into battle. *Deōs*, the fear of injury, loses out to *aidōs*, the fear of disgrace. "Thus, heroism is for Homer a definite social task," Redfield puts it, "and the heroes are a definite social stratum." These distinguished men, the warriors, make up the governing and propertied class, upon which depends the protection and maintenance of the whole community. Sarpedon in his speech to Glaucus acknowledges that the privileges of a warrior both mark his special status and compel him to fight when he is needed (*Iliad* 12.310–28). Combat "is the crucial social act, for in combat the survival of the collectivity is at stake. . . . a man stands his ground because he shrinks from betraying his fellows."[14] And so the actual deeds and character of the hero need not, probably should not, have stimulated the audience to emulation; but the social nature of those deeds, the sense of mutual obligation imposed by the warrior's code, did constitute a model of behavior for the *Iliad's* audience. And while the Odysseus of the *Odyssey* may seem a rather private character compared to an Achilles or a Hector or a Nestor, his homecoming and vengeance on the suitors illustrate a new valuation of the household and accompanying system of justice which advances and modernizes the social model set up by the older epic tradition.

But even in the just society that the *Odyssey* and Hesiod's *Works and Days* look forward to, the notion of the battle, the contest, as the arena in which, by fighting one another, geniuses both spur one another on to greater endeavors and protect the people against one another, never yields to any vision of the Peaceable Kingdom. "Every talent must unfold itself in fighting," Nietzsche assures us. When a great personality is removed from the contest by his successors he degenerates: "the Greek was incapable of enduring fame and happiness. . . . he was unable to endure fame without any further contest, or the happiness at the end of the contest." Without the contest, the hero and civilization would sink back into savagery.[15] As an armchair hero, Nietzsche quite rightly insists there can be no armchair heroes: "so popular morality also separates strength from expressions of strength, as if there were a neutral substratum behind the strong man, which was *free* to express strength or not to do so. But there is no such substratum. . . . the deed is everything."[16]

No civilization without strife: no strife without passion: "very differently from St. Paul and the Jews, the Greeks directed their idealistic tendency precisely toward the passions and loved, elevated, gilded, and deified them. Evidently, passion made them feel not only happier but also purer and more divine."[17] But passion, particularly Greek passion, cannot be discharged in action without the risk, even the certainty, of error. In a different context, Redfield excuses the tragic hero for making an error that, while not forced upon him, is nevertheless the kind of error a good man would make, under difficult circumstances: "Tragedy is thus grounded in meditation on action and the conditions of action."[18] And Auden expresses pretty much the same view about at least the Homeric world—"a world without guilt for its tragic flaw is not a flaw in human nature, still less a flaw in an individual character, but a flaw in the nature of existence."[19]

The hero, when he makes the epic (not tragic) mistake that causes his downfall, does so under conditions that might drive any man to his limits and beyond, into error. But only a hero, not just any man, would find himself in those circumstances. And so only a hero would make a hero's kind of mistake, one made when the passions of a god (which have elevated him above the common, unambitious run of men) have driven him to exceed the limits that keep him a man—indeed, have blinded him to his mortal limitations. The first word of the *Iliad* is *wrath (mēnin)*; and the poem, although packed with action, is a prolonged meditation on the causes and effects of the hero's emotions—how those emotions make him a hero and ensure his immortality, but also how they hasten his death. He is both a product and a victim of hubris. The chief emotion that animates him is *philotimia*, which equates self-love with honor: the hero is blameless; if misfortunes occur it must be the fault of others or of fate; but others are always ready to haul down the hero whose *philotimia* has gotten him into trouble.[20]

The *Odyssey* offers its hero and its audience a way out of heroic error. The poem begins with the word *man (andra)*; and while even more packed with action than the *Iliad*, it considers the possibility and then the actuality of a hero who could, almost but not quite always, restrain his passions with the help of a goddess when their expression would not serve his best practical interests and release them with the help of a woman at precisely the right moment. Odysseus' enemies, not the hero himself, traffic in hubris.

Doubtless the great mass of Homer's later listeners and readers—in the sixth and subsequent centuries, by which time he was regarded by them as the educator of Greece—did not draw such connections of character and plot as I have. The average Greek, like the average European or American, reduced the epic tellings of the myths to romanticized profundities, relieved them of all distinctions and precisions, and equated them with the tedious proverbs which (as Paul Valéry's lucubrations led him to conclude) stock the bottom of every mind. But such connections and distinctions did concern the tragedians, who wrote plays not about action but about choice and error, that is, about the human conditions of action.

Tragic Heroes

Tragedy—the genre, not the event—was invented according to Gerald Else under the following conditions. In the second half of the sixth century the tyrant Pisistratus, having on his third try seized power in Athens, instituted economic and political reforms to better the lot of the people vis-à-vis the landowners. He also gave the common citizen something to take pride in: he

enhanced and enlarged the all-Athenian festival, the Panathenaea, from a simple service in the cult of the city's divine patroness to a festival with major
athletic contests and lots of free meat, where everybody was honored just for
being Athenian. Since the gods are made in the image of man, one can safely
entertain both us and them at the same time; and so Pisistratus seems to have
instituted the recitation of the complete *Iliad* and *Odyssey*, along with a competition of rhapsodes who gave dramatic expression to the frequent passages of
dialogue, at the Great Panathenaea, every four years, for Athena and the audience's delectation. He also glorified the City Dionysia—for Dionysus was a
god of the people, giving them relief from toil and the hope of salvation—by
commissioning a certain Thespis, probably a choral poet, to create a new art
form. Blending the plots of epic with the songs of dithyrambic verse, the dialogue and characterization of the rhapsodes' performance of Homer, and the
didactic tone of some local poetry, Thespis came up with a tragedy: he staged,
with sung commentary and choral dancing, the disasters, not the triumphs, of
the great old families of myth.[21]

The great old families of Athenian politics had been giving Pisistratus
problems. For the sake of the tyranny (and later, after his sons' fall from power,
for the sake of the democracy) their influence had eventually to be curtailed.
"Accordingly the dead of the great families were reduced to the level of the
ordinary unimportant dead, by restrictions in regard to grave-cult and burial
customs," Martin Nilsson writes. The grave-cults could be tended in their
ancestral form only for those heroes who were public property, lest a family
have religious interests which elevated it above other families and distinguished
its fate from the fate of the state. The Homeric idea of the dead as mere shades
was impressed upon the people.[22] And so the periodic recitation of Homer fitted
in beautifully with Pisistratus' plan to level out private holdings of economic
and religious power. The Homeric tradition had deviated from the mainstream
of Greek religion because the emigrants to Ionia—the provenance of the
poems—could not carry with them the grave-sites and old bones of their ancestors into exile from the mainland. The hero thus escaped from the repetitious-
ness of cult to grow into the ever-changing great man of literature who belonged
to all Greeks, not merely to his immediate family.

But the passions of those great men who romp joyfully across the wide
plains of the past came to seem out of place within the walls of the Archaic
and classical city-state. Consider this possibility—that, after instituting the
regular recitation of Homer, partly in order to replace the local heroes of powerful clans with the distant panhellenic ones of *Iliad* and *Odyssey* fame, Pisistratus ordered Thespis to invent drama in order to counteract the bad effect
the epic versions of Achilles and others might be having on the demos: tragedy
was calculated to promulgate an interpretation of the heroic way as a way to be

shunned by the people, to ensure that they stayed satisfied being mere people and did not rock their despotic helmsman out of the ship of state.

The propaganda, however, did not always succeed. The lovers Harmodius and Aristogeiton (a veritable sixth-century Achilles and Patroclus) took exception to the second-generation tyrant Hippias and his brother Hipparchus. Miffed over a private slight, they determined to kill the oppressors, botched the plot, and were executed; but shortly thereafter they were heroized into icons of freedom-fighters.

"The Tragic Hero," Auden writes, "is not an ideal [like the Homeric Hero] but a warning, and the warning is addressed not to an aristocratic audience, i.e., other potentially heroic individuals, but to the *demos*, i.e., the collective chorus."[23] In play after play the Chorus remarks how grateful they are to the gods for having kept them middle-class or women or slaves, insignificant and far from fortunate compared to the protagonist or antagonist, since those tall trees in the civic forest are always the first to be struck by bolts from the Olympian blue. Not from the very first but from as early as the sixth or fifth century the hero and the society he supposedly served had a falling-out: individuation not only risks but requires alienation from the mass of men. Women, then, made excellent tragic heroes—Clytemnestra, Electra, Antigone, Helen. You could admire their spunk all you liked but still had to admit their rebellious cases were safely hopeless in a world ruled by men.

The Greeks, even while they shunned the fates of the heroes, could not but admire heroic passions and recognized that (in Nietzsche's words about a Christian, bourgeois, context), "The praise of virtue is the praise of something privately harmful—the praise of instincts that deprive a human being of his noblest selfishness and the strength for the highest autonomy."[24] The Greeks were never so wholly resigned to the inadvisability of the heroic, independent way as Freud was; for surely the psychoanalyst would have judged the hero a neurotic, one of those rebellious, unstable types who cannot sufficiently repress his instincts for the sake of a smoothly functioning civilization but who, if we are all lucky, can sublimate his antisocial urges in heroic derring-do.

Jean-Pierre Vernant has argued that the writing down of choral odes led to a shift in the function of myth, a separation of the author and audience from the text that was out of keeping with the immediateness of oral performance. Myth lost value in its own fluid right but gained value as a fixed "other" compared to which our actions, "conceived as imitative, can reveal their meaning and fall into position on the scale of values." But the paradigmatic nature of mythological texts did not prevent a constant tension from obtaining in the theater between the heroes of the far-off past and the citizens of the polis who made up the classical audience. The polis had to find some way to integrate into its culture the actions and curses that tore apart the legendary royal houses.

And so, according to Vernant, the hero in tragedy ceases to serve as a model and becomes an object of debate, the embodiment of the enigma of the human condition. "Myth in its original form provided answers without ever explicitly formulating the problems. When tragedy takes over the mythical traditions, it uses them to pose problems to which there are no answers."[25] The hero's career always had a beginning *(archē)* but in tragedy it lost the epic sense of a compelling goal *(teleutē):* where once there had been a definite answer to the questions implicitly posed by that beginning, now there crept in a distressingly wide range of possibilities. Eventually tragedy proved inadequate to fulfill this new, inquisitional function of myth and some fresh heroes made their way onto the literary scene—the philosopher, the artist, and finally the analysand as hero—looking for genres to inhabit.

The Freudian Hero

In *Totem and Taboo* Freud suggests that in tragedy the Chorus, a brotherhood of citizens, and the lonely suffering hero represent the primal horde and the father. Originally the horde, not the hero, was guilty of rebelliousness; but the hero, by acting out the crime of the horde and assuming their guilt for them, became their redeemer. Thus the story of Christ, who suffered and died for the sins of all men, provided the subject matter for a revival of drama in the Middle Ages.[26] Later, in *Group Psychology and the Analysis of the Ego*, Freud revised and elaborated his hero myth in a long postscript written under the influence of Otto Rank: after the band of sons had slain the father, the first of them to take the father's place was the first epic poet, who made this advance in his imagination and invented the myth of the hero:

> The hero was a man who by himself had slain the father—the father who still appeared in the myths as the totemic monster. Just as the father had been the boy's first ideal, so in the hero who aspires to the father's place the poet now created the first ego ideal. The transition to the hero was probably afforded by the youngest son, the mother's favorite, whom she had protected from paternal jealousy, and who, in the era of the primal horde, had been the father's successor. In the lying poetic fancies of prehistoric times the woman, who had been the prize of battle and the temptation to murder, was probably turned into the active seducer and instigator of the crime. . . . The myth, then, is the step by which the individual emerges from group psychology.

And the poet, Freud adds, finds his way back to the group by recounting the hero's deeds.[27]

Freud's explanation is not quite an explanation of ancient mythology but more nearly a hero myth of his own, consisting as it does not of an analysis of the myths but of illustrations for his theory of the connection between the Oedipus complex and the first stages of civilization. The paradigmatic hero myth for Freud contains no heroes at all but only gods and Titans: it is the myth of Zeus' overthrow of his father Cronus, with the help of his mother Rhea, in order to save his brethren and to put himself in his father's place. Oddly enough, however, the Freudian myth (perhaps because heroes are the sons of gods or would like to be) contains exactly the right ingredients for an explanation of the mortal hero's rise to prominence: the group dominated, if not actually suppressed, by a stronger male whom they would like to overthrow; the bumptious and talented member of that group, a narcissistic *Wünderkind* who wants simultaneously to aid the group and aggrandize himself; the hero's victory, after which he becomes an ideal for the horde (insofar as he is now a fantasy figure) but also becomes a new tyrant himself and the object of envy (insofar as he is still a real man); and the psychological solution to this ambivalence of the group toward its hero—their internalization of him as an ego-ideal.

Freud's system works even for Pisistratus—the tyrant as hero and as patron of poets albeit no poet himself. He broke free from the aristocracy to take the part of the common people against the paternal, oppressive nobility, advanced himself and his family while improving the lot of the group, and found it politic to offer the people the poeticized set of popular heroes in place of the former, exclusive heroes of local family-cults. (He could not actually set himself up as a hero, although he probably expected to become one after his death.) Then he found the Homeric ego-ideals unsuitably freewheeling for the needs of a stable polis, and so he commissioned the invention of a set of falling and fallen idols—the heroes of tragedy.

The details of the hero's career in general, and of several careers in particular, will have to wait a few pages; but all of the ingredients in Freud's myth can be matched by those details. The analysts Friedman and Gassel, however, go too far when in a Freudian way they find an evolution in the conflated unconscious of three heroes, Oedipus, Orestes, and Odysseus: the primal horde achieves a state of security under the dominance of a vengeful father; there follows the revolt of a son, along with a sense of guilt over the patricide and incest, acts of self-punishment, and the establishment of rigorous taboos (Oedipus); eventually a hero reacts against the taboo, denies the incest by acts of substitution, and relinquishes his claims to mother (Orestes); finally the primal father returns, is accepted back by his community and family and especially by his son, and the old days of peace and happiness as promised by Zeus are restored (Odysseus).[28] A pretty myth but, once again, not an analysis;

for instead of drawing distinctions in the several stories, our two analysts-turned-mythographers fabricate a whole new story out of works by at least three very different authors, composed over at least three hundred years.

Whereas Freud seems most interested in the act of revolt against a male and the function played by idealization of the hero in the machinery of the soul, Jung and his followers concern themselves more with the cause of individuation, the rise of a single consciousness out of the collective murk, and the difficulties of this task as it is allegorized in the hero's quest (a quest provides a more protracted test than a revolt). And of course in Freud's view, the dangers that beset the heroic upstart are mostly of a male kind—the jealous horde of brothers, the paternal oppressor—while the only female on the scene, the hero's mother, had, by cosseting him and protecting him from his father, given him the strength and courage he needed to stage a revolt. Freud writes off the transformation of this one woman from the prize of battle to shrewish inspiratrix as a pack of poet's lies. For Jung, however, the dangers the hero meets along his way turn out to be mostly maternal ones, for that collective un- or semi-conscious that he has sworn to rise above manifests itself as the primal mother.

Both Freud and Jung owed much to Nietzsche on the subject of the hero and the emergence of consciousness, "the necessity of sacrilege imposed upon the titanically striving individual:

> Each, taken as an individual, has right on its side, but nevertheless has to suffer for its individuation, being merely a single one beside another. In the heroic effort of the individual to attain universality, in the attempt to transcend the curse of individuation and to become the *one* world being, he suffers in his person the primordial contradiction that is concealed in things, which means that he commits sacrilege and suffers. [29]

The theory of the birth of tragedy that was current in Nietzsche's day, and even in Freud's and Jung's, although now discredited as fact still has some use as a myth—the story that tragedy was born when the chorus-leader of the dithyramb (a narrative hymn) separated himself from the Chorus and became the protagonist of what thereby became tragedy. Nietzsche understood the Chorus as "the symbol of the whole excited Dionysian throng," and the source of Dionysian discharges into the world of images. The protagonist of a tragedy—originally the god Dionysus (although a god, he was Nietzsche's favorite hero and the face behind all the masks of the various tragic figures)—embodies the *principium individuationis* who separates himself from the Dionysian mass and suffers the consequences. [30] Tragedy in Nietzsche's view thus provides the spectator with either an anti-model or a model—depending on your point of view: for the would-be *Ubermensch*, the superman, the hero, can be taken as a model despite his sufferings; for the crowd, however, his career is nothing but the summation of all they wish to avoid. (The task of the hero subsumes even the work of the artist: "The tragedians wrote in order to triumph. Their whole art is unthinkable without the contest: Hesiod's good Eris, ambition, gave wings to their genius."[31])

Jung deploys the vocabularies of myth and of depth psychology to surround much the same meaning: "The self is the hero, threatened already at birth by envious collective forces. . . . In its psychological meaning, individuation is an *opus contra naturam*, which creates a *horror vacui* in the collective layer and is only too likely to collapse under the impact of the collective forces of the psyche."[32] Jung (on the subject of *Genesis*) conceives of every step toward greater consciousness as "a kind of Promethean guilt: through knowledge, the gods are as it were robbed of their fire, that is, something that was the property of the unconscious powers is torn out of its natural context and subordinated to the whims of the conscious mind." The man who possesses this knowledge "has raised himself above the human level of his age" and suffers the vengeance of the gods in the form of loneliness, "for never again can he return to mankind."[33] Prometheus, although a Titan, one of the divine race that preceded the Olympian, was a kind of culture hero and even artist-hero: he may have been the creator of mankind, sculpting it out of clay, and in any case he helped it to cheat the gods out of the edible portion of the constant sacrifices that were keeping men hungry; and he stole fire from heaven, where it had been reserved only for the gods, and gave it to men who before had shivered in the cold and eaten raw food like animals. Zeus punished Prometheus for this philanthropy by having him nailed to a cliff in the Caucasus where a vulture eats his liver out every day and every night he grows it back again (Hesiod, *Theogony* 507–616; *Works and Days* 47–105; and elsewhere). According to Freud's interpretation of the myth, Prometheus by bringing fire to man had renounced an instinct to urinate on it and put it out; and so Zeus saw to it that his liver, the seat of the passions, would be devoured daily and, like the erotic desires, be renewed daily. For primal man, the attempt to quench fire with urine was symbolically a pleasurable struggle with another phallus. Heracles, also a culture hero and the savior of Prometheus, "put out" a water monster, the Hydra, with firebrands; this "reverse" is the same as Prometheus' deed.[34]

Prometheus is yet another who helped the horde achieve its rightful place vis-à-vis the oppressor and who suffered the fate of a hero. But Prometheus left man in an uncomfortable intermediate position—in Nietzsche's words: "Man is a rope, fastened between animal and superman—a rope over an abyss."[35] This favorite of Prometheus, this man as Superman, is, like any hero, more prone to commit serious error than the common run of men. Whereas the

Homeric hero's error proceeds from excessive pride and self-confidence, the philosophical Superman's downfall comes from too much forethought—*mētis*, the eponymous virtue of Prometheus:

> Consciousness gives rise to countless errors that lead an animal or a man
> to perish sooner than necessary, "exceeding destiny," as Homer puts it. If
> the conserving instincts were not so very much more powerful, and if it
> did not serve on the whole as a regulator, humanity would have to perish
> ... of its consciousness. ... At bottom, every high degree of caution in
> making inferences and every skeptical tendency constitute a great danger
> for life. [36]

Nietzsche displays the intellectual's penchant for laying all mistakes at the feet of the intellect. But why can't the unconscious make mistakes too?

Note that Nietzsche almost completely internalizes heroic action;[37] Jung, too, regards an actual deed as only a manifestation of a psychic process; Freud, however, in his concrete way insists on the necessity of action, of the revolt against the father, as central to both the hero's career and the maturation of the soul. But can the hero of a Greek tragedy—the original model for psychological man—himself be called psychological man?

Roland Barthes argues (did Roland Barthes ever argue?) that there was no psychology in Greek drama: "here passion has no interior density, it is entirely extroverted, oriented toward its civic context."[38] Freud, of course, insisted that psychoanalysis could be applied to uncover the buried truth in many fields of human endeavor, since it aims to uncover what is unconscious in mental life, wherever mental life is to be found. That word *applied* causes difficulty: can we know whether we are reading our modern sense of the soul into the tragedies—a psychological fallacy to add to the intentional fallacy—or are truly detecting the imprint and shape of the soul inevitably left like a potter's thumbprint on any human product? Can the psyche, after all, do anything without reproducing itself?

Where others have found depths as profound as those Heraclitus claimed for the soul and the cosmos (Nature must have a place to hide herself) Barthes sees only open plains: "However paradoxical it may seem, *myth hides nothing*: its function is to distort, not to make disappear. There is no latency of the concept in relation to the form: there is no need of an unconscious to explain myth." A Parisian vote, then, cast for the case of façade as all. Barthes as an aesthetician and aesthete is repulsed by anything beneath the surface, by "this disease of thinking in essences, which is at the bottom of every bourgeois mythology of man."[39] The Viennese vote goes quite the other way. For Freud, every little thing—innocent-seeming or not—is symptomatic of some deeper, far-from-innocent other thing. For Jung, too, everything we do or that happens to us is rather a token of something else.

The average Greek, of course, would not have understood Barthes' and Freud's positions nor the difference between them: myth for him was something to be *used*, and analysis (whether two-dimensional or three-dimensional, semiological or psychological) of myth was not useful. The myths provided the common man with textbook illustrations of his little, personal case, whatever that case might be—assurances that the petty and seemingly meaningless course of his life had some prototype in the past which legitimized its details and direction. The profundity of myth was all up front, unless an artist cared to add more.

The myths are in one sense empty forms waiting to be filled by any poet or man in the street who cares to refer his particular case to their general pattern. Since these stories have, by definition, been told time and again (variations aside), and are a product of the folk and carriers of phylogenetic memory traces, their idealized forms suit them to our analogic desire. Myth in its most available form is vulgar, ready to be had by anybody, flat but deceptive: anyone who thinks that by referring his life to a myth he has given either myth or his life depth is mistaken. He has only bestowed a glorious and lasting temporality on the momentary present, enclosed his life in amber, and added one more globule of grandeur to the worry beads of human existence. It is the hero's profound desire to escape, if he can, from time; and the artist's desire to make his telling of a myth so much his own that it and its hero can never be stolen from him by an audience. This is what Euripides finally managed to do, and did it so skillfully that he destroyed myth but left most of the spectators unaware of what they had lost.

The Homeric hero and the tragic hero are necessary analogies for psychological man in the early stages of his career. But once the old challenges have been met, the old roads travelled to their bitter ends, the modern hero is faced with Pound's challenge to poets—"Make it new." That new career, however, will have to wait until the final two chapters of this book. For now the old ways still concern us.

The Rankian Hero

Otto Rank applied Freud's theory of the horde and his own of the trauma of birth to a variety of heroic legends, and he discovered the standard form of the saga: the hero comes of distinguished parents, but various difficulties— dire prophecy of what he will do to his father, exposure in infancy, salvation by animals or peasants, an obscure upbringing—precede his coming into his own; he grows up and takes vengeance on his father or a substitute; and finally he achieves a high position and honor. This career, Rank points out, matches the common childhood fantasy of every boy, not just of the neurotic who imagines he was adopted by parents beneath his proper station; for the true hero of myth or romance is the ego—"which finds itself the hero, through its first heroic act, i.e., the revolt against the father. The ego can only find its own heroism in the days of infancy, and it is therefore obliged to invest the hero with its own revolt, crediting him with the features which make the ego a hero. . . . Myths are, therefore, created by adults, by means of retrograde childhood fantasies, the hero being credited with the mythmaker's personal infantile history."[40] The ego of the child behaves like the hero of myth and endeavors to replace the real parents with fantastic ones and to recapture the happy days of yore when his mother was the dearest and most beautiful woman and his father the strongest man; the two parent-couples of the hero myth correspond to the real and imaginary parents of the child's fantasy. We begin to daydream of ascending the social scale almost as soon as we attain an infantile consciousness.[41]

But what if it is the myth-reader, not the myth-maker, who credits the innocent hero with an alien past? Only by attending as closely as possible to the versions of a story—the folk's, the artists' many versions, and our own as readers—can we hope to escape from the labyrinth of myth. Rank mistakes the original for the ultimate tyranny which the hero must conquer: the hero is persecuted, while still in the womb, by his father who doesn't want him to come into the world at all. "The rest of the hero's fate is nothing but the working out of this situation, namely, the reaction to a specially severe birth trauma, which has to be mastered by over-compensating achievements, among which the most prominent is the regaining of the mother." All the hero's deeds are directed at getting back into the "primal situation," to regaining residence in the womb. Whatever magical invulnerability the hero is gifted with is a kind of permanent uterus he has brought with him into the world. His father is his chief opponent on this quest.[42]

While Rank sought all the answers in the past, Jung was always looking to the future, to the day when his patient would have mastered the heroic, the adult stride. Joseph Henderson defines the nature and function of the hero in the terms of depth psychology: the hero symbolizes the more comprehensive identity of the whole psyche, that which supplies the strength the personal ego lacks, and the myth of the hero serves to develop the individual's ego-unconsciousness. But he warns that the image of the hero had best not be identified with the ego itself; rather, it symbolically enables the ego to separate itself from the archetypal images of its parents.[43]

The birth and career of the individual soul corresponds to the heroic pattern. In Jung's own words—"the hero symbolizes a man's *unconscious* self, and this manifests itself empirically as the sum total of all archetypes and therefore includes the archetype of the father and of the wise old man. To that extent the hero is his own father and his own begetter." A similar confusion of progenitors reigns on the mother's side: "the hero is not born like an ordinary mortal because his birth is a rebirth from the mother-wife. That is why the hero so often has two mothers."[44] (A pedantic note: the classical hero, in fact, more often has two fathers than two mothers.)

Once out of the womb and grown up the hero starts on the way of his second birthing. The process—ostensibly a quest for some irrelevant object, but in fact a search for himself—often takes the form of a night-sea journey, from east to west, symbolizing the transit of the sun and anticipating the hero's own renewal and elevation to a higher level of humanness. (On a darker note, Freud thought Theseus' adventure in the labyrinth was "a representation of anal birth: the twisting paths are the bowels and Ariadne's thread is the umbilical cord."[45]) On his way the hero meets many monsters, but as his main feat he overcomes "the monster of darkness: it is the long-hoped-for and expected triumph of consciousness over the unconscious."[46] The battle with this maternal dragon symbolizes the ego's triumph over regressive trends. The hero must realize the existence of his shadow-side and learn to draw strength from it. He must come to terms with the shadow's destructive powers if he is to become mean enough to overcome the dragon of legend.[47]

The willingness of an individual to expose himself first to the dark forces of his shadow side and then to the blandishments of the monster is not found in all men. It takes a hero, according to Jung, to give way constructively to his regressive longing and purposely expose himself to the maternally monstrous abyss. The true test of the hero is in his not being devoured, in his frequent conquest of the monster.[48] Nearly all monsters represent the unconscious, which is feminine; heroes represent consciousness, which is male. The hero must create himself by doing battle with his enemy, his origins—"The making of fire in the monster's belly suggests as much, for it is a piece of apotropaic magic aimed at dispelling the darkness of unconscious."[49] What Slater takes as a rather special case—the conflict between the Greek hero and the monster, based on a fear of women that originated in the peculiar family structure of the Greeks and the ambivalence of mother and son toward each other—Jung regards as the universal, necessary, and even redeeming pattern of the soul's journey from the cave to the light.

One great danger awaits the hero after he has met and overcome a series of hostile forces ranged by the wayside. The idealism that drives him on may, after a few successful encounters, lead to overconfidence as it did, Henderson observes, in the case of Icarus. But the risk of overweening pride *(hubris)* comes with the heroic territory: "for if a young man does not strive for a higher goal than he can safely reach, he cannot surmount the obstacles between adolescence and maturity."[50] The hero, by definition, is one who goes out to meet and draw energy from his meeting with forces more powerful than himself to an unknown degree. "He corresponds to what I call the 'mana personality.' The latter has such an immense fascination for the conscious mind that the ego all too easily succumbs to the temptation to identify with the hero, thus bringing on a psychic inflation with all its consequences."[51] The archetype of the hero invades a soul, occupies it, swells it beyond the bounds of the human: "It causes exaggeration, a puffed-up attitude (inflation), loss of free will, delusion, enthusiasm in good and evil alike."[52] The hero, then, may offer himself as a model for the individuating self, but the self should not take the offer too literally. The ego must preserve its sovereignty and independence from the model.

Jung seems to say that ego-inflation may also derive from the ego's identification with that most elusive part of the self, the anima or animus. The women the hero meets on his quest, then, pose a special danger; for when a man masters the anima, his ego becomes a mana-personality—draws to itself the power belonging to the anima—which is a dominant of the collective unconscious in the archetypal form of the hero or saint. The archetype now takes possession of the conscious personality—"for by inflating the conscious mind it can destroy everything that was gained by coming to terms with the anima." Every step in the process of individuation thus entails a secondary, retrograde danger, for after every success the ego feels it has become a little more godlike.[53] The real gods, however, take their vengeance on this false god: even if the identification of the self with the archetype does not lead the ego directly into disaster, the hero turns into a flat, static persona, the mere mask of a great man; and he may as well be dead.

In *Psychological Types* Jung makes a distinction between the mechanisms by which introverts and extroverts suffer inflation. Introverts, it seems, identify their whole selves with the ego, whereas extroverts identify themselves with that most public part of the self, the persona.[54] In *Two Essays*, however, it would seem that the persona is the location of everybody's ego-inflation— "a mask worn by the collective psyche, a mask that *feigns individuality*, making others and oneself believe that one is individual whereas one is simply acting a role through which the collective psyche speaks."[55] (Jung never explores the implications of this statement for depth psychology's borrowings from Greek tragedy: that behind the mask of the hero there would be nothing to analyze and the mask itself only an aid for meditation on the archetypes.) Since the process of individuation, for which the hero is the prototype, results in public maturation as well as private development, must the persona not claim a major share in the problem? And may the only difference in this regard between introvert and extrovert be that the one, unless a psychopath, expects to have less of an effect on the world than the other; the extrovert may have a bit more success in realizing his delusions.

One other aspect of ego-inflation requires our attention. Since the process of learning leads to suffering which is supposed to lead back to learning—as the choral songs of Aeschylus and Sophocles and the analysts tell us—the hero, who by definition must suffer to achieve his goal, may account himself a greater man than one who suffers less or even enjoys a prosperous, healthy, happy life. And just as a Christian may relish the afflictions which he thinks render him more justified before the Lord than his canker-less neighbor, the hero may grow fond of the laborious quest in a manner that is sick—may hope that he never reaches his Ithaca, because a quest bounded by an unattainable goal does not satisfy his craving for life, as it should, but rather assuages his fear of a life beyond this particular journey's end.

The anima is actually the savior of the hero, both coming to his aid when he has exhausted all his masculine resources and, after his triumphs, softening his soul when heroic sclerosis threatens to set in. The damsel in distress—so typical of heroic myth—only *seems* to deflect the hero from his straight-arrow flight; she is actually his anima calling to him for mutual aid, now that he has left mother behind. Henderson gives an example: The labyrinth in Theseus' myth represents the matriarchal realm that can be crossed only by those ready for initiation into the world of the collective unconscious. The rescue from the labyrinth of the maiden in distress, Ariadne, "symbolizes the liberation of the anima figure from the devouring aspect of the mother image. Not until this is accomplished can a man achieve his first true capacity for relatedness to women."[56] The moral of Henderson's story may be a felicitous one, even though he reverses the facts. Ariadne helped Theseus, not the other way around—by showing him how to find his way through the labyrinth, kill her brother the Minotaur, and then get back out; and Theseus ungratefully abandoned her on Naxos, where Dionysus found and married and heroinized her.

The anima, or her mythological representative, supports the hero against the hostile avatars of the Goddess; so Athena gives Heracles the strength and direction he needs to survive Hera's persecution. As Slater suggests in another context, the Greeks couldn't believe a man could get the better of a woman without help from another woman.[57] Some of the monsters that the hero encounters turn out—once he has had the courage to confront them—to be only paper tigresses: finding this out is also a part of his growing up. Mortal women, once possessed, become attributes of the hero; Heracles on his deathbed makes his son promise to marry his spear-won mistress Iole; the heroic seed now permanently resident in her womb, according to the ancient genetic theory of telegony, must be kept within the family (Sophocles, *Women of Trachis* 1226–29).

Heroes have no more success than the common run of men in making good marriages. While the marriage may be the object of his quest (Odysseus), more often it is merely a political move (Theseus), the payment of a debt left over from his quest (Jason), or a sign of collapse into respectable stability (Menelaus). Nietzsche insists on the last explanation: "What becomes of the 'Wandering Jew' whom a woman adores and makes stable? He merely ceases to be eternal; he gets married, he is of no further use to us. Translated into reality: the danger for artists, for geniuses . . . is woman; adoring women confront them with corruption."[58] But Odysseus, as we shall see, is a different case entirely.

Campbell's Hero

Joseph Campbell, in many ways the most naive of Jung's explainers (a role he might very well deny), is probably the most honest. His *The Hero with a Thousand Faces* draws heroes from the world's mythologies in one simple yet concrete narrative. The quest has a practical purpose: "The effect of the successful adventure of the hero is the unlocking and release again of the flow of life into the body of the world." In ancient times this energy undoubtedly helped to coordinate the individual with society and to strengthen the group; but today all potential for meaning resides in the individual, and so myth has acquired a purely personal value.[59]

Campbell lists about fifteen major incidents in the career of the hero. To begin with, the hero feels himself a chosen one. As Sartre writes in his autobiography, *The Words*, "I had taken precautions against accidental death, that was all; the Holy Ghost had commissioned me to do a long and exacting job, he had to leave me time enough to carry it out. . . . we [Death and I] had made a date; if I showed up too soon, it wouldn't be there yet."[60] The chosen one, in Campbell's narrative, must begin his quest by separating himself from the ordinary world: "The first work of the hero is to retreat from the world of secondary effects to those causal zones of the psyche where the difficulties really reside . . . " and he must break through to a direct experience of the archetypal images. Psychoanalysis, religious teaching, and myth all remove the hero from his ordinary milieu and thus from the enterprises and distractions offered to him by his culture. At the village boundary the hero crosses the threshold into the world of adventure.[61] Adventure will set him free to become great by protecting him from the annoyances of the mediocre life: the palace roof that needs repair, the palace plumber who must be dealt with. The tribe and its tribulations have been left behind; only one man exists.

The quest is thus a closed as well as a profoundly open situation. To our infantile and foetal longings for the womb we can attribute the appeal of islands, caves, ships, mountain cabins, tree houses, writers' studies, painters' ateliers, closets of one sort or another, safari tents. Such isolated sites not only delight us with their furnishings but shelter us from everything else in the world which is not privileged to have been included. The traveler may enjoy the best of both worlds, exploring the *exotic* with the tight weight of *en*closed independence clasped in his hand: thus the romance of luggage.

The hero, now on his way, is often tempted from the true path by an offer of earthly pleasures,[62] just as the Buddhist traditionally encounters the best of the world he is giving up. But the hero must first prove himself by a series of sacrifices before he ever has a chance to unsheath his sword.

At and beyond the threshold of adventure the hero encounters a series of opponents and helpers. Even apparent disasters may turn out to be only tests or provocations to heroic action. Woman, often encountered at the nadir of the hero's cycle, comprises the greatest test of all, as much one of interpretation as of performance. In Campbell's words "Woman, in the picture language of mythology, represents the totality of what can be known. The hero is the one who comes to know. As he progresses in the slow initiation which is life, the form of the goddess undergoes for him a series of transfigurations: she can never be greater than himself, though she can always promise more than he is yet capable of comprehending."[63] Woman provides the text, but in code; the hero must break the code, but gently, and possess the text in which has been written more than he ever hoped to know. Some texts, however, are deadly: The Sirens tempt Odysseus with knowledge (*Odyssey* 12. 189–91); Ovid calls them "learned," *doctae sirenes* (5. 535); in late antiquity the sobriquet *siren* could be applied to any glib and learned man (*Palatine Anthology* 9. 184 and elsewhere).[64] Sensuality seems to be commingling with wisdom.

Campbell makes a valiant attempt to bridge the Jung-Freud abyss on the subject of women.

> The mythical marriage with the queen goddess of the world represents the hero's total mastery of life; for the woman is life, the hero its knower and master. And the testings of the hero, which were preliminary to his ultimate experience and deed, were symbolical of those crises of realization by means of which his consciousness came to be amplified and made capable of enduring the full possession of the mother-destroyer, his inevitable bride. With that he knows that he and the father are one: he is in the father's place.[65]

After the hero's union with the goddess (sacred marriage) he is recognized by his creator (atonement with the father), apotheosized or perhaps ("if the powers have remained unfriendly to him") bereft of the boon he has won. Finally he must return to the ordinary world, either as emissary of the transcendental powers or as fugitive; he re-crosses the threshold and, if he has held on to the boon, restores the world with its elixir.[66]

As thorough and noble an attempt to write the Ur-myth as Campbell's has been, it still reminds one of those farinaceous accounts of the idyllic life of some primitive tribe—who turn out, when visited by an impartial observer, to be riddled with yaws and goiter, to pad about on splayed feet, to subsist entirely on yams, and to practice a system of usury based on snails' shells. Few heroes ever go as far as Joseph Campbell thinks they do; few enjoy happy, healthy marriages or the equivalent; many indulge in craven or criminal acts somewhere along the way.

Classical Exemplars

Let us look at a few episodes from the long-running careers of Heracles, Jason, Theseus, and Odysseus. Their whole life-cycles may be said roughly to correspond to the narrative pattern laid out by Campbell (albeit without suiting the optimistic tenor of his prose) and may be consulted in any handbook of mythology.

Heracles had no grave; his reward for distinguished labors—in service to his cousin Eurystheus, at the command of Apollo, as penance for killing his wife and children in a fit of madness laid on him by his enemy Hera—was to be turned into a god: a painful process, since his mortal portion had first to be burned away by poison and the funeral pyre. He was the only hero to receive both Olympian and chthonian sacrifice and his fate was thought to symbolize man's striving for immortality by way of great deeds. Through his association with hot springs he was a healer, but through those same springs he commanded a direct channel to the Underworld.[67]

He was a man of antithetical parts, "on the margin between culture and nature," as one scholar remarks of Homeric heroes, or potentially occupying "both polarities at the same time," as another scholar remarks of tragedic heroes.[68] No hero found that border-country more difficult to traverse than Heracles did: while he always worked for the side of culture, his virtues periodically turned into his vices and toppled him into the darker realms of the cosmos and of himself. In Freudian terms, the ego-istic hero does battle with the irrational forces of the wilderness (the id, the many monsters of his labors) for the sake of the sometimes equally irrational forces of civilization (the superego, the universal polis of mankind). He is a bulwark pounded from both sides.

How many animal aspects there are to Heracles! Kirk notes: his hairiness, his lion-skin armor, his club, his ravenous appetites for food and drink and sex. He is the smooth man Gilgamesh and the hairy man Enkidu all rolled into one hero wrestling with himself.[69] The physique of the centaurs—the horsemen whose lives touch Heracles' so many times—expresses the same dichotomy: all man above, all beast below the waist. Cheiron and Pholus, those wild old centaurs of Magnesia, distill wisdom for the young heroes in their charge and herbal panaceas for all mankind; but your average, bad centaur wields a rough club and exhibits a herculean weakness for the ladies and a tendency to go berserk after two sips of freshly tromped wine.

Heracles had as difficult a struggle with his female side as with his male. The *ne plus ultra* of strength and virility, he is periodically thrown into a weak and womanish posture. His labors were set him by the weak Eurystheus, Queen Omphale of Lydia made him dress as a woman and forced him to spin, his priests dressed as women on certain occasions, and sometimes he was called *misogynos*, "woman-hater."[70] Never one to tarry over the preliminaries of love, he swived the fifty daughters of King Thespius in one drunken night. Lust for a young woman, Iole, got him into trouble with his wife, Deianeira: Long ago the centaur Nessus had tried to rape Deianeira; Heracles shot him with one of his arrows poisoned with the venom of the Lernaean Hydra; before he died Nessus told Deianeira that his blood and ejaculate were a love potion, to be applied topically; she collected the ingredients in a vial, and now for fear of losing Heracles' love to his mistress anointed his linen with it. The Hydra's poison, by way of the arrow, the blood and semen of the centaur, and Deianeira's foolishness, destroyed Heracles (acting on his flesh like napalm). In his death scene in Sophocles' *Women of Trachis* Heracles laments that he once cleaned up the woods and seas (of beasts); that he defeated the Nemean lion, the Hydra, the Erymanthian boar, Cerberus, and the dragon of the Hesperides; that he survived the violence of these beasts and the fight with the Earth-born Giants, only to be brought down by a woman—one utterly unlike a man—without even a sword (lines 1012–13, 1090–1111, 1051–63, 1026–28). The violence and lust of Heracles' nature (projected onto a centaur) combined with his misunderstanding of women, foolish or otherwise, to destroy him.

Only with Athena did he maintain a long-term relationship. She could always spot a winner, sided with him from the beginning, and backed him all the way to Olympus. The earthly course of their relationship is portrayed on the metopes of the temple of Zeus at Olympia, which depict the twelve labors of Heracles. She directs him, lends him spiritual support and on occasion a helping hand, but never actually does his work for him. Only once do they touch—her foot accidentally brushes his. He grows older, wearier, as the labors go on; she never loses her girlish looks, having put aside her helmet so we can observe the unwrinkling front of a goddess. Athena (or now and then Hera or Aphrodite) serves as the hero's soul-mate, the feminine force he can resort to when no masculine one suffices to propel him through and out of danger. Finally, in a number of vase-paintings, she introduces Heracles to the exclusive circle of the gods, beseeching her father Zeus, with a tug on his beard, to accept the newcomer. Once an immortal, Heracles marries one of his mother's servants, Hebe—*Youth* personified.

Heracles thus has something to offer everyone by way of example: the buffoon, the ignoble savage, the humble and obedient servant of mankind, the exalted one who has transmuted the lead of his labors on earth into the gold of immortality on Olympus. Like the Einstein of Barthes' *Mythologies* who "reconciles the infinite power of man over nature with the 'fatality' of the sacrosanct, which man cannot yet do without,"[71] Heracles compensates for his successes and immortality with his tragic overreaching and his "death."

Theseus, too, although favored by Athena, brought his life to a bitter end—and without the sweet codicil of a seat on Olympus. He abandoned one woman (Ariadne) after she was of no further use to him in his career (more a political career as organizer of Attica than a quest, although the theme of a journey with a boon at the end does wind its way through his life), was betrayed by another's lust (Phaedra) for his son, enjoyed adventures with a series of others (Hippolyte, Helen, Persephone), but never came to terms with women, never cultivated a woman in his life. Plutarch records "other stories also about marriages of Theseus which were neither honorable in their beginnings nor fortunate in their endings ... " and mentions four or five by way of example (*Theseus* 29.1–2). Indeed, his domestic affairs were distinguished by failure at every turn—with mistress, wife, son, father, stepmother, and other relatives. He ended his days alone on the rocky island of Scyros, where he fell or was pushed off a goat path and over a cliff.

Jason was blessed with the favor of at least two goddesses: Hera who liked him from the start and planned to use him against her enemy, his impious uncle Pelias, persuaded Aphrodite to endow him with good looks and irresistible charm. (Athena, too, turns up in some scenes on vases to lend him moral support.) Hypsipyle, queen of the Lemnian women (famed for murdering their husbands), fell in love with him and helped him and his fellow Argonauts on their quest for the golden fleece. Then Medea, the young witch of Colchis, abandoned home and family, killed a brother, and ensured her father's loss of power, in order to save Jason's life and procure him the fleece. In Medea, Jason carried off more of a woman than he could ever be a match for. Despite numerous demonstrations of her power and her temper, when a barbarian mate seemed a drawback to his already faltering career he foolishly tried to put her aside. Done out of his birthright in northern Greece, he planned to marry the princess of Corinth and succeed to her father's throne. Medea devised a way to dissolve both princess and king into a burning mass and thus ended Jason's chances to advance his career without her. She rode off in a winged chariot to a new life in Athens, and he ended his life ignominiously in Corinth—the hero as burnt-out case. A piece of his old ship the Argo, rotting, broke off and split his silvering pate as he dozed alongside in the shade.

The epic or tragic hero defines himself through his opponents. When they have been disposed of, he tends to fade away as a personage. Whether as victor or vanquished, he is a superannuated man, even if still in his prime. Never having taken the time out to make his soul, he seems not to have one, once the reflecting glass of conflict has been removed. Without surveying all the Greek heroes and mapping their careers, I wish to suggest by way of a few examples that most of these savage noblemen come to grief through lack of understanding of woman. They defeat many monsters in the course of their quests; but those victories so often give them the false confidence that they have comprehended what they have only impaled. The quest—if the hero takes it as no more than a series of physical events and does not bother to project an inner journey onto the outer one—will lead him to a bitter end, in which the female forces he supposedly conquered in his youth seem to rise up from their beds or their graves and take revenge not for his victories but for his stupidity. Only by making a dynamic peace with woman, the external and the internal one, can the hero mediate between the warring forces of nature and culture and coordinate the elements of his antinomical self. One hero stands out as a success with women and as a success at the end.

The One Who Finished Last Was Best

The details of Odysseus' journey often remind one of Jason's and of journeys in general—the voyage into an unknown region past monsters and natural wonders, the band of faithful companions, the various women who help the hero reach his goal, the death of old ways and the rebirth of a new self (from Hades, from the west, from the vortex of Charybdis, across the threshold of the Cyclop's cave). The resemblance is only superficial: the poet of the *Odyssey* may have adapted much of his plot from earlier accounts of the voyage of the Argonauts. But Jason's quest was for an intrinsically worthless object, a golden fleece; Odysseus', for his homecoming (*nostos*, as in *nostalgia*). Achilles had to choose between *nostos* and *kleos* ("fame"), but Odysseus got both. [72] When he takes over the poet's role in Book 8 and sings his own story to the court at Phaeacia, he anticipates the career of the hero as artist, who commemorates his own deeds, preserves his own fame; and when in Book 21 the actual poet compares Odysseus' stringing of the bow to the stringing of a lyre, *he* anticipates the artist as hero. Odysseus is not alone, despite his doubled role. Penelope, by proposing the contest of the bow and giving him the only possible means of defeating the suitors, is responsible for his *nostos* and thus for his fame as the man who came home after twenty years, killed his rivals, and found his wife faithful as on the day he left her. He, of course, as the man worth waiting for, could claim responsibility for her faithfulness. Whence this talent of husband and wife for each other?

Noos or *nous* ("mind," "wit," and much more) and *nostos* ("return") may come from the same root; thus can the attainment of one's past be identified with the getting of wisdom. The companions lost their *nostos* because of their lack of *noos* (*nepioi* the poet calls them, "foolish children"); Odysseus achieved *his* return because of his ample intelligence.[73] Genius is born *and* made. Odysseus' natural wit was developed by his education before the Trojan War and by his adventures on the way home. The women he experienced between Troy and Ithaca offered him not mere interludes but opportunities to learn more *noos* (*Odyssey* 1.3); to acquire the sort of intelligence that the Greeks associated with weaving, tricks, riddles, disguises, potions, and feminine guile; to become the man who was a match for Penelope, herself the match for any man; and finally to be worthy of the prize that *she*—bow in hand—offers *him*. Adventure in the *Odyssey* has been transmuted into a kind of wisdom, knowledge of others into knowledge of oneself that makes one worthy of others. This is the quest psychoanalysts talk of when they talk about a hundred other heroes' flimsy careers.

Or do we read our twentieth-century aspirations toward the light into the dark thoughts of Homer's Odysseus? Others have done so. Witness Cavafy's Odysseus who never wants to reach his goal ("pray your road is long"); or Tennyson's restless personage ("I am become a name"); or Kazantzakis' manic wanderer ("Even my island moves under my feet like the angry sea") who winds up in Antarctica! But Homer's man came home and meant, after a brief expiatory pilgrimage, to stay there.

To answer the question posed at the beginning of this chapter, the heroes of legend can serve usefully as paradigms of behavior, but not for long. Until, say the sixth century B.C. for Greek civilization, by which time the problem of coordinating the rising individual's desires with civilization's conservative requirements exceeded the resources of myth to provide answers: Achilles and even Odysseus lacked the elasticity to respond to those antipodal tugs. The way out for the modern middle-aging hero with a newly acquired but useless boon on his hands is to abandon his physical quest for a spiritual one: to do something which the eminently practical Odysseus never did but nevertheless continues to suggest to us.

9

Eros and Psyche

"O dear Phaedrus, where are you coming from and where are you going now?"

—Plato, *Phaedrus*

Y OU CAN'T ALWAYS TELL a hero at first glance, and the greatest battles may be of a kind that would barely have caught the notice of the old, epic audience. At the turn of the fifth century into the fourth—and with the deaths of Euripides and Sophocles, the trial and execution of Socrates, the creation of a guilt-culture within a shame-culture, the failure of either Athens or Sparta to resume their flourishings after thirty years of war between them, the ultimate defeat of the city-state by the mounted genius of Macedon, the subsequent imposition of a kingdom on Greece, and the rise of individualism among the prosperous urban classes—with all of this happening at the end of the Classical Age and the beginning of the Hellenistic, the hero found he had to don new guises and disguises, to strike out in new directions. In short, he realized that his vocation was now himself.[1]

Freedom once construed, in an age of immediate democracy, as an ideal to be realized within the body politic, has been forced, in ages of despotism and bureaucratic democracy, to go underground to find work—within the soul of man, where creativity depends not simply on courage and endurance but on reflection and interpretation, on intelligence and consciousness. Such changes do not occur quickly. But already in the themes and characters of fifth-century tragedies we have seen modern, psychoanalytical concerns adumbrated. The time must have been ripe for one generation to consider putting the ideals of previous generations on the shelf. When Plato attacks the poets, he is really attacking the whole way of life, habit of thought, and system of values which they, particularly Homer, had enshrined in their verse.[2] The rise in literacy may

211

have had much to do with this. About the time *Oedipus the King* was first produced, sons were becoming more literate than their fathers.[3] Marshall McLuhan assures us that literate man is a private creature with a discrete and stable inner world, whereas in the closed, tribal society of pre-literate Homeric man that abstraction called the self may not yet have been thought of.[4]

A sense of glorious destiny saved Achilles and Odysseus from hopelessness. And while many tragic heroes appear utterly tragic indeed, the questions posed in the plays were to a large extent answered by the situation of the audience: do not despair, *you* needn't suffer like this, *you* can find safety in citizenship. But the time came when there were no more city-states to serve and all destined destinies had been accomplished and even would-be heroes lacked the imagination to invent more.[5]

If the hero does think of something to do, he will not escape a new sort of shame or (depending on how you look at it) guilt. In Nietzsche's view, "The free human being is immoral because in all things he is *determined* to depend upon himself and not upon a tradition: in all the original conditions of mankind, 'evil' signifies the same as 'individual,' 'free,' 'capricious.' "[6] While performance once upon a time—for the original heroes—meant public service, for the new heroes it suggests rather self-indulgence of a rigorous sort: for the philosopher, the artist, the *Übermensch* or Superman of Nietzschean fame and Nazi infamy, and the analysand. The bad name Socrates, as the first such private hero, acquired for the new breed has not been shed by analytical man. Just as Nietzsche told his nonexistent audience, "Do not understand me too quickly," Freud feared, in Bruno Bettleheim's words, that "psychoanalysis would be destroyed if it was widely accepted without being widely understood." And his fear was justified: "it has come to be assumed that psychoanalysis advocated 'letting it all hang out,' all over the place, all the time. 'Know thyself' has become 'Do whatever you please.' "[7]

The Rankian Artist

Of the four new heroes I have posited, philosopher, artist, superman, and analysand, Freud would have regarded the artist as coming closest to deserving obloquy. But what makes one an artist is the ability to pull up just short of "letting it hang out" and to convert private concerns into the raw material for public art. The artist, according to Freud, has developed himself from a near-neurotic who is obsessed by powerful instinctual needs and the desire for wealth, fame, power, women. He transforms his desires and fantasies into art and thus leads himself back to reality: "he understands how to work over his daydreams in such a way as to make them lose what is too personal about them and repels strangers, and to make it possible for others to share in the enjoyment of them. He understands, too, how to tone them down so that they do not easily betray their origin from proscribed sources."[8] The primary function of art, then, may be symbolically to reconcile competing pressures. The artist can relax the psychic censorship of conscious life and allow the repressed to have its say. He sounds the clarion of victory for the ego, the critic Frederick Crews writes, "if not in 'happy endings' then in the triumph of form over chaos, meaning over panic, mediated claims over naked conflict, purposeful action over sheer psychic spillage."[9] Freud makes a similar observation, but from the therapist's point of view: "If a person who is at loggerheads with reality possesses an *artistic gift*. . . . , he can transform his phantasies into artistic creations instead of into symptoms. In this manner he can escape the doom of neurosis and by this roundabout path regain his contact with reality."[10] Artists, having begun their struggles at the same point as neurotics, succeed in taking the giant step from sick soliloquy to culturally acceptable oratory. "Literature," as Philip Rieff reductively puts it, "is merely the craft some personalities develop at exhibiting their deeper emotions."[11]

Artists, however, even those who lead far from exemplary lives (Villon, Byron, Gaugin, Mailer) may show us the way out of our neuroses, encourage us to establish real order where they themselves, in some instances, could create only the illusion of order. Paul Ricoeur qualified Freud's pronouncements on the common ground between psychoanalysis and art: works of art "are not simply projections of the artist's conflicts, but the sketch of their solution. Dreams look backward, toward infancy, the past; the work of art goes ahead of the artist; it is a prospective symbol of his personal synthesis and of man's future, rather than a regressive symbol of his unresolved conflicts."[12]

Otto Rank, too, disagreed with Freud on the subject of creativity—which he understood not as a neurotic symptom, but the highest form of living, an expression of a quite un-Freudian self-determination and of the desire for immortality, a veritable overcoming of our first fear which was of life not of death. In *Art and Artist* he asserts that the artist is a conquering hero in the truest sense.[13] Originally, however, back in the dismal days of our tribal beginnings, it was not the attempts by individual artists to attain personal immortality which bodied forth musical, literary, or sculptural productions; rather the primitive longing for abstraction both created the notion of the soul and gave aural or tactile form to that notion in art. Eventually, a conflict arose between the tribe's collective belief in immortality and the personal consciousness of the artist. Christ temporarily relieved the budding genius of Western man from the duty of making himself over, for the figure of Christ constituted no model hero but, instead, the victim who volunteered the development of everyone's personality.

Only at the close of the Middle Ages and the beginning of the Renaissance was individual genius freed from the tyranny of the collective spirit; but the artist still needs to keep the various communal ideologies handy, if only to exercise the force of his personality by overcoming them.[14]

The individual, Rank continues, appoints himself an artist but then, through the compulsion to work and achieve, must justify his self-election: he raises himself above the community by his inclusion in the genius-type, very much as an object is alienated from its natural surroundings by artistic stylization. Creativity thus begins with the making of the individual personality into the self of the artist. Both the neurotic and the artist, unlike the average man, tend to exercise their wills to create themselves. But the neurotic does not go beyond the destructive preliminary work; he idealizes himself and then wallows in self-criticism. The artist, the antithesis of the self-destructive neurotic, although he criticizes himself nevertheless accepts his personality. We must ultimately pay for an aggrandizement of life; but the neurotic, afraid of making the final payment, death, consistently restricts his life, the loan: he aims at self-preservation by restricting his experience. The neurotic avoids life; the artist uses it in his art, where he really lives himself out: he does not produce his calling so much as himself becomes it. Through creation (and here Rank comes close to speaking of sublimation) he can be sure of keeping the less ruly matters of life under control. The inhibitions that artists complain about in the process of creation and its intervals are merely the ego's necessary—not neurotic—protections against being swallowed by demon creativity. Even the true artist may suffer a neurotic collapse after a great production, through a sense of guilt arising from the arrogance of creative masterfulness. And the artist may have his troubles with success, because even though he has won it through his art it is still a success in that very life from which he has fled to art as a refuge. The revolutionary artist creates collective values and is himself finally collectivized by the community; throughout their careers, great artists resist the threat of this dissolution of their selves by plotting new creations, new revolts. But eventually success and fame complete the cycle of conflict between individual and group: the individual acquires immortality through success, and the community, in its turn, appends to itself the immortality won by the individual.[15]

The artist requires not only an ideology suited to his individualism—the genius-concept—but also a more restricted audience, his Muse, for whom alone he creates. (This is the reverse of the classical situation, in which the poet was the only auditor of his guiding Muse: "Tell *me*, O Muse," Homer begged, so that he might then repeat her story to his audience.) Classical art, in general, depends on the conformity of the ideology of art with the ideology of culture and thus does not allow the personal revolt necessary for the creation of the artist-hero. Nevertheless Rank, somewhat inconsistently, interprets the saga of Oedipus as the Greek artist's revolt against the average man's experience of the preordained parental relation: the myth symbolizes the striving for independence in human development, which paradoxically can be achieved only by the hero or poet deliberately making what is universally fated into part of his own, very personal, experience. [16]

In "The Double as Immortal Self," a chapter in his last book, *Beyond Psychology*, Rank made an interesting addendum to the subject of the artist as hero: "Among such specially endowed individuals [those chosen by destiny, heroes and artists], really deviates, the twin stands out as the one who was capable of bringing with him into earthly existence his living double and thus had no need to procreate himself in any other form." Twins appear to have created themselves independently of natural fertility and consequently seem able to create something new, something not found in nature—namely, culture. The heroic type emerged from the cult of twins, and so twinship symbolizes the self-creative tendency. The artist-hero creates a spiritual double in his own image—his work. He abjures the naive belief in the automatic survival of his physical double, his son, who in any case portends the father's passing: he thus labors for the double of immortality, through his artistic achievements, rather than submitting to the double of death, through the natural order of the generations. [17]

Nietzsche, ever the salvationist, seems to anticipate both Freud's realistic and Rank's idealistic positions when he praises the models literature offers us:

> Only they [artists] have taught us to esteem the hero that is concealed in everyday characters; only they have taught us the art of viewing ourselves as heroes—from a distance and, as it were, simplified and transfigured— the art of staging and watching ourselves. Only in this way can we deal with some base details in ourselves. Without this art we would be nothing but foreground and live entirely in the spell of that perspective which makes what is closest at hand and most vulgar appear as if it were vast, and reality itself. [18]

Nietzsche manages to have his hero both Freud's and Rank's ways, because he defines health not as an accidental lack of disease but as the experience of having overcome infection and the heightened ability to do so again. The sick man writes books, often about heroes, whereas the true hero keeps healthy silence.

Nietzsche himself invented the ultimate mythological hero for his readers to emulate, the *Übermensch*, someone yet to exist—the man, specifically the philosopher, who has transcended himself and thereby becomes the highest instance of humanity. The Superman or near-Superman is the true goal of the race. Such single great human beings occur at random, not as the result of a breeding program; nor do they serve the best interests of society, of the race, or even of the individual himself. "No man explores into his own nature," Norman Mailer explains, "without submitting to a curse from the root of biology since existence would cease if it were natural to turn upon oneself."[19] Or, as Nietzsche himself puts it: "At times, our strengths propel us so far forward that we can no longer endure our weaknesses and perish from them."[20]

Of course Nietzsche's creation falls short of reality. "His Superman," Auden writes, "who combines the self-consciousness of a man with the self-assurance of an animal, is a chimaera."[21] But perhaps the elusiveness of the paradigm makes it all the more useful. Nietzsche rails against resting content with the status quo. His quarrel is with time: "What does a philosopher demand of himself first and last? To overcome his time in himself, to become 'timeless.' With what must he therefore engage in the hardest combat? With whatever marks him as a child of his time."[22]

If nature takes an interest in the development of the individual, of the Superman, then there must be a nature to which one can be true. One can feel compelled to self-transcendence only if a daimon, a genius, an archetype, or the ground of Being itself is urging one on into an as yet uncreated future. Nietzsche, however, would have denied the existence of a guiding principle, preferring as he did to romanticize his loneliness into an ideology. He thereby anticipated the existentialists' myth of the anti-hero but abjured the gods of the Greek philosophers.

The Platonic Philosopher

The Homeric hero's career had a fixed content—the quest for glory in battle, with all the attendant ceremony that swirls around a noble warrior. Eventually the quest was transmuted into a spiritual and personal one, when fighting had become a job for mercenaries, not citizens, and the hero's career simply a way of his being true to himself or to some principles fixed in the firmament far above this world's shift and flux. The hero separated himself from the group that had raised him and asserted, like the true ancestor of the analysand, that he found service to the group and atonement with it an insufficent consolation for the labor and pain of existence.[23] In this individualistic revolt Odysseus prefigured Socrates, and both spiritually fathered Apuleius' Lucius—a character who, in a novel of the second century A.D., was transformed into an ass and overheard an old lady tell a young girl the myth of

Cupid and Psyche. This, the least tribal, the most personal of all the classical myths, seems not only to fit its particular protagonist's case, and perhaps the novelist's case as well, but to prefigure the myth of analysis. (Guilt may now be supposed to matter more than shame; and, according to Plato and Socrates, the problem of evil ought to have disappeared. But the old literary forms, most of them mythomorphic and shame-ridden, always remain to be dealt with.)

Plato has many ways to tell a myth—science-fictions for the structure of the world (Atlantis, the reverse cosmos), allegories to extend the power of his dialectic out over our imaginations (the prisoners in the cave, the chariot of the soul), and little dramas in which Socrates himself lays hold of myth and like a questing hero embarks on the path of Eros leading through human life to the world of the forms.[24] The mythomorphic vein was still being mined in Plato's day; and, if the silver ran out, a good poet (Plato's first vocation) could change the leftover lead of the sagas into pure philosophic gold. Hence, Plato equips Socrates with many of the traditional traits of the Homeric warrior, but in forms modified to sustain the new, philosophic content of the hero's role. For the Socratic philosopher the discernment of rational standards, patterns, and paradigms is not only the road to the reflective life but also the mimetic way to Virtue. But even for an individual questing along new heights of moral speculation there are still older figures for him to model himself on. Plato found the domain of the soul as challenging a battlefield as the, by his time, almost meaningless assembly; this new world needed myth for its shores to be made accessible to the likes of mere men, and Socrates—who was himself *entheos*, "enthused"—was the very hero to animate the saga of Virtue and the forms.

In the agonistic Greek world of politicians, sophists, athletes, and poets, Plato's Socrates stands out as the most erotically powerful intellectual in Athens. Plato, the philosopher as distinguished author rather than as hero, enjoyed a superior sense of breeding and reserve over his rather vulgar mentor. But Plato's attitude toward his heritage was far from unquestioning. He resented the old timocracy and shame-culture memorialized by Homer, and in his more utopian moods, he was determined to eradicate its lingering influence. The men of that culture had killed Socrates; and Friedländer draws attention to how Plato's mind was attracted again and again, by the defeat of Socrates before the Athenian court, to the myth of the judgment of the dead in a world beyond.[25] Much has been made of Plato's attacks on poetry and drama. Bennett Simon claims Plato "saw that myth does not allow one to free oneself from endless repetition and reenactment of old problems and conflicts."[26] Such freedom as this may be claimed by analytical man, child of a different time. Plato, however, grew up on the myths. He was, in fact, unable to escape their influence but realized their rhetorical efficacy; and, once he thought he had solved the political dilemma fancied that the outer world could be rendered as self-consistent and ethically pure as the inner world: he would happily have forced the citizens of his utopias into very circumscribed lives indeed.

Socrates enjoys the full range of heroic attributes and encounters: a noble descent from Daedalus (*Euthyphro* 11 B–C); self-control *(egkrateia)* and virtue *(aretē)*; endurance of heat and cold and various other privations, but also (unlike the other heroes—say, Heracles) resistance to the temptations of wine and boys (*Symposium* 176 C, 219 E); a set of monsters to defeat, namely, the Sophists; a protégé, just as Heracles' nephew Iolaus served as squire and helpmeet; and a distinguishing weapon (like Odysseus' bow or like Heracles' bow, club, and impenetrable lion skin): dialectic—a weapon which Socrates purloined from the armory of the sophists and maliciously wields in the service of truth and metaphysical, if not earthly, justice.

The course of Socrates' life is pursued, in Plato's dialogues, toward a goal that, while mysterious, is embedded in a permanence beyond the unreliability of mortal existence. Diogenes Laertius once wrote some verses to Socrates which described him as *en Dios ōn*, "being in the house of Zeus" (2.45)—thus implying that, like Heracles, he had successfully completed his labors and gone to his heavenly, his heroic, reward. And Xenophon, in his *Memorabilia*, has Socrates recall Prodicus' essay on Heracles' passage from childhood to youth: while the future hero was sitting in a quiet spot, wondering whether to take the path of Virtue or that of Vice, two women approached and described the ways open to him (2.1.21–34). Virtue's path sounds like the way taken by Socrates, who thus suggests he is like Heracles, the model traveller on the highway of Life.

As the hero seeks to improve the physical world or break trail for the spirit of man, his deeds and very nature attract new enemies, who line up on the side of either a decadent status quo or a decline into chaos. In the *Apology* Socrates describes how his interlocutors have attacked him whenever he showed they knew nothing; he would have been surprised had it been otherwise, but one ought to be fearless and care only if one is doing right or wrong. Should all the demi-gods who fought at Troy be considered craven for doing their duties by their own lights? He, Socrates, was assigned his station by the god—to spend his life in philosophy and in examining himself and others (23 D–24 B, 28 B–30 A). In the absence of any viable saintly or psychoanalytical metaphor, Socrates' image of himself can only be regarded as a heroic one. Nowhere else, in Plato's dialogues or in Socrates' ostensible consciousness of the meaning of his own life, is his mythic role so explicitly suggested. Plato has given the heroic model a new life, while relieving it of the dread of shame that was largely responsible for the old hero's tragic irrationality. Euripides had, by this time, introduced new standards of realism and guilt into the old, inflexible, shame-governed world of the myths. But Plato went well beyond the problem posed by the juxtaposition of mythic and contemporary worlds on Euripides' stage, and *doubt*

exchanged guilt (in the form of aporetic questioning) for shame and substituted a peculiar form of eros (in the person of Socrates) for the wrath and might of the *Iliad*'s heroes.

While adopting a heroic posture, Socrates also turns his back on the heroism of the old school. After drinking his poison, he tells his friends there must be no weeping; he has sent the women away for this very reason (*Phaedo* 177 D–E). This new male world of bravery and silence is far removed from the Homeric vale of tears and halls of boasting. The Homeric hero boasts of his imperfections, but Socrates' very sobriety at the end of the *Symposium* is a warning that the old temptations can find no purchase on the smooth virtue of the philosopher-hero.

The hero should have a divine patroness, to save him when he has exhausted his resources, to restrain him from barging in where even daimons fear to tread; and Socrates received instruction from two mortal women. Aspasia, a former courtesan and the most interesting woman in Athens, taught rhetoric to both Socrates and Pericles (*Menexenus* 235 E–236 C); and Diotima, the witch from Arcadia, gave Socrates lectures, very early in his career as a thinker, on the mysteries of Eros. Fate, after having revealed itself in the form of a divine protector of a hero (like Odysseus' Athena) eventually develops into the personal daimon.[27] As Socrates matures, in life and in Plato's account of him, into a more philosophically rounded hero, he leaves behind his mortal patronesses and comes to recognize and rely on a divine, internal one—his "voice" or daimon. Athena, too, increases her aid to Odysseus and Heracles as their travels and labors progress; and so the voice of Socrates' daimon—although he has heard it since childhood (*Apology* 31 C–D)—plays a greater role as he enters the critical stages of his career. It becomes more an intimate of his soul than merely a visiting counselor, it corresponds to the feminine part of the hero himself, and it emerges as the key both to Socrates' poise and to his erotic power.

The hero's distinguishing genius seems determined by his noble, often semi-divine birth or by some unexplained *moira* ("fate" in the sense of one's allotment in life). In the just universe that the Greek philosopher claims as his context there must be some explanation besides noble birth for his election to a hero's fate. At the end of the *Republic* we learn that the daimon does not choose the soul, but rather the soul selects its daimon (617 E). The philosopher-hero, then, was not a passive, unconscious psyche picked at random for the role from some ectoplasmic chorus line, but rather an already sentient being who deliberately sought that role, which at critical moments of his career may be personified as his daimon. Personal effort and wisdom bring the reward of an improved soul, an improved relationship with the daimonic. As Socrates has progressed in conversations with his soul, he has become almost a daimon or something divine himself.

The philosopher-governors of the *Republic* (the Supermen of Plato's utopia) depart after their work here is done, to the Isles of the Blessed; and the state should establish memorials and sacrifices to them, as to daimons if the priestess of Apollo approves, or if she does not approve then as to holy and godlike men (7. 540 B–C). Here in this passage, more clearly than anywhere else in the dialogues, the philosopher approaches the status of a mythological hero, one of those to whom libations were undoubtedly poured at the symposia held once a month in Plato's Academy. And if Athenaeus' *Deipnosophistai, Table Talk of the Sages*, is to be believed, Athena (the daimon of Odysseus) and Eros (one form of Socrates' daimon) were worshipped together at the Academy (13. 561 D–E)—a fact Plato never mentions.

In the *Symposium* Socrates becomes identified with Eros as well as with a daimon. Like Love, Socrates is ugly but desires the beautiful; he is poor, shoeless, a good hunter, always weaving some stratagem, midway between wisdom and ignorance. Like a daimon, Socrates acts as a messenger and interpreter between gods and men—an intermediate being and an intermediary. Heroes (*hēmitheoi*, "demi-gods") and mules (*hēmionoi*, half-asses, mentioned in the *Apology*) are caught in cosmological and zoological halfway states; and philosophers have similarly made it only halfway up the road from ignorance to wisdom. Alcibiades clinches the certification of Socrates as a daimon by saying that he looks like a satyr, specifically like a silenus figure in a sculptor's shop— the kind with a hollow belly that opens up to reveal images of the gods (215 A– C). Which gods? Certainly Dionysus, whom satyrs and sileni attend. Now, asses and mules carry the god and his wineskins, and sometimes they couple with the satyrs. Plato may be not only describing the bright side of Socrates' erotic daimonism (heroes and gods) but also slyly alluding to its dark side— that he was hung like a mule. The philosopher's superego balances, across the fulcrum of his ego, with his all-too-often neglected id.

Phaedrus and Pausanias, in their speeches in the *Symposium*, imply that heroic endeavor requires Eros. The hero's physiognomy usually expresses a restrained form of Love: he is "good and noble" (*kalos k'agathos*). But despite his well-proportioned good looks, his Eros often leads him on violent and sexual rampages. Socrates, on the other hand, despite his quite unheroic appearance and Dionysiac potential, remains the unmoved mover of his companions. The trivializing, gustatory anecdotes of, say, Heracles and the fifty daughters of King Thespius have been replaced by the story of Socrates holding out for a long night against Alcibiades. Socrates almost transcends the heroic and here resembles the older, bearded, sober Dionysus who sits quietly on a campstool while his inspired revelers whirl dervishly around him. Like the god of drink himself, Socrates cannot get drunk.

The madness of wine derives from a greater *mania*, of which physical Eros, too, is a manifestation. Madness comes from the god and is superior to sanity which is of human origin (*Phaedrus* 244 A–C). Madness proves the wholeness of Socrates' soul, where his real battles have been waged; and his possession by the divine is an earnest of his possession of the divine after death. Such a personality takes his inspiration wherever he can find it: Socrates explained to a startled Charmides, who found him dancing alone at home, that this was the more convenient way to do it (Xenophon, *Symposium* 2.17–19). The incident suggests that many would have called Socrates worse than *atopos*, "eccentric"—but truly an *idiotēs*, an "idiot," a private and ignorant person and therefore a social outlaw. (Psychoanalysis offers a socially acceptable opportunity for fifty minutes of private, idiotic but inspired, chanting, on appointment.)

Heroes are necessarily exposed to greater dangers than the general run of men. Alcibiades suggests, by claiming a resemblance between Socrates and Marsyas (the satyr who was flayed alive for daring to compete on the pipes with Apollo), that Socrates' excessive confidence in dialectic can turn his peculiar virtue into the mirror-imaged flaw of so many epic and tragic downfalls. Alcibiades traces a deficient eros in Socrates (*Symposium* 215 B, 222 A–B);[28] despite the hero's access to archetypal femininity through his patroness, he is likely to be the coldest as well as the most erotic character on the scene—erotic, surely, because he is the coldest, like Narcissus or Jason. Socrates as model of the whole man must also serve as model of the deficient man—a warning to us that these heroic roles have already been filled and we can go about our business with due attention to the warmth of quotidian detail and the construction of our souls.

Socrates' heroic coldness emanates from the employment of his second weapon, irony—for the ironist is an outsider, a resident alien even at home. This fleeting and elusive attitude suits the mythological exemplar, for mythology is fiction mixed with truth (*Republic* 2. 382 E). Only the duplicity of irony and the duplicity of myth can pretend to compensate for the essential reticence of reality. Nature's privileges of evasion, however, are not to be exercised for long by mere mortals, and there comes a time when we wish Socrates would drop his devices for keeping friends and enemies alike at a distance. But even the night before his execution, when he admits his ignorance of what he shall soon have to face on the other side, an essential coldness renders him deficient in simple human responses. The philosopher has learned the uses of irony— even more impenetrable than Odysseus' disguise as a beggar—not, ultimately, from the hero but from the epic poet, who needs to speak publicly yet cannot risk being completely understood lest he suffer expulsion from his patron's court or worse. The poet must encode his message in such a way that his text will be understood in one, safe, way by his immediate audience and another, fuller and truer but potentially dangerous, way by his fellows in art. The poet ensures his fame by constructing levels of meaning in his text unsuspected at the original performance. Unlike Homer or Euripides, Socrates failed to keep his irony and hubris undetected by the demos. Plato learned from his master's mistakes and claimed never to have written down his best work, since books can fall into the wrong hands.

In his coldness, Socrates resembles no hero more closely than Odysseus. In the *Lesser Hippias* Plato's Socrates argues that Odysseus is a better hero than Achilles, since he lies (or speaks the truth) entirely by design (365 B, 371 A–E). The ironic man, like the Cretan liar (another one of Odysseus' disguises), cannot help but prevaricate; his eloquence is of a kind full of safe truths that mislead by masquerading as the whole truth and thus distract the uninitiated from the true doctrines of the philosopher, draw them away from the *Schadenfreude* and about-to-be-enacted vengeance of the hero. Like Odysseus addressing the suitors as he prepares to shoot them down, Socrates mockingly praises the sophists just before doing them in.

In the myth of Er in Book 10 of the *Republic* the souls of those about to be reincarnated choose the forms they will take. Odysseus, after having selected a lot which could just as well fit Socrates—that of a private citizen, one without any ambition—drinks, along with his fellow revenants, of the River Lethe and washes his memory clean (621 A–B). This symbolic washing, like the sleep during which the drink will take effect, is a *rite de passage* marking the hero's entry into the world that awaits him at the end of his quest. Thus, Odysseus enjoys a last bath just before he returns to Penelope's arms, and Gilgamesh is given a splendid ablution before his tragic return from the Land of the Living to Uruk. Toward the end of the *Phaedo* (115 A) Socrates also expresses a desire to bathe, ostensibly so that he would not trouble the women with washing his corpse. In fact, he is behaving like an epic warrior to the end, one about to enter an Elysium reserved for the greatest heroes of myth.

Apuleius' Wanderer

After his death, Socrates' daimon enjoyed almost as much popularity as the philosopher himself did. Both Plutarch and Apuleius wrote monographs on the demi-god. E. R. Dodds believes that the refinement and spread of monotheism led to a growing belief in daimons, because pagans and Christians alike "needed an accessible mediator between themselves and the High God."[29]

(You can befriend or be patronized by one of a multiplicity of gods, who must develop personal characteristics in order to assert their individualities: in diversity is the chance to find a divine soul-mate. But the one and only deity cannot stoop to playing favorites.) Apuleius, an amateur Neo-Platonic philosopher whose syncretistic faith in the goddesses verged on monotheism, describes the divine powers of a middle kind, operating between the firmament and the earth, through whom word of our desires and deserts passes to the gods (*On the God of Socrates* 6–8). Philosophers were often known to pass themselves off as daimons: Epictetus, for example, observed in the first or second century A.D. that the true Cynic philosopher knows that he has been sent by Zeus as a messenger to men to show them how they have gone astray in good and evil (3. 22.23). And Apuleius, too, continued the same line of speculation about daimons, in his rhetorical showpiece, the *Florida* (10), where he cites Amor as one of the "middle powers of the gods." In his essay on Socrates he also calls Love a daimon, one whose task is to rouse us to consciousness (16); and in his novel, the *Golden Ass*, He apparently invented the myth of Cupid (Amor, Love) and Psyche (Soul) in its full narrative form. This, despite all the fuss made over it, is not a precise philosophical allegory but an imprecise, a poetic not dialectical, myth in the best tradition of Plato, extending not a logical line of argument but a Rabelaisian, picaresque account of the author's conversion from a dissolute life to one of joyous service to the goddess Isis.

Few interpreters have been content to deal with this book on its own straightforwardly idiosyncratic level. The monads of myth, Kerenyi asserts, break down into various mysticisms at the end of a culture.[30] In Apuleius' day, the late second century A.D., paganism was about to die out in the Roman Empire, Christianity to win the day. The more intellectual proponents of one mysticism were eager to claim as their own all the more attractive myths of their sundry competitors. Feats of allegorical interpretation not seen again until the Renaissance were performed on, among other texts, the *Golden Ass*. Of late, Jungians have claimed the novel as their own, discounted the possibility that its author was a consciously articulate artist, and discovered archetypal symbols crouching behind the arras of every episode.

What is this book about and what should we make of it? First, the style: an elaborate, semi-archaic, glowing diction laid down in a convoluted word order for the delectation of an audience that enjoyed rhetorical flourishes. For the most part, *we* are not such an audience and suspect a complex writer like Apuleius of "blocking," of trying to hide something which, with good, sincere analytical acumen, we think we can force him to face up to. He is not, however, blocking, but on the contrary giving us all he's got—although refusing all the while to don a flat, antiseptic style in order to record his protagonist's case history. Hugh Kenner understands these things: "Scrupulous homespun prose,

the plain style of narrative fidelity, was a late and temporary invention, affirming
the temporary illusion that fact and perception, event and voice are separable.
. . . Rhetoric in all its play is the human norm, the denotative plain style one
of its departments merely."[31] Apuleius was an ironist—much of what he says
means other than what it seems to. This assertion skirts close to the intentional
fallacy: how can we know what an author intended?—all we can talk about is
his text. But Apuleius' interpreters commit the unintentional fallacy and ascribe
all his carefully turned phrases and episodes to daydream work. Irony is beyond
their range, as it is beyond that of all computational theorists: a switch cannot
mean "on" when it reads "off." But we know from Plato and Euripides and the
rhetoricians that it very well can. The best literature declines to submit whole-
heartedly to the authority of the reader, just as the best patients, for fear of being
emptied and reduced to ciphers, keep a bit of themselves tucked safely away
from the probing thumbs of too simple an analyst.

The essential plot shows multifarious involutions which match the work's
style: Our first-person narrator, one Lucius (apparently Apuleius himself), is
traveling in Thessaly, a part of the world renowned for its magical practices. He
starts an affair with Fotis, the servant of some acquaintances who are putting
him up. The mistress of the house turns out to be a witch; and Lucius, who
has always been a curious chap, persuades Fotis to borrow milady's flying
ointment. But Fotis grabs the wrong jar; and instead of being turned briefly into
a bird he becomes an ass—permanently so unless he can chew the antidote of
rose petals. For various reasons he doesn't manage to get a bite of roses this
season and has to spend nearly a year in an ass's skin until they are in bloom
again. His new form disgusts him, except that he enjoys the wonderful enlarge-
ment of his ears (for curiosity's sake) and his penis (for sensuality's).

He is stolen by a band of robbers and while in their possession overhears
their crone tell a kidnapped maiden the tale of Cupid and Psyche, to divert her
until the ransom arrives. After the tale has been told, the maiden is rescued by
her fiancé. They marry and live happily for a while, but come to a tragic end:
Lucius, having acquired bad luck from the slave girl Fotis, has been spreading
it to others.

He goes on to serve many masters and suffer many torments, almost dying
a number of times. Eventually, his luck turns with the seasons; he meets a
noblewoman wishing to make love to him; news of this spreads, his master
arranges for him to copulate in the arena with a condemned murderess as a
preliminary, before she is thrown to the wild beasts. But he flees from this
perverted display and is rescued by the goddess Isis, who appears to him that
night at full moon in his refuge by the seashore; she tells him to step forward
next day at her festival, boldly eat from the high priest's crown of roses, and be

transformed back into a man. Then he must be initiated into her mysteries, put aside sensuality and serve her, and thus be saved from the caprices of fortune.

Lucius' transformations in their way parallel Psyche's in the crone's story: Psyche is the most beautiful girl in the world, but no man dares to woo her. Following an oracle of Apollo's, her father sets her on a rock for a winged viper to take as his bride. But the viper is Love (personified as Eros in Greek, Cupid in Apuleius' Latin), who disobeys the orders of his jealous mother Venus (Aphrodite) that he drive Psyche ("Soul") to fall in love with some fool, and instead wafts her down on the west wind to his palatial retreat deep in a deserted valley. He visits her only in the dark, and she is never permitted to see him. Psyche's evil sisters visit her several times and, out of jealousy of her luxurious home and lusty lover, convince her that the mystery man is a dragon and that she must slay him before he eats her. One night, while Cupid sleeps in the dark bedchamber, she draws out a lamp and a razor from a hiding-place, but once she sees him she cannot bring herself to kill him. As she gazes at the precious youth lying next to her, she draws out one of his arrows from the quiver and accidentally pricks herself on the arrowhead: thus, she falls in love . . . with Love. He awakes and leaves her—forever, he says in a fit of pique. She tries to kill herself but fails, does kill her wicked sisters, is hounded out of hiding by Venus and set a series of impossible tasks, which with good luck and much help from daimons and animals she manages to perform. Her last task is to descend to the Underworld, like a true hero, and fetch back a bit of Persephone's beauty in a box. She foolishly disobeys instructions, gives in to curiosity, and opens the box on her way back up to the light. A deep sleep settles upon her, and she would have perished on the road. But Cupid has been missing her, goes looking, finds and revives her with a second, this time deliberate, scratch of his arrow. Jupiter makes her immortal, she and Cupid are formally married in the presence of all the gods and goddesses, and shortly thereafter Psyche gives birth to the child she has been carrying throughout her wanderings. Its name is *Voluptas*—Joy. This soul in torment is delivered by pure love from the power of blind fortune, personified by the goddess of sensuality, and discovers spiritual joy within herself.

Much is going on in this novel as a whole and in this tale in particular—Apuleius has seen to that. Pagans, Christians, and analysts have all elaborated their interpretations from suggestions made by the author himself. The respectable householders of the safe and stable world inherited by the successors of Alexander the Great, leading adventureless lives themselves, gobbled up tales of the loves and adventures of others; and expanded trade to Asia and Europe excited stay-at-home imaginations.[32] The novel and the travel book were born.

Apuleius' fears and longings likewise tottered between mutability and stability; he sought a way to transcend the shifts of personal fortune, in a world made large enough to dwarf any epic hero, and to save, at least, himself. Who could hope for more in a bureaucratic empire? In a world where everything changes (or never was what it seemed to be), Lucius' final metamorphosis achieves a sublime fixity.[33]

Salvation implies sin, Apuleius' attitude to which reflects the Greek (even the modern Greek), the heroic, and the analytic attitudes. What counts is not—as in the Christian view of life—the perfect endeavor but rather the performance productive of either enlightenment or good work. The right insight is worth any amount of pain or effort.

Lucius pretends the tale he has overheard is no more than a diverting story. But we know that the myth not only elaborates his particular career (as reflected in the realm of the divine) but also comforts any soul in torment with a vision of Soul's progress, through an initiatory gauntlet of adventures, to a true and mysterious union with the ground of Being. And Soul, while apparently estranged from the natural world around her, is in fact supported by that world. Psyche tries to drown herself, but the stream throws her up. And the woodland god Pan—teacher and herdsman of initiates in the mysteries of Dionysus—advises her not to kill herself but worship and thus placate Cupid (5.25). The mysteries of nature shade off into the more urbane mysteries of Roman religiosity. Cupid has told the uninitiated Psyche not to try to see his shape (forma) out of sacrilegious curiosity (5.6). As Psyche is married to Cupid, Carl Schlam observes, "so Lucius the mystēs takes on the role of Osiris joined to the goddess by sacred bonds."[34] And Psyche's search for her husband recalls Isis's search for Osiris. (Apuleius, as a worshipper of Isis, made the story of Cupid and Psyche illustrate the myth of Isis and Osiris and the experience of an initiate into the Egyptian mysteries. But many of the elements of the story partake of a common body of folklore and will not work for a comprehensive Isiac interpretation—except at the end, where Psyche travels the road of trials.[35]) The labors of Psyche, several of them bridal tests set by a wicked mother-in-law-to-be, also suggest the rites of a chthonian cult such as Demeter and Kore's at Eleusis.[36] Indeed Psyche's nubile naiveté and general predicament match Kore's. One may descend to the Underworld either to sacrifice a life and promote fertility, or else to gain wisdom, or both: Voluptas, Joy, hēdonē in Greek, the child of Cupid and Psyche, stands for sensuality and spirituality. In Lucretius' philosophical poem On the Nature of Things, voluptas can refer to physical pleasure, but it also denotes Mother Nature as a moving force; similarly in Plato's Symposium, divine pleasure, eros, confers philosophic enlightenment and religious blessedness.[37] Love reappears for Psyche in a crisis, to insist on the necessity of divine enlightenment (what Christians call grace) and on the soul's vulnerability before fortune.[38]

underworld deities

Something goes wrong, or right, with the sex roles in this tale. Psyche's fate parallels Lucius'; but she's a woman and he's a man. Isis, a goddess, saves Lucius; Cupid, a god albeit no he-man, rescues Psyche, whose name must be feminine in Greek but could take either a masculine or feminine form in Latin (*animus* or *anima*)—the masculine being by far the more usual to express the range of concepts which we and the Greeks associate with *soul*. (Apuleius gives his heroine a Greek name, Psyche, but also refers to her with both the Latin words; and where translations give "Psyche," the text sometimes reads "daughter," or "sister," or just plain "girl.") Apuleius, bound by this confusion of genders, makes use of it. If Psyche's fate mirrors, not matches, Lucius', should not their genders and saviors' genders also mate, not coincide? To prepare himself for the goddess and come home again to human form, Lucius must make it up with the feminine powers he has so voluptuously abused. To get herself a divine spouse and attain to divinity in her own right, Psyche must also make it up with the darker side of those same feminine powers; but she also needs to toughen her male side through a series of heroic adventures: to assault her mysterious husband she had, as Apuleius metaphorically puts it, to alter her sex (5.22); and later she must adopt manly courage (*masculum animum*) in order to hand herself over to angry Venus (6.5).

Lucius' sexuality has as much to do with the success of his quest as Odysseus' sexuality does with his. In the *Golden Ass*, James Tatum points out, Apuleius creates his own version of the *Odyssey*, with his alter ego as hero. In his *Apology*, he casts himself as Socrates, defends the philosophical way of life, and expressly compares himself to Odysseus as well as to the philosopher hero. In his essay *On the God of Socrates* (924), a goddess delivers the protagonist from misfortune, just as one does in the eleventh book of the *Golden Ass*. Because of his *curiosity*, Odysseus serves as the mythological paradigm of the philosopher and scientist; and the Odyssean way of life satisfies our thirst for adventures and marvels. But the *simplicity* of the Socratic life encourages us to leave behind earthly complexities. And joy, delight, *voluptas*—the third great quality of the philosopher in Apuleius' book—leads us to pursue transcendent ideals.[39] The fable of Psyche, hung like a mirroring sky over the course of Lucius' quest, reflects past estimates of the warrior and of the philosopher as hero, and it even manages to catch the shadowy outline of that future paladin, the analysand. In the lives of all of these characters Eros plays a starring role.

Interpreting Apuleius

Such a suggestive novel has attracted its interpreters. Their tendencies have been either to take the myth of Cupid and Psyche entirely out of context or to connect it item for item with Lucius' own fate. In the battle between Christian and pagan apologists, allegory was a popular weapon, and Greek mythology and philosophy a common arsenal of allegory. The pagans interpreted the myths allegorically in order to make them acceptable to the ethical and cosmological principles of Greek philosophy. The Christians, in turn, allegorized Homer and Plato in order to herd these favorite authors of their schooldays into the fold of the saved. The Jewish philosopher Philo even tried by allegory to reconcile the Hebrew scriptures with Greek philosophy. Plotinus, the greatest of the Neo-Platonics, made only casual use of the allegorical interpretations of Plato current in his day, but his student Porphyry took those same interpretations very seriously indeed and applied them right and left. The pagan religion had never boasted a coherent theology, but the later Neo-Platonists tried to endow it with one—complete with daimons—based on the inspired writings of Plato. They tried to find a place in their system for every super-natural being that adorned the last revisions of Greco-Roman myth and cult and to produce an atlas of the spirit. At the same time they assumed that the structure of reality corresponded exactly to the way Plotinus' mind had worked.[40]

Apuleius must take the blame for some of his symbolism-appeal. As a Neo-Platonist himself, he knew what the game was about. Although he seems to have invented the full-blown myth of Cupid and Psyche, the motif of the two lovers goes back at least to Plato's day: they are first found together in the late fifth century on an Etruscan gem. Plato drew on a common stock of images for his chariot of the soul and its ill-matched horses, like good and bad erotes, hauling the charioteer now back to earth, now up to the heavens. On the monuments, however, either Psyche or Eros may drive the team, and later antiquity associated Plato's ideas and narrative in the *Phaedrus* with this repertoire of images.[41] The Neo-Platonist interpretation of Apuleius envisages Psyche and her two sisters as the tripartite soul of Platonist psychology: the desirous (base) and the spirited (noble) parts tugged the rational in opposite directions.[42]

Plato's soul wears bird's wings, but by late Hellenistic times the standard wings issued to the soul in art are those of a butterfly. Eros appears with a papilionine Psyche on gold earrings from the fourth or third century. And by the time of Aristotle, *psychē* could mean a particular kind of butterfly (*History of Animals* 551 a 14). Eros sometimes drives Dionysus' chariot, and he and Psyche play Dionysus and a maenad or Ariadne in the frescoes in the house of the Vettii. Dionysus had roused the mortal girl from a deathlike sleep to an immortal life with him as her husband in the heavens; and vintage and harvest scenes have often been used to convey the joys of salvation. Eros and Psyche were associated with this pattern of apotheosis and rebirth in Hellenistic and Roman art. Apuleius has Bacchus play bartender at their wedding. The frescoes from Boscoreale, through representations of Dionysus and Ariadne and of Cupid and Psyche, express these same ideas of salvation by initiation into mysteries and of the union of the divine and the mortal. About the time Apuleius was writing, Eros and Psyche began to appear on sculpted sarcophagi; their embrace became an emblem of the soul's salvation, the promise of afterlife; and the Dionysiac associations of the pair were expanded on. Eros purifies the soul of bodily concerns, and so before the embrace can occur the soul may be tormented and almost burnt to a crisp.[43]

On the other hand, if Eros can save the soul from a deathlike sleep, then he has also acquired some features of a god of death. Since Eros loosens or breaks the bond between body and soul, he was identified as late as the Renaissance with Death himself; the agonies of Psyche before she comes to rest in the arms of Eros, moreover, resemble a death-struggle.[44] Recall that Psyche made up the third in a sisterly trio. In "The Theme of the Three Caskets" Freud concludes that such a woman (and he mentions Psyche by way of example) is always death in disguise; and where no such identification can be made, it is because Death has made the easy transformation into its opposite.[45]

Freud's death-force, Thanatos, is also ready to change places with Eros, but only when the soul has loosened its hold on the connection-making faculty. Death in the Cupid and Psyche story, however, and the death of Socrates in Plato's dialogues, is a real as well as a metaphorical match for a powerful Eros. Of course, the soul must expire symbolically before achieving rebirth at a higher level of consciousness, but Plato actually meant his myth of the soul's rise toward the forms to fit the facts. Eros, love, desire, *amor, cupido*—whatever you call it—drives the soul, both in the *Symposium* and the *Phaedrus*, first toward the particular, but then toward the more general objects of desire, and finally to that most general category of all, the forms, which cannot be encountered at terrestrial symposia. To become a lover in the Platonic and even Neo-Platonic sense is ultimately to give one's self up to death, so that the soul (*eidōlon*, "phantom") can come home to the forms (*eidos* or *idea*).

Although the enlarged sexuality of psychoanalytic theory closely resembles the Eros of Plato, the libido has no salvational, inspirational, "enthusing" function in Freud's model of the soul. There is nothing beyond this life, to Freud's way of thinking, toward which the soul should be raised. Except death—and that is that and no more than that. On the other hand, Jung insists that it is the Will to Power (rather than Thanatos) which constitutes the shadow-side of Eros: "Where love reigns, there is no will to power." Thus for Jung a giving of oneself to the cosmic flow, not on a deathbed but in the midst of life, precipitates the glimpsing of the hypostases of the universe.

Apuleius never intended that his tale would make interpretation-fodder for the Christians, whom he portrayed as a sect of low-class troublemakers, but

the Christians did not exempt Cupid and Psyche from service in their apolo-
getics. Fulgentius Planciades, for example, took Psyche's native city as the
world, her royal parents as God and matter, her elder sisters as the flesh and
free will, and Psyche herself as the soul itself. Venus becomes lust, which orders
desire (Cupid) toward the soul. And so on.[46] Adherence to a single, possessible,
truth has led true believers to trust that everything everywhere is always mani-
festing that truth. But the old gods have been known to take a modicum of
vengeance on their interpreters: certain humanists of the Renaissance went so
far with Neoplatonic exegesis in reconciling Greek myths with the Bible that
the distinction between the two sets of texts was obscured and Christian dogma
itself had to be made palatable by allegory.[47]

Erich Neumann has worked out the most famous Jungian interpretation
of the tale of Cupid and Psyche. While Bachofen ignores the details and sees
in the plot only the purification of a genderless soul,[48] Neumann discerns a
myth of the feminine, "a later and higher stage of feminine initiation than that
embodied in the Eleusinian mysteries," a struggle between opposing aspects of
a woman's psychology and between the feminine and the masculine principles
of the soul—and the consequent emergence of Psyche from the dark realm of
girlish unconsciousness.[49]

As P. G. Walsh points out, Neumann seems often to be analyzing some
original folktale behind Apuleius' distinctly literary account rather than the
Latin text actually before him.[50] In particular, when Psyche raises the lamp and
sees Eros, Neumann interprets this in line with his great monomyth, as "the
awakening of Psyche as the psyche, the fateful moment in the life of the feminine, in which for the first time woman emerges from the darkness of her
unconscious and the harshness of her matriarchal captivity and, in individual
encounter with the masculine, loves, that is, recognizes, Eros."[51] Venus, as the
"old parent of the nature of things" (4.30)—the mother-goddess of feminine
fertility and feminine unconsciousness—has wanted to keep Psyche in bondage
to wifework. But the accidental, enrapturing, scratch of the arrow alters the
status of Psyche from passive to active, from merely beloved to lover.

Robert A. Johnson, in a less ambitious but more practical Jungian analysis of the tale, supports Neumann's reading. Eros is a woman's animus and so,
"Eros held Psyche in a state of unconscious animus possession in paradise until
she lighted the lamp of consciousness and then, as animus, he flew back into
the inner world." Like a good animus, Eros mediates for Psyche between the
conscious and unconscious (Venus) parts of her personality. And the ram's
fleece which she must gather as one of her tasks is also a masculine symbol,
the Logos; but unlike Jason, who has to retrieve a whole skin-full of fleece to
prove his hero-hood, Psyche needs only a few tufts—for too much would hinder
her psychic progress, just as too much of the feminine would impede a man.[52]

Neumann has noticed that Eros doesn't want an adult, awakened Psyche: "The unconscious tendency toward consciousness (here toward consciousness in the love relationship) was stronger in Psyche than everything else, even than her love for Eros—or so, at least, the masculine Eros would have said." Both the bad feminine (the matriarchal aggression of Venus) and the good animus compel her to emerge from the darkness. Psyche's act—attempted murder, realized Love, the acquisition of knowledge—leads to the pain of individuation, in which the personality experiences itself, in relation to another, as other. Psyche wounds both herself and Eros, dissolves their original, paradisiacal but unconscious bond, and prepares the way for a conscious, loving encounter. (Here Neumann refers to Aristophanes' myth in the *Symposium*—in which human beings have descended from the splitting apart of a once whole race of Siamese twins, so that love consists of each man or woman's desire and pursuit of his or her original other half. But Plato has Socrates and Diotima discredit the myth, since Platonic love cannot restrict itself to, nor find, ultimate satisfaction in a one and only, but must rise above the particularities of the flesh.[53])

Psyche's development manifests an archetypal process; the relationship between her and Eros in the dark suits the archetypal relation between man and woman. The feminine, the creative, principle precipitates a change in this psycho-sexual stand-off. The conservative, masculine principle, Eros, strives of course to preserve the status quo; but ultimately it must relinquish its egoistic leadership and permit the soul to be guided by the totality, which is to say, by the unconscious. Psyche, not Eros himself, transforms the boy god into dragon, monster, husband, sleeper, redeemer.[54] Feminine individuation leads to the proper union of woman with her proper lover, just as Lucius' individuation, in turn, leads to his being made worthy of union with the feminine in the person of Isis. Which is to make all this more clear than Neumann himself ever finds it convenient to do.

Whereas Neumann analyzes "Cupid and Psyche" in isolation from the rest of the novel in which it is set and takes it as a model-myth for the problems of feminine psychology, Marie-Louise von Franz interprets the tale in its context—as illustrative therefore of the problems of Lucius' masculine psychology. Psyche, that is, represents not the Feminine's feminine side, as in Neumann's scheme, but rather the Masculine's feminine, the anima.[55]

Von Franz seems to take the position that behind the thin disguise of the main character lurks the neurotic personality of the author; her book really winds up psychoanalyzing Apuleius himself. She starts with the little we know of his life, in particular his marriage to an older woman, and proposes that he suffered from a positive mother-complex but projected the concomitant, negative complex onto his character Lucius. Apuleius' way of patching odd stories into his main plot, moreover, reminds her not of the traditional techniques of

story-telling but of that Jungian *abaissement du niveau mental,* or lowering of
the wall of consciousness against the unconscious. She concludes that the novel
is more the product of the author's unconscious associations than of his logical
reflections and conscious artistry. And so, she believes, she may treat the inserted
stories as though they were dreams and the episodes as though they
were fantasies. [56]

Lucius, Apuleius, one and the very same, has trouble with insides and
outsides, with listening to the Collective Unconscious and then realizing his
fantasies within himself. For example—because Lucius cannot see the anima
as something inside himself, the robbers plan to sew the girl, Charite, up in
his belly and thereby to force the feminine principle into him. Charite and her
fiancé constitute the counter-half of a marriage quaternity to match the inner
Cupid and Psyche. But the mortal couple, Lucius learns, are eventually killed;
Cupid and Psyche retire to Olympus and thus are never brought into the real
world and cannot unite the two worlds: Lucius remains in his dream world and
fails to make the archetypes real. [57] Von Franz writes two different psychic
prescriptions: one must block out the distractions of daily life and make room
for the archetypes, and then one must adapt the archetypes to the practical
demands of ordinary life.

Lucius, she continues, also shares a number of faults with Cupid and
Psyche. In his monograph *On the God of Socrates,* Apuleius describes how
the gods live in the great beyond, apart from us and from each other, and how
only the daimons can influence or be influenced by us. Lucius must come to
terms with such daimons as Eros and Psyche before he can meet the goddess
Isis. The bad side of Eros is the *puer aeternus,* the eternal boy, and Lucius
Apuleius resembles this archetype: a bit of a homosexual, a bit of a Don Juan,
in need of an older woman to tell him what to do (Venus, Apuleius' own wife).
Psyche, on the other hand, with her curiosity and penchant for the kind of
magic by which divine powers are abused rather than served, resembles Lucius'
anima. But finally, both Lucius and Psyche are saved from themselves: "That
Psyche (the anima of men) succeeds in holding the waters of the Styx in a vessel
signifies that when we are in touch with the depths of our unconscious psyche
we can be creative." And Lucius at last returns to himself when he turns directly
to the unconscious, drops his conscious defenses, and allows the fourfold goddess to reveal herself to him and restore him to human form. Thus he begins
to realize the archetype of the Self. [58]

In contrast to Neumann and others, James Hillman does not analyze the
myth but uses it as an illustrative centerpiece for his *Myth of Analysis,* in which
he advocates the generation of a creative, Jungian psychology to replace the
reflective, Freudian brand of analysis. For his revolutionary purposes he finds
the traditional myths of psychoanalysis—of Oedipus, say, and the night-sea

journey—inadequate. "The heroic age in psychology is past. The hero of consciousness is now further along." Having tended to and secured his maleness he must now find his female soul, and that is what "Cupid and Psyche" is about. Reflection is not nor does it necessarily lead to creativity. To define the aim of psychotherapy as "becoming conscious" suggests that insight for its own sake has some value. "And which of us by taking thought can add one cubit to his stature?"[59]

Freud set stricter limits for analysis than Hillman does. Self-knowledge frees one, as far as possible within the confines of culture, from obsessive behavior; if the analysand enjoys some creative potential, he may then seek to exercise it on his own, may learn constructively to sublimate his neurotic tendencies, once the analyst has helped him to wake up to himself. Knowledge leads to control which makes freedom possible. Neither happiness nor creativity may lurk in the shadows of one's destiny, but analysis can at least dispel some of the gloom and provide the illumination requisite for great deeds.

Hillman differs: "Reflection may make consciousness, but love makes soul."[60] It would follow that the analyst's job is to teach his patient how to love. But the analysand may begin independently, through contemplating Hillman's version of the myth of Cupid and Psyche. Examining Merkelbach's scholarly *Roman und Mysterium*, Hillman takes the author's failure to mention the birth of *Voluptas* and to relate the ending to the rest of the novel as "final evidence for the inadequacy of the historical and literary method in providing sufficient amplification for psychology."[61]

He concentrates on Psyche's pain and suffering: "a girl is tortured into womanhood, as a man's anima is awakened through torment into psyche." Love endures a similar transformation: Eros must regress "into a state of burning unrest . . . to realize he has found his mate, Psyche." For our psyches to mate with the creative and bring something to birth, we need to accept our "loss of primordial love through betrayal and separation and also our wrong relation to eros. . . . Neurosis becomes initiation, analysis the ritual, and our developmental process in psyche and eros, leading to their union, becomes the mystery." Love must transmute fear and compulsion into a higher feeling. This cannot occur in the Oedipus myth, for there compulsion overcomes love; but in the Cupid and Psyche myth love overcomes compulsion.[62]

Hillman is onto something here. Bruno Bettleheim, too, notes how the one myth forms a counterpart to the other: In the Oedipus story a father fears his son will replace him and tries to avert this by destroying the boy; in the myth of Psyche a mother, Venus, fears that a young girl will replace her in the affections of mankind and of her son, and she therefore tries to destroy the girl. The Oedipus story ends tragically, but the Psyche story happily—since a mother's jealousy toward her son's beloved can be more openly acknowledged and more easily resolved than a father-son rivalry.[63] Freud, in fact, chose as his monomyth one suited to a pessimistic interpretation of human relationships and events; Hillman picks a story of salvation.

Even the most painful setbacks in the career of Psyche (matters that Freud would have brooded long on) in Hillman's view only serve to redeem the soul from its childish naiveté. "Eros is born of Chaos [in Hesiod's account], implying that out of every chaotic moment the creativity of which we have been speaking can be born." (Hesiod's *Chaos*, however, is not "chaos," but a "gulf" or "yawning" out of which everything could quite naturally stream.) The destructive aspect of eros works to prevent the *hieros gamos* ("holy mating") by insisting upon 'the other,' by sticking his arrow into a third one, a rival: "the triangles of eros educate the psyche out of its girlish goodness." Love that has failed in the outside world turns inward and becomes part of the soul.[64] Hillman, while following Apuleius' account less carefully than von Franz, declares the soul's, the hero's, the analysand's task to be the opposite of the one she lays down for us: not the abandonment of life in a private dream world, but rather the adaptation and modification of reality to the personal needs of each soul. Hillman, oddly enough, has come close to a statement of Freud's on the subject of Psyche's lost love for Eros:

> When it happens that a person has to give up a sexual object, there quite often ensues an alteration of his ego which can only be described as a setting up of the object inside the ego, as it occurs in melancholia. . . . At any rate the process, especially in the early phases of development, is a very frequent one, and it makes it possible to suppose that the character of the ego is a precipitate of abandoned object-cathexes and that it contains the history of those object-cathexes.[65]

Hillman could justify his optimism by pointing out that Soul gets her true love in the end. And Freud bolstered his pessimism by interpreting Psyche as Death, a demon whom Hillman insists on taking metaphorically: the box containing a bit of Persephone's beauty "refers to an underworld beauty that can never be seen with the senses. It is the beauty of the knowledge of death. . . . Psyche must 'die' herself in order to experience the reality of this beauty."[66]

Advancements over the simple hero; a story of soul-making; a psychological death and rebirth; the union of Eros and Psyche. Are these psychic myths to be experienced only by analysands (our modern heroes) in the presence of analysts (our modern daimons)? Hillman thinks not. Analysis is necessary but not sufficient: "We have been looking for love for the soul. That is the myth of analysis. We have been going to analysis during this past century for soul-making. Where else was one to find the psyche taken seriously?" Unfortunately, little value was accorded to what happened between eros and psyche in the course of therapy: the erotic experience of analysis was called transference and treated analytically, i.e., as requiring the submission of Eros (or Dionysus) to Apollo. Consciousness's gain was imagination's loss. The answer to the need for a new process of soul-making—what neurosis has been calling out for all along—is the integration of female inferiority through the metaphorical perspective of archetypal psychology. And something else is needed, too; but Hillman does not specify what that something else is. Although he demands a *"revision of psychology in terms of the Gods,"* he never makes a practical suggestion.[67]

Is Freudian psychology really inferior to this? Is it not too late for those of us who have learned the lessons of nineteenth- and twentieth-century literature and philosophy and psychology to return to an ego-less practice of religion? Have the charlatans and psychopaths of recent cultic scams and slaughters taught us nothing? Analytic man suspects everything, and rightly so. Consider this from Philip Rieff: "Psychoanalysis supplied an individual and secular substitute for communal and religious vocation. Where nothing can be taken for granted, and the stupidity of social life no longer saves, every man must become something of a genius about himself."[68] Replace "psychoanalysis" with "philosophy" and Nietzsche could have written this.

Psychoanalysis, or analytical reflectiveness, approximates—on a purely private level—the Socratic ideal of the examined life, which in ancient times required a commitment to utopian politics from the philosopher. Analytic man cherishes his privacy (that precious notion which neither Ancient nor Modern Greek has exactly the right word for); whether social concerns can once again penetrate his idiosyncratic one is up to the course of history to determine. Even Socrates and Plato found in the end that the most they could do was to save their own souls and leave an example behind for others to imitate. Similarly, the heroes and heroines of the myths have left us their exemplary successes and disasters. Perhaps the greatest profit one can take from the limited application of the myths to the analytic process itself accrues not from the Jungian emphasis on ends and answers but from the Freudian reliance on methods and questions. Plato and Socrates thought sin was a matter of ignorance, virtue of knowledge; this, in reverse, constitutes the guiding principle of analysis: the only good comes from knowing, and that, as Oedipus well knew, is a hard road to walk. One doesn't get more soul simply by demanding it.

10

Myth, Therapy, and Culture

T HE USES AND ABUSES of classical mythology in psychoanalysis and psychology are implicated with the issue of the emergence of psychological man. This paladin of consciousness contrives to begin his anything but tidy career when mythological man begins to refine a sense of himself as Other, personified by a labile but gently consolidating double. Achilles by slaying his enemy fixes his own death. Odysseus in disguise contends with Odysseus about to reveal himself, and with Penelope. Oedipus cross-examines everyone but the murderer. Things are no longer what they seemed to be. Helen, it turns out, never went to Troy. Medea argues with herself and loses, and wins. Dionysus could pass for Pentheus; Pentheus, for Dionysus. Ovidian man turns into Ovidian woman, and Ovidian woman turns into a tree, a bird, a cloud.

The residue of all these mutant sports of nature settles about an emblematic visage: the monster, shadow-side of the self, playful and ironic conjunction of hominoid and theriomorph. Woman, like monster, appears as predator and herself victim of raging hormonal imbalance, more psychological a creature than man. Only half human; half, for lack of a better category, bestial. Other than herself, never out of disguise, as reliable as the Cretan liar. Consumer of raw rather than cooked and thus most natural yet most unnatural.

Spirits and demigods rise up from the palm grove of an ancient oasis and migrate across the sand dunes of the centuries. A god out of the East, Dionysus, the savior as charlatan, comes to marshal them in the service of Love, which is also the service of Death; while from his plushly ascetic cave near the top of Mt. Parnassus, Apollo descends to claim the worship of his fellow narcissists, his skin-deep brethren.

Through the welter of all these primping personages the hero wends his or her way, changing as he goes, first a warrior, then a wife—then, in turn, a philosopher, an artist, and at last a mental patient who goes over the wall of the communal asylum and checks himself into his own care.

What (the question comes down to) does myth have to do with us, or we with it?

Philoctetes

I think we know most of the uses of myth in the ancient world: Entertainment value aside, as a collection of types and personas mythology proved itself in helping to organize every man's impressions of and judgments on the world and its inhabitants. It supplied role models of public service and heroic endeavor for those aspiring to become great statesmen or generals. It gave the Greek and Roman world several prototypes of the artful rhetorician. And, taken as a whole and in conjunction with its various other uses and influences, mythology constituted a force that tugged the aberrant individual back into line with his society's requirements. The myth of the outcast and wounded Philoctetes, specifically Sophocles' play by that name, illustrates all of these uses.

When it had come time for Heracles to leave the earth and ascend to his reward on Olympus, only Philoctetes (or, some say, Philoctetes' father) dared light the pyre that would consume Heracles' mortal portion and set him free from his suffering. His wife had mistakenly put a lethal ointment on his shirt and he was being broiled alive; only a "death" of a sort could release him. In gratitude for Philoctetes' singular service, Heracles willed him his bow—the legacy, apparently, of a culture-hero and a symbol of man's achievement in defeating and shaping nature, given to Philoctetes so that he might carry on the good work.[1]

Some years later, Philoctetes set out with the rest of the heroes on the expedition to Troy, to retrieve the stolen Helen; but on the way, on a little island called Chryse, he accidentally trespassed on a sacred precinct and was bitten by the guardian snake. (Jung thinks that the nymph of the place was Philoctetes' anima and that she turned into a snake and bit him in order to make him conscious of her.[2] Indeed, the suffering hero does refer to his disease, nosos, as "she" at lines 758–59, but this may be only the accident of the noun's gender.) The wound festered but never killed him. The Greeks could not stand the putrid odor from his foot nor his cries of agony when the pain was upon him, and so they marooned him on the deserted island of Lemnos. But ten years later they found they needed him and his bow to defeat the enemy bowman Paris and make possible the sack of Troy; Odysseus and Neoptolemus, the son of Achilles, came to bring him back—for it was the will of Zeus that Troy should fall. Philoctetes refused to go. Neoptolemus at first agreed to help the wily Odysseus trick Philoctetes into coming with them, but his noble sympathies soon got the better of him and he sided with the wounded hero. Philoctetes, it seemed, would remain forever in isolation, Troy would never fall, and the will of Zeus would be thwarted. But in the closing scene of the play, the immortal Heracles, the only personage Philoctetes would listen to, descends from Olympus and tells him he must go to Troy and that there he will find a cure for his wound, at the healing hands of the sons of Asclepius. Philoctetes packs up his bow and arrows and leaves.

In the course of the play some interesting comparisons are worked out. At one point, feeling himself betrayed by Neoptolemus, Philoctetes prays to Hephaestus; Odysseus, his enemy, a fifth-century rhetorician if ever there was, responds that Zeus is the god here (986–90). Philoctetes, a mythic figure himself, is being told to abandon a mythological model. Both Hephaestus and Philoctetes are cripples; both were cast out by aristocratic societies and were isolated on Lemnos. Hephaestus had sided with Hera against Zeus on the matter of her persecution of Heracles, and so Zeus threw him out of heaven; but Hephaestus then sent Hera a magic throne that trapped her when she sat in it. The gods begged him to come back and free her, offering him a place once again in their society, but he refused. Finally Dionysus persuaded him to return by getting him so drunk he didn't care where he went (Pausanias 1.20.3).[3] Dionysus seems to have won a place among the Olympians as his reward for this service.

Like Hephaestus, Philoctetes opposes the plans of Zeus; and he, too, is needed back by his peers because of a device and a special skill. He must abandon the attitude of the outcast god, look to the socializing ways of Zeus as laid down for him by his personal hero Heracles. Unlike Heracles, who was destined for a seat among the gods, Philoctetes will not find relief from his pain in fire, although he longs to plunge himself into the volcano that crowns Lemnos (799–800, 1210–17). But like Heracles, like Dionysus, like even Hephaestus, he must eventually settle himself in that aristocratic society of his peers from which he has long felt an outsider. Neoptolemus' heroic model is his father Achilles—a noble but savage man who in a fit of pique divorced himself from his peers and sat and sulked alone on the beach while his fellow Greeks died on the plains of Troy. Neoptolemus, too, was renowned for his savagery in the sack of Troy (he beat Priam to death with the body of Hector's young son). Sophocles, then, seems to have dramatized in this play several practical lessons for the Greeks of the late fifth century: you must choose the right hero to model your career on (a culture-hero like Heracles, not an outsider like Hephaestus or a narcissist like Achilles); and you can fulfill yourself only by aligning your will with the needs of society, even if it once rejected you and now no longer deserves you.

Edmund Wilson expressed one point of view when he claimed Philoctetes' disability was in a sense responsible for his heroic superiority—the wound went with the bow.[4] But others have argued rather that, according to the classical point of view, great virtue or genius can overcome, or succeed despite, a disability—in contrast to the notion that a desocializing handicap is in fact the precondition for superiority.[5] The great man, some still believe today, has achieved great things by sublimating a social or physical disadvantage which made his youth a hell and led to his determination to rise above it. In other words, the ancient hero was part of the social fabric, although he may have grown up in peasant obscurity; the modern hero is always on his way out of town. Philoctetes, at the close of Sophocles' play, rides back into the community.

Nietzsche expressed the antique attitude as well or better than he did that of his own age: "The origin of custom lies in two ideas: 'the community is worth more than the individual' and 'an enduring advantage is to be preferred to a transient one'; from which it follows that the enduring advantage of the community is to take unconditional precedence over the advantage of the individual . . . even over his survival."[6] In the so-called guilt culture of Sophocles' last days, the voice of most men's consciences still spoke for the common weal; and the Pindaric remonstrance to become the person that you are did not have the anti-social tone Nietzsche wished to give it when he altered the old dictum "virtue is the health of the soul" by the insertion of two possessive pronouns, specifying "your virtue" and "your soul."[7] Sanity has been, and always will be, measured more by a standard of social conformity than by one of personal mental hygiene. R. D. Laing puts the case for the sociopaths fairly: "I suggest, therefore, that *sanity or psychosis is tested by the degree of conjunction or disjunction between two persons where the one is sane by common consent.*"[8] But Evelyn Waugh, the good citizen and good churchman speaks, without benefit of italics, for society: "It requires constant effort to keep within the world order and our contemporaries are too lazy to make the effort."[9] The Greeks thought man a political, by which they meant a social, animal. Laing and Nietzsche, and Marcuse too,[10] have suggested this is mere bourgeois propaganda. But Freud thought that unlimited happiness is not in our natures and that it comes, if at all, from the "satisfaction of needs which have been dammed up to a high degree, and it is from its nature only possible as an episodic phenomenon." We derive little pleasure from a state of equilibrium but may derive much from the resolution of a tension.[11] Society, far from restricting our happiness, may, in Freud's somewhat perverted and mechanistic view, make it possible by opposing it. And, to return to the Greeks, the hero may become a hero only when forced to divert or channel his energies into tasks of others' choosing. Heracles had to be harnessed as much for his own good as for society's. The rankest anarchist would be lost without an order to oppose.

Psychoanalysis in its most general, least mechanistic application provides the practitioner with a multiple-entry visa for access to his neuroses and back again to the less than serene playing fields of sanity. It seeks to enable the patient to master instinctual forces hostile to his survival in society and to civilize himself at the least possible cost or sacrifice of activity.[12] Society, Nietzsche noted, calls him good who gladly does what is customary and beneficial to it;[13] and H. L. Mencken had a penchant for mocking democracy for its fear, not so much of the wicked man, as of the superior and outstanding man, of the virtual aristocrat. But surely the Greeks had a fondness as well as a hatred for that rare beast they were the first to denominate *hero*. In the hero they could prophylactically discharge all their higher impulses, at second hand, with no risk to their persons or their status in the eyes of their neighbors. So what if a few queer souls took the epic business seriously and rose to do great deeds? These men could be cultivated as long as their activities helped secure the man in the street from the monstrous dangers lurking just across the bridge and over the nearest hill; and they could be cut down to the measure of the meanest in the mob as soon as they made the least slip in performance.

And the heroes? They needed fame and that substantial repute which rests with the insubstantial masses to bestow. Achilles in his blackest choler was pleased to be begged to return by the Greeks who had offended him. And Philoctetes, had the Trojan war lasted much longer, would soon have committed some gaff and the army of his peers would undoubtedly have sent him packing, as an upstart, back to the island they had so charitably rescued him from. But it didn't happen that way; the war ended and Philoctetes went home healed. What sort of physicians did he place his body and soul in care of, and what would his alternatives have been should they have failed in their ministrations?

Asclepius

Machaon and Podalirius, the mythical sons of Asclepius, the god or hero of medicine—in later days they would have been doctors who took Hippocrates as the hero of their trade—presumably found the right herbs to apply to the snake bite, drained the poison, and terminated sepsis. What if they had not succeeded? Could a god have helped Philoctetes?

The princess Coronis bore Asclepius to Apollo. He was raised by the centaur Chiron and taught the techniques of folk medicine, which he later raised to a sort of science and handed down to his two sons by a certain Xanthe or Epione. But he exceeded the proper duties of a physician, and, with a vial of Gorgon's blood given him by Athena, he raised Hippolytus, Theseus' son, from the dead. Zeus, disturbed by this supra-medical precedent, struck Asclepius with a thunderbolt (Diodorus 4.71.1–4; Vergil, *Aeneid* 7.765–73). But, somehow, the dead mortal came to be worshipped as a living, revivifying god, often in the form of a snake. He thus has much in common with Heracles, another mortal who earned divinity and whom, in fact, he once treated for a hip injury (Pausanias 3.19.7 and 20.5); their deifications were often mentioned in the same breath.

In cult, as distinguished from myth, Asclepius seems to have begun life as a daimon. "Hail to healer Asclepius, most famous daimon," reads an anonymous inscription of the fourth century B.C.[14] Apuleius attests that he was everywhere ranked among the daimons who have guided their lives wisely and been worshipped afterwards as divinities (*On the God of Socrates* 15.153). He enjoyed many fine sanctuaries, particularly at Epidaurus, Kos, and Pergamum, sanatoriums really, where his cult was more or less associated with actual medical treatment and schooling. The progress of ancient medicine was often skewed by philosophical presuppositions and religious tendencies. Doctors in the Greek world did not hesitate to tell a patient they could not help him, both in order to avoid failure and the subsequent loss of repute and custom, and because a cure was available at the sanctuary of Asclepius. The god's rate of success seems to have been as good as the physicians'. His temples were bedizened with thanks offerings, usually in the shape of the organ or limb that had been healed—everything from eyes and ears to someone's rear end (on a relief in the Athens National Museum, number 5222). Socrates' death-bed debt of a cock to Asclepius may have been for the healing dream which promised him a fair arrival in paradise (*Phaedo* 118 A; *Crito* 44 A–B).

Representations of Asclepius himself show a god as wise as Zeus, but more concerned and sympathetic with a mortal's lot, the sort of deity an up-and-coming individual of the Hellenistic Age could relate to. The god often took the form of his snake—a symbol of healing since it can shimmy out of its old, dead skin and emerge as a shiny new being—*elaphe longissima*, the only constrictor in Europe. Called the Aesculapian snake today, it belongs to a type known as the rat snakes, for their favored food—an appropriate diet for the healing god's totem. The Romans introduced it from its native southeastern Europe and Asia Minor to isolated spots throughout northern Europe, as a guardian of their famous baths. The lyre-shaped posture which the males assume when they duel for a mate inspired the snake-entwined caduceus of the medical profession.[15] Dogs, too, inhabited the sanctuaries, since they were said to heal wounds by licking them.

Asclepius as a healer accrued the powers of a vanquisher of death. He was associated with moisture, as one who postpones the dryness of death; taking the waters was often part of the cure he prescribed. The spring at Pergamum was reputed to be particularly salubrious and is still sweet-watered. Some evidence also connects him with the vine and vintage; he was commonly mentioned, in inscriptions and prayers, with Dionysus.[16]

Pilgrims to his shrines relied chiefly on incubation for their cures: sleeping the night in his temple or in a special chamber nearby, where a dream would come to them as if by magic (that is, automatically) and, if not heal them outright, then tell them what regimen would effect a certain cure. Such a practice is also known in Japanese Shintoism.[17] In Greece today, troubled worshippers in at least one village may spend the night in a church, some awake and some asleep; and St. George may appear to them in their dreams or as an apparition, to offer his advice on their problems.[18] And according to Kerenyi, small children in Greece are sometimes "made to pass the night in a kind of 'temple sleep' at the feet of the wonder-working Mother of God."[19]

Divine dreams—as opposed to those caused by physical factors—might occur to one at any time and require the services of an interpreter,[20] but the dreams of Asclepius did not need elucidation. You paid no fee for your incubation; no secret approach or hieratic dress or mysterious rites were involved. Amid sober, almost trivial, surroundings, the god simply appeared, on demand, almost any night, and worked on you in your sleep or in a strange state halfway to sleep: he healed you of the ailment then and there, operating just as a human physician would, or he prescribed the correct treatment.[21] Belief in the envy of the gods was fading toward the end of the fifth century. Freed from jealousy and hatred, a god might become the friend and adviser of an average man; expensive intermediaries might even be dispensed with—although some still accused Asclepius of selling health and life (Pindar, *Pythian* 3.54–58; Libanius, *Declamationes* 34.23–26).

The Therapy of *Logos*

This natural and benevolently spontaneous dream-therapy accords with the Jungian view of such matters—where the patient, with the help and co-operation of a therapist, relates his neuroses to elements of the collective unconscious, which reveals itself to him according to certain personal, cultural, and cosmic codes—more than it does with the Freudian attitude. Jung believed that the psyche has a natural religious function; therapy consists in getting in touch and coming to terms with this function or god: from this a healing will spontaneously eventuate. In many cases one probably does: getting on with it, as consciously as possible, may be the best therapy of all for any but the truly insane.

For Freud, however, the dream work was "the process which has brought about the distortion of unconscious dream-thoughts into the manifest content of the dream."[22] Dreams may manifest the symptoms of an illness; not a form of healing *per se*, they may discharge our antisocial, instinctual wishes and so make civilization possible.[23] The mental life of the healthy person differs only quantitatively from that of the neurotic: "dreams appear to be the only symptoms he is capable of forming."[24]

Neurotic symptoms disappear as soon as the unconscious processes from which they are invariably constructed have become conscious. The task of psychoanalysis is thus "to make conscious everything that is pathogenetically unconscious." For by bringing what is unconscious into consciousness, "we remove the preconditions for the formations of symptoms, we transform the pathogenic conflict into a normal one for which it must be possible somehow to find a solution."[25] We are fully conscious only of that which we can formulate verbally, *pace* the objections of painters, musicians, and dancers. Such is the logical and practical basis of the "talking cure," as Freud first called psychoanalysis. Verbal mastery (naming the beasts, in paradise or in the wilderness) leads to psychical mastery, which leads, as Freud noted about religious personifications, to a sense of physical mastery.[26] The words we rely on may not convey the truth about the world at large, but they may still protect us against a hostile universe, one that in fact grows more alien the more we have seemed to delimit it with words. The greatest heroes may be those who, in difficult situations, can still deliver themselves of their words with aplomb.

But if we borrow too many of the words from one source, then we may enjoy their power, too, only on loan. Freud admitted he was not a good analyst, that he got tired of people, was more interested in working out technical problems than in therapy.[27] There is little evidence that the talking cure took on most patients. Psychotherapy is a psychodrama of narrative rather than of action.[28] The words, like the actions, if they are to be effective must come from the psychodramatists; but most patients are not literate enough to supply their own scripts.

The therapy of the word, borrowed or original, goes way back. Socrates tells Charmides that he has learned from a disciple of Zalmoxis (perhaps a Thracian god of the dead) that the maladies of the body cannot be cured without treating the soul with certain charms—namely, rational discourse (*Charmides* 156 D–157 A). In the *Phaedrus* Socrates actually compares the art of healing to rhetoric and asserts that the health of the soul, the desired belief and virtue, requires the proper training and discourse (270 A–B). Pedro Laín Entralgo credits Plato with the invention of a verbal psychotherapy, for having resolved the *epōdē*, or magic charm, into its magical element (superstitious charms), beseeching element (prayers to the gods), and its rational.[29] It is the last which the Platonic Socrates elaborates, in the course of the dialogues, into a discourse which forms the way of Virtue—a process, not unlike psychoanalysis, of healing the soul of life. A lower sort of reason, promulgated orally, helps to keep the masses of Plato's ideal state in line; a higher sort of reason, learned both orally and from writings, sets the higher sort of man (the philosopher) free, eventually, from the masses. The therapeutic word performs both a socializing and desocializing function. In Plato's lifetime, Greek culture seems to have been completing the move from pure orality, through a stage of literacy as a craft, to a state where the cultivated Greek public constituted a community of readers;[30] where the word, when written, could isolate a man from his fellows as well as, when spoken, unite him.

In the polis, speech had been the most powerful political tool. *Logos*, the reasoning word, sustained society and provided the avenue to success for the superior members of society. In Jean-Pierre Vernant's words—

> Greek reason was not so much the product of human commerce with
> things as of the relations of human beings with one another. It developed
> less through the techniques that apply to the world than through those
> that give one person a hold over others, and whose common instrument
> is language: the art of the politician, the rhetorician, the pedagogue. . . .
> In its limitations as in its innovations, it is the creature of the city.[31]

The street life of ancient Athens or Thebes was a welter of disputatious voices. In antiquity the problem of discovering the therapeutic role of the word was, Walter Ong believes, the opposite of the problem in Freud's day: not to establish the physical and psychological effectiveness of speech, but to sort out therapeutic discourse from the daily din of words.[32] Platonic diaeresis—constant backtracking and quibbling in a conversation, to get subject matter, definitions, categories, and logic straight—derives from the clear-thinking literate's need to survive and get ahead in oral argumentation. The Anglo-Saxon is stunned in Greece today by the way a simple request for a receipt can precipitate an hour of confused dispute. How could so many easily excited, conflicting wishes and fears have been resolved in antiquity except by submission of the individuals' *logoi* to the logos of the state? And once a year that submission was ritually dramatized, in the tragedies produced at the festival of Dionysus.

Aeschylus fulfilled the fears of the audience, with a solution at the end of his *Oresteia* that saves the state but not the individual. Sophocles offered no such tragic relief from his spectacles, merely a resignation to suffering as a hero or to undistinguished security as a member of the chorus. Euripides probably enjoyed the worst audiences, for he eschewed both solution and resignation in his heroes' and heroines' duels with society, and thereby subverted the social contract under which his audience hoped to operate. His choruses no longer sustain the culture but disrupt it.

Myth, Psychoanalysis, and Literature

Is the mythopoeic imagination, in K. K. Ruthven's words, "an expression of our freedom to invent alternative realities, or is it merely an agent of those powerful forces (personal and traumatic, or racial and primordial) which determine our lives?" Freud thought the latter; the Greeks would have agreed and perhaps have added society and the gods to the list of forces that have hired myth's services. The former possibility, however, is the first article of faith for such as the adopted sons of J. R. R. Tolkien. Let Ruthven speak again: "When writers come to realize that they must not expect to grow away from myth, but towards it, Romanticism triumphs and the child once more becomes father to the man."[33] Jung and his followers want the imaginative freedom this possibility allows, but the security and fatedness of the other as well.

Again and again, Jung bore witness that "myth is the natural and indispensible intermediate stage between unconscious and conscious cognition."[34] An understanding, or merely a recognition, of our lives as projections of myths is thought somehow to conduct our imaginations beyond the stuffy concerns of daily business to a simpler, purer realm of archaic powers and attainable perfections. Some need more help than others: "As is often the case with mythological material," the Jungian analyst Edward Whitmont admits, "our patients' personal associations were sparse. At such times the analyst has to draw on his own knowledge of mythology."[35] That is, the analyst once again lends the analysand a language in which to express himself, or to which he is encouraged to adapt experiences and emotions he is too inarticulate to describe in his own way.

From event to remembrance a revision always takes place in the mind of the memoirist, and between the erasures and insertions in even the most conscientious chronicle the truth has been known to slip away. Freud found an analogy between the screen memories of childhood and the screen memories of the race, myths.[36] This did not trouble him, since for his purposes a faulty memory served as well, or better, than an accurate one, and he regarded the language of myth as simply an older dialect of his own, psychoanalytic, language. Both Freud and Jung found the meaning they extracted from myth inevitable—as indeed it was—and presumed to teach their patients the language behind all languages.

But do objects and events inevitably attain the status of myth? Roland Barthes thinks not: "Ancient or not, mythology can only have an historical foundation, for myth is a type of speech chosen by history: it cannot possibly evolve from the 'nature' of things."[37] And so the only way to make a dynamic use of it, "a use endowed with responsibility," is to grasp the historical specificity of the myth, to perform the play authentically or to read the text accurately;

only by understanding the past can we master it.[38] Such understanding, psychoanalytically directed or otherwise, is an enemy of myth—an enemy like Nietzsche's Socrates who destroyed myth by persistently asking for the definitions which it cannot abide, which it both ante- and post-dates. Such an understanding, however, also befriends myth, for by comprehending its specificities, we preserve it; by distinguishing its language from ours, we recover the etymologies of many of our own words and gestures and thus learn to bespeak our particular concerns more fluidly and precisely—to make sure the psychoanalytic quest remains ours and not the guiding physician's.

Rollo May echoes the ideology of many psychologists when he advises that therapy should help the patient weed out the pseudomyths from the walled garden of his soul, so that he can then cultivate a personal myth.[39] But few patients possess the verbal and imaginative resources necessary to create private mythologies which help, rather than hinder, their passage through the real world. And so they fall victim to the myths of others, more glibly powerful than they, analysts of one or another school, or fickle students of one or another ruling idea.

Freud recognized the variation possible in symbolism; depending on the individual's associations and history, the symbol enjoys a unique content: only through the associative technique can the analyst determine the individual's psychical situation and accurately interpret his dreams.[40] The essentially humanistic and philosophical nature of his thinking encouraged Freud to show the soul how it could become aware of itself, free from many of the dark forces that ride it, and so more fully human.[41] This, if it is a therapy at all, is one in which the patient must be prepared to work far harder than the physician; he must at times resist the physician; he must cherish his contacts with history and with his present realities as a check against the seductiveness of the physician's ideas and language. For he cannot subsume as much of his soul as possible into his ego,[42] his I, to translate literally, without balking before the invitation every school of analysis issues for its patients to surrender what of themselves they have rescued from the caverns of the unconscious to a darkly ordered set of psychological principles.

Myth constitutes a communal language, available, illuminating, comforting, exhalting. But few patients have the strength and intelligence to maintain their integrity, to be true to themselves, while voicing the old mythic patterns; to develop their own, dreadfully personal, styles—which is to say, to create souls or egos within which to dwell, or by which to maintain an equilibrium, after the old, authoritarian, guilt- and shame-ridden communities have proved suffocating. "Freud has bred a generation," Rieff acknowledges, "no longer willing to commit itself, as Freud himself did, to the belief that culture must be accepted as the despotic and inescapable god."[43] Freud's attempt to reconcile each individual to living without the comforts of communal strictures finally comes to resemble Nietzsche's commands to live without "truth," "good," and "evil." But while Freud (in the process of discovering the common man) morosely concluded that the despotism of culture must be submitted to, Nietzsche (in the process of creating the Superman) gloriously declined to bend his knee to civilization and receive its comforts.

Freud loved mythology but despised religion. Myth does not make the same demands upon us as religion does, but asks only for our attention, not for our belief. Myth remains passive, an analysable artifact, like a dream; religion aggressively imposes a passivity on us before its dogmas and precepts. Jung and his followers treat myth as only the occasional manifestations, through narrative, of some cosmic religion. Thus, in the last analysis, Freud seems to be more nearly the optimist, working always to set us as free as possible from the swarming tyrannies of the world; and Jung is the more passive one, the mechanist, according to whom we are born with tendencies and dispositions that direct our behavior from cradle to catafalque, in a closed psychic system.[44] Jung starts with a certainty and explores its intricacies. Freud, however, finds satisfaction in precise approximations to the truth, a sign of the ego's strength being its ability "to pursue constructive work further in spite of the absence of final confirmation."[45]

A knowledge of psychoanalysis, then, constitutes the metaeducation of modern man—for the purpose, Freud said, of "overcoming the residues of childhood."[46] (But Jung would have countered that it was to give direction to the second half of life.) As with Socratic philosophy, that education is distinguished, not by the possession of a body of knowledge, but by the experience of a process, one as much of the abandonment of opinions as the adoption of them. The process of education is indistinguishable from the acquisition of a discourse: for only a discourse can lead us out of ourselves, separate us from ourselves and from the rest of the world, and then provide a bridge across that distance. When psychiatry does not aspire to become pharmacology, it displays a hunger for metaphor which cannot be satisfied in the sterile atmosphere of the laboratory, where all chance connections are forbidden. Metaphor feeds on chance connections: and so the psychiatrist has little choice but to return to the asphodel fields of Greek mythology, abundant with coincidences and happenstances that turn out to have been destinies in the making.

Those destinies, however, were fixed, finally and forever, only in the handbooks of mythology—not quite in the actual literature, where they enjoy both an oral fluidity and a textual independence. Psychoanalytic theory relies on the fixity of the data; myth must therefore be refined and stabilized before it is soluble in theory. An antagonism exists between analysis and literature: in analysis, consciousness must discover the unconscious, so that our emotional *molten material beneath earth's crust*

life may be integrated into our intellectual life; but in literature, and in life, the unconscious should rather feed consciousness, inspire it to creatively mold the magma welling up from below. The labor of analysis is essential, if we are to have a chance at freedom and at writing our own roles in life. And it is, of course, a never-ending job, but it is not one to occupy us fully for more than a few of our middle years, unless we are a Freud or a Jung; for the constant analytic reference of our lives to styleless myth, Greek or Viennese, ceases after a while to be useful unless it is made the substratum of a sportive, inventive something else that takes up where the myths end. An adventure, admittedly, that few are qualified or eager for. But without the shiver of joy that shoots up the spine as one feels words, newly minted and perfectly apt, tripping down one's tongue and into the clear morning air or onto the fresh white page— without this Eden-bright sense of the creation of language anyone, even a hero, will be headed off at the pass by some tired old fate.

Both analytic and literary discourse have been calculated to bestow freedom on the speaker, but that gift is finally beyond the rhetorical range of the analytic. The conflict between myth and literature is only a skirmish in the great war between determinism and freedom, between a morbidity before and a delight in the dilemma of existence. A myth, *qua* myth, generalized, tidy, and closed, leaves us no room for freedom—of interpretation, of characterization, of invention. But a literary telling, mythical or fictional, revels in precisely what the handbook summary has left out of its account: ambiguity, duplicity, irony, playfulness, openness. We readers and interpreters of ourselves as characters in the myths vacillate between, on the one hand, the comfort of confinement offered by an entry in the archetypal encyclopedia of human behavior and, on the other hand, the terrifyingly blank pages of the unwritten text of our lives. We, like the poets and tragedians, feel ourselves drawn to and drawn into the old plots—until the saga is just about to close over us for good. And then we must break free, like willful little fascicles from the binding of a codex called tradition, assert our individualities against the retrospective future of the race, and take the road which Oedipus seems not to have noticed the signpost for, the road to Daulis.

Notes

Chapter 1—Oedipus and His Kind

1. *The Interpretation of Dreams* pp. 295–96.
2. Ibid., p. 294.
3. Sigmund Freud, *The Origins of Psychoanalysis: Letters to Wilhelm Fliess*, trans. Eric Mosbacher and James Strachey (New York: Basic Books, 1954), p. 223.
4. Sigmund Freud, *Three Essays on the Theory of Sexuality*, trans. James Strachey (New York: Basic Books, 1975), p. 92, n. 1.
5. *Five Lectures on Psycho-Analysis*, p. 47.
6. *Totem and Taboo*, pp. 125–26.
7. Ibid., p. 132.
8. Ibid., pp. 141–45, quotations 142 and 143.
9. Ibid., p. 146.
10. Ibid., p. 152.
11. Ibid., pp. 148, quotation 154.
12. *The Future of an Illusion*, p. 43.
13. *Civilization and Its Discontents*, p. 78.
14. *The Ego and the Id*, p. 27.
15. *Totem and Taboo*, p. 156.
16. *The Ego and the Id*, p. 27.
17. *Totem and Taboo*, pp. 155–56.
18. Joel Friedman and Sylvia Gassel, "The Chorus in Sophocles' *Oedipus Tyrannus*," *Psychoanalytic Quarterly* 19(1950), 213–14, 225–26.
19. Quoted by Ronald Clark, *Freud, the Man and the Cause* (New York: Random House, 1980), p. 355, from Anna Quindlen, *The New York Times*, 7 May 1977.
20. *Totem and Taboo*, p. 159.
21. *An Outline of Psycho-Analysis*, p. 62.
22. Bruno Bettleheim, "Freud and the Soul," *The New Yorker*, 1 March 1982, p. 67.
23. Karl Abraham, "The Rescue and Murder of the Father in Neurotic Phantasy-Formations" and "Dreams and Myths," in *Clinical Papers and Essays on Psychoanalysis*, trans. Hilda Abraham and D. R. Ellison (New York: Basic Books, 1955), pp. 69, 161–62, 180.
24. One who was not so haunted was Ludwig Wittgenstein; see "Conversations on Freud," in *Lectures and Conversations* (Berkeley: University of California Press, 1966), p. 51.
25. *Totem and Taboo*, p. 151.
26. Ibid., pp. 153–54.
27. *The Interpretation of Dreams*, p. 290 and see pp. 657–58; *The Psychopathology of Everyday Life*, p. 218.

28. Quoted by Carl Jung, *Symbols of Transformation* (CW 5), p. 32 and n. 45.

29. E. R. Dodds, *The Greeks and the Irrational* (Berkeley: University of California Press, 1951, reprint 1968), pp. 44–49, 61 n. 103, quotation 46.

30. *The Interpretation of Dreams*, p. 297.

31. Artemidorus, *The Interpretation of Dreams*, trans. Robert White (Park Ridge, New Jersey: Noyes Press, 1975), and see p. 81.

32. Dodds, pp. 61–62 n. 105.

33. Erich Fromm, "The Oedipus Complex and the Oedipus Myth" in Ruth Anschen (ed.), *The Family* (New York: Harper and Bros., 1949), p. 424.

34. Sigmund Freud, *Moses and Monotheism*, trans. Katherine Jones (New York: Vintage Books, n.d.), p. 128.

35. George Devereux, "Why Oedipus Killed Laius," *International Journal of Psycho-Analysis* 34(1953), 138.

36. *Beyond the Pleasure Principle*, pp. 15–16.

37. *The Future of an Illusion*, p. 18.

38. See E. R. Dodds, "On Misunderstanding the *Oedipus Rex*," in *The Ancient Concept of Progress* (New York: Oxford University Press, 1973), pp. 64–77; and Bernard Knox, *Oedipus at Thebes* (New Haven: Yale University Press, 1957), pp. 3–52.

39. Knox, pp. 7–8.

40. I. Galdston, "Sophocles Contra Freud," *Bulletin of the New York Academy of Medicine* 30(1954), 805, 809, 812–15.

41. Thomas Gould, "The Innocence of Oedipus: The Philosophers on *Oedipus the King*," *Arion* 4(1965), 386, 586ff.; 5(1966), 478ff., 490–92.

42. Lionel Casson, *Travel in the Ancient World* (Toronto: Hakkert, 1974), pp. 69–71.

43. Peter Green, *The Shadow of the Parthenon* (Berkeley: University of California Press, 1972), p. 41.

44. *Introductory Lectures on Psychoanalysis*, p. 331.

45. *An Outline of Psycho-Analysis*, p. 47 n. 1.

46. Sigmund Freud, "Psychoanalysis," *SE* 18, p. 252.

47. Sigmund Freud and D. E. Oppenheim, *Dreams in Folklore*, trans. A. M. O. Richards (New York: International Universities Press, 1958), pp. 13–14.

48. H. Trosman, "Freud's Cultural Background," *Psychological Issues* 9(1976), 46–70.

49. W. H. Auden, "Greatness Finding Itself," *Forwards and Afterwords* (New York: Vintage Books, 1974), p. 79.

50. *The Interpretation of Dreams*, p. 295.

51. Clark, pp. 281–82.

52. *Five Lectures on Psycho-Analysis*, pp. 23, 29.

53. *Introductory Lectures on Psychoanalysis* (Norton), p. 245, quotation pp. 293, 291; and see *Beyond the Pleasure Principle*, p. 12.

54. Max Schur, *Freud: Living and Dying* (New York: International Universities Press, 1972), pp. 19–22.

55. *Introductory Lectures on Psychoanalysis*, p. 206.

56. Paul Ricocur, *Freud and Philosophy* (New Haven: Yale University Press, 1970), p. 189.

57. See *Civilization and Its Discontents*, pp. 16ff.

58. "A Case of Homosexuality in a Woman," *Sexuality and the Psychology of Love*, pp. 154–55.

59. *The Psychopathology of Everyday Life*, p. 21.

60. *Introductory Lectures on Psychoanalysis*, p. 178.

61. Philip Rieff, ed., *Delusion and Dream and Other Essays* (Boston: Beacon Press, 1956), p. 5.

62. Ibid., pp. 4–5.

63. Roland Barthes, *Camera Lucida*, trans. Richard Howard (New York: Farrar, Straus and Giroux, 1981), p. 8.

64. Auden, "The Greeks and Us" in *Forwards and Afterwords*, p. 28 n. 1.

65. See Friedrich Nietzsche, *Beyond Good and Evil*, trans. Walter Kaufmann (New York: Vintage Books, 1966), p. 9, section 1.1.

66. Philip Rieff, "The Analytic Attitude," *Encounter* 17:6(June 1962), 24.

67. See Rieff *Delusion and Dream*, pp. 16–17.

68. *The Psychopathology of Everyday Life*, p. 68.

69. *An Outline of Psycho-Analysis*, p. 44, quotation pp. 48–49.

70. *Introductory Lectures on Psychoanalysis*, pp. 181–82, 114.

71. Rieff *Delusion and Dream*, p. 8.

72. K. K. Ruthven, *Myth* (London: Methuen, 1976), p. 10.

73. André Green, *The Tragic Effect: The Oedipus Complex in Tragedy*, trans. Alan Sheridan (London: Cambridge University Press, 1979), pp. 18–19.

74. John Jones, *On Aristotle and Greek Tragedy* (London: Oxford University Press, 1962), pp. 44–45.

75. Philip Vellacott, *Sophocles and Oedipus* (Ann Arbor: University of Michigan Press, 1971), pp. 104ff.

76. *Three Essays on the Theory of Sexuality*, pp. 60–61.

77. Richard Caldwell, "The Blindness of Oedipus," *International Review of Psycho-analysis* 1(1974), 207, 216.

78. *Three Essays on the Theory of Sexuality*, p. 92 n. 1.

79. *The Future of an Illusion*, p. 5.

80. *The Psychopathology of Everyday Life*, pp. 136, 146–47, 154.

81. *Five Lectures on Psycho-Analysis*, p. 27.

82. Friedrich Nietzsche, *The Birth of Tragedy*, trans. Walter Kaufmann (New York: Vintage Books, 1967), pp. 68–69.

83. From a letter to Goethe dated 11 November 1815; quoted by Sandor Ferenczi, *Sex in Psychoanalysis*, trans. Ernest Jones (New York: Basic Books, 1950), p. 254.

84. Quoted by Rieff "The Analytic Attitude," 24.

85. *The Freud/Jung Letters*, ed. William McGuire, trans. Ralph Manheim (Princeton: Princeton University Press, 1974), p. 428, 12 October 1911; *The Psychopathology of Everyday Life*, pp. 255–56.

Chapter 2—The Afterbirth

1. Jean-Paul Sartre, *The Words*, trans. Richard Frechtman (New York: Vintage Books, 1981), p. 21.

2. Alfred Kazin, "The Language of the Pundits," in *Hidden Patterns*, ed. Leonard and Eleanor Manheim (New York: MacMillan, 1966), pp. 37–39.

3. Clyde Kluckhohn, "Myth and Ritual," *Harvard Theological Review* 35(1942), 46.

4. Erich Fromm, *The Forgotten Language* (New York: Grove Press, 1951), p. 7.

5. *The Viking Portable Nietzsche*, trans. Walter Kaufmann (Harmondsworth: Penguin Books, 1959), p. 30.

6. Mark Kanzer, "On Interpreting the Oedipus Plays," in *The Psychoanalytic Study of Society*, vol. III, ed. Warner Muensterberger and Sidney Axelrod (New York: International Universities Press, 1965), p. 36.

7. Karl Abraham, "The Rescue and Murder of the Father in Neurotic Phantasy-Formations" and "Two Contributions to the Study of Symbols," in *Clinical Papers and Essays on Psychoanalysis*, trans. Hilda Abraham and D. R. Ellison (New York: Basic Books, 1955), pp. 70, 72, 73, 85.

8. *Gargantua and Pantagruel*, trans. J. M. Cohen (Harmondsworth: Penguin Books, 1955), p. 38.

9. Michel Bréal, *Mélange de mythologie et de linguistique* (Paris: Hachette, 1877), pp. 163–85.

10. Géza Roheim, "The Oedipus Complex, Magic and Culture," in *Psychoanalysis and the Social Sciences* II (New York: International Universities Press, 1950), pp. 178ff., 214.

11. Géza Roheim, *The Gates of the Dream* (New York: International Universities Press, 1952), p. 530.

12. Géza Roheim, "Teiresias and Other Seers," *Psychoanalytic Review* 33(1946), 314–15.

13. Richard Caldwell, "The Blindness of Oedipus," *The International Review of Psycho-Analysis* 1(1974), 208, 215.

14. M. St. Clair, "A Note on the Guilt of Oedipus," *Psychoanalytic Review* 48(1961), 114.

15. Simone de Beauvoir, *The Second Sex*, trans. H. M. Parshley (New York: Vintage Books, 1974), p. 51.

16. *The Psychopathology of Everyday Life*, p. 255.

17. *The Freud/Jung Letters*, ed. William McGuire, trans. Ralph Manheim (Princeton: Princeton University Press, 1974), p. 428, letter dated 12 October 1911.

18. *The Psychopathology of Everyday Life*, p. 255.

19. *Introductory Lectures on Psychoanalysis*, pp. 308, 424.

20. George Devereux, "Why Oedipus Killed Laius," *International Journal of Psycho-Analysis* 34(1953), 132–41; see also his "The Self-Blinding of Oidipous in Sophokles: *Oidipous Tyrannos*," *Journal of Hellenic Studies* 93(1973), 36–49.

21. Edmund Leach, *Claude Lévi-Strauss* (Harmondsworth: Penguin, 1976), pp. 85–86.

22. *Sexuality and the Psychology of Love*, p. 185.

23. Sigmund Freud, *The Origins of Psychoanalysis*, trans. Eric Mosbacher and James Strachey (New York: Basic Books, 1954), p. 289, letter dated 1 August 1899.

24. *The Ego and the Id*, p. 23.

25. Theodor Reik, "Oedipus and the Sphinx," *British Journal of Medical Psychology* 1(1921), 189–92.

26. *The Ego and the Id*, p. 22.

27. See *Group Psychology and the Analysis of the Ego*, p. 37.

28. René Girard, *Violence and the Sacred*, trans. Patrick Gregory (Baltimore: The Johns Hopkins University Press, 1977), pp. 174–92.

29. Robert Graves, *The Greek Myths* (London: Cassell, 1958), pp. 375–77.

30. J. J. Bachofen, *Myth, Religion, and Mother Right*, trans. Ralph Manheim (Princeton: Princeton University Press, 1967).

31. Carl Robert, *Oidipus* (Berlin: Weidmann, 1915), pp. 44–45; W. A. Lessa, "On the Symbolism in Oedipus," in *The Study of Folklore*, ed. A. Dundes (Englewood Cliffs: Prentice-Hall, 1965), p. 116.

32. George Devereux, "The Sociopolitical Functions of the Oedipus Myth," *Psychoanalytic Quarterly* 32(1963), pp. 205, 209.

33. Erich Fromm, "The Oedipus Complex and the Oedipus Myth," in *The Family*, ed. Ruth Anschen (New York: Harper and Bros., 1949), pp. 425–45, quotation p. 426; *The Sane Society* (New York: Holt, Rinehart and Winston, 1955), pp. 42–44, quotation p. 43.

34. Harry Slochower, "Oedipus: Fromm or Freud," *Complex* 8(1952), 60; also Barbara Lefcowitz, "The Inviolate Grove," *Literature and Psychology* 17(1967), 79; C. Rado, "*Oedipus the King*, an Interpretation," *Psychoanalytic Review* 43(1956), 230.

35. Ivan Linforth, *Religion and Drama in Oedipus at Colonus* (Berkeley: University of California Press, 1951), pp. 94–97.

36. Slochower, 60; Lefcowitz, 81.

37. Mark Kanzer, "The Passing of the Oedipus Complex in Greek Drama," *International Journal of Psycho-Analysis* 29(1948), 132.

38. Lester Golden, "Freud's Oedipus: Its Mytho-Dramatic Basis," *American Imago* 24(1967), 278.

39. Mark Kanzer, "The Oedipus Trilogy," *The Yearbook of Psychoanalysis*, vol. III (New York: International Universities Press, 1951), p. 77; see Mario Carlinsky, "The Oedipus Legend and *Oedipus Rex*," *American Imago* 15(1958), 91–95; and Golden, 277.

40. Kanzer, "The Oedipus Trilogy," 69, 75; and Kanzer, "The Passing of the Oedipus Complex," 133.

41. Rado, 229–33; H. van der Sterren, "The King Oedipus of Sophocles," *International Journal of Psycho-Analysis* 33(1952), 343–49.

42. Robert Stein, "The Oedipus Myth and the Incest Archetype," in *Spectrum Psychologiae*, ed. C. T. Frey (Zurich: Rascher and Cie., 1965), pp. 18–28, quotation p. 21.

43. Otto Rank, *The Trauma of Birth* (New York: R. Brunner, 1952), pp. 144–45.

44. Ibid., p. 44, quotation p. 43; see his *Das Inzest-Motiv in Dichtung und Saga* (Leipzig and Vienna: Deuticke, 1912), pp. 40–42, 256–58, 585–91.

45. Otto Rank, "The Emergence of the Social Self," in *Beyond Psychology* (New York: Dover Books, 1958), pp. 122–24, quotation p. 123.

46. Otto Rank, "Forms of Kinship and the Individual's Role," in *Modern Education*, excerpted in his *The Myth of the Birth of the Hero and Other Writings* (New York: Vintage Books, 1964), pp. 306–12, quotation p. 309.

47. A. J. Levin, "The Oedipus Myth in History and Psychiatry," *Psychiatry* 11(1948), 283–99.

48. Luis Feder, "Adoption Trauma: Oedipus Myth/Clinical Reality," *International Journal of Psycho-Analysis* 55(1974), 491–93.

49. Sofie Lazarsfeld, "Did Oedipus Have an Oedipus Complex," *American Journal of Orthopsychiatry* 14(1944), 226–29.

50. N. Atkins, "The Oedipus Myth, Adolescence and the Succession of Generations," *Journal of the American Psychoanalytic Association* 18(1970), 860–75, quotation, 862.

51. Leonard Schengold, "The Parent as Sphinx," *Journal of the American Psychoanalytic Association* 11(1963), 725–51.

52. Matthew Besdine, "The Jocasta Complex, Mothering and Genius: Parts I and II," *Psychoanalytic Review* 55(1968), 271–75, 574, 595.

53. Claude Lévi-Strauss, *Structural Anthropology*, trans. Claire Jacobson and Brooke Schoepf (New York: Basic Books, 1963), pp. 217, 215, 216.

54. K. K. Ruthven, *Myth* (London: Methuen, 1976), p. 41.

Chapter 3—Electra and Other Monsters

1. Marie-Louise von Franz, *Puer Aeternus*, 2nd ed. (Santa Monica: Sigo Press, 1981), p. 175.

2. Richard Caldwell, "The Misogyny of Eteocles," *Arethusa* 6(1973), 218.

3. Edward Whitmont, *The Symbolic Quest* (New York: G. P. Putnam's Sons, 1969), p. 201.

4. Von Franz, pp. 175–76.

5. Roland Barthes, *Mythologies*, trans. by Annette Lavers (New York: Hill and Wang, 1972), p. 135.

6. Ibid., p. 120.

7. C. Hopkins, "Assyrian Elements in the Perseus-Gorgon Story," *American Journal of Archaeology* 38(1934), 357.

8. Robert Parker has recently argued in *Miasma* (Oxford: Clarendon Press, 1983) that the view that pollution fears settled over Greece like a cloud in the post-Homeric period (for the best presentation of which, see E. R. Dodds, *The Greeks and the Irrational*, chapter 2) is largely based on a comparison of genres—epic with tragedy. And "the prominence of murder pollution in tragedy is a consequence of its preferred subject matter." In other fifth-century genres, like the poems of Pindar, pollution fears are as slight as in Homer (p. 16). But surely tragedy was the most popular fifth-century genre and its concerns reflect the hopes and fears of its immense audience.

9. Otto Rank, *The Trauma of Birth* (New York: R. Brunner, 1952), p. 149.

10. Marie Delcourt, *Oedipe, ou la légende du conquérant* (Paris: Bibliothèque de la Faculté de Philosophie et Lettres de l'Université de Liège, Fasc. CIV, 1944), pp. 110–27.

11. Ibid., pp. 1–2.

12. Rank, pp. 144–50.

13. Erich Neumann, *The Origins and History of Consciousness*, trans. by R. F. C. Hull (Princeton: Princeton University Press, 1954), pp. 162–63 and cf. pp. 153–57.

14. *Symbols of Transformation* (CW 5), pp. 235–36 and n. 42, 204; cf. also pp. 417–420.

15. Ibid., p. 271.

16. Erich Fromm, *The Sane Society* (New York: Holt, Rinehart and Winston, 1955), pp. 40–43.

17. *History of Consciousness*, p. 156.

18. *Symbols*, p. 374.

19. "Medusa's Head," in *Sexuality and the Psychology of Love*, ed. by Philip Rieff (New York: Collier Books, 1963), pp. 212–13.

20. J. C. Flugel, "Polyphallic Symbolism and the Castration Complex," *International Journal of Psycho-Analysis* 5(1924), 166–75.

21. Isador Coriat, "A Note on the Medusa Symbolism," *American Imago* 2(1941), 281–85.

22. Philip E. Slater, *The Glory of Hera* (Boston: Beacon Press, 1968), pp. 3–74, see, too, "The Greek Family in History and Myth," *Arethusa* 7(1974), 9–44.

23. R. and E. Blum, *Health and Healing in Rural Greece* (Palo Alto: Stanford University Press, 1975), pp. 49–50.

24. See Leon Balter, "The Mother as Source of Power: Three Greek Myths," *Psychoanalytic Quarterly* 38(1969), 223.

25. George Devereux, "Greek Psuedo-Homosexuality and the 'Greek Miracle,' " *Symbolae Osloenses* 42(1967), 69–92.

26. Noted by Slater *Glory of Hera*, p. 13: Bruno Bettleheim, *Symbolic Wounds* (London: Thames and Hudson, 1955), pp. 232–33.

27. Simone de Beauvoir, *The Second Sex*, trans. H. M. Parshley (New York: Vintage Books, 1974), p. 217.

28. Patrick Leigh Fermor, *Mani* (New York: Harper and Brothers, 1958), pp. 184–89.

29. Edward Phinney, "Perseus' Battle with the Gorgons," *Transactions and Proceedings of the American Philological Association*, 102(1971) 452.

30. Slater, *Glory of Hera*, pp. 309–10, 391.

31. Slater, *Glory of Hera*, pp. 88–94, 53–55; "The Greek Family," 39.

32. "The Mother as Source of Power," 226.

33. K. J. Dover, *Greek Homosexuality* (New York: Vintage Books, 1978), pp. 98–102.

34. Karl Abraham, "The Spider as a Dream Symbol," *Selected Papers of Karl Abraham*, trans. Douglas Bryan and Alix Strachey (New York: Basic Books, 1953), p. 331.

35. I recall first reading of this in a book by Gerald Durrell, but see J. L. Cloudsley-Thompson, *Spiders, Scorpions, Centipedes and Mites* (Oxford: Pergamon Press, 1968), p. 217.

36. See Michael J. O'Brien, "Orestes and the Gorgon: Euripides' *Electra*," *American Journal of Philology* 13(1964), 13–39.

37. R. P. Winnington-Ingram, "Clytemnestra and the Vote of Athena," *Journal of Hellenic Studies* 68(1948), 145–46.

38. "On Narcissism," in *Sexuality and the Psychology of Love*, p. 79.

39. *Introductory Lectures on Psychoanalysis*, p. 290.

40. Ronald Clark, *Freud, the Man and the Cause* (New York: Random House, 1980), pp. 51–52.

41. *Introductory Lectures on Psychoanalysis*, p. 333.

42. In *Sexuality and the Psychology of Love*, pp. 183–93.

43. Ibid., pp. 194–211, especially p. 198.

44. *New Introductory Lectures on Psychoanalysis*, p. 114.

45. *An Outline of Psychoanalysis*, pp. 50–51.

46. *New Introductory Lectures*, p. 114.

47. "Some Consequences of the Anatomical Distinction between the Sexes," in *Sexuality and the Psychology of Love*, pp. 192–93; see, too, Simone de Beauvoir, pp. 45–47.

48. In *Freud and Psychoanalysis* (CW 4), pp. 153–55, 168.

49. "Psychoanalysis and Neurosis" in CW 4, pp. 245–47.

50. *Aion* (CW 9.2), p. 15.

51. *Two Essays on Analytical Psychology* (CW 7), pp. 208–209; and see Whitmont, pp. 201, 210.

Chapter 4—Daimon and Archetype

1. Blum, Richard and Eva, *Health and Healing Rural Greece* (Stanford, California: Stanford University Press, 1975), p. 197.

2. I have relied here upon John Cuthbert Lawson's *Modern Greek Folklore and Ancient Greek Religion* (Cambridge: Cambridge University Press, 1910), Patrick Leigh Fermor's *Mani* (New York: Harper and Bros., 1958).

3. Giuseppe di Lampedusa, *Two Stories and a Memory*, trans. Archibald Colquhoun (New York: Grosset and Dunlap, 1968).

4. C. G. Jung, *Memories, Dreams, Reflections*, ed. Aniela Jaffé, trans. Richard and Clara Winston (New York: Vintage Books, 1965); hereafter, *MDR*.

5. See Jolande Jacobi, *Complex, Archetype, Symbol in the Psychology of C. G. Jung*, trans. Ralph Manheim (Princeton: Princeton University Press, 1959), pp. 33–34 and her references there; also Jacobi, *The Psychology of C. G. Jung* (New Haven: Yale University Press, 1973), p. 39.

6. *CW* 11, par. 140, pp. 82–83.

7. *CW* 9.1, par. 150, pp. 76–77.

8. Edward Whitmont, *The Symbolic Quest* (New York: G. P. Putnam's Sons, 1969), p. 15.

9. Joseph Campbell, *The Hero with a Thousand Faces*, second ed., (Princeton: Princeton University Press, 1968), p. vii.

10. *CW* 8, pp. 213–14.

11. Jacobi, *Psychology of C. G. Jung*, p. 47; see also pp. 49–50, 58.

12. Sigmund Freud, *Moses and Monotheism*, trans. Katherine Jones (New York: Vintage Books, 1967), p. 127.

13. *Introductory Lectures on Psychoanalysis*, pp. 150–51, 199, 362, 371; quotation p. 199.

14. *An Outline of Psycho-Analysis*, pp. 23–24.

15. Jacobi, *Psychology of C. G. Jung*, pp. 49–50, 58.

16. *CW* 8, par. 417, pp. 213–14.

17. *CW* 9.1, par. 155, pp. 79–80. *Four Archetypes* (Princeton: Princeton University Press, 1969), p. 13.

18. *CW* 9.1, par. 80, pp. 37–38.

19. Whitmont, *Symbolic Quest*, pp. 189–90.

20. Ibid., pp. 202, 211.

21. Sean O'Faolain, *Vive Moi* (London: Rupert Hart-Davis, 1967), p. 169.

22. *CW* 9.1, pars. 80–81, pp. 37–38. Jacobi, *Complex, Symbol, Archetype*, p. 59.

23. *CW* 6, par. 401, pp. 236–37; *CW* 13, par. 199, pp. 162–63.

24. Jean-Pierre Vernant, "The Reason of Myth," in *Myth and Society in Ancient Greece*, trans. Janet Lloyd (Atlantic Highlands, NJ: Humanities Press, 1980), pp. 218–19.

25. Jacques Lacan, *Écrits*, trans. Alan Sheridan (London: Tavistock, 1977), p. 195.

26. Vernant, pp. 75–77.

27. *An Outline of Psycho-Analysis*, p. 19.

28. Jung, *MDR*, pp. 150–51.

29. Ibid., p. 329.

30. Ibid., p. 3.

31. *CW* 16, par. 179, pp. 78–79.

32. Philip Rieff, *The Triumph of the Therapeutic* (New York: Harper and Row, 1966), p. 45.

33. Claude Lévi-Strauss, *Structural Anthropology*, trans. Claire Jacobson and Brooke Schoepf (New York: Basic Books, 1963), p. 18.

34. Edmund Leach, *Claude Lévi-Strauss* (Harmondsworth: Penguin Books, 1976), pp. 22, 45.

35. Lévi Strauss, pp. 213ff., 229.

36. Claude Lévi-Strauss, *Mythologiques I: Le cru et le cuit* (Paris: Plon, 1964), p. 20.

37. Carl Sagan, *The Dragons of Eden* (New York: Ballantine Books, 1978), pp. 62–65, 135–60.

38. *CW* 11, par. 140, pp. 82–83.

NOTES 259

39. E. R. Dodds, *The Greeks and the Irrational* (Berkeley: University of California Press, 1951, reprint 1968); Bruno Snell, *The Discovery of the Mind*, trans. T. G. Rosenmeyer (New York: Harper and Row, 1960); Julian Jaynes, *The Origin of Consciousness in the Breakdown of the Bicameral Mind* (Boston: Houghton Mifflin, 1977).

40. Snell, p. 31.

41. Dodds, p. 14.

42. Jaynes, pp. 103–4.

43. Ibid., pp. 201–2.

44. Søren Kierkegaard, *The Sickness unto Death* (pub. with *Fear and Trembling*), trans. Walter Lowrie (Princeton: Princeton University Press, 1968), p. 146.

45. In this and the following paragraph I draw freely from Walter Ong, *Orality and Literacy* (London: Methuen, 1982); Eric Havelock, *Preface to Plato* (Cambridge, Mass.: Harvard University Press, 1963), "Prologue to Greek Literacy," in *Lectures in Memory of Louise Taft Sample* (Norman, Okla.: University of Oklahoma Press, 1973), pp. 229–91, *The Literate Revolution in Greece and Its Cultural Consequences* (Princeton: Princeton University Press, 1982). Ong, p. 127.

46. Ong, pp. 140–41, 133; Havelock, *Literate Revolution* p. 137.

47. Ong, pp. 48–49, 23–24, 70–71, 151–55; Havelock, *Preface to Plato*, pp. 115, 49.

48. Havelock, *Literate Revolution*, pp. 73–74.

49. Ong, p. 154.

50. Ong, pp. 105, 41; Havelock, *Preface*, pp. 197–233, 254–305.

51. Ong, pp. 178–79; Havelock, *Literate Revolution*, p. 23.

52. CW 8, pars. 406, 650; pp. 222, 362.

53. Quoted by Jacobi, *Psychology of C. G. Jung*, p. 92, from T. Wolff, *Studien zu C. G. Jungs Psychologie* (Zurich, 1959), pp. 99–100.

54. *Symbols of Transformation* (CW 5), par. 388, pp. 255–56.

55. The literature on whether or not Penelope recognizes Odysseus is extensive: see Robert Fitzgerald's afterword to his translation of the *Odyssey* (Garden City: Anchor Books, 1963), pp. 497–503.

56. See Samuel Butler's *The Authoress of the Odyssey* (Chicago: University of Chicago Press, 1967), and Robert Graves's *Homer's Daughter* (Garden City: Doubleday, 1955).

57. Dodds, pp. 40–43.

58. Paul Friedländer, *Plato*, 2, trans. Hans Meyerhoff (Princeton: Princeton University Press, 1969), p. 37 and p. 35 for Goethe quotation.

59. Dodds, p. 17.

60. Friedländer, p. 41.

61. Søren Kierkegaard, *The Concept of Irony*, trans. Lee Capel (Bloomington: Indiana University Press, 1968), p. 192.

62. *Scriptores Physiognomici Graeci et Latini*, ed. Richard Foerster (Leipzig, 1900), vol. I, pp. vii ff.

63. A. H. Armstrong, *An Introduction to Ancient Philosophy* (Boston: Beacon Press, 1963), p. 152.

64. *On the God of Socrates* 7–8, trans. by James Tatum in his *Apuleius and the Golden Ass* (Ithaca, NY: Cornell University Press, 1979), p. 54.

65. Charles Segal, *Landscape in Ovid's Metamorphoses*, Hermes Einzelschriften 23 (Wiesbaden: Franz Steiner, 1969), p. 15 and cf. p. 75.

66. Rieff, *Triumph*, p. 119.

67. Jacobi, *Complex, Archetype, Symbol*, p. 62.

Chapter 5—Dionysus

1. W. K. C. Guthrie, *The Greeks and Their Gods* (Boston: Beacon Press, 1955), p. 146, calls Otto's *Dionysus* (1933) both a contribution to religious history and itself a document of the cult; see Walter F. Otto, *Dionysus*, trans. Robert Palmer (Bloomington: Indiana University Press, 1965).

2. Robert Eisner, "Some Anomalies in the Myth of Ariadne," *Classical World* 71(1977), 175–77.

3. Axel W. Persson, *The Religion of Greece in Prehistoric Times* (Berkeley: University of California Press, 1942), pp. 80–82, ring nos. 25–26. Also Robert Eisner "Ariadne in Art," *Rivista di Studi Classici* 25(1977), 165–82; and Eisner, "Some Anomalies."

4. Robert Eisner, "The Temple at Ayia Irini: Archaeology and Mythology," *Greek, Roman and Byzantine Studies* 13(1972), 23–33. J. Caskey, "Excavations in Keos, 1960–61," " . . . 1963," and " . . . 1964–65," *Hesperia* 31(1962), 263; 33(1964), 314; 35(1966), 363.

5. Jane Harrison, *Prolegomena to the Study of Greek Religion* (N.Y.: Meridian Books, 1957), p. 373.

6. Gerald F. Else, *The Origin and Early Form of Greek Tragedy* (Cambridge, Mass.: Harvard University Press, 1965).

7. On this and the connection of Dionysus and goats with the question of the year-god, or *eniautos daimon*, see Walter Burkert, "Greek Tragedy and Sacrificial Ritual," *Greek, Roman and Byzantine Studies* 7(1966), 100, 113, 115.

8. L. R. Farnell, *Cults of the Greek States*, 5 vols. [1896] repr. (Chicago: Aegean Press, 1971). Martin P. Nilsson, *A History of Greek Religion*, 2nd ed., trans. F. J. Fielden (N.Y.: Norton, 1964). H. W. Parke, *Festivals of the Athenians* (Ithaca: Cornell University Press, 1977).

9. E. R. Dodds, *The Greeks and the Irrational* (Berkeley: University of California Press, 1951, reprint 1968), pp. 155–56; and Dodds' references there (nn. 125, 131, 132, 134) to Pausanias 8.37.5; Plato, *Meno* 81 B.C., *Laws* 701 C, 854 B; Olympiodorus to *Phaedo* 84.22ff.

10. E. R. Dodds, "Maenadism in the *Bacchae*," *Harvard Theological Review* 33(1940), 171ff.

11. Porphyry, *On Abstinence* 4.19; compare Strabo 10.466. Guthrie, *Greeks and Their Gods*, pp. 51, 155, 157, 45.

12. Robert Graves, "What Food the Centaurs Ate," in *Steps* (London: Cassell's, 1958), pp. 320–43.

13. Marcel Detienne, *Dionysus Slain*, trans. Mireille and Leonard Muellner (Baltimore: John Hopkins University Press, 1979), pp. 36–39; also Guthrie, pp. 46–47, and J. D. Pendlebury, *The Archaeology of Minoan Crete* (London: Methuen, 1939), p. 9, for the Palaikastro hymn to Zeus.

14. Dodds, *The Greeks and the Irrational*, pp. 76–77, and see p. 69.

15. William James, *Varieties of Religious Experience* (New York: The Modern Library, 1936), p. 387.

16. Otto, pp. 95–102.

17. Parke, p. 98.

18. Carl Kerenyi, *Dionysos*, trans. Ralph Manheim (Princeton: Princeton University Press, 1978), p. 303.

19. Friedrich Nietzsche, *The Birth of Tragedy*, trans. Walter Kaufmann (N.Y.: Vintage Books, 1967), pp. 99–100.

20. *The Will to Power*, trans. Walter Kaufmann and R. J. Hollingdale (N.Y.: Vintage Books, 1968), p. 435, no. 822.

21. *Birth of Tragedy*, p. 60.

22. Ibid.

23. *Will to Power*, p. 428, no. 811.

24. Ibid., p. 521, no. 1005.

25. *Birth to Tragedy*, p. 73.

26. *Will to Power*, p. 540, no. 1050; and *Birth of Tragedy*, p. 39.

27. C. G. Jung, *Memories, Dreams, Reflections*, trans. Richard and Clara Winston (N.Y.: Vintage Books, 1965), pp. 102–3.

28. *CW* 6, pp. 139, 140, 141.

29. *CW* 6, p. 142.

30. James Hillman, "Dionysus in Jung's Writings," in *Facing the Gods*, ed. by the author (Irving, Texas: Spring Publications, 1980), p. 154.

31. Ibid., pp. 151–63.

32. "Senex and Puer," in *The Puer Papers*, ed. James Hillman (Irving, Texas: Spring Publications, 1979), p. 26.

33. James Hillman, *The Myth of Analysis* (N.Y.: Harper and Row, 1972), p. 44, and p. 34.

34. Ibid., p. 39.

35. Ibid., pp. 215–93, especially 225, 238, 241.

36. Ibid., pp. 242, n. 54, and 243.

37. Ibid., pp. 290–93.

38. Ibid., pp. 94, 258–82.

39. Philip Slater, *The Glory of Hera* (Boston: Beacon Press, 1971), p. 227.

40. Herbert Marcuse, *Eros and Civilization* (Boston: Beacon Press, 1966), p. 111.

41. Norman O. Brown, *Life Against Death* (Middletown, CT: Wesleyan University Press, 1959), p. 321.

42. *Beyond the Pleasure Principle*, p. 21.

43. Garfield Tourney, "Freud and the Greeks: A Study of the Influence of Classical Greek Mythology and Philosophy upon the development of Freudian Thought," *Journal of the History of the Behavioral Sciences* 1(1965), 81ff., 85.

44. *New Introductory Lectures on Psychoanalysis*, p. 84.

45. Garfield Tourney, "Empedocles and Freud, Heraclitus and Jung," *Bull. Hist. of Medicine* 30(1956), 109–123. Freud's "Analysis Terminable and Interminable," in *Therapy and Technique*, ed. Philip Rieff (N.Y.: Collier Books, 1963), pp. 263–64.

46. William Sale, "The Psychoanalysis of Pentheus in the *Bacchae* of Euripides," *Yale Classical Studies* 22(1972), 74–79.

47. Charles Segal, "Pentheus and Hippolytus on the Couch and on the Grid," *Classical World* 72(1978), 140.

48. Philip Rieff, *Freud: The Mind of the Moralist*, 3rd ed. (Chicago: University of Chicago Press, 1979), p. 34.

49. Dodds, *The Greeks and the Irrational*, p. 159 and n. 19.

50. E. R. Dodds, *Introduction to Euripides' Bacchae*, 2nd ed. (Oxford: Oxford University Press, 1960), p. xliv.

51. *The Ego and the Id*, p. 15; and see *New Introductory Lectures*, pp. 68–69.

52. *Beyond the Pleasure Principle*, p. 23.

53. *New Introductory Lectures*, p. 67.

54. *Beyond the Pleasure Principle*, p. 4.

55. *The Ego and the Id*, p. 43.

56. Ibid., pp. 24, 26.

57. Ibid., pp. 46, 38–39.

58. Ibid., p. 39.

59. Ibid., p. 48.

60. Ibid., pp. 19, 20, 64.

61. Philip Rieff, "Introduction" to his collection of Freud's papers in *General Psychological Theory* (N.Y.: Collier Books, 1963), pp. 15–16.

62. *An Outline of Psycho-Analysis*, p. 7.

63. *The Ego and the Id*, pp. 43, 46, 44.

64. Freud, "The Instincts and Their Vicissitudes," in *General Psychology Theory*, pp. 91–97.

65. *The Ego and the Id*, p. 37.

66. *Eros and Civilization*, p. 29. Bruno Bettleheim in "Freud and the Soul," *New Yorker*, March 1, 1982, pp. 38–39, 88–89 objects to the word *instinct*; Freud's *Trieb* is better translated by "drive."

67. *Beyond the Pleasure Principle*, pp. 31–35.

68. Ibid., pp. 34, 40, 49, 44.

69. Lou Andreas-Salomé, *The Freud Journal of Lou Andreas-Salomé*, trans. Stanley Leavy (New York: Basic Books, 1964), p. 142.

70. Kerenyi, *Dionysos*, pp. 204–5.

71. Dodds, *The Greeks and the Irrational*, p. 213.

72. Segal, p. 142.

73. Kerenyi, *Dionysos*, p. 82, on the *Etymologicum Gudianum*. The Ionian word *zagrē* means a pit for the capture of animals.

74. R. P. Winnington-Ingram, *Euripides and Dionysus* (Cambridge: Cambridge University Press, 1948), p. 169.

75. Rieff, *Freud*, pp. 32–33.

76. Ibid., pp. 28–35; Edward Glover, *Freud or Jung* (New York: Norton, 1950), pp. 52–71.

77. *Group Psychology and the Analysis of the Ego*, pp. 6, 44–45, 55–56.

78. Dodds, *The Greeks and the Irrational*, p. 170 and n. 71: "Euripides, in his description of the normal rite (*Bacchae*, 135ff.), appears to recognize only one male celebrant, who is identified with the god."

79. *Group Psychology*, p. 56, n. 1; see *Totem and Taboo*, p. 144.

80. *Beyond the Pleasure Principle*, p. 36.

81. Dodds, *The Greeks and the Irrational*, p. 176.

82. Rieff, "Introduction" to Freud's *General Psychological Theory*, p. 19.

83. Freud, "On Narcissism," in *General Psychological Theory*, p. 75.

84. Dodds, *The Greeks and the Irrational*, p. 76.

85. John Jones, *On Aristotle and Greek Tragedy* (Oxford: Oxford University Press, 1962), pp. 45–46, 270.

Chapter 6—Apollo and His Boys

1. Friedrich Nietzsche, *The Birth of Tragedy*, trans. Walter Kaufmann (N.Y.: Vintage Books, 1963), p. 52.

2. *New Introductory Lectures*, p. 71.

3. "Civilized Sexuality and Modern Nervousness," in Freud's *Sexuality and the Psychology of Love*, ed. Philip Rieff (N.Y.: Collier Books), p. 25.

4. W. K. C. Guthrie, *The Greeks and Their Gods* (Boston: Beacon Press, 1955), p. 203.

5. Norman Mailer, *Genius and Lust* (New York: Grove Press, 1976), p. 185.

6. Cited by Guthrie, *Greeks and Their Gods*, pp. 183–84.

7. *An Outline of Psychoanalysis*, p. 7.

8. "On Narcissism," in Freud's *General Psychological Theory*, ed. Philip Rieff (N.Y.: Collier Books), pp. 69, 70.

9. Ibid., pp. 73–74.

10. Philip Slater, *The Glory of Hera* (Boston: Beacon Press, 1971), pp. 160–61.

11. K. J. Dover, *Greek Homosexuality* (New York: Vintage Books, 1980).

12. Victoria Hamilton, *Narcissus and Oedipus: The Children of Psychoanalysis* (London: Routledge and Kegan Paul, 1982), p. 117.

13. *Leonardo da Vinci and a Memory of His Childhood*, p. 50.

14. Hans Licht, *Sexual Life in Ancient Greece*, trans. J. H. Freese (London: The Abbey Library, 1932), pp. 193–94.

15. E. R. Dodds, *The Greeks and the Irrational* (Berkeley: University of California Press, 1951), p. 142.

16. L. R. Palmer, *Minoans and Mycenaeans*, 2nd ed. (N.Y.: Alfred A. Knopf, 1965), p. 343 and fig. 46.

17. *The Greeks and the Irrational*, pp. 146, 209, p. 210 for the quotation.

18. H. Spotnitz and P. Resnikoff, "The Myths of Narcissus," *Psychoanalytic Review* 41(1954), 174–75.

19. *The Greeks and Their Gods*, pp. 86–87. L. R. Farnell, *Cults of the Greek States* (Oxford: Oxford University Press, 1896; repr. Chicago: Aegean Press, 1971), IV, pp. 125, 264.

20. Farnell, *Cults*, IV, p. 266, interprets the evidence the other way: the mournful part of the festival was pre-Hellenic, the joyful part Apollo's contribution.

21. Farnell, *Cults*, IV, p. 120; A. J. Evans, *Journal of Hellenic Studies*, Mycenaean Tree and Pillar Cult, 21(1901), 148.

22. Ann V. Rankin, "Euripides' Hippolytus: A Psychopathological Hero," *Arethusa* 7(1974), 76ff.

23. R. P. Winnington-Ingram, *Euripides and Dionysus* (Cambridge: Cambridge University Press, 1948), p. 40.

24. Jean J. Smoot, "Hippolytus as Narcissus," *Arethusa* 9(1976), 38 and ref. there to Freud, *SE* XX, p. 99.

25. "On Narcissism," p. 75.

26. *Genius and Lust*, p. 188.

27. Lou Andreas-Salomé, *The Freud Journal of Lou Andreas-Salomé*, trans. Stanley Leavy (New York: Basic Books, 1964), p. 109.

28. *Genius and Lust*, p. 189.

29. Hamilton, p. 128.

30. Conon, *Narrations* 24; *Fr. Gr. Hist.* 1.26; Photius, ed. R. Henry, vol. 3, 1962.

31. *Civilization and its Discontents*, pp. 66–70.

32. Ibid., p. 85.

33. Ibid., pp. 79–80.

34. "Civilized Sexual Morality and Modern Nervousness," in *Sexuality and the Psychology of Love*, p. 29.

35. Sigmund Freud, *The Origins of Psychoanalysis: Letters to Wilhelm Fliess*, trans. Eric Mosbacher and James Strachey (N.Y.: Basic Books, 1954), pp. 209–10.

36. Friedrich Nietzsche, *On the Genealogy of Morals*, trans. Walter Kaufmann (N.Y.: Vintage Books, 1969), p. 84, section 2.16.

37. *The Will to Power*, trans. Walter Kaufmann and R. J. Hollingdale (N.Y.: Vintage books, 1968), p. 527, no. 1019.

38. *Genealogy of Morals*, pp. 93–94.

39. Ibid., pp. 84–85.

40. *The Origins of Psychoanalysis: Letters to Wilhelm Fleiss*, p. 335.

Chapter 7—The Great Mothers

1. C. G. Thomas, "Matriarchy in Early Greece: The Bronze and Dark Ages," *Arethusa* 6(1973), 173.

2. For a well-balanced appraisal of matriarchy by a modern anthropologist, see Joan Bamberger, "The Myth of Matriarchy," in *Woman, Culture, and Society*, ed. by Michelle Rosaldo and Louise Lamphere (Palo Alto: Stanford University Press, 1974), pp. 263–80.

3. E. A. S. Butterworth, *Some Traces of the Pre-Olympian World in Greek Literature and Myth* (Berlin: De Gruyter, 1966).

4. Simon Pembroke, "Women in Change: The Function of Alternatives in Early Greek Tradition and the Ancient Idea of Matriarchy," *Journal of the Warburg and Courtald Institute* 30(1967), 35.

5. Freud, "Female Sexuality," in *Sexuality and the Psychology of Love*, p. 195.

6. Leonard Farnell, *Cults of the Greek States* (Oxford: Oxford University Press, 1896; repr. Chicago: Aegean Press, 1971), II, pp. 456, 443, and 572, n. 55; W. K. C. Guthrie, *The Greeks and Their Gods* (Boston: Beacon Press, 1955), p. 101.

7. Farnell, p. 521.

8. Edward Phinney, "Perseus' Battle with the Gorgons," *Transactions and Proceedings of the American Philological Association* 102(1971), 446; Martin Nilsson, *Geschichte der griechischen Religion*, 3rd ed., (Munich: Beck, 1967), I, p. 227.

9. See Martin Nilsson, *A History of Greek Religion* (New York: W. W. Norton, 1964), pp. 9–37.

10. Farnell, pp. 446, 448, 481, 290, 253–54, quotation 257.

11. Freud, "Great Is Diana of the Ephesians," *SE* XII, pp. 342–44.

12. G. Zuntz, *Persephone: Three Essays on Religion and Thought in Magna Graecia* (New York: Oxford University Press, 1971), p. 13.

13. James Mellart, "Deities and Shrines of Neolithic Anatolia," *Archaeology* 16(1963), 32, fig. 1.

14. Guthrie, pp. 211, n. 1; 100, n. 3; 101.

15. Farnell, p. 429.

16. Cf. Axel Persson, *The Religion of Greece in Prehistoric Times* (Berkeley: University of California Press, 1942), p. 151.

17. Walter Burkert, *Structure and History in Greek Mythology and Ritual* (Berkeley: University of California Press, 1979), pp. 102–3 and ref. there to Helck; Bernice Engle, "The Amazons in Ancient Greece," *Psychoanalytic Quarterly* 11(1942), 522.

18. S. H. Hooke, *Middle Eastern Mythology* (Harmondsworth: Penguin Books, 1963), pp. 20–23, 39–41; Burkert, p. 101; James Pritchard, *The Ancient Near Eastern Texts* (Princeton: Princeton University Press, 1950), pp. 52ff.; Samuel Noah Kramer, *Mythologies of the Ancient World* (Garden City: Doubleday, 1961), pp. 106–15. *The New Golden Bough*, ed., Theodor H. Gaster (New York: New American Library, 1964), is the easiest form in which to consult James Frazer's work.

19. Jean-Pierre Vernant, *Myth and Society in Ancient Greece*, trans. Janet Lloyd (Atlantic Highlands, NJ: Humanities Press, 1980), pp. 131–32.

20. Ibid., p. 146 and *passim*; Marcel Detienne, *The Gardens of Adonis* (Atlantic Highlands, NJ: Humanities Press, 1977).

21. Elizabeth Weigert-Vowinkel, "The Cult and Mythology of the Magna Mater from the Standpoint of Psychoanalysis," *Psychiatry* 1(1938), 370, 372.

22. Jung, *Symbols of Transformation* (CW 5), pp. 204–5.

23. Marie-Louise von Franz, *Puer Aeternus*, 2nd ed. (Santa Monica: Sigo Press, 1981), pp. 130–32.

24. Leon Balter, "The Mother as Source of Power: Three Greek Myths," *Psychoanalytic Quarterly* 38(1969), 266–71.

25. Randall Jarrell, "Robert Graves and the White Goddess," *The Third Book of Criticism* (New York: Farrar, Straus and Giroux, 1979), p. 99. Robert Graves, *The White Goddess* (New York: Vintage Books, 1959).

26. Carl Kerenyi and C. G. Jung, *Essays on a Science of Mythology*, trans. R. F. C. Hull (Princeton: Princeton University Press, 1969), p. 116.

27. Carl Kerenyi, *Dionysos*, trans. Ralph Mannheim (Princeton: Princeton University Press, 1978), pp. 26–27.

28. Carl Kerenyi and C. G. Jung, *Essays on a Science of Mythology*, p. 118–19; and *Eleusis*, trans. Ralph Mannheim (New York: Pantheon Books, 1960), p. 55.

29. See Raymond J. Clark, *Catabasis* (Amsterdam: Gruner, 1979), pp. 15 ff, 93–94.

30. Martin Nilsson, *Greek Folk Religion* (New York: Harper and Row, 1961), pp. 52–55 and cf. 59, n. 31; N. J. Richardson, *The Homeric Hymn to Demeter* (New York: Oxford University Press, 1974), pp. 13, 284 at line 399.

31. Vernant, *Myth and Society*, pp. 133, 138–39.

32. Farnell, vol. III, pp. 147–50; Nilsson, p. 48.

33. T. B. L. Webster, *From Mycenae to Homer*, 2nd ed. (New York: W. W. Norton, 1964), pp. 43, n. 2; 44.

34. Nilsson, p. 61, fig. 24; cf. Kerenyi, *Eleusis*, p. 35.

35. Jung, *Aion* (CW 9.2), pp. 12–13.

36. *Nietzsche Reader*, ed. and trans. by R. J. Hollingdale (Harmondsworth: Penguin Books, 1977), p. 275 — *Zarathustra* I, "Of Old and Young Women;" *Gay Science*, trans. Walter Kaufmann (New York: Vintage Books, 1974), p. 129; *Thus Spoke Zarathustra*, trans. R. J. Hollingdale (Harmondsworth: Penguin Books, 1969), pp. 83–84.

37. Freud, "Some Psychological Consequences of the Anatomical Distinction Between the Sexes," in *Sexuality and the Psychology of Love*, p. 193; *Outline of Psychoanalysis*, p. 45; *New Introductory Lectures on Psychoanalysis*, p. 119.

38. Simone de Beauvoir, *The Second Sex*, trans. H. M. Parshley (New York: Vintage Books, 1974), p. xviii.

39. Sigmund Freud, *Moses and Monotheism*, trans. Katherine Jones (New York: Vintage Books, n.d.), pp. 105–106.

40. Freud, *Three Essays on the Theory of Sexuality*, trans. James Strachey (New York: Basic Books, 1962), pp. 92–96; cf. *Totem and Taboo*, p. 17; quotation, *New Introductory Lectures on Psychoanalysis*, p. 118.

41. Freud, *New Introductory Lectures on Psychoanalysis*, p. 117; "Female Sexuality," in *Sexuality and the Psychology of Love*, p. 206; quotation, *Totem and Taboo*, p. 152.

42. Jacques Derrida, discussion of Jean-Pierre Vernant, "Greek Tragedy: Problems of Interpretation," *The Languages of Criticism and the Sciences of Man*, ed. by Richard Macksey and Eugenio Donato (Baltimore: Johns Hopkins University Press, 1970), p. 194.

43. Richard Caldwell, "Psychoanalysis, Structuralism and Greek Mythology," *Phenomenology, Structuralism, Semiology*, ed. Harry Garvin (*Bucknell Review*, April 1976), pp. 220–22.

44. Philip Slater, *The Glory of Hera* (Boston: Beacon Press, 1968), pp. 190, 187, 135.

45. Weigert-Vowinkel, p. 359 for refs to: Ernest Jones, "Das Mutterrecht und die sexuelle Unwissenheit der Wilden," *Imago* 13(1927), pp. 199–222; T. Reik, "Die Pubertätsriten der Wilden," *Probleme der Religiopsychologie* (Leipzig, 1919), pp. 58ff.

46. J. Friedman and S. Gassel, "Orestes: A Psychoanalytic Approach to Dramatic Criticism," *Psychoanalytic Quarterly* 20(1951), 426–33.

47. Sartre, *No Exit and Other Plays* (New York: Vintage Books, 1955), p. 74.

48. Herbert Fingarette, "Orestes: Paradigm Hero and Central Motif of Contemporary Ego Psychology," *Psychoanalytic Review* 50(1963), 440, 442–44.

49. Jung, *Memories, Dreams, Reflections*, pp. 201–2.

50. Jung, *Four Archetypes* (excerpted from CW 9.1), p. 19.

51. *Viking Portable Nietzsche*, trans. Walter Kaufmann (Harmondsworth: Penguin Books, 1968), p. 58, from *Human, All too Human*.

52. Jung, *Four Archetypes*, p. 24.

53. Jung, *Psychology and Alchemy* (CW 12), p. 25.

54. Erich Neumann, *The Great Mother*, trans. Ralph Mannheim, 2nd ed. (Princeton: Princeton University Press, 1963), p. 13.

55. Ibid., pp. 138, 39, quotation 149.

56. Ibid., p. 148.

57. Jung, *Four Archetypes*, p. 30.

58. Neumann, *Great Mother*, p. 168.

59. Jung, *Symbols of Transformation* (CW 5), p. 186.

60. Neumann, *Great Mother*, p. 35.

61. *The Second Sex*, p. xix.

62. *The Gay Science*, p. 298, section 354.

63. *The Second Sex*, p. 89.

64. Ibid., pp. xx, xxi.

65. Ibid., p. 54, quotation pp. 157–60.

66. Ibid., p. 159.

67. Neumann, *Great Mother*, p. 272.

68. *Second Sex*, p. 289.

69. Ibid., p. 290.

Chapter 8—The Hero and the Quest

1. Thomas Mann, "Freud and the Future," *Essays of Three Decades*, trans. H. T. Lowe-Porter (New York: Alfred Knopf, 1971), p. 424.

2. Erwin Rohde, *Psyche* I, trans. from the eighth edition by W. B. Hillis (New York: Harper and Row, 1966), p. 116.

3. Martin Nilsson, *Greek Folk Religion* (New York: Harper and Row, 1961), pp. 18–19.

4. Martin Nilsson, *A History of Greek Religion*, second ed., trans. F. J. Fielden (New York: W. W. Norton and Co., 1964), p. 194.

5. Ibid., pp. 233–37.

6. Martin Nilsson, *The Mycenaean Origin of Greek Mythology* (Berkeley: University of California Press, 1972).

7. Eric Havelock, "Prologue to Greek Literacy," *Lectures in Memory of Louise Taft Semple*, (Norman, Okla.: University of Oklahoma Press, 1973), p. 269.

8. Isabel Colegate, *The Shooting Party* (New York: Avon Books, 1981), p. 108.

9. Moses Finley, *The World of Odysseus*, second revised edition (Harmondsworth: Penguin Books, 1979), p. 59.

10. James Redfield, "Foreword" to Gregory Nagy, *The Best of the Achaeans. Concepts of the Hero in Archaic Greek Poetry*, (Baltimore: Johns Hopkins, 1979), pp. x–xi.

11. Finley, p. 28.

12. Redfield, p. ix.

13. W. H. Auden, *Forwards and Afterwords* (New York: Vintage Books, 1974), pp. 18–19.

14. James Redfield, *Nature and Culture in the Iliad* (Chicago: University of Chicago Press, 1970), pp. 115, 99–100, 119.

15. *The Viking Portable Nietzsche*, trans. Walter Kaufmann (Harmondsworth: Penguin Books, 1968), pp. 36, 39.

16. *On the Genealogy of Morals*, trans. Walter Kaufmann (New York: Vintage Books, 1969), p. 45.

17. *The Gay Science*, trans. Walter Kaufmann (New York: Vintage Books, 1974) p. 190.

18. Redfield *Nature and Culture*, p. 128.

19. Auden, p. 18.

20. R. and E. Blum, *Health and Healing in Rural Greece* (Stanford: Stanford University Press, 1975), pp. 227, 24, 42; and D. Tomasic, "Personality Development of the Dinaric Warriors," *Psychiatry* 8(1945), 449–93.

21. Gerald Else, *The Origin and Early Form of Greek Tragedy* (Cambridge, Mass.: Harvard University Press, 1965).

22. Nilsson, p. 252 and p. 136.

23. Auden, p. 19.

24. *The Gay Science*, p. 93, section 1.21.

25. Jean-Pierre Vernant, *Myth and Society in Ancient Greece*, trans. Janet Lloyd (Atlantic Highlands, NJ: Humanities Press, 1980), pp. 194, 196.

26. *Totem and Taboo*, pp. 155–56.

27. *Group Psychology and the Analysis of the Ego*, p. 68.

28. J. Friedman and S. Gassel, "Odysseus: the Return of the Primal Father," *Psychoanalytic Quarterly* 21(1952), 223.

29. *The Birth of Tragedy*, trans. Walter Kaufmann (New York: Vintage Books, 1967), pp. 72, 71.

30. Ibid., p. 65.

31. *The Viking Portable Nietzsche*, p. 58.

32. *Four Archetypes* (from CW 9.1), pp. 80–81.

33. *Two Essays in Analytical Psychology* (CW 7), pp. 156–57, n. 1.

34. Sigmund Freud, "The Acquisition of Power Over Fire," *SE* 22, pp. 189–92.

35. *Thus Spoke Zarathustra*, trans. R. J. Hollingdale (Harmondsworth: Penguin Books, 1969), p. 43, Prologue, section 4.

36. *The Gay Science*, pp. 84; 171–72.

37. Ibid.

38. Roland Barthes, *Critical Essays*, trans. Richard Howard (Evanston, Illinois: Northwestern University Press, 1972), p. 63.

39. Roland Barthes, *Mythologies* (New York: Farrar, Straus and Giroux, 1975), pp. 121, 75.

40. Otto Rank, *The Myth of the Birth of the Hero*, trans. F. Robbins and S. Jelliffe (New York: Vintage Books, 1964), pp. 65, 68–69, quotation p. 84.

41. Ibid., pp. 71–72, 89.

42. Otto Rank, *The Trauma of Birth* (New York: R. Brunner, 1952), p. 106.

43. Joseph Henderson, "Ancient Myths and Modern Man," in *Man and His Symbols* (New York: Dell, 1964), pp. 101, 120.

44. *Symbols of Transformation* (CW 5), pp. 333, 321.

45. *New Introductory Lectures on Psychoanalysis*, p. 23.

46. Jung, "Psychology of the Child Archetype," *Essays on a Science of Mythology* (Princeton: Princeton University Press, 1969), p. 86 (from CW 9.1, par. 284).

47. Henderson, p. 112 and p. 111.

48. *Two Essays* (CW 7), p. 287.

49. *Symbols of Transformation* (CW 5), p. 348.

50. Henderson, pp. 112–13.

51. *Symbols of Transformation* (CW 5), p. 392.

52. *Two Essays* (CW 7), pp. 70–71.

53. Ibid., pp. 228–29, 233.

54. *The Viking Portable Jung*, ed. Joseph Campbell (Harmondsworth: Penguin Books, 1976), p. 234.

55. *Two Essays* (CW 7), p. 281.

56. Henderson, p. 117.

57. Philip Slater, *The Glory of Hera* (Boston: Beacon Press, 1968), pp. 182–83; "The Greek Family in History and Myth," *Arethusa* 7(1974), 32.

58. *The Case of Wagner* (published with *The Birth of Tragedy*, p. 161.

59. Joseph Campbell, *The Hero with a Thousand Faces*, second edition (Princeton: Princeton University Press, 1968), pp. 40, 348.

60. Jean-Paul Sartre, *The Words*, trans. Bernard Frechtman (New York: Vintage Books, 1981), p. 197.

61. Campbell, pp. 167, 17, 164, 78–81.

62. Ibid., p. 186, n. 159.

63. Campbell, p. 116.

64. Hugo Rahner, *Greek Myths and Christian Mystery*, trans. Brian Battershaw (London: Burns and Oates, 1963), pp. 356–57.

65. Campbell, pp. 120–21.

66. Ibid., p. 246.

67. Geoffrey Kirk, *The Nature of the Greek Myths* (Harmondsworth: Penguin Books, 1974), p. 190 with reference there to J. H. Croon, *The Herdsman of the Dead* (Utrecht, 1952).

68. Redfield, *Nature and Culture in the Iliad*, p. 103; the other, Charles Segal, "Pentheus and Hippolytus on the Couch and on the Grid," *Classical World* 72(1978), 132.

69. Kirk, pp. 206–9.

70. Ibid., p. 198; Bernice Engle, "The Amazons in Ancient Greece," *Psychoanalytic Quarterly* 11(1942), 536; Plutarch, *On the Pythian Oracle, Greek Questions* 58.

71. Barthes, p. 70.

72. Nagy, p. 39.

73. Douglas Frame, *The Myth of Return in Early Greek Epic* (New Haven: Yale University Press, 1979), pp. 4, 33.

Chapter 9—Eros and Psyche

1. Susan Sontag, ed., *A Barthes Reader* (New York: Hill and Wang, 1982), pp. xxxiii–xxxiv, describes a not dissimilar egocentrism in Barthes.

2. See Eric Havelock, *Preface to Plato* (Cambridge, Mass.: Harvard University Press, 1963), chapters 2–8; A. W. H. Adkins, *Merit and Responsibility* (Oxford: Oxford University Press, 1960), p. 238.

3. Bennett Simon, *Mind and Madness in Ancient Greece* (Ithaca: Cornell University Press, 1978), p. 189, drawing on Eric Havelock, "Prologue to Greek Literacy," in *Lectures in Memory of Louise Taft Semple* (Norman, OK: University of Oklahoma Press, 1973).

4. Marshall McLuhan, *The Gutenberg Galaxy* (New York: New American Library, 1969).

5. See W. H. Auden, "The I Without a Self," in *The Dyer's Hand* (New York: Vintage Books, 1968), p. 168.

6. *Daybreak*, trans. R. J. Hollingdale (Cambridge: Cambridge University Press, 1982), p. 10.

7. Bruno Bettleheim, "Freud and the Soul," *New Yorker*, March 1, 1982, p. 63.

8. Freud, *Introductory Lectures on Psychoanalysis*, pp. 375–76.

9. Frederick Crews, *Psychoanalysis and Literary Process* (Cambridge, Mass.: Winthrop, 1970), p. 13.

10. *Five Lectures on Psycho-Analysis*, p. 50.

11. Philip Rieff, *Delusion and Dream* (Boston: Beacon Press, 1956), p. 12.

12. Paul Ricoeur, *Freud and Philosophy*, trans. Denis Savage (New Haven: Yale University Press, 1970), p. 175.

13. Otto Rank, *The Myth of the Birth of the Hero and Other Writings*, trans. F. Robbins, Smith Jelliffe, *et al.* (New York: Vintage Books, 1959), pp. 139ff., 148, 263ff.

14. *Art and Artist*, in *The Myth of the Birth of the Hero and Other Writings*, pp. 116–18, 155, 122–24.

15. Ibid., pp. 132, 139, 142, 148, 144, 271, 190, 192, 203–4, 216, 221–27.

16. Ibid., pp. 152, 163–67.

17. Otto Rank, "The Double as Immortal Self," in *Beyond Psychology* (New York: Dover Books, 1958), pp. 91–92, 99–100.

18. *The Gay Science*, trans. Walter Kaufmann (New York: Vintage Books, 1974), p. 133.

19. Norman Mailer, *Cannibals and Christians*, abridged ed. (London: Granada, 1979), p. 124.

20. *The Gay Science*, p. 101.

21. W. H. Auden, *Forwards and Afterwords* (New York: Vintage Books, 1974), p. 408.

22. *The Case of Wagner*, trans. Walter Kaufmann (New York: Vintage Books, 1967), p. 155.

23. Simon, p. 278.

24. Paul Friedländer, *Plato 1: An Introduction*, 2nd. ed. (Princeton: Princeton University Press, 1969), pp. 207–8; and Robert Eisner, "Socrates as Hero," *Philosophy and Literature* 6(1982), 106–18, where much of this material on Socrates is presented in expanded form.

25. Freidländer, p. 175.

26. Simon, p. 273.

27. Geoffrey Kirk, *Homer and the Epic* (Cambridge: Cambridge University Press, 1965), p. 95.

28. Stanley Rosen, *Plato's Symposium* (New Haven: Yale University Press, 1968), pp. 293–94.

29. E. R. Dodds, *Pagan and Christian in an Age of Anxiety* (Cambridge: Cambridge University Press, 1965), p. 384, n. 1.

30. Carl Kerenyi (and C. G. Jung), *Essays on a Science of Mythology*, trans. R. C. F. Hull (Princeton: Princeton University Press, 1969), p. 23.

31. Hugh Kenner, *Joyce's Voices* (Berkeley: University of California Press, 1978), p. 94.

32. W. W. Tarn, *Hellenistic Civilization*, 3rd ed., rev. G. T. Griffith (London: Edward Arnold, Ltd., 1952), chapters 7 and 8 on trade and travel writing.

33. Carl Schlam, *Cupid and Psyche: Apuleius and the Monuments* (University Park, Pennsylvania: The American Philological Association, 1976), p. 3; James Tatum, *Apuleius and the Golden Ass* (Ithaca: Cornell University Press, 1979), p. 89.

34. Schlam, p. 35.

35. Rheinhold Merkelbach, *Roman und Mysterium in der Antike* (Munich and Berlin: Beck, 1927, reissued 1962); see P. G. Walsh, *The Roman Novel* (Cambridge: Cambridge University Press, 1970), pp. 221–22.

36. Tatum, p. 59.

37. Schlam, p. 38; Lucretius, *De rerum natura* 2.172, 3.28.

38. Tatum, p. 61.

39. Ibid., pp. 119–22.

40. A. H. Armstrong, *An Introduction to Ancient Philosophy* (Boston: Beacon Press, 1947), pp. 197–99.

41. Schlam, pp. 4, 31.

42. P. G. Walsh, p. 220 and n. 2.

43. Meleager, *Greek Anthology* 5.57; 12.80, 132; Schlam, pp. 4, 8, 20–24, 5, 10, 32.

44. Edgar Wind, *Pagan Mysteries in the Renaissance*, rev. ed. (London: Faber and Faber, 1968), pp. 158, 160, and n. 29.

45. Included in *Character and Culture*, pp. 67–79, esp. 75–77.

46. Walsh, p. 218.

47. Jean Seznec, *The Survival of the Pagan Gods*, trans. Barbara Sessions (New York: Pantheon Books, 1952), p. 99.

48. J. J. Bachofen, *Myth, Religion and Mother Right*, trans. Ralph Mannheim (Princeton: Princeton University Press, 1967), pp. 44–48.

49. Erich Neumann, *Amor and Psyche*, trans. Ralph Mannheim (Princeton: Princeton University Press, 1971), *passim*, quotation p. 148.

50. Walsh, p. 220.

51. Neumann, pp. 77–78.

52. Robert A. Johnson, *She* (New York: Harper and Row, 1977), pp. 52–53, quotation p. 38.

53. Neumann, pp. 80–81, 85–86.

54. Ibid., pp. 108–9, 150–51.

55. Marie-Louise van Franz, A *Psychological Interpretation of "The Golden Ass" of Apuleius,* 2nd ed. (Irving, Texas: Spring Publications, 1980), p. 62.

56. Ibid., pp. 61–62, 64–65.

57. Ibid., pp. 112, 63.

58. Ibid., pp. 76, 85, 139, 145; quotation, p. 98.

59. James Hillman, *The Myth of Analysis* (New York: Harper and Row, 1978), pp. 57–58, 84.

60. Ibid., p. 106.

61. Ibid., p. 103.

62. Ibid., pp. 94–95.

63. Bettleheim, p. 57.

64. Hillman, pp. 97–98.

65. Freud, *The Ego and the Id,* p. 19.

66. Hillman, p. 102.

67. Hillman, pp. 297–98.

68. Philip Rieff, "The Analytic Attitude," *Encounter* 17.6(June 1962), 23.

Chapter 10—Myth, Therapy, and Culture

1. G. Karl Galinsky, *The Heracles Theme* (Oxford: Basil Blackwell, 1972), pp. 52–53.

2. *Symbols of Transformation* (CW 5), pp. 294–95.

3. Ulrich von Wilamowitz-Moellendorf, "Hephaistos," *Nachrichten von der Königlichen Gesellschaft der Wissenschaften zu Göttingen,* Philologisch-historische Klasse, 1895, pp. 217–45 (*Kleine Schriften* 5, 2, 5ff.); Jane Henle, *Greek Myths* (Bloomington: University of Indiana Press, 1973), pp. 43–45.

4. Edmund Wilson, *The Wound and the Bow* (Oxford: Oxford University Press, 1947), p. 287.

5. Oscar Mandel, *Philoctetes and the Fall of Troy* (Lincoln: University of Nebraska Press, 1981), p. 35.

6. From *Human, All too Human,* quoted in *A Nietzsche Reader,* ed. and trans. R. J. Hollingdale (Harmondsworth: Penguin Books, 1977), p. 82.

7. *The Gay Science,* trans. Walter Kaufmann (New York: Vintage Books, 1974), pp. 176, 219; Pindar, *Pythian* 2.73.

8. R. D. Laing, *The Divided Self* (New York: Random House, 1969), p. 37.

9. *The Letters of Evelyn Waugh* (New Haven: Ticknor and Fields, 1980), p. 215, 27 December 1945.

10. Herbert Marcuse, *Eros and Civilization* (Boston: Beacon Press, 1966), pp. 5, 83.

11. *Civilization and Its Discontents,* pp. 23–24.

12. See "Analysis of a Phobia in a Five-Year-Old Boy," in *The Sexual Enlightenment of Children,* p. 181; *Five Lectures on Psycho-Analysis,* p. 53.

13. In *Human, All too Human,* quoted in *A Nietzsche Reader,* p. 75.

14. E. J. and L. Edelstein, *Asclepius* (Baltimore: The Johns Hopkins University Press, 1945), quotation vol. 1, pp. 327–28, and see vol. 2, p. 99; see also Ludwig Edelstein, *Ancient Medicine,* ed. and trans. O. and C. L. Temkin (Baltimore: The Johns Hopkins University Press, 1967), pp. 244–45.

15. Guido Majno, *The Healing Hand* (Cambridge, Massachusetts: Harvard University Press, 1975), p. 203; Kenneth Porter, *Herpetology* (Philadelphia: W. B. Saunders, 1972), p. 388; Karl Schmidt and Robert Inger, *Living Reptiles of the World* (New York: Doubleday, 1957), p. 211, pl. 96.

16. Edelstein, *Asclepius*, vol. 2, p. 222; Arnobius, *Adversus Nationes* 7.32.

17. C. A. Meier, *Ancient Incubation and Modern Psychotherapy*, trans. Monica Curtis (Evanston, Illinois: Northwestern University Press, 1967), p. 54.

18. R. and E. Blum, *The Dangerous Hour* (New York: Scribners, 1970), pp. 62–63.

19. Carl Kerenyi, *Asklepios*, trans. Ralph Mannheim (New York: Pantheon Books, 1959), p. 88.

20. Edelstein, *Ancient Medicine*, p. 241.

21. Edelstein, *Asclepius*, vol. 2, pp. 149–51; Meier, p. 60; George Bean, *Aegean Turkey* (New York: Praeger, 1966), p. 90, claims a sacrifice and loose white clothing were required of the incubant.

22. *Five Lectures on Psycho-Analysis*, p. 36.

23. Ibid., p. 46; Jacob Arlow, "Ego Psychology and the Study of Mythology," *Journal of the American Psychoanalytic Association* 9(1961), 378–79.

24. *Introductory Lectures on Psychoanalysis*, p. 457.

25. Ibid., p. 273, quotations pp. 279 and 435.

26. *The Future of an Illusion*, p. 22.

27. Reminiscence of Abram Kardiner, quoted by Ronald Clark, *Freud, the Man and the Cause* (New York: Random House, 1980), p. 281.

28. M. Askew, "Classical Tragedy and Psychotherapeutic Catharsis," *Psychoanalysis and the Psychoanalytic Review* 47(1960), 120.

29. Pedro Laín Entralgo, *The Therapy of the Word in Classical Antiquity*, trans. L. J. Rather and J. M. Sharp (New Haven: Yale University Press, 1970), p. 126.

30. Walter Ong in the "Foreword" to Laín Entralgo's *Therapy of the Word*, p. xiv; Eric Havelock, *Preface to Plato* (Cambridge, Massachusetts: Harvard University Press, 1963), especially chapters 2–8.

31. Jean-Pierre Vernant, *The Origins of Greek Thought* (Ithaca: Cornell University Press, 1982), p. 132.

32. See Walter Ong's "Foreword" in Laín Entralgo, p. x.

33. K. K. Ruthven, *Myth* (London: Methuen, 1976), pp. 24–25, quotation p. 55.

34. Carl Jung, *Memories, Dreams, Reflections*, trans. R. and C. Winston (New York: Vintage Books, 1965), p. 311.

35. Edward Whitmont, *The Symbolic Quest* (New York: Putnam, 1969), p. 110.

36. *The Psychopathology of Everyday Life*, pp. 47–48.

37. Roland Barthes, *Mythologies*, trans. Annette Lavers (New York: Farrar, Straus and Giroux, 1975), p. 110.

38. Roland Barthes, "Putting on the Greeks," *Critical Essays*, trans. Richard Howard (Evanston, Illinois: Northwestern University Press, 1972), p. 66.

39. Rollo May, "Values, Myths, and Symbols," *American Journal of Psychiatry* 132(1975), 705.

40. Bruno Bettelheim, "Freud and the Soul," *New Yorker*, March 1, 1982, p. 72; Sigmund Freud, "Some Additional Notes on Dream Interpretation as a Whole," *SE* XIX (1925), pp. 125–38, esp. 128–29.

41. Bettelheim, p. 52.

42. Ibid., p. 84; Freud, *New Introductory Lectures on Psychoanalysis*, pp. 67–71 and *passim*.

43. Philip Rieff, "The Analytic Attitude," *Encounter* 17.6, June 1962, 28.
44. Edward Glover, *Freud or Jung?* (New York: W. W. Norton, 1950), p. 138.
45. *Introductory Lectures on Psychoanalysis*, p. 51.
46. *Five Lectures on Psycho-Analysis*, p. 48.

Bibliography

T HIS BIBLIOGRAPHY attempts to be complete for all works cited in the Notes and in addition to refer the reader to a number of works not cited but which deserve notice. For the major psychoanalytical writings I refer if possible to convenient editions: in the case of Jung, the various volumes of the *Collected Works (CW)*, translated by R. G. F. Hull and published by Princeton University Press in the Bollingen Series, may be found in many trade bookstores; the comparable *Standard Edition* of *The Complete Psychological Works of Sigmund Freud (SE)*, edited by James Strachey and published in London in seventeen volumes by Hogarth Press (1955–68), is not so popularly distributed, and so I cite, where possible, the individual volumes published in the Strachey translation by W. W. Norton and the various volumes of *The Collected Papers* series published by Collier under the editorship of Philip Rieff. Square brackets enclose date of original publication in German or, in the case of ancient authors, accepted date of composition. If any work is cited by a short title or abbreviation in the notes, I have indicated this in the Bibliography. References to Greek and Latin sources are to the Oxford Classical Texts for poetry and to the Loeb Classical Library for prose and for the Greek Anthology, unless otherwise noted.

Abraham, Karl. *Clinical Papers and Essays on Psychoanalysis.* Translated by Hilda Abraham and D. R. Ellison. New York: Basic Books, 1955.
———. "The Spider as Dream Symbol." In *Selected Papers of Karl Abraham.* Translated by Douglas Bryan and Alix Strachey. New York: Basic Books, 1953.
Aeschylus. [fl. early 5th century B.C.] See *Complete Greek Tragedies.*
Alderman, Harold. "Oedipus the King: A Hermeneutic Tragedy." *Philosophy and Literature* 5 (Fall 1981) 176–85.
Andreas-Salomé, Lou. *The Freud Journal.* 1912–13. Translated by Stanley Leavy. New York: Basic Books, 1964.
———. "Narzismus als Doppelrichtung." *Imago* 7 (1921), 361–86. English translation by Stanley Leavy in *Psychoanalytic Quarterly* 31 (1962) 1–30.
Anzieu, Didier. "Oedipe avante le complexe, ou De l'interprétation psychanalytique des mythes." *Les Temps Modernes* 22, no. 245 (1966) 675–715.
Arlow, Jacob A. "Ego Psychology and the Study of Mythology." *Journal of the American Psychoanalytic Association* 9 (1961) 371–393.

Armstrong, A. H. *An Introduction to Ancient Philosophy*. Boston: Beacon Press, 1963.

Arrowsmith, William. "Nietzsche on Classics and Classicists (Part III)." *Arion* 2 (1963) 5–31.

Artemidorus. *The Interpretation of Dreams*. [A.D. 2nd century] Translated by Robert J. White. Park Ridge, N.J.: Noyes Press, 1975.

Arthur, Marylin. "Origins of the Western Attitude Toward Women." *Arethusa* 6.1 (1973) 7–58.

Askew, M. "Classical tragedy and psychotherapeutic catharsis." *Psychoanalysis and the Psychoanalytic Review* 47.3 (1960) 116–22.

Atkins, N. "The Oedipus Myth, Adolescence and the Succession of Generations." *Journal of the American Psychoanalytic Association* 18 (1970) 860–75.

Auden, W. H. *The Dyer's Hand*. New York: Vintage Books, 1968.

———. *Forewords and Afterwords*. 1973. Reprint. New York: Vintage Books, 1974.

Bachofen, J. J. *Myth, Religion, and Mother Right*. Translated by Ralph Mannheim. Princeton University Press, 1967.

Balter, Leon. "The mother as source of power: three Greek myths." *Psychoanalytic Quarterly* 38 (1969) 217–74.

Bamberger, Joan. "The Myth of Matriarchy," in *Women, Culture, and Society*. Edited by Michelle Rosaldo and Louise Lamphere. Stanford: Stanford University Press, 1974.

Barchilon, J. "Beauty and the Beast. From myth to fairy tale." Psychoanalysis and the Psychoanalytic Review 46.4 (1959) 19–29.

Barnes, Hazel E. *The Meddling Gods*. Lincoln: University of Nebraska Press, 1974.

Barthes, Roland. *A Barthes Reader*. Edited and with an introduction by Susan Sontag. New York: Hill and Wang, 1982.

———. *Camera Lucida*. Translated by Richard Howard. New York: Hill and Wang, 1981.

———. *Critical Essays*. Translated by Richard Howard. Evanston, Illinois: Northwestern University Press, 1972.

———. *Mythologies*. Selected and translated by Annette Lavers. New York: Hill and Wang, 1972.

Baynes, H. G. *Mythology of the Soul*. 1940. Reprint. London: Rider & Co., 1969.

Bean, George. *Aegean Turkey*. New York: Praeger, 1966.

Beauvoir, Simone de. *The Second Sex*. Translated by H. M. Parshley. New York: Vintage Books, 1974.

Beazley, J. D. *Attic Red-Figure Vase-Painters*. 2nd ed. Oxford: Clarendon Press, 1963.

Besdine, Matthew. "The Jocasta Complex, Mothering and Genius: Parts I and II." *Psychoanalytic Review* 55 (1968) 259–77, 574–600.

———. "The Jocasta Complex, Mothering and Woman Geniuses." *Psychoanalytic Review* 58 (1971), 51–74.

Bettleheim, Bruno. "Freud and the Soul." *New Yorker*, March 1, 1982, pp. 52–93.

Blum, R. and E. Blum. *The Dangerous Hour: The Love and Culture of Crisis and Mystery in Rural Greece*. New York: Scribners, 1970.

———. *Health and Healing in Rural Greece*. Stanford: Stanford University Press, 1975.

Bréal, Michel. *Mélange de mythologie et de linguistique*. Paris: Hachette, 1877.

Brown, Norman O. *Hermes the Thief*. Madison: University of Wisconsin Press, 1947.

―――. *Life Against Death*. Middletown, Conn.: Wesleyan University Press, 1959.

Bunker, Henry Alden. "The Feast of Tantalus." *Psychoanalytic Quarterly* 21 (1952) 355–72.

―――. "Mother-murder in myth and legend." *Psychoanalytic Quarterly* 13 (1944) 198–207.

―――. "Tantalus: A Pre-oedipal Figure of Myth." *Psychoanalytic Quarterly* 22 (1953) 159–73.

Burkert, Walter. "Greek Tragedy and Sacrificial Ritual." *GRBS* 7 (1966) 87–122.

―――. *Structure and History in Greek Mythology and Ritual*. Berkeley: University of California Press, 1979.

Butler, Samuel. *The Authoress of the Odyssey*. Chicago: University of Chicago Press, 1967.

Butterworth, E. A. S. *Some Traces of the Pre-Olympian World in Greek Literature and Myth*. Berlin: De Gruyter, 1966.

Caldwell, Richard. "The Blindness of Oedipus." *International Review of Psychoanalysis* 1 (1974), 207–18.

―――. "The Misogyny of Eteocles." *Arethusa* 6 (1973), 197–231.

―――. "The Pattern of Aeschylean Tragedy." *Transactions and Proceedings of the American Philological Association* 101 (1970) 77–94.

―――. "Psychoanalysis, Structuralism and Greek Mythology." *Phenomenology, Structuralism, Semiology, Bucknell Review*. (April 1976) 209–30.

―――. "The Psychology of Aeschylus' *Supplices*." *Arethusa* 7 (1974) 45–70.

―――. "Selected Bibliography in Psychoanalysis and Classical Studies." *Arethusa* 7 (1974) 115–34.

Campbell, Joseph. *The Hero with a Thousand Faces*. 2nd ed. Princeton: Princeton University Press, 1968.

Carlinsky, Mario. "The Oedipus Legend and *Oedipus Rex*." *American Imago* 15 (1958) 91–95.

Cassirer, Ernest. *Language and Myth*. Translated by Suzanne Langer. New York: Dover, 1953.

―――. *The Philosophy of Symbolic Forms. 2: Mythical Thought*. Translated by Ralph Mannheim. New Haven: Yale University Press, 1955.

Casson, Lionel. *Travel in the Ancient World*. Toronto: Hakkert, 1974.

Clark, Raymond. *Catabasis*. Amsterdam: Gruner, 1979.

Clark, Ronald. *Freud, the Man and the Cause*. New York: Random House, 1980.

Cloudsley-Thompson, J. L. *Spiders, Scorpions, Centipedes and Mites*. Oxford: Pergamon Press, 1968.

Colegate, Isabel. *The Shooting Party*. New York: Avon, 1981.

The Complete Greek Tragedies. 4 vols., hardbound; 9 vols., paperbound. Edited by David Greene and Richmond Lattimore. Translated by Grene, Lattimore, *et alii*. Chicago: The University of Chicago Press, 1953–59.

Cook, Albert. *Myth and Language*. Bloomington: Indiana University Press, 1980.

Coriat, Isador H. "A Note on the Medusa Symbolism." *American Imago* 2 (1941) 281–85.

––––––– . "A Note on the Sexual Symbolism of the Cretan Snake Goddess." *Psychoanalytic Review* 4 (1917) 367–68.

Crews, Frederick, *Psychoanalysis and Literary Process.* Cambridge, Mass.: Winthrop, 1970.

Delcourt, Marie. *Oedipe, ou la légende du conquérant.* Paris: Bibliothèque de la Faculté de Philosophie et Lettres de l'Université de Liège, Fasc. CIV, 1944.

DeLeuze, Gilles and Guattori, Felix. *Anti-Oedipus: Capitalism and Schizophrenia.* Translated by Robert Hurley, Mark Seem, and Helen Lane. New York: Viking, 1977.

Derrida, Jacques. "Greek Tragedy: Problems of Interpretation." In *The Languages of Criticism and the Sciences of Man.* Edited by Richard Macksey and Eugenio Donato. Baltimore: Johns Hopkins University Press, 1970.

de Saussure, Raymond. "Le complexe de Jocaste," *Internationale Zeitschrift für Psychoanalyse* 6 (1920) 118–22.

Detienne, Marcel. *Dionysos Slain.* Translated by Mireille and Leonard Muellner. Baltimore: Johns Hopkins University Press, 1979.

––––––– . *The Gardens of Adonis.* Translated by Janet Lloyd. Atlantic Highlands, NJ: Humanities Press, 1977.

Deutsch, Helene. *A Psychoanalytic Study of the Myth of Dionysus and Apollo.* New York: International Universities Press, 1969.

Devereux, George and Weston La Barre. "Art and Mythology: A General Theory." In *Studying Personality Cross-culturally.* Edited by B. Kaplan. New York: Harper & Row, 1961.

Devereux, George. "A Counteroedipal Episode in Homer's *Iliad.*" *Bulletin of the Philadelphia Association for Psychoanalysis* 4 (1954) 90–97.

––––––– . *Dreams in Greek Tragedy: An Ethno-Psycho-Analytical Study.* Oxford: Blackwell, 1976.

––––––– . "Penelope's Character." *Psychoanalytic Quarterly* 26 (1957) 378–86.

––––––– . "The Psychotherapy Scene in Euripides' *Bacchae.*" *Journal of Hellenic Studies* 90 (1970) 35–48.

––––––– . "Retaliatory Homosexual Triumph over the Father." *International Journal of Psycho-Analysis* 41 (1960) 157–61.

––––––– . "The Self-Blinding of Oidipous in Sophokles: *Oidipous Tyrannos.*" *Journal of Hellenic Studies* 93 (1973) 36–49.

––––––– . "The Sociopolitical Functions of the Oedipus Myth." *Psychoanalytic Quarterly* 32 (1963) 205–14.

––––––– . "Why Oedipus killed Laius." *International Journal of Psycho-Analysis.* 34 (1953) 132–41.

Dodds, E. R. *The Ancient Concept of Progress.* New York: Oxford University Press, 1973.

––––––– . *The Greeks and the Irrational.* 1951. Berkeley: University of California Press, 1968.

———— . "Maenadism in the *Bacchae*." *Harvard Theological Review* 33 (1940) 155–76.

———— . *Pagan and Christian in an Age of Anxiety*. Cambridge: Cambridge University Press, 1965.

Dover, K. J. "Classical Greek Attitudes to Sexual Behavior." *Arethusa* 6 (1973) 59–73.

———— . *Greek Homosexuality*. Cambridge: Harvard University Press, 1978. Reprint. New York: Vintage Books, 1980.

———— . *Greek Popular Morality in the Time of Plato and Aristotle*. Berkeley: University of California Press, 1974.

Draenon, Stanley. *Freud's Odyssey: Psychoanalysis and the End of Metaphysics*. New Haven: Yale University Press, 1982.

du Bois, Page. *Centaurs and Amazons*. Ann Arbor: University of Michigan Press, 1982.

Dunbabin, T. J. *The Greeks and their Eastern Neighbors*. London: Society for the Promotion of Hellenic Studies, 1957.

Edelstein, Ludwig. *Ancient Medicine: Selected Papers of Ludwig Edelstein*. Edited and translated by O. Temkin and C. L. Temkin. Baltimore: Johns Hopkins University Press, 1967.

Edelstein, E. J. and L. *Asclepius*. 2 vols. Baltimore: Johns Hopkins University Press, 1945.

Eisner, Robert. "Euripides' Use of the Mythic Code." *Arethusa* 12 (Fall 1979) 153–74.

———— . "Socrates as Hero." *Philosophy and Literature* 6 (1982) 106–18.

———— . "Some anomalies in the Myth of Ariadne." *Classical World* 71 (1977) 175–77.

———— . "The Temple at Ayia Irini: Archaeology and Mythology." *Greek, Roman and Byzantine Studies* 13 (1972) 22–33.

Else, Gerald. *The Origin and Early Form of Greek Tragedy*. Cambridge, Mass.: Harvard University Press, 1965.

Engle, Bernice. "The Amazons in Ancient Greece." *Psychoanalytic Quarterly* 11 (1942) 512–54.

———— . "Lemnos, Island of Women." *Psychoanalytic Review* 32 (1945) 353–58.

Euripides. [5th century B.C.] See *Complete Greek Tragedies*.

———— . *Bacchae*, 2nd ed. Edited by E. R. Dodds. Oxford: Oxford University Press, 1960.

Farnell, Leonard Richard. *Cults of the Greek States*. Oxford: Oxford University Press, 1896. 5 vols. Reprint. Chicago: Aegean Press, 1971.

———— . *Greek Hero Cults and Ideas of Immortality*. 1921. Reprint. New York: Oxford University Press, 1970.

Feder, Lilian. *Ancient Myths in Modern Poetry*. Princeton: Princeton University Press, 1971.

———— . *Madness in Literature*. Princeton: Princeton University Press, 1980.

Feder, Louis. "Adoption Trauma: Oedipus Myth/Clinical Reality." *International Journal of Psycho-Analysis* 55 (1974) 491–93.

Feldman, Thalia. "Gorgo and the Origins of Fear." *Arion* 4 (1965) 484–94.

Felman, Shoshana. *Literature and Psychoanalysis*. Baltimore: Johns Hopkins University Press, 1982.

———. "Beyond Oedipus: The Specimen Story of Psychoanalysis." *Modern Language Notes* 98 (1983) 1021–53.

Ferenczi, Sandor. "Symbolic Representation of the Pleasure and Reality Principles in the Oedipus Myth." In *Sex in Psychoanalysis*. 1916. Reprint. Translated by Ernest Jones. New York: Basic Books, 1950.

———. "The Symbolism of the Head of Medusa." In *Further Contributions to the Theory and Technique of Psychoanalysis*. New York: 1952. Originally appeared in *Zeitschrift für Psychoanalyse* 9 (1923) 69ff.

Fermor, Patrick Leigh. *Mani*. New York: Harper and Brothers, 1958.

Festugière, A. J. *Personal Religion Among the Greeks*. Berkeley, University of California Press, 1954.

Fingarette, Herbert. "Orestes: Paradigm Hero and Central Motif of Contemporary Ego Psychology." *Psychoanalytic Review* 50 (1963) 437–61.

Finley, Moses. *The World of Odysseus*. 2nd revised edition. Harmondsworth: Penguin Books, 1979.

Flugel, J. C. "Polyphallic Symbolism and the Castration Complex." *International Journal of Psycho-Analysis* 5 (1924) 155–96.

Foley, Helene. "The Masque of Dionysus." *Transactions and Proceedings of the American Philological Society* 110 (1980) 107–33.

Fontenrose, Joseph. *The Delphic Oracle*. Berkeley: University of California Press, 1978.

———. *Python*. Berkeley: University of California Press, 1959.

———. *The Ritual Theory of Myth*. Folklore Studies 18. Berkeley: University of California Press, 1966.

Frame, Douglas. *The Myth of Return in Early Greek Epic*. New Haven: Yale University Press, 1978.

Franz, Marie-Louise von. *Problems of the Feminine in Fairytales*. Zurich: Spring Publications, 1972.

———. *A Psychological Interpretation of "The Golden Ass" of Apuleius*. 2nd ed. Irving, Texas: Spring Publications, 1980.

———. *Puer Aeternus*. 2nd ed. Santa Monica: Sigo Press, 1981.

Frazer, James. *The New Golden Bough*. Edited by Theodor H. Gaster. New York: New American Library, 1964.

Freud, Sigmund. "The Acquisition and Control of Fire." [1932] *Standard Edition* 22, pp. 187–93.

———. *Beyond the Pleasure Principle*. [1920] Translated by James Strachey. New York, W. W. Norton, 1961.

———. *Character and Culture*. Edited by Philip Rieff. New York: Collier Books, 1963.

———. *Civilization and Its Discontents*. [1930] Translated by James Strachey. New York: W. W. Norton, 1961.

———. "Creative Writers and Daydreaming." [1907] *Standard Edition* 9, pp. 143–48.

——— and D. E. Oppenheim. *Dreams in Folklore*. [1911] Translated by A. M. O. Richards. New York: International Universities Press, 1958.

_____ . *Five Lectures on Psychoanalysis*. [1910] Translated by James Strachey. New York: W. W. Norton, 1977.

_____ and Carl Jung. *The Freud/Jung Letters*. Edited by William McGuire and translated by Ralph Mannheim. Princeton: Princeton University Press, 1974.

_____ . *The Ego and the Id*. [1923] New York: W. W. Norton, 1960.

_____ . *The Future of an Illusion*. [1927] New York: W. W. Norton, 1960.

_____ . *General Psychological Theory*. Edited by Philip Rieff. New York: Collier Books, 1963.

_____ . "Great is Diana of the Ephesians." [1911] *Standard Edition* 12, pp. 342–44.

_____ . *Group Psychology and the Analysis of the Ego*. [1921] New York: W. W. Norton, 1959.

_____ . *The Interpretation of Dreams*. [1st ed., 1900; 7th ed., 1922] Translated by James Strachey. New York: Avon Books, 1965.

_____ . *Introductory Lectures on Psychoanalysis*. [1917] Translated by James Strachey. New York: W. W. Norton, 1966.

_____ . *Leonardo da Vinci and a Memory of his Childhood*. [1910] Translated by Alan Tyson. New York: W. W. Norton, 1964.

_____ . *Moses and Monotheism*. [1937] Translated by Katherine Jones. New York: Vintage Books, 1967.

_____ . *New Introductory Lectures on Psychoanalysis*. [1933] Translated by James Strachey. New York: W. W. Norton, 1965.

_____ . "On the Universal Tendency to Debasement in the Sphere of Love." [1912] *Standard Edition* 11, pp. 179–90.

_____ . *The Origins of Psychoanalysis: Letters to Wilhelm Fliess*. Edited by Marie Bonaparte, Anna Freud, and Ernst Kris, and translated by Eric Mosbacher and James Strachey. New York: Basic Books, 1954.

_____ . *An Outline of Psycho-Analysis*. [1940] Translated and newly edited by James Strachey, 1969.

_____ . *The Psychopathology of Everyday Life*. [1901] Translated by Alan Tyson and edited by James Strachey. New York: W. W. Norton, 1965.

_____ . *The Sexual Enlightenment of Children*. Edited by Philip Rieff. New York: Collier Books, 1963.

_____ . *Sexuality and the Psychology of Love*. Edited by Philip Rieff. New York: Collier Books, 1963.

_____ . "Some Additional Notes on Dream-Interpretation as a Whole." [1925] "Some Additional Notes on Dream-Interpretation as a Whole." *Standard Edition* 19, pp. 125–38.

_____ . *Therapy and Technique*. Edited by Philip Rieff. New York: Collier Books, 1963.

_____ . *Three Case Histories*. Edited by Philip Rieff. New York: Collier Books, 1963.

_____ . *Three Essays on the Theory of Sexuality*. [1905] Translated and newly edited by James Strachey. New York: Basic Books, 1975.

_____ . *Totem and Taboo*. [1912–13] Translated by James Strachey. New York: W. W. Norton, n.d.

Friedländer, Paul. *Plato*. 2nd ed. 3 vols. Translated by Hans Meyerhoff. Princeton: Princeton University Press, 1969.

Friedman, Joel and Sylvia Gassel. "The Chorus in Sophocles' *Oedipus Tyrannus*." *Psychoanalytic Quarterly* 19 (1950) 213–26.

———. "Odysseus: The Return of the Primal Father." *Psychoanalytic Quarterly* 21 (1952) 215–23.

———. "Orestes: A Psychoanalytic Approach to Dramatic Criticism." *Psychoanalytic Quarterly* 20 (1951) 423–33.

Friedrich, Paul. *The Meaning of Aphrodite*. Chicago: University of Chicago Press, 1978.

Fromm, Erich. *The Forgotten Language: An Introduction to the Understanding, of Dreams, Fairy Tales and Myths*. New York: Grove Press, 1951.

———. "The Oedipus Complex and the Oedipus Myth." In *The Family*. Edited by Ruth N. Anschen. New York: Harper and Brothers, 1949.

———. *The Sane Society*. New York: Holt, Rhinehart and Winston, 1955.

Galdston, I. "Sophocles Contra Freud: A Reassessment of the Oedipus Complex." Bulletin of the New York Academy of Medicine 30 (1954) 803–17.

Galinsky, G. Karl. *The Herakles Theme*. Oxford: Basil Blackwell, 1973.

Gilman, Sandor. *Difference and Pathology: Stereotypes of Sexuality, Race, and Madness*. Ithaca, N.Y.: Cornell University Press, 1985.

Girard, René. *Violence and the Sacred*. Translated by Patrick Gregory. Baltimore: Johns Hopkins University Press, 1977.

Glenn, Justin. "Psychoanalytic Writings on Greek and Latin Authors, 1911–60." *Classical World* 66 (1972) 129–45.

———. "Psychoanalytic Writings on Classical Mythology and Religion: 1909–1960." *Classical World* 70 (1976–77) 225–47.

Glover, Edward. *Freud or Jung?* New York: W. W. Norton, 1950.

Golden, Lester. "Freud's Oedipus: Its Mytho-dramatic Basis." *American Imago* 24 (1967) 271–82.

Gold, Thomas. "The Innocence of Oedipus: The Philosophers on *Oedipus the King*." *American Imago* 4 (1965) 363–86, 582–611; and *Arion* 5 (1966) 478–525.

———. *Platonic Love*. London: Routledge and Kegan Paul, 1963.

Graves, Robert. *The Greek Myths*. 4th ed. London: Cassell's, 1965.

———. *Homer's Daughter*. Garden City: Doubleday, 1955.

———. *Steps*. London: Cassell's, 1958.

Green, André. *The Tragic Effect: The Oedipus Complex in Tragedy*. Translated by Alan Sheridan. Cambridge: Cambridge University Press, 1979.

Green, Peter. "Sex and Classical Literature." In *The Sexual Dimension in Literature*. Edited by Alan Bold. New York: Barnes and Noble, 1982.

———. *The Shadow of the Parthenon*. Berkeley: University of California Press, 1972.

Greenson, Ralph. *The Technique and Practice of Psychoanalysis*. New York: International Universities Press, 1967.

Guépin, J-P. *The Tragic Paradox: Myth and Ritual in Greek Tragedy*. Amsterdam: Hakkert, 1968.

Guthrie, W. C. K. *The Greeks and Their Gods*. 1949. Reprint. Boston: Beacon Press, 1969.

Hamilton, Victoria. *Narcissus and Oedipus: The Children of Psychoanalysis*. London: Routledge and Kegan Paul, 1982.

Harrison, Jane. *Themis*. 2nd ed. Cambridge: Cambridge University Press, 1927.

Havelock, Eric. *The Greek Concept of Justice*. Cambridge, Mass.: Harvard University Press, 1978.

――――. *The Literate Revolution in Greece and its Cultural Consequences*. Princeton: Princeton University Press, 1982.

――――. *Preface to Plato*. Cambridge, Mass.: Harvard University Press, 1963.

――――. "Prologue to Greek Literacy." In *Lectures in Honor of Louise Taft Semple*. Norman, Oklahoma: University of Oklahoma Press, 1973.

――――. "The Socratic Self as it Is Parodied in Aristophanes' *Clouds*." *Yale Classical Studies* 22 (1972) 1–18.

Hesiod. *Theogony*. [700 B.C.] Edited by M. L. West. Oxford: Clarendon Press, 1966.

Hillman, James, ed. *Facing the Gods*. Irving, Texas: Spring Publications, 1980.

――――, ed. *Puer Papers*. Irving, Texas: Spring Publications, 1979.

Hooke, S. H. *Middle Eastern Mythology*. Harmondsworth: Penguin Books, 1963.

Hopkins, C. "Assyrian Elements in the Perseus-Gorgon Story." *American Journal of Archaeology* 38 (1934) 341–58.

Howe, Thalia. "Illustrations to Aeschylus' Tetralogy on the Perseus Theme." *American Journal of Archaeology* 57 (1953) 269–75.

――――. "The Origin and Function of the Gorgon-Head." *American Journal of Archaeology* 58 (1954) 209–21.

Hyman, Stanley Edgar. "The Ritual View of Myth and the Mythic." In *Myth*. Edited by Thomas Sebeok. Bloomington: Indiana University Press, 1955.

Jacobi, Jolande. *Complex, Symbol and Archetype*. Translated by Ralph Mannheim. Princeton: Princeton University Press, 1959.

――――. *The Psychology of C. G. Jung*. Translated by Ralph Mannheim. New Haven: Yale University Press, 1973.

James, William. *The Varieties of Religious Experience*. New York: The Modern Library, 1936.

Jarrell, Randall. *The Third Book of Criticism*. New York: Farrar, Straus and Giroux, 1979.

Johnson, Robert A. *She*. New York: Harper and Row, 1977.

Jones, Ernest. *Hamlet and Oedipus*. 1910. Reprint. New York: W. W. Norton, 1976.

Jones, John. *On Aristotle and Greek Tragedy*. Oxford: Oxford University Press, 1962.

Jung, C. G. *Analytical Psychology, Its Theory and Practice*. 1935. Reprint. New York: Vintage Books, 1970.

――――. *The Collected Works of C. G. Jung*. 20 vols. Princeton: Princeton University Press. Translated by R. C. F. Hull. Vol. 5, *Symbols of Transformation* [1911/1952] (2nd ed., 1967). Vol. 6, *Psychological Types* [1921] (1971). Vol. 7, *Two Essays on Analytical Psychology* [1917–66] (2nd ed., 1966). Vol. 8, *The Structure and Dynamics of the Psyche* [1916–57] (1960). Vol. 9, Part 1, *The Archetypes and the Collective Unconscious* [1934–55] (1959). Vol. 9, Part 2, *Aion* [1951] (2nd ed., 1968). Vol. 10, *Civilization in Transition* [1918–59] (2nd ed., 1970). Vol. 11, *Psychology and Religion: West and East* [1930–54] (2nd ed., 1969). Vol. 12, *Psychology and Alchemy* [1936–51?] (2nd ed., 1968). Vol. 13, *Alchemical Studies* [1929–54] (1968). Vol. 14, *Mysterium Coniunctionis* [1955–56] (2nd ed., 1970). Vol. 16, *The Practice of Psychotherapy* [1921–46] (1954). Cited as CW.

———— and Karl Kerenyi. *Essays on a Science of Mythology.* Revised ed. Translated by R. C. F. Hull. Princeton: Princeton University Press, 1969.

————. *Four Archetypes.* From CW 9.1. Princeton: Princeton University Press, 1969.

————, Joseph Henderson, Marie-Louise von Franz, Aniela Jaffé, and Jolande Jacobi. *Man and His Symbols.* 1964. Reprint. New York: Dell, 1978.

————. *Memories, Dreams, Reflections.* [1961] Edited by Aniela Jaffé. Translated by Richard and Clara Winston. New York: Vintage Books, 1965.

————. *Modern Man in Search of a Soul.* [?–1932] 1933. Reprint. Translated by W. S. Dell and Cary Baynes. New York: Harcourt Brace Jovanovich, n.d.

————. *The Viking Portable Jung.* Edited by Joseph Campbell. Translated by R. C. F. Hull. Harmondsworth: Penguin Books, 1976.

Kanzer, Mark. "The Oedipus Trilogy." In *The Yearbook of Psychoanalysis,* vol. 7. New York: International Universities Press, 1951.

————. "On Interpreting the Oedipus Plays." In *The Psychoanalytic Study of Society,* vol. 3. Edited by Warner Muensterberger and Sidney Axelrad. New York: International Universities Press, 1965.

————. "The Passing of the Oedipus Complex in Greek Drama." *International Journal of Psycho-Analysis* 29 (1948) 131–34.

Kaufmann, Walter. "Nietzsche Between Homer and Sartre: Five Treatments of the Orestes Story." *Revue Internationale de Philosophie* 18 (1964) 50–73.

Kenner, Hugh. *Joyce's Voices.* Berkeley: University of California Press, 1978.

Kerenyi, Karl. *Asklepios.* Translated by Ralph Manheim. New York: Pantheon Books, 1959.

————. *Dionysos.* Translated by Ralph Manheim. Princeton: Princeton University Press, 1978.

————. *Eleusis: Archetypal Image of Mother and Daughter.* Translated by Ralph Manheim. New York: Pantheon Books, 1960.

————. *Hermes, Guide of Souls.* Translated by Murray Stein. Zurich: Spring Publications, 1976.

————. *The Heroes of the Greeks.* Translated by H. J. Rose. London: Thames and Hudson, 1957.

————. *Prometheus.* Translated by Ralph Manheim. New York: Pantheon Books, 1963.

Kierkegaard, Søren. *The Concept of Irony.* Translated by Lee Capel. Bloomington: Indiana University Press, 1968.

————. *Fear and Trembling* and *The Sickness Unto Death.* Translated by Walter Lowrie. Princeton: Princeton University Press, 1968.

Kirk, Geoffrey. *Homer and the Epic*. Cambridge: Cambridge University Press, 1965.
———. *The Nature of the Greek Myths*. 1974. Reprint. Harmondsworth: Penguin Books, 1978.
Klein, Melanie. *Our Adult World*. New York: Basic Books, 1963.
Kluckhohn, Clyde. "Myth and Ritual: A General Theory." *Harvard Theological Review* 35 (1942) 45–79.
Knox, Bernard. *Oedipus at Thebes*. New Haven: Yale University Press, 1957.
Kouretas, D. "From Freud to Hippocrates." *Psychiatric Communications* 2 (1959) 34–35.
Kramer, Samuel Noah. *Mythologies of the Ancient World*. Garden City: Anchor Books, 1961.
Laín Entralgo, Pedro. *The Therapy of the Word in Classical Antiquity*. Translated by L. J. Rather and J. M. Sharp. New Haven: Yale University Press, 1970.
Laing, R. D. *The Divided Self*. New York: Random House, 1969.
Lampal-de Groot, Jeanne. "The Evolution of the Oedipus Complex in Women." In *Psychoanalysis and Female Sexuality*. Edited by Hendrik Ruitenbeek. New Haven: College and University Press, 1966.
Lampedusa, Giuseppe di. *Two Stories and a Memory*. Translated by Archibald Colquhoun. New York: Grosset and Dunlap, 1968.
Lawson, John Cuthbert. *Modern Greek Folklore and Ancient Greek Religion*. Cambridge: Cambridge University Press, 1910.
Lazarsfeld, Sofie. "Did Oedipus Have an Oedipus Complex?" *American Journal of Orthopsychiatry* 14 (1944) 226–29.
Leach, Edmund. *Claude Lévi-Strauss*. Revised edition, 1974. Reprint. Harmondsworth: Penguin Books, 1976.
———. *The Structural Study of Myth and Totemism*. London: Tavistock, 1967.
Lefcowitz, Barbara. "The Inviolate Grove." *Literature and Psychology* 17 (1967) 78–86.
Lessa, W. A. "On the Symbolism in Oedipus." In *The Study of Folklore*. Edited by A. Dundes. Englewood Cliffs, N.J.: Prentice-Hall, 1965.
Levin, A. J. "The Oedipus Myth in History and Psychiatry." *Psychiatry* 11 (1948) 283–99.
Lévi-Strauss, Claude. *Structural Anthropology*. Translated by Claire Jacobson and Brooke Grundfest. New York: Basic Books, 1963.
Levy, Gertrude. *The Gate of Horn*. London: Faber and Faber, 1948.
Licht, Hans. *Sexual Life in Ancient Greece*. Translated by J. H. Freese. London: The Abbey Library, 1932.
Linforth, Ivan. *Religion and Drama in "Oedipus at Colonus."* Berkeley: University of California Press, 1951.
MacDowell, Douglas. *Athenian Homicide Law*. Manchester: Manchester University Press, 1963
Mailer, Norman. *Cannibals and Christians*. Abridged ed. London: Granada, 1979.
———. *Genius and Lust*. New York: Grove Press, 1976.
Majno, Guido. *The Healing Hand*. Cambridge, Mass.: Harvard University Press, 1975.

Manheim, Leonard and Eleanor. *Hidden Patterns: Studies in Psychoanalytic Literary Criticism.* New York: MacMillan, 1966.

Mann, Thomas. "Freud and the Future." In *Essays of Three Decades.* Translated by H. T. Lowe-Porter. New York: Knopf, 1971.

Marcuse, Herbert. *Eros and Civilization.* 1955. Reprint. Boston: Beacon Press, 1974.

May, Rollo. "Values, Myths, and Symbols." *American Journal of Psychiatry* 132 (1975) 703–6.

McCary, W. Thomas. *Childlike Achilles.* New York: Columbia University Press, 1982.

McCluhan, Marshall. *The Gutenberg Galaxy.* 1962. Reprint. New York: New American Library, 1969.

———. *Understanding Media.* 2nd ed. New York: New American Library, 1964.

McGinty, Park. *Interpretation and Dionysos.* The Hague: Mouton, 1978.

Meier, C. A. *Ancient Incubation and Modern Psychotherapy.* Translated by Monica Curtis. Evanston, Illinois: Northwestern University Press, 1967.

Mellart, James. "Deities and Shrines of Neolithic Anatolia." *Archaeology* 16 (1963) 29–38.

Miller, A. "An Interpretation of the Symbolism of Medusa." *American Imago* 15 (1968) 389–99.

Mitchell, Juliet. *Psychoanalysis and Feminism.* New York: Pantheon Books, 1974.

Mylonas, George E. *Eleusis and the Elusinian Mysteries.* Princeton: Princeton University Press, 1974.

Nagy, Gregory. *The Best of the Achaeans.* Baltimore: Johns Hopkins University Press, 1979.

Neumann, Erich. *Amor and Psyche: The Psychic Development of the Feminine: A Commentary on the Tale by Apuleius.* Translated by Ralph Manheim. Princeton: Princeton University Press, 1971.

———. *The Great Mother.* 2nd ed. Translated by Ralph Manheim. Princeton: Princeton University Press, 1963.

———. *The Origins and History of Consciousness.* Translated by R. C. F. Hull. Princeton: Princeton University Press, 1954.

Newell, H. W. "Hippocratic Use of Psychotherapy." *Bulletin of the Philadelphia Association for Psychoanalysis* 3 (1953) 75–78.

Nietzsche, Friedrich. *Beyond Good and Evil.* Translated by R. J. Hollingdale. Harmondsworth: Penguin Books, 1973.

———. *The Birth of Tragedy* and *The Case of Wagner.* Translated by Walter Kaufmann. New York: Vintage Books, 1967.

———. *Ecce Homo.* Translated by R. J. Hollingdale. Harmondsworth: Penguin Books, 1979.

———. *The Gay Science.* Translated by Walter Kaufmann. New York: Vintage Books, 1974.

———. *On the Genealogy of Morals.* Translated by Walter Kaufmann. New York: Vintage Books, 1969.

———. *Philosophy in the Tragic Age of the Greeks.* Translated by Marianne Cowan. South Bend, Indiana: Gateway Editions, 1962.

_____ . *Schopenhauer as Educator.* Translated by James Hillesheim and Malcolm Simpson. South Bend, Indiana: Regnery/Gateway, 1965.

_____ . *Twilight of the Idols and The Anti-Christ.* Translated by R. J. Hollingdale. Harmondsworth: Penguin Books, 1968.

_____ . *The Viking Portable Nietzsche.* 1954. Reprint. Edited and translated by Walter Kaufmann. Harmondsworth: Penguin Books, 1976.

Nilsson, Martin P. *The Dionysiac Mysteries of the Hellenistic and Roman Age.* Stockholm: Lund, 1957.

_____ . *Greek Folk Religion.* 1940. Reprint. New York: Harper and Row, 1961.

_____ . *A History of Greek Religion.* 2nd ed., 1952. Reprint. New York: W. W. Norton, 1964.

_____ . *The Mycenaean Origin of Greek Mythology.* 2nd ed., 1925. Reprint. Berkeley: University of California Press, 1972.

Nin, Anais. *Journals of Anais Nin, 1931–1934.* Edited by Gunther Stuhlman. London: Peter Owen, 1966.

Nock, Arthur Darby. *Conversion.* Oxford: Oxford University Press, 1933.

O'Brien, Michael. "Orestes and the Gorgon." *American Journal of Philology* 13 (1964) 13–39.

O'Faolain, Sean. *Vive Moi.* London: Ruper Hart-Davis, 1967.

Ong, Walter J. *Orality and Literacy.* New York: Methuen, 1982.

Onians, R. B. *The Origins of European Thought About the Body, the Mind, the Soul, the World, Time, and Fate.* 2nd ed. Cambridge: Cambridge University Press, 1954.

Otto, Walter F. *Dionysos, Myth and Cult.* Translated by Robert Palmer. Bloomington, Indiana: Indiana University Press, 1965.

Palmer, Leonard. *Minoans and Mycenaeans.* 2nd ed. New York, Knopf, 1965.

Parke, H. W. *Festivals of the Athenians.* Ithaca, N.Y.: Cornell University Press, 1977.

Parker, Robert. *Miasma.* Oxford: Clarendon Press, 1983.

Pembroke, Simon. "Last of the Matriarchs: A Study in the Inscriptions of Lycia." *Journal of the Economic and Social History of the Orient* 8 (1965) 217–47.

_____ . "Women in Change: The Function of Alternatives in Early Greek Tradition and the Ancient Idea of Matriarchy." *Journal of the Warburg and Courtauld Institutes* 30 (1967) 1–35.

Peradotto, John. "Oedipus and Erichthonius: Some Observations on Paradigmatic and Syntagmatic Order." *Arethusa* 10 (1977) 85–101.

Persson, Axel W. *The Religion of Greece in Prehistoric Times.* Berkeley: University of California Press, 1942.

Phinney, Edward. "Perseus' Battle with the Gorgons." *Transactions and Proceedings of the American Philological Association* 102 (1971) 445–63.

Plass, Paul. "Eros, Play, and Death in Plato," *American Imago* 26 (1969) 37–55.

Pomeroy, Sarah. "A Classical Scholar's Perspective on Matriarchy." In *Liberating Women's History.* Edited by Berenice Carroll. Urbana, Illinois: University of Illinois Press, 1975.

_____ . *Goddesses, Whores, Wives, and Slaves.* New York: Schocken Books, 1975.

Pritchard, James, ed. *The Ancient Near East: An Anthology of Texts and Pictures.*

1958. Reprint. Princeton: Princeton University Press, 1969.

Rabelais, François. *Gargantua and Pantagruel.* Translated by J. M. Cohen. Harmondsworth: Penguin Books, 1955.

Rado, C. "*Oedipus the King,* An Interpretation." *Psychoanalytic Review* 43 (1956) 228–34.

Raglan, Lord Fitzroy. *The Hero.* 1936. Reprint. New York: Vintage Books, 1956.

Rahner, Hugo. *Greek Myths and Christian Mystery.* Translated by Brian Battershaw. London: Burns and Oates, 1963.

Rank, Otto. *Beyond Psychology.* 1941. Reprint. New York: Dover Books, 1958.

———. *The Double.* Translated and edited by Harry Tucker. Chapel Hill, N.C.: University of North Carolina Press, 1971.

———. *Das Inzest-Motiv in Dichtung und Saga.* Leipzig: Deuticke, 1912.

———. *The Myth of the Birth of the Hero.* 1914. Reprint. Translated by F. Robbins and Smith Jelliffe. Edited by Philip Freund. New York: Vintage Books, 1964.

———. *The Trauma of Birth.* 1929. Reprint. New York: R. Brunner, 1952.

Rankin, Ann. "Euripides' Hippolytus: A Psychopathological Hero." *Arethusa* 7 (1974) 71–94.

Rankin, H. "Socrates' Approach to Thanatos," *American Imago* 21 (1964) 111–28.

Redfield, James M. *Nature and Culture in the Iliad.* Chicago: University of Chicago Press, 1975.

Reik, Theodor. *Dogma and Compulson* 1951. Reprint. Westport, Conn.: Greenwood Press, 1973.

———. "Modern Medusa." *American Imago* 8 (1951) 323–28. Reprinted in *The Secret Self.* New York: Farrar, Straus and Young, 1952.

———. *Myth and Guilt.* New York: George Braziller, 1957.

Rein, D. "Orestes and Electra in Greek Literature." *American Imago* 11 (1954) 33–50.

Richardson, N.J. *The Homeric Hymn to Demeter.* [late 7th century B.C.?] Oxford: Clarendon Press, 1974.

Richter, Gisela. *Animals in Greek Sculpture.* New York: Oxford University Press, 1930.

Ricoeur, Paul. *Freud and Philosophy: An Essay in Interpretation.* New Haven: Yale University Press, 1970.

Rieff, Philip. "The Analytic Attitude." *Encounter* 17 (June 1962) 22–28.

———, ed. *Delusion and Dream.* Boston: Beacon Press, 1956.

———. *Freud: The Mind of the Moralist.* 3rd ed. Chicago: University of Chicago Press, 1979.

———. *The Triumph of the Therapeutic.* New York: Harper and Row, 1966.

Robert, Carl. *Oidipous.* Berlin: Weidmann, 1915.

Roberts, Patrick. "Euripides: The Dionysiac Experience." In *The Psychology of Tragic Drama.* London: Routledge and Kegan Paul, 1975.

Rohde, Erwin. *Psyche.* 1925. Reprint. Translated from the 8th ed. by W. B. Hillis. New York: Harper and Row, 1961.

Roheim, Géza. "The Anthropological Evidence and the Oedipus Complex." *Psychoanalytic Quarterly* 21 (1952) 537–42.

———. *The Gates of the Dream.* New York: International Universities Press, 1952.

_____ . "The Oedipus Complex, Magic and Culture." In *Psychoanalysis and the Social Sciences, II*. New York: International Universities Press, 1950.

_____ . "The Song of the Sirens." *Psychiatric Quarterly* 22 (1948) 18–44.

_____ . "Teiresias and Other Seers." *Psychoanalytic Review* 33 (1946) 314–34.

Rosen, Stanley. *Plato's Symposium*. New Haven: Yale University Press, 1968.

Russo, Joseph and Bennett Simon. "Homeric Psychology and the Oral Epic Tradition." *Journal of the History of Ideas* 29 (1968) 483–98.

Ruthven, K. K. *Myth*. London: Methuen, 1976.

Sagan, Carl. *The Dragons of Eden*. 1977. Reprint. New York: Ballantine Books, 1977.

St. Clair, M. "A Note on the Guilt of Oedipus." *Psychoanalytic Review* 48 (1961) 111–14.

Sale, William. "The Psychoanalysis of Pentheus in the *Bacchae* of Euripides." *Yale Classical Studies* 22 (1972) 74–79.

Sartre, Jean-Paul. *No Exit and Other Plays*. New York: Vintage Books, 1955.

_____ . *The Words*. Translated by Bernard Fechtman. New York: Vintage Books, 1981.

Savory, Theodore. *Arachnida*. London: Academic Press, 1964.

Schlam, Carl. *Cupid and Psyche: Apuleius and the Monuments*. University Park, PA: The American Philological Association, 1976.

Schur, Max. *Freud: Living and Dying*. New York: International Universities Press, 1972.

Sebeok, Thomas. *Myth: A Symposium*. Bloomington, Indiana: Indiana University Press, 1955.

Segal, Charles. *Dionysiac Poetics and Euripides' "Bacchae."* Princeton: Princeton University Press, 1982.

_____ . "Etymologies and Double Meanings in Euripides' *Bacchae*." *Glotta* 60 (1982) 81–93.

_____ . "Pentheus and Hippolytus on the Couch and on the Grid: Psychoanalytic and Structuralist Readings of Greek Tragedy." *Classical World* 72 (November 1978) 129–48.

_____ . "Sophocles." In *Ancient Writers: Greece and Rome*. New York: Scribner's, 1982.

Seznec, Jean. *The Survival of the Pagan Gods*. Translated by Barbara Sessions. New York: Pantheon Books, 1952.

Shengold, Leonard. "The Parent as Sphinx." *Journal of the American Psychoanalytic Association* 11 (1963) 725–51.

Sherwin-White, Susan. *Ancient Cos*. Hypomnemata 51. Göttingen: Vanderhoeck and Ruprecht, 1978.

Silk, M. S. and J. P. Stern. *Nietzsche on Tragedy*. Cambridge: Cambridge University Press, 1981.

Simon, Bennett. *Mind and Madness in Ancient Greece*. Ithaca, N.Y.: Cornell University Press, 1978.

Slater, Philip. *The Glory of Hera*. 1968. Reprint. Boston: Beacon Press, 1971.

_____ . "The Greek Family in History and Myth." *Arethusa* 7 (1974) 9–44.

Slochower, Harry. "Oedipus: Fromm or Freud." *Complex* 8 (1952) 52–64.

Smoot, Jean J. "Hippolytus as Narcissus: An Amplification." *Arethusa* 9 (1976) 37–51.

Snell, Bruno. *The Discovery of the Mind.* Translated by T. G. Rosenmeyer. New York: Harper and Row, 1960.

Sophocles. [fl. 445–406 B.C.] See *Complete Greek Tragedies.*

Spotnitz, H. "The Prophecies of Teiresias." *Journal of the National Psychological Association for Psychoanalysis* 3 (1955) 37–43.

―――― and P. Resnikoff. "The Myths of Narcissus." *Psychoanalytic Review* 41 (1954) 173–81.

Stein, Robert. "The Oedipus Myth and the Incest Archetype." In *Spectrum Psychologiae.* Edited by C. T. Frey. Zurich: Rascher and Cie, 1965.

Stevans, Anthony. *Archetype: A Natural History of the Self.* London: Routledge and Kegan Paul, 1982.

Stewart, Harold. "Jocasta's Crimes." *International Journal of Psycho-Analysis* 42 (1961) 424–30.

Stone, Merlin. *When God Was a Woman.* New York: Dial Press, 1976.

Storr, Anthony. *C. G. Jung.* New York: Viking Press, 1973.

Stuart, G. L. *Narcissus: A Psychological Study of Self-Love.* New York: MacMillan, 1955.

Szasz, Thomas. *The Myth of Mental Illness.* New York: Harper and Row, 1961.

Tarn, W. W. *Hellenistic Civilization.* 3rd ed. Revised by G. T. Griffith. London: Edward Arnold, 1952.

Tatum, James. *Apuleius and the Golden Ass.* Ithaca, N.Y.: Cornell University Press, 1979.

Thomas, C. G. "Matriarchy in Early Greece: The Bronze and Dark Ages." *Arethusa* 6 (1973) 173–95.

Tourney, Garfield. "Empedocles and Freud, Heraclitus and Jung." *Bulletin of the History of Medicine* 30 (1956) 109–23.

―――― . "Freud and the Greeks: A Study of the Influence of Classical Greek Mythology and Philosophy Upon the Development of Freudian Thought." *Journal of the History of the Behavioral Sciences* 1 (1965) 67–85.

Trosman, H. "Freud's Cultural Background." *Psychological Issues* 9 (1976) 46–70.

van der Sterren, H. "The King Oedipus of Sophocles." *International Journal of Psycho-Analysis* 33 (1952) 343–51.

Vellacott, Philip. *Sophocles and Oedipus.* Ann Arbor: University of Michigan Press, 1971.

Vernant, Jean-Pierre. "From Oedipus to Periander: Lameness, Tyranny, Incest in Legend and History." Translated by Page duBois. *Arethusa* 15 (1982) 19–38.

―――― . *Myth and Society in Ancient Greece.* Translated by Janet Lloyd. Atlantic Highlands, N.J.: Humanities Press, 1980.

―――― . "Oedipe sans Complexe." *Bulletin de Psychologie* 31 (1978) 730–40.

―――― and Marcel Detienne. *Greek Culture and Society.* Translated by Janet Lloyd. Atlantic Highlands, N.J.: Humanities Press, 1978.

―――― and P. Vidal-Naquet. *Mythe et Tragédie en Grèce Ancienne.* Paris: Maspero, 1973.

Veszy-Wagner, Lilla. "Orestes the Delinquent: The Inevitability of Patricide." *American Imago* 18 (1961) 371–81.

Walcot, Peter. *Hesiod and the Near East*. Cardiff: University of Wales Press, 1966.

Walsh, P. G. *The Roman Novel*. Cambridge: Cambridge University Press, 1970.

Wasson, R. Gordon, Albert Hoffman, and Carl Ruck. *The Road to Eleusis: Unveiling the Secrets of the Mysteries*. New York: Harcourt Brace Jovanovich, 1978.

Watson-Williams, Helen. *André Gide and the Greek Myths*. Oxford: Clarendon Press, 1967.

Waugh, Evelyn. *The Letters of Evelyn Waugh*. New Haven: Ticknor and Fields, 1980.

Webster, T. B. L. *From Mycenae to Homer*. 2nd ed. New York: W. W. Norton, 1964.

Weigert-Vowinkel, Edith. "The Cult and Mythology of the Magna Mater from the Standpoint of Psychoanalysis." *Psychiatry* 1 (1938) 347–78.

West, M. L. *Early Greek Philosophy and the Orient*. Oxford: Clarendon Press, 1971.

Whitmont, Edward. *The Return of the Goddess*. New York: Crossroads, 1982.

———. *The Symbolic Quest*. New York: Putnam's, 1969.

Whyte, Lancelot Law. *The Unconscious Before Freud*. New York: Basic Books, 1960.

Wilson, Edmund. *The Wound and the Bow*. Oxford: Oxford University Press, 1947.

Wind, Edgar. *Pagan Mysteries in the Renaissance*. Revised ed. London: Faber and Faber, 1968.

Winnington-Ingram, R. P. "Clytemnestra and the Vote of Athena." *Journal of Hellenic Studies* 68 (1948) 130–47.

———. *Euripides and Dionysus*. Cambridge: Cambridge University Press, 1948.

Wittgenstein, Ludwig. *Lectures and Conversations*. Edited by Cyril Barrett. Berkeley: University of California Press, 1966.

Woodward, Jocelyn. *Perseus: A Study in Greek Art and Legend*. Cambridge: Cambridge University Press, 1937.

Zeitlin, Froma. "Cultic Models of the Female: Rites of Dionysus and Demeter." *Arethusa* 15 (1982) 129–57.

Zuntz, G. *Persephone: Three Essays on Religion and Thought in Magna Graecia*. Oxford: Oxford University Press, 1971.

Index

THE ROAD TO DAULIS

was composed in 10-point Electra and leaded 2 points on a Linotron 202
by Partners Composition;
with initial capitals and display type set in Bernhard Modern Roman by Dix Type;
printed by sheet-fed offset on 50-pound, acid-free Glatfelter Eggshell Cream,
Smyth sewn and bound over binder's boards in Joanna Arrestox B,
by Maple-Vail Book Manufacturing Group, Inc.,;
with dust jackets printed in two colors by New England Book Components
and published by

SYRACUSE UNIVERSITY PRESS

Syracuse, New York